INTRODUCTION TO
21ST CENTURY COUNSELING

Introduction to
21st Century Counseling

A Multicultural and Social Justice Approach

S. Kent Butler, Anna Flores Locke,
and Joel M. Filmore, Editors

cognella®
SAN DIEGO

Bassim Hamadeh, CEO and Publisher
Amy Smith, Senior Project Editor
Abbey Hastings, Production Editor
Emely Villavicencio, Senior Graphic Designer
Stephanie Kohl, Licensing Coordinator
Jaye Pratt, Interior Designer
Natalie Piccotti, Director of Marketing
Kassie Graves, Vice President of Editorial
Jamie Giganti, Director of Academic Publishing

Cover image: Copyright © 2009 iStockphoto LP/Qweek.

Printed in the United States of America.

3970 Sorrento Valley Blvd., Ste. 500, San Diego, CA 92121

Brief Contents

Detailed Contents

CHAPTER 9

MULTICULTURAL TECHNIQUES IN COUNSELING

Michelle D. Mitchell and Michael Brooks

CHAPTER 16

Preface

SOMETIMES YOU MUST FORGE YOUR OWN PATH

To whom much is given, much is required. While this may sound biblical, it really is not about that. It is about the purpose of being a competent counselor, a culturally competent counselor. The *Introduction to 21st Century Counseling: A Multicultural and Social Justice Approach* serves to provide cultural competence. Its unique approach offers a new culturally responsive perspective to counseling. The viewpoint offered in the text proffers to an entire generation of future counselors and counselor educators a narrative of voices that has not been offered before, namely the focusing of intentionality and an enlightened inclusion of the Multicultural and Social Justice Counseling Competencies (MSJCC) throughout its pages.

A myriad of amazing things occur when you begin the journey of becoming a counselor, especially during the very important Introduction to Counseling course. Many students enter the course with a very limited sense of what they are about to embark on. Some believe that they are the best advice givers because they heard somewhere in their lives that they "always know what to say and give the best advice," often followed by "You should consider being a counselor." It is a struggle at first to get students to embrace the true meaning and purpose of a counselor, to embrace being with their clients and not simply providing all the answers to their problems, to recognize that their role is to help clients in their journey find the "aha moment" for themselves. This is a chore for counseling faculty indeed, but once students learn that they are not in the room to give advice they actively enter into their journey to becoming. It is at this point when many students jump straight into the self-imposed imposter syndrome paradox. This mode of operandi is often difficult to navigate. However, once a student becomes more secure in their abilities and realizes they are not a pretender, that they honestly know what they are doing, is the time when their future clients will benefit from the best self they have become.

So, what does this all mean? What does it mean when you, as a student, are asked to self-reflect? How do you not rebel, especially if you are of the mind-set that you already know who you are? How dare any professor tell you that you may not. But to be honest, this is the challenge most instructors and supervisors face with each new cohort of students: how to help minds and perceptions already set see inside their Johari's window, how to help break the stubbornness so that students come away from glimpses deep inside with the realization of the actual growth and development that occurred. Counselor education programs are a great place to recognize what is inside, to discover one's self, to embrace who one truly is, and to understand what it is that they stand for. Perhaps professors are culturally responsive interior designers, who help to influence one's journey and ultimately help future counselors decide which curtains to hang.

As you forge your own path, introduction courses are a great place to start aligning yourself with your purpose to serve and understanding yourself so you may in turn understand your clientele. Having knowledge of the myriad of worldviews and cultures will impact your ability to develop therapeutic rapport that will lead to positive mental wellness outcomes for your clients. Also, by learning about yourself and developing counseling skills will move you into integrating your professional identity; helping you to move past the imposter and the play acting to actually "becoming" a counselor. It will bring you to the recognition that the counselor lives within you. That counseling actually has the power to become an innate part of you; becomes a part of your soul. Much like driving a car many years after you took lessons, counseling is instinctual, your abilities and you merge and become one!

OVERVIEW OF THE BOOK

This edited body of work, entitled *Introduction to 21st Century Counseling: A Multicultural and Social Justice Approach*, is designed to provide culturally responsive instructors with an evidenced-based teaching tool for graduate students taking an Introduction to Counseling course. The core counseling principles offered throughout the book are infused with aspects of the MSJCC. The endorsement of the MSJCC by the American Counseling Association (ACA), Association for Multicultural Counseling and Development (AMCD), and Association for Spiritual, Ethical and Religious Values in Counseling (ASERVIC) makes this book timely. The book provides counselor educators, supervisors, and practitioners with innovative 21st-century perspectives that enhance teaching and position students to successfully navigate their work with diverse clientele.

This book is a restatement of existing knowledge but separates itself from the rest because it provides cutting-edge narratives of historically oppressed voices. This book deviates from the norm: Traditionally other texts are written from ethnocentric perspectives; our book is written from a multicultural lens. The assumption, in this text, is that we are all creatures of intersecting identities (e.g., racial/ethnic, sexual/affectional, able/disabled, religious/nonreligious, gender-conforming/non-gender-conforming, immigrant/native) and that being a person of multiple identities must be viewed as the norm. The emphasis is on normalizing that which is already the norm as a way of destigmatizing what heretofore has been considered a stigmatizing status or identity. This text focuses on removing Westernized ideologies that are oppressive.

Competing titles pretty much all stem from the same narrative; however, many are written entirely from an ethnocentric approach to counseling. Some rely on the premise that counseling is linear and that students only need to learn counseling theories and techniques to be good counselors. The flaw in this ideology is that they do not teach counselors-in-training to embrace differences. The assumption is that all counselors and clients think and act in similar ways and that if helping professionals utilize proper techniques they will help a person move toward their personal wellness. While each of the existing texts has many strengths and weaknesses, what stands out clearly is that they leave little room for alternative voices. While multiculturalism is often presented in a fragmented fashion within our profession, we believe that multiculturalism should, in fact, be the foundation of counseling and infused throughout.

The approach we are taking with this textbook is unique in that we have paired seasoned experts and rising stars within the counseling community, who together will set the stage for the next generation of helping professionals. The MSJCC are infused into each chapter, intently focused on developing the awareness, knowledge, skills, and actions necessary to be a culturally responsive counselor in today's world.

Due to the strong authorship aligned to produce this text, students will be able to draw from a wealth of life experiences and expertise. Our experiential pedagogical approach deliberately stems from a culturally focused paradigm designed to enlighten, challenge, and inspire students to understand themselves, others, and the world around them.

ACKNOWLEDGMENTS

To see this project through to completion has been overwhelming. From the steadfastness of our publishers at Cognella, especially Kassie Graves, who believed in this project from day one, and Amy Smith who helped us navigate through the edits and the edits and the edits to come with this phenomenal package that reverberates multicultural excellence. We cannot leave out the authors, musicians as it were, because they took the challenge of incorporating multicultural and social justice principles into their individual master-pieces and made the pages sing with a resonance so bright, so assuredly embracing equity, inclusion, and diversity. We thank each and every one of our phenomenal authors for sharing their gifts on this project. There are too many to name here, but the reader will find your brilliance through the written words on the pages that follow. It is with great appreciation that we applaud the time and effort everyone involved expended to this very innovative, if not timely, book well positioned to have a profound impact on the entire counseling profession.

With much gratitude, Dr. Anna Flores Locke would like to thank her social justice mentor, Carla Adkison-Johnson. She dedicates the "*Professional Identity Development With Multicultural and Social Justice at Its Core*" chapter stating, "You helped me find my social justice voice. In this chapter, you freed that voice so that I could put in writing my social justice aspirations for the counseling profession. I was blessed to have you as my writing mentor on this chapter."

Lastly, Dr. S. Kent Butler would like to thank his extraordinary family for their love, patience, and support during the long nights and inordinate amounts of time spent on the computer accomplishing this task. To my co-editors, it takes a village to build something that is meaningful and that will last; we are building the future and leaving our indelible mark on the counseling community. I am encouraged that professors and practitioners will come to embrace this book as they support counselors-in-training in finding themselves and becoming the best counselors and social justice advocates that they can be! Our profession will always beckon us to think outside of the box and to help create an inclusive society where we all have equitable access to exceptional counselors, helping professionals who truly care about their communities and the mental wellness of their clients. Finally, much thanks to Joel Filmore for being the brainchild behind the concept and inviting me to the table, we did it!

CHAPTER 1

INTRODUCTION TO MULTICULTURAL AND SOCIAL JUSTICE COUNSELING

Anna Flores Locke, Nyack College

S. Kent Butler, University of Central Florida

Aseelah Davis, Nyack College

Anthony Pacifico, Seton Hall University

Gelawdiyos Haile, University of Central Florida

LEARNING OBJECTIVES
1. Learn about the origins of the counseling field and the importance of multiculturalism and social justice in practice.
2. Learn about the effects of power and privilege on counseling.
3. Learn the importance of action and why counselors are called to be social justice advocates.
4. Learn about the multicultural and social justice counseling competencies' significance to the counseling profession.

LEARNING OUTCOMES
1. Learn the history of multiculturalism and social justice counseling.
2. Learn the importance of infusing multiculturalism and social justice principles and actions into their practice as they actively develop their professional identity.
3. Understand the importance of social justice advocacy within the realm of counseling.

According to the U.S. Census Bureau, it is projected that by 2030 one in five Americans will be over the age of 65; by 2044, more than half of all Americans will belong to ethnic groups not classified as White American; and by 2060, one in five Americans may be foreign born (Colby & Ortman, 2015). In addition, approximately 4.1% of the U.S. adult population will be identified as lesbian, gay, bisexual, or transgender, and that percentage is growing (Newport, 2018). A myriad of cultural identities exists, and each will not have opportunity to be explored within this text; however, it is important to acknowledge that each intersectionality will have an impact on American society. The rapidly changing demographics are providing our nation with a much more global and multiculturally enriched populace. As a result, the majority of people in the United States will have identities that are not classified as White, male, able-bodied, Christian, and young. It is vital that the counseling community embrace the impending changes to society and begin amending current counseling theories, perspectives, and intervention that historically only reflected the White male perspective (Crethar & Ratts, 2008). It is the intention of this textbook to support counselors-in-training to develop into culturally responsive and social justice–minded helping professionals. From this space, professional counselors will be able to critically read and adapt professional literature so that it informs their work with diverse clientele.

As you begin to learn about how multiculturalism and social justice will shape your counselor identity and the work you do with clients, families, and communities, we want you to reflect on the diversity in your own life. Take an assessment of the demographics of the students in your class: Are they predominantly White American or from diverse ethnic and racial backgrounds? Think about where you grew up and where you currently live: What cultural diversity have you encountered in your lifetime? For all of us, we have encountered some form of diversity—in racial and ethnic groups, in affectional and sexual orientation, in socioeconomic status, religious or spiritual beliefs, in gender and age, and in many other identities.

Multiculturalism is all around us and will continue to be an integral part of our life and counseling experiences into the 21st century. As counselors become more adept in their roles it will be vital for them to ask themselves the following questions: How will you adapt current empirically based treatment modalities so that you are ethically responsive to ever-changing demographic scenarios? How will you counsel within a multicultural environment that does not fit the model client represented within most of our counseling theories and often outdated interventions? How will you respond when a Lesbian female in her 70s walks into your counseling office? This textbook will use the multicultural and social justice counseling competencies (MSJCC) to equip counselors-in-training with the awareness, knowledge, skills, and action methodologies required to be multiculturally competent and social justice change agents.

THE IMPORTANCE OF MULTICULTURALISM AND SOCIAL JUSTICE IN COUNSELING

Because our world is diverse, multiculturalism is central to counseling. Counseling is defined as "a professional relationship that empowers diverse individuals, families, and groups to accomplish mental health, wellness, education, and career goals" (Kaplan et al., 2014, p. 366). According to Pedersen (1988), "All counseling is to some extent multicultural … because culture is within each person" (p.vii). Further, "culture … is a personal orientation to each decision, behavior, and action in our lives" (Pedersen, 1988, p. vii). Thus, counselors must consider the influence of the client's cultural context to interpret their behavior accurately and to provide effective and competent treatment (Pedersen, 1988;). To do otherwise is harmful to clients and maintains the status quo that ethnocentric counseling theories and interventions apply to all clients, regardless of cultural background (Crethar & Ratts, 2008).

Multicultural competency has emerged at the forefront of the counseling profession over the course of the last 30 years (Vasquez, 2010). Cultural competence is achieved when counselors understand the role that culture plays within a counseling relationship, appreciate and have a thirst to learn and immerse themselves into diverse environments, and have the wherewithal to genuinely connect with the cultural worldviews of others (Vasquez, 2010). To provide guidance and a culturally attuned perspective to mental health practitioners, the Multicultural Counseling Competencies (MCC) were developed. In 1992, the American Counseling Association (ACA) endorsed the MCC and challenged the profession to utilize the conceptual framework to effectively teach and practice multicultural competence. In 2015, in an effort to incorporate the influence of power and privilege within the counseling relationship the Association for Multicultural Counseling and Development (AMCD) commissioned a revision of the MCC and the MSJCC emerged (Ratts et al., 2016). Stemming from a socioecological model, the MSJCC proffer an updated context for counselors to utilize as they become more multiculturally competent. The addition of action to awareness, knowledge, and skills provides a solid framework for counselors as they proactively advocate for change within oppressive systems (Ratts et al., 2016).

The Importance of Taking Action as Professional Counselors

According to critical race theory (CRT) scholars, the United States has systemically evolved into an oppressive environment that does not readily embrace individuals, families, and communities of varying cultural identities that do not meet the status quo (Delgado & Stefancic, 2012). Founded and normed on the values of White Christian men, this country prides itself on individualism, merit, and competition (Katz, 1985). As a result, White men who are young, able-bodied, heterosexual, and Christian have unearned assets: power and privilege (McIntosh, 1992). One consequence of having power and privilege is that citizens are often governed by culturally encapsulated behaviors and/ or ethnocentric worldviews.

Cultural encapsulation is the tendency to operate from a monocultural worldview and to dismiss variations in how people from differing cultures view the world. Bizumic and Duckitt (2012), concur and proffer that it relates to the ideology of ethnocentrism, a sense of ethnic group self-importance and self-centeredness, where one's ethnic group is central, and all other ethnic groups fail in comparison. Ethnocentrism ultimately leads to the devaluing and disadvantaging of other ethnic groups (Bizumic & Duckitt, 2012), which results in oppressive practices aimed at sustaining White supremacy and privilege (Delgado & Stefancic, 2007; Valdes, 2005).

Since the counseling profession is embedded within U.S. mainstream society, it is not immune to the effects of racism and systemic oppression (D'Andrea & Daniels, 1991). As a result, counseling's pioneering theories and subsequent interventions utilized throughout the profession and taught in counselor education programs often represent viewpoints that place a strong emphasis on White American values and beliefs. To this end, research representing the experiences of a myriad of ethnic and cultural backgrounds highlight that ethnocentric leaning theories and treatment models are ineffective and may cause harm (Hanna et al., 2000; Vasquez, 2010).

Case in Point

As the United States expanded across the North American continent in creation of a new nation, it became very evident that Native Americans inhabitants of this land were a barrier to their progress. Past president Andrew Jackson stated,

> That those tribes cannot exist surrounded by our settlements and in continual contact with our citizens is certain. They have neither the intelligence, the industry, the moral habits, nor the desire of improvement, which are essential to any favorable change in their condition. Established in the midst of another and a superior race, and without appreciating the causes of their inferiority or seeking to control them, they must necessarily yield to the force of circumstances and ere long disappear. (Parrillo, 2013, p. 22)

Deeply embedded in this statement is a racist narrative: that the White race is superior in intelligence, industry, morality, and their desire to improve. By virtue of this belief, the U.S. government instituted and enacted policies that systematically dismissed the life experiences and well-being of Native Americans, Blacks, Asians, Latinos, and a host of other racial groups. Native Americans were forced off their lands and forced to assimilate to White American culture. Those that persevered did so at great costs; the results from this injustice were devastating and are still evident today.

Imagine experiencing such pain and anguish under an oppressive and colonizing government; imagine not having the communal coping mechanisms available because your tribe was forced to live on reservations. Additionally, Native American children were placed into boarding schools, forced to cut their hair, and banned from speaking their native languages or practicing their cultural norms and traditions. Residual effects of these efforts are very evident in current Native American environments. For example, many live in impoverished locations and lack adequate access to common everyday resources such as food and the internet. Inadequate food resources may potentially have aversive effects on their overall health and nutrition. Inadequate internet access may consequently create an inability to apply for jobs and as a result contribute to the high rates of unemployment and poverty many Native Americans face. Similarly, alcohol abuse has long been a problematic behavior within this Indigenous community. Assimilation has taken its toll. White oppressors not only capitalized on the lands where Native

Americans resided; they also built easy access stores and warehouses that inexpensively sold enormous amounts of alcoholic beverages to Native Americans, thus contributing to the rising and alarming alcoholism rates suffered by the community. Alcohol addiction has become an epidemic and has plagued the Native American culture (Young, 1993). When counseling a Native American, this sociohistorical and political situation must be considered to ensure the client experiences no harm or invalidation.

EFFECTS OF ACCULTURATION

Ideally America should be a place where everyone's culture is acknowledged and accepted equally without the expectation to acculturate to a dominant culture, perceived or otherwise accepted. For America to exist as an ethical, inclusive, and thriving multicultural society it is vital that we examine the toxic seeds that have been planted throughout our history (e.g., slavery, racism, colonialism, classicism, sexism, etc.). We must tackle the residual effects of these seeds by planting new seeds of equality, cultural acceptance, and social justice for all American citizens and noncitizens. Toxicity comes in many forms. One such seed that needs further examination is acculturation and the disservice it has done to society.

America has existed with marginalized individuals in a constant struggle—fighting for equality, seeking to live and walk in their truth—with cultural identities that freely embrace traditions, customs, and native languages. When marginalized individuals are oppressed and forced to acculturate into American culture it often results in a denial of their ethnic distinctiveness. Similar to their Native American counterparts, Latin and Asian Americans also have not escaped the debilitating effects of not embracing one's identity. As an example, first-, second-, and third-generation Latinx (Latino/a) and Asian American communities mostly speak English and minimally use their native tongue to communicate outside of the family. Africans were forcibly held captive and taken from their homelands, stripped of their languages and traditions, sold into slavery, given slave names, and relegated to work under harsh conditions on plantations for slave masters who completely disregarded their human rights. In the Black community some individuals, in an effort to elevate, even tried to "pass" as White in order to achieve better opportunities and acceptance in American society. Many African Americans straightened and permed their hair and or were told to cut their locks (hair braids) in order to be more accepted, obtain employment, and or fit into corporate America (Landor & Smith, 2019). Despite efforts to acculturate and fit in African Americans continue to experience disparity and marginalization (Goldsmith et al., 2007).

Ultimately, acculturation only serves to increase the social gap in America and weaken the preservation of one's cultural identity. In contrast, multiculturalism closes this gap, giving individuals the opportunity to embrace their own humanity. Culturally competent counselors are primed to support clients experiencing acculturation issues and may be strong social justice advocates in the eradication of social systems designed to decrease one's level of attainment in this country. Counselors are also well suited to help heal the pain and suffering of past manipulations embedded deeply into the psyche of oppressed and marginalized clients.

COUNSELING IS POLITICAL

Policies and laws dictate our lives and create the social systems in which we function, so counseling should be viewed as political and social justice must emerge as an integral part of treatment plans designed to help clients affected by unfair guidelines and regulations (Crethar & Ratts, 2008). In order to elicit change, social justice efforts must recognize and confront the injustices and systemic oppression that adversely affect clients' well-being. Counselors must equip themselves with the knowledge and skills and take the action necessary to help clients and communities pursue a better future (Crethar et al., 2008).

Considered the fifth force in counseling, social justice follows multiculturalism, which is widely accepted as the fourth force. To put these forces into perspective from a counseling point of view, psychodynamic is considered the first, followed by behavioral and humanism, each contributing in significant ways to the mental wellness of clients. To this end, Crethar and Ratts (2008) describe social justice as a multifaceted approach where counselors promote human development and intentionally confront inequities that negatively impact and alter life experiences. Social justice–minded counselors espouse four critical principles, equity, access, participation, and harmony (Crethar & Ratts, 2008), in their advocacy work. Equity refers to the fair distribution and access of resources, services, power, information, rights, and responsibilities to all members of society. Access is the key to a socially just world because it allows for self-determination and healthy human development. Participation is successful when every person has the right to control their personal narratives and make the decisions that impacts their lives. Harmony occurs when the best possible outcomes for the entire community are realized (Crethar & Ratts, 2008). Social justice is an integral part of multiculturalism and promotes values for a healthier society and counseling practices that are culturally responsive (Crethar & Ratts, 2008). These principles are well positioned to work seamlessly with the MSJCC.

Endorsed by the ACA, the MSJCC provides culturally responsive counselors with a useful praxis from which to engage in social justice–oriented counseling practices. The MSJCC are the backbone of this textbook. Every chapter integrates the competencies into the content and showcases how to incorporate them successfully into a counselor's professional identity. The next section explains the MSJCC and their context in this textbook.

MSJCC EXPLAINED

Ratts et al. (2016) introduced the MSJCC to the counseling profession and outlined how four developmental domains: (a) counselor self-awareness, (b) client worldview, (c) counseling relationship, and (d) counseling and advocacy. These domains help culturally competent counselors effectively work with their clientele. Interwoven in the first three developmental domains, there are four aspirational competencies: (a) attitudes and beliefs, (b) knowledge, (c) skills, and (d) action. We will briefly highlight the four developmental domains and follow that with an in-depth overview of the four aspirational competencies.

Counselor Self-Awareness

The MSJCC framework underscores the intersectionality that shapes individuals' identities; to improve on their awareness counselors must make a concentrated effort to increase reflexivity (Ratts et al., 2016). To this end, a counselor's consciousness and ability to acknowledge and articulate their biases, worldviews, and experiences lay the foundation for meaningful interactions and understanding value differences with clients (Sue et al., 1992). This increased self-awareness aids in counselor acceptance of client worldviews. Deeply processing and reflecting on one's own life ultimately helps counselors gain a clearer understanding of how their clients' marginalized or privileged cultural identities shaped them. This collaboration also strategically allows counselors to home in on and embrace mindfulness, especially as this concept relates to their strengths and limitations.

Client Worldview

A counselor's deep self-reflection and increased self-awareness enables them to honor and respect their clients' worldview (Ratts et al., 2016). Being attuned to their clients' worldview entails recognizing and understanding marginalized or privileged statuses and how societal treatment has impacted client identity development.

Counseling Relationship

Counselors' genuine interest in the lived experiences of their clients will build a foundation for the most important pillar of counseling: the counseling relationship. Counselor recognition of how their privileged or marginalized status influences the counseling relationship will provide the foundation that fosters a therapeutic climate. Counselors' attunement to the social status of their clients will also proffer further insight into how the dynamic benefits or hinders the therapeutic relationship. Strong collaborative counseling relationships ensure that appropriate, often mutually agreed on, interventions that benefit clients individually and within their social systems.

Counseling and Advocacy

Once counselors operate from a subjective lens that respects client worldviews, they strategically integrate their level of knowledge into culturally attuned best practices that accurately conceptualize client concerns from a systemic perspective. Counselors practicing from a MSJCC framework develop an awareness that enables them to employ advocacy interventions and strategies (Singh et al., 2012). The counseling and activism aspect of MSJCC empowers counselors to advocate for their clients on a myriad of levels (e.g., community, institutional, and global) (Ratts et al., 2016). Attuned counselors will proactively and relentlessly advocate and dismantle inequitable social and systemic barriers that hinder their clients' forward progression (Ratts, 2009).

Ratts and his colleagues (2016) outlined the following four aspirational competencies in the MSJCC.

Attitudes and Beliefs

Attitudes and beliefs involve counselors acknowledging their own identity and how they are similar or dissimilar to their clients, recognizing the influences of social status on the counseling relationship. The MSJCC provides a framework that aids counselors in recognizing biases, value systems, and worldviews and broadens their curiosity to learn.

Knowledge

Knowledge involves understanding the impact of systemic barriers, stereotypes, and biases related to counselor and client privileged or marginalized statuses and accurately integrating salient multicultural theories and interventions. In addition, embracing intersectionality, worldviews, and how individuals define their identity may positively influence the counseling relationship. Ultimately, knowledge involves finding effective means of communicating with clients.

Skills

Critical thinking is required when utilizing **skills** that delve into the intricacies of the counselor–client relationship. Reflexivity may help practitioners develop a level of understanding that analyzes, recognizes, acknowledges, and articulates the impact of one's worldview on lived experience. Moreover, being culturally responsive and attuned will afford counselors the opportunity to administer multiculturally relevant assessments because conceptualizing clients appropriately and creating accurate treatment plans are vital components that lead to client wellness.

Action

Action encompasses immersing oneself into cultural activities to better facilitate one's biases and prejudices, especially as they relate to worldviews, societal roles, and economic status. Action also includes participating in multiculturally inspired professional development trainings and workshops related to counseling. To this end, it is important to continue assessing and articulating client strengths and limitations through a cross-cultural lens. It includes strategic communications that take initiative and create opportunities to engage in difficult dialogues about societal status and its impact on therapeutic relationships.

As the MSJCC emphasizes advocacy in the form of social justice action, the role of the counselor as an ally and advocate is of vital importance to our global society. You might be wondering how one participates in social justice advocacy or what that means in your role as a counselor. The following section will provide a framework from which to begin integrating a social justice perspective into your counselor identity.

ROLE OF COUNSELOR AS ADVOCATE

Although significant strides are made within the confines of the therapeutic environment, professionals have recognized the need to move beyond the walls of their counseling space and actively engage in the communities they serve (Vera & Speight, 2003). In other words, counseling professionals must engage in advocacy efforts working with and/or on behalf of clients to address systemic barriers impacting the clients' wellness (Toporek & Daniels, 2018). The ACA advocacy competencies provide a framework from which to achieve this goal.

The competencies describe the necessary counselor skills, knowledge, and behavior that can be implemented to address systemic barriers facing clients, client groups, and communities (Toporek & Daniels, 2018; Lewis et al., 2003). They are organized around two dimensions: extent of client involvement and level of advocacy intervention. To have an empowering experience with the client, counselors must act with or on behalf of them and engage in collaborative activities. The intersection of these two dimensions is reflected in six advocacy domains: empowerment, client advocacy, community collaboration, systems advocacy, collective action, and social/political advocacy (Toporek & Daniels, 2018). Readers are encouraged to refer to the original document on the advocacy competencies (that can be found on https://www.counseling.org/docs/default-source/competencies/aca-advocacy-competencies-updated-may-2020.pdf?sfvrsn=f410212c_4) for a more thorough understanding on them.

SUMMARY, INSIGHTS, AND ACTIONS

Because the counseling profession has deemed advocacy a necessary professional activity and skill, to be effective counselors we must diligently ensure that the tenets are engrained within our core beliefs and can be drawn on without hesitation (Decker et al., 2015). The multicultural and social justice competencies incorporate this aspect of advocacy and ask all counselors to take action in their professional role. We are certain that the knowledge readers gain throughout the rest of this book will provide the tools necessary for the successful integration of multiculturalism and social justice into their professional identities.

In summary, the chapter provided readers with evidenced-base information that highlights the importance of multiculturalism and social justice to counseling; spoke to the effects of acculturation within the United States; shared the nuances of counseling as a political weapon; briefly outlined the MSJCC; and provided useful information on how counselors can become strong social justice advocates.

Throughout the rest of the textbook, the MSJCC will anchor each chapter. Readers will be provided with innovative and timely competency-related case studies that apply to the topic covered in that chapter. We are excited to share with you the following topics as they are expertly presented by some of counseling's phenomenal heavyweights:

- Historical Overview of the Counseling Profession
- Professional Identity
- Counseling Relationships
- Professional Settings
- Professional Roles
- Client Worldview and Intersectionality
- Counseling Theories
- Clinical Techniques
- Ethics and Ethical Behaviors
- Crisis and Trauma
- Research and Writing
- Testing, Assessment, and Diagnosis
- Wellness
- Creativity
- Licensure

The textbook also provides readers with a chapter full of valuable resources to further support learning. In closing, it is the editors' hope that the information provided will support your journey to becoming a strong culturally responsive and competent counselor.

REFLECTION AND DISCUSSION QUESTIONS

1. Reflect on the diversity of your class/cohort and discuss the myriad identities represented within this environment. Share how this diversity effects your learning and experience of this course.
2. When discussing or studying about Eurocentric power and privilege in the United States (or your country of origin), what feelings and thoughts arise? What are the best ways for students to process these feelings and thoughts?
3. What does social justice in counseling mean to you? What does it mean to become a multiculturally competent counselor?
4. Do you find the MSJCC helpful? Why or why not?
5. What do you believe will be your greatest hurdle as you engage with this textbook and work toward developing a culturally competent counseling identity?

ADDITIONAL READINGS AND RESOURCES

1. Critical Race Studies in Education Association
2. Association for Multicultural Counseling and Development
3. Counselors for Social Justice
4. American Educational Research Association
5. Ali, S. R., Liu, W. M., Mahmood, A., & Arguello, J. (2008). Social justice and applied psychology: Practical ideas for training the next generation of psychologists. *Journal for Social Action in Counseling and Psychology, 1,* 1–13.
6. Bemak, F., & Chung, R. C. Y. (2011). Applications in social justice counselor training: Classroom without walls. *The Journal of Humanistic Counseling, 50,* 204–219. https://doi.org/10.1002/j.2161- 1939.2011.tb00119.x
7. Brady-Amoon, P., Makhija, N., Dixit, V., & Dator, J. (2012). Social justice: Pushing past boundaries in graduate training. *Journal for Social Action in Counseling Psychology, 4,* 85–98.
8. Collins, S., Arthur, N., & Brown, C. (2013). Critical incidents in graduate student development of multicultural and social justice competency. *Academic Journal of Interdisciplinary Studies, 2,* 105–115. https://doi.org/10.5901/ajis.2013.v2n9p105
9. Ratts, M. J. (2009). Social justice counseling: Toward the development of a fifth force among counseling paradigms. *Journal of Humanistic Counseling, Education & Development, 48*(2), 160–172. https://doi.org/10.1002/j.2161-1939.2009.tb00076.x
10. Toporek, R. L., Lewis, J. A., & Crethar, H. C. (2009). Promoting systemic change through the ACA advocacy competencies. *Journal of Counseling & Development, 87,* 260–268. https://doi.org/10.1002/j.1556-6678.2009.tb00105.x
11. Toporek, R. L., & Liu, W. M. (2001). Advocacy in counseling: Addressing race, class, and gender oppression. In D. B. Pope-Davis & H. L. K. Coleman (Eds.), *The intersection of race, class, and gender in multicultural counseling* (pp. 285–413). SAGE.

REFERENCES

Bizumic, B., & Duckitt, J. (2012). What is and what is not ethnocentrism? A conceptual analysis and political implications. *Political Psychology, 33*(6), 887–909.

Colby, S., & Ortman, J. (2015). *Projections of the size and composition of the U.S. population: 2014–2060.* U.S. Census Bureau. https://www.census.gov/content/dam/Census/library/publications/2015/demo/p25-1143.pdf

Crethar, H.C. & Ratts, M.J. (2021). *Why social justice is a counseling concern.* https://www.counseling.org/docs/default-source/Government- Affairs/why_social_justice_is_a_counseling_concern-1.pdf?sfvrsn=2

D'Andrea, M., & Daniels, J. (1991). Exploring the different levels of multicultural counseling training in counselor education. *Journal of Counseling and Development, 70*(1), 78–85. https://doi.org/10.1002/j.1556-6676.1991.tb01565.x

Decker, K. M., Manis, A. A. & Paylo, M. J. (2015). Infusing social justice advocacy into counselor education: Strategies and recommendations. *The Journal of Counselor Preparation and Supervision, 8*(3). http://dx.doi.org/10.7729/83.1092

Delgado, R., & Stefancic, J. (2012). *Critical race theory: An introduction* (2nd ed.). New York University Press.

Goldsmith, A.H.; Hamilton, D.; Darity, W. (2007). From dark to light: Skin color and wages among African-Americans. *Journal of Human Resources 42* (4). 701–738.

Hanna, F.J.; Talley, W.B.; Guindon, M.H. (2011). The power of perception: Toward a model of cultural oppression and liberation. *Journal of Counseling and Development, 78* (4). 430–441. https://doi.org/10.1002/j.1556-6676.2000.tb01926.x.

Kaplan, D.M.; Tarvydas, V.M.; Gladding, S.T. (2014). 20/20: A vision for the future of counseling: The new consensus definition of counseling. *Journal of Counseling and Development. 92* (3), 366–372. https://doi.org/10.1002/j.1556-6676.2014.00164.x.

Katz, J. (1985). The sociopolitical nature of counseling. *The Counseling Psychologist, 13*(4), 615–624.

Landor, A.M. & Smith, S.M. (2019) Skin-tone trauma: Historical and contemporary influences on the health and interpersonal outcomes of African Americans. *Perspectives of Psychological Science. https://doi.org/10.1177%2F1745691619851781*

Lewis, J. A., Arnold, M. S., House, R., & Toporek, R. L. (2003). *ACA advocacy competencies.* https://www.counseling.org/docs/default-source/competencies/aca-advocacy-competencies-may-2020.pdf?sfvrsn=85b242c_4

McIntosh, P. (1992). *White privilege and male privilege: A personal account of coming to correspondences through work in women's studies.* Wellesley College Center for Research on Women.

Newport, F. (2018). *In U.S., estimate of LGBT population rises to 4.5%.* Gallup. Retrieved February 21, 2021, from https://news.gallup.com/poll/234863/estimate-lgbt-population-rises.aspx.

Parrillo, V.N. (2013). *Diversity in American.* (4th ed.). Paradigm.

Pedersen, P. A (1988). *Handbook for Developing Multicultural Awareness.* American Association for Counseling and Development.

Ratts, M. J., Singh, A. A., Nassar-McMillan, S., Butler, S. K., & McCullough, J. R. (2016). Multicultural and social justice counseling competencies: Guidelines for the counseling profession. *Journal of Multicultural Counseling and Development, 44*(1), 28–48. https://doi.org/10.1002/jmcd.12035

Singh, A. A., Merchant, N., Skudrzyk, B., Ingene, D., Hutchins, A. M., & Rubel, D. (2012). Association for specialists in group work: Multicultural and social justice competence principles for group workers. *Journal for Specialists in Group Work, 37*(4), 312–325. https://doi.org/10.1080/01933922.2012.721482

Sue, D. W., Arredondo, P., & McDavis, R. J. (1992). Multicultural counseling competencies and standards: A call to the profession. *Journal of Counseling & Development, 70*(4), 477–486. https://doi.org/10.1002/j.1556-6676.1992.tb01642.x

Toporek, R.L. & Daniels, J. (2018). *American Counseling Association Advocacy Competencies.* https://www.counseling.org/docs/default-source/competencies/aca-advocacy-competencies-updated-may-2020.pdf?sfvrsn=f410212c_4.

Valdes, F. (2005). Legal reform and social justice: An introduction to LatCrit theory, praxis and community. *Griffith Law Review, 14*(2), 148–173.

Vera, E. M., & Speight, S. L. (2003). Multicultural competence, social justice, and counseling psychology: Expanding our roles. *The Counseling Psychologist, 31*, 253–272. http://dx.doi.org/10.1177/ 0011000003031003001

Young, T. (1993). Alcoholism prevention among Native-American youth. *Child Psychiatry and Human Development, 24*(1), 41–47.

CHAPTER 2

HISTORICAL OVERVIEW OF COUNSELING

Harriet L. Glosoff, Professional Counseling Program, Texas State University

Monica Band, Mindful Healing Counseling Services, LLC

LEARNING OBJECTIVES

1. Learn about historical events in the United States that have influenced the development of the counseling profession.
2. Understand how the evolution of the counseling profession and its related professional organizations reflects sociopolitical and mental health needs movements within society.
3. Review pieces of federal legislation and other regulations related to equitable access of counseling services for marginalized and underserved populations in different treatment settings (e.g., community, residential, school, etc.).
4. Understand how to become advocates on behalf of the counseling profession and the communities they serve.

LEARNING OUTCOMES

1. Readers will identify major historical events and describe how these relate to the counseling and advocacy intervention domain of the multicultural and social justice counseling competencies.
2. Readers will analyze how federal and state legislation and policies affect the availability, equity, and accessibility of counseling services to individuals from marginalized groups.
3. Readers will map out the current American Counseling Association (ACA) organizational structure to include international, national, state, and division leadership.
4. Readers will review the competencies that have been endorsed by ACA (www.counseling.org/knowledge-center/competencies) since the 1990s. Readers will select at least one set of competencies (other than the MSJCC), discuss how the chosen document relates to the domains of the MSJCC and what actionable efforts they will commit to in order to meet these competences.

5. Readers will demonstrate an understanding that developing into a multicultural and social justice counselor is an ongoing commitment and evolution of their identity by reviewing current issues that impact clients' well-being and professional counselors' ability to provide services. They will choose one current issue and engage in an act of advocacy on behalf of the counseling profession or clients.

As we begin, we would like to note that this chapter will differ from others in this textbook in that we will focus primarily on the developmental domain of counseling and advocacy, rather than review all domains on the multicultural and social justice counseling competencies (MSJCC). We will begin by sharing an overview of the counseling profession's roots in the social events and movements of the early 20th century in the United States. We follow this with a brief review of significant factors by decades, from the 1930s to the present, that influenced the profession's development. We end this chapter by highlighting some current issues in the counseling profession.

COUNSELING PROFESSION: ROOTS IN EARLY 20TH-CENTURY EVENTS AND SOCIAL MOVEMENTS

There is not a single point in time that the counseling profession was "born." Caplow (1996) noted that, among other things, to be considered a profession, an occupation must (a) establish a professional society or association, (b) develop standards for training programs and a vehicle to enforce those, and (c) create a code of ethics and standards for admitting and regulating practitioners. Although counseling did not meet most of Caplow's criteria to be considered a profession until the 1950s and beyond, the profession has emerged over time, with roots going back to the early 20th century. At that time, the United States experienced several societal shifts due to population growth, industrialization and urbanization, World War I, a growing immigrant population, and social reforms (Glosoff et al., 2020). At that same time, the counseling profession was influenced by social movements such as the vocational guidance, school guidance, mental hygiene, and mental health movements of the early 20th century.

The advocacy and social justice roots of our profession can be seen in those early movements. For example, Frank Parsons, considered by most as the parent of the vocational guidance movement, now commonly referred to as career counseling, created the Vocational Bureau of Boston in 1908 to help the growing population of immigrants in their search for work (Glosoff et al., 2020). Additionally, Parsons created a systematic approach by considering people's interests, skills, and qualifications for careers, laying a foundation for the trait theory of career counseling (Erford, 2014). He also proposed a plan for educating career counselors (Glosoff et al., 2020). Shortly after Parsons opened the Vocational Bureau, the National Vocational Guidance Association (NVGA) was founded (1913), exemplifying one of Caplow's (1996) criteria for the establishment of a profession. The NVGA would later become one of the first four professional counseling organizations to come together in 1952 to found the American Personnel and Guidance

Association (APGA), the first name of what we now know as the American Counseling Association (ACA).

World War I also impacted the vocational guidance movement. The U.S. Army ordered that psychological tests (e.g., the Army Alpha and Beta IQ tests) be developed to screen personnel. After that, psychological testing became commonplace in U.S. education, business, and personnel offices—so much so that testing was often used synonymously with counseling (Glosoff et al., 2020). Additionally, World War I inspired the promulgation of three U.S. federal acts that attempted to address issues service members faced while reintegrating into society. The first, in 1917, was the Smith-Hughes Act. This act established the Federal Board for Vocational Education, which later administered the veteran and civilian vocational rehabilitation programs.

In 1918, the Soldiers Rehabilitation Act created a vocational rehabilitation program for disabled World War I veterans. The Federal Board for Vocational Education administered the act. In 1920, the Smith-Fess Act (also known as the Civilian Vocational Rehabilitation Act) established the first vocational rehabilitation program for civilians, not just veterans, with disabilities (Peterson, 2020). Peterson (2020) noted that the Smith-Fess Act is considered by many to be the beginning of the rehabilitation counseling specialty.

At the same time Parsons was working in Boston, Jesse B. Davis, a principal, incorporated vocational guidance into his high school in Grand Rapids, Michigan. Shortly after, the Grand Rapids school district followed suit and created a citywide vocational guidance department. Similar vocational services programs were created in several other regions of the country throughout the 1920s (Glosoff et al., 2020). During that same period, based on surveys of school-leaving children and their subsequent employment experiences, Anna Reed reported that public schools were not adequately preparing students for most businesses (Reed, 1917). She proposed that vocational guidance become an integral part of the Seattle school curriculum (Reed, 1917). Eli Weaver also proposed that students need guidance before entering the workforce but took an approach different from Reed's. Weaver organized a guidance program for boys in the New York City schools and had them work on farms during the summer to gain work experience. Although Reed and Weaver took different approaches to working with youth, they both recognized the need for a systematic guidance system to help students from differing backgrounds access work experience and information. It was also during the 1920s that counselors in school systems from New York and Boston were expected to help all students make education and career decisions and that school counselors were first certified in those cities.

The early 1920s also saw the emergence of the mental hygiene movement. Erford (2014) noted that there was a shift in the stigma around mental illness, prompted in part by Clifford Beers (1908), who published *A Mind That Found Itself*, his autobiography about his experiences with being treated for mental health problems under wretched conditions in psychiatric institutions. His work laid a foundation for the formation of advocacy, such as the creation of the National Mental Health Association, which he founded in 1909. William Healy, a psychiatrist and criminologist who was also a reformer in corrections, established the Juvenile Psychopathic Institute in Chicago. This was the first community-based psychiatric clinic (Snodgrass, 1984). Although it was not until the 1960s that the "deinstitutionalization" movement began in earnest, its roots can be traced back to Healy and Beers's work, including establishing the National Committee on Mental Hygiene in 1909 (Scull, 2018). The committee's mission was to develop measures that would prevent mental illness, promote mental health, provide support to people dealing with mental health issues, and reform psychiatric treatment. The committee was the precursor to the National Mental Health Association, which later became Mental Health America in 2006.

FACTORS ACROSS THE DECADES THAT INFORMED THE COUNSELING PROFESSION: THE 1930S TO 1990S

In the next sections we present a summary of key factors by decade (from the 1930s to the present) that have informed and influenced the counseling profession, counselor identity, and advocacy on behalf of the profession and the consumers of counseling services across work settings. In each decade, we highlight examples of societal events that shaped our profession and acts of advocacy by individual counselors or organizations to make social and legislative changes. In alignment with the MSJCC (Ratts et al., 2016), these sociopolitical movements have systemic impacts on counselors' lives and the communities they serve. We have attempted to weave in our profession's historical and current knowledge, much like an intricate tapestry, to equally honor our history and recognize the future of our profession. It is important to note that what we present is not an exhaustive list of events and legislation due to page limitations.

1930s–1940s

The Great Depression, World War II, and the advent of new guidance and counseling theories significantly shaped the counseling profession. There was growth in vocational, or career, counseling, beyond focusing on occupational choices (Lee, 1966) and mental health counseling. We encourage readers to consider how Williamson and his colleagues' work and the passage of the legislation noted throughout this chapter are acts of advocacy.

During the 1930s, the Great Depression led to a heightened focus on researching and developing vocational/career counseling strategies as millions of adults and young people lost their jobs. E.G. Williamson and colleagues at the University of Minnesota built on the foundational work on a trait factor theory of career developed by Frank Parsons. They proposed the Minnesota point of view, or Minnesota model, an empirically based strategy to help the students at the university and people who were unemployed learn about their traits, interests, and skills and use this knowledge to make effective vocational decisions (Lynch & Maki, 1981). The model was a directive one. It emphasized counselors' role as mentors and teachers and dominated the counseling field during much of the 1930s and 1940s.

Lee (1966) noted that Edward Thorndike and John Brewer's work began to broaden the focus of counseling. Like what Anna Reed and Eli Weaver proposed in the 1920s, Brewer advocated integrating guidance into the school curriculum. He proposed that school systems were responsible for preparing students for life post-graduation (Brewer, 1932). This preparation included making vocational decisions and being guided by counselors about courses and life skills needed to live as emerging adults.

The counseling profession's roots in assessment, career, mental health, and rehabilitation counseling continued to occur during and after World War II. As in the First World War, the government needed help selecting the most suited individuals for different jobs within the military and related industries (Ohlsen, 1983). Counselors and psychologists were hired to conduct testing. In addition to performing tests to help place military personnel, counselors and psychologists were needed on the front lines and then at home to help soldiers deal with shell shock or battle fatigue (now known as posttraumatic stress disorder) (Cummings, 1990). Cummings (1990) noted that to meet that need, the government created basic training and began credentialing research-oriented psychologists and new medical school graduates.

The Veterans Administration (VA) also created counseling centers in their hospitals (Shertzer & Stone, 1986). The VA coined the term *counseling psychology* and created "counseling psychology positions and training programs to fill these positions" (Glosoff et al., 2020, pp. 11–12). Further, they provided stipends and paid internships to train mental health professionals to provide counseling services. However, they did establish that the entry-level for these positions as a doctorate (Cummings, 1990), which essentially placed restrictions on the hiring of counselors, the majority of whom had master's degrees.

Although reviewing counseling theories beyond this chapter's scope, no history of the counseling profession can be considered complete without noting the influence of Carl Rogers and his work during the 1940s and 1950s. Rogers believed that clients were experts about their lives and did not need to be directed by counselors, challenging the directive, counselor-centered approach of the Williamson and Freudian psychoanalysis. Rather than serving in the role of teacher, Rogers proposed that counselors serve as nonjudgmental mirrors for their clients. Gibson and Mitchell (2008) remarked that Rogers shifted the focus of counseling to how to use the counseling relationship (or how we interact) to help clients affect change. Following, we provide a brief overview of federal legislation enacted in the 1930s and 1940s that influenced the counseling profession's development.

Examples of Federal Legislation/Policies

The U.S. Congress passed three significant pieces of legislation related to career or employment services during the 1930s. The Wagner O'Day Act, establishing the U.S. Employment Services, passed in 1933. The George-Dean Act, enacted in 1936, established continued federal grants to support a nationwide vocation education program (created by the Smith-Hughes Act of 1917) (Sweeney, 2001). In 1938, the U.S. Office of Education established the Occupational and Information Guidance Services Bureau (Sweeney, 2001), which researched vocational guidance issues and stressed the need for school counseling (Glosoff et al., 2020).

During the 1940s, legislation passed focused on both vocational and mental health counseling. In 1944, the U.S. Employment Service opened 1,000 offices across the country staffed by employment counselors. In 1946, the George-Barden Act was passed to establish counselors' training programs, focusing on vocational counseling. This helped set a precedent for funding the preparation of counselors. That same year, the National Institute for Mental Health (NIMH) was established, and the National Mental Health Act was passed (Hershenson et al., 1996). That act authorized funds for research, demonstration, and training to prevent and treat mental health disorders (Hershenson et al., 1996). The NIMH continued to provide training stipends for students in PhD programs, and they asked the American Psychological Association (APA) to create training standards (Cummings, 1990). Cummings (1990) noted that those standards "may well have been the first step in the eventual credentialing process" (p. 486) for psychologists. At that same time, those standards precluded most counselors. It would not be until 2006, when the Veterans Benefits, Healthcare, and Information Technology Act was passed, that master's-level professional counselor would meet the criteria to be hired by the VA. Later in this chapter, we will take a closer look at our profession's efforts to assist veteran populations.

1950s

Aubrey (1977) wrote, "If one decade in history had to be singled out for the most profound impact on counselors, it would be the 1950s" (p. 292). During this decade, the APA established Division 17, the Society of Counseling Psychology; the American Personnel and Guidance Association was established as a professional organization separate from APA; significant federal legislation was passed that impacted the development and recognition of specialty of school counseling; and there was continued research and development of new guidance and counseling theories.

Professional Associations and Professional Identity

One of the most significant developments in the counseling profession was the American Personnel and Guidance Association's (APGA) founding in 1952. Between 1952 and 1992, the name of the association changed twice. From 1952–1983 it was known as APGA. In 1983, the name was changed to the American Association for Counseling and Development (AACD) to represent its members' work more accurately. In 1992, the association's governing council changed the name to the American Counseling Association (ACA).

When this chapter was submitted for publication, the ACA had 18 divisions; 22 interest networks; 56 state and territorial branches in the United States, Europe, and Latin America; and four regional assemblies. We will present information about the ACA throughout the remainder of the chapter, trying to capture how it, its divisions, and other professional associations have developed and influenced professional counselors.

Also, to make it easier for readers, we will refer to the association as ACA throughout most of this chapter. We encourage readers to review the ACA website for information (www.counseling.org) about the divisions, interest networks, branches, and governing structure, and for a review of its milestones (www.counseling.org/about-us/about-aca/our-history/aca-milestones).

Before ACA was established, the Council of Guidance and Personnel Associations (CGPA) was a federation comprised of organizations that all had interests in vocational guidance, education guidance, psychology, and personnel. At the 1950 convention of the council, a committee presented a plan to unify these different organizations. In 1951, the NVGA and the American College Personnel Association (ACPA) (two of the CGPA organizations) approved the plan. They joined together as a new organization, the Personnel and Guidance Association (PGA) (McDaniels, 1964). The next year, 1952, the name was changed to the American Personnel and Guidance Association (APGA) with the following for founding partners (or divisions): the ACPA, the National Association of Guidance Supervisors and College Trainers (now the Association for Counselor Education and Supervision, ACES), the NVGA (now the National Career Development Association), and the Student Personnel Association for Teacher Education (now titled the Association for Humanistic Counseling). The founding of ACA was significant in meeting one of Caplow's (1996) first criteria to be considered a profession. Two additional divisions were established during this decade: the American School Counselors Association (1953, one of the two largest divisions until its disaffiliation from ACA in 2018) and the Division of Rehabilitation Counseling (now the American Rehabilitation Counseling Association) and reflected the focus on vocational, educational, and rehabilitation counseling that was prevalent in the previous decade.

The same year that ACA was founded as a home for professional counselors, the APA created the Society of Counseling Psychology, known as Division 17. Members of Division 17, like members of ACA, were more interested in typical growth and development compared to their colleagues in clinical psychology, who tended to work with individuals with more severe and chronic mental disorders. Members of both ACA and APA Division 17 shared interests in vocational counseling and humanistic therapy, and many affiliated with both ACA and APA. A major distinction between counseling and counseling psychology was and continues to be the requirement of a doctoral degree to practice independently as a psychologist compared to professional counselors who can practice with a master's degree. Sweeney (2001) wrote that in the 1970s the APA began to establish state legislation that limited the practice of counseling to doctoral-level psychologists or to other mental health professionals who worked under their supervision. We discuss the ramifications of the APA initiative to limit the practice of counseling in the section on the 1960s–1970s.

Examples of Federal Legislation

Thorazine was first used to treat symptoms of severe mental disorders. Because symptoms were better managed, many people who had been treated in state hospitals were released into communities. However, communities were not well set up to provide the necessary services, nor were they prepared to meet the needs of World War II veterans. The Vocational Rehabilitation Act (VRA) was passed in 1954, in part to address those needs. Congress required that funds be allocated for training counselors who specialized in working with people with disabilities (psychological and physical). The Mental Health Study Act was passed in 1955 "to study and make recommendations on mental health and mental illness in the U.S" (National Institute of Mental Health [NIMH], 2017), establishing the Joint Commission on Mental Illness and Health. The act "authorized NIMH to study and make recommendations on mental health and mental illness in the U.S. The act also authorized the creation of the Joint Commission on Mental Illness and Health" (NIMH, 2017, para. 7).

The launching of the Soviet Union's first space satellite, Sputnik I, led to the enactment of the National Defense Education Act (NDEA) in 1958. The act funded school counseling programs focused on encouraging students to go into science and math fields. The NDEA provided grants to offer counseling in high schools and authorized contracts to colleges and universities to train counselors to work in schools. This was significant in the developing standards for the preparation of professional counselors, and the number of counselors hired by schools across the country rose dramatically.

1960s–1970s

The 1960s–1970s was a tumultuous time in the United States. The Vietnam War, the civil rights movement, the assassinations of Martin Luther King and Robert Kennedy, and the women's movement brought attention to social issues. It was also a decade of the Johnson administration's Great Society initiatives to develop social service agencies, leading to the opportunity for legislation that impacted counseling services across different settings. Major works related to cross-cultural counseling written by pioneers such as William Cross, Paul Pedersen, and Derald Sue were published in counseling and psychology journals, reflecting a growing focus in counseling on cultural issues.

Professional Associations

ACA continued to add divisions that reflected changes in the country and meet its members' interests. For example, the Association for Non-White Concerns in Personnel and Guidance (ANWIC) was added as a division in 1972 to address the concerns about minority representation within APGA and the counseling profession and the social movements that were occurring in the 1960s and 1970s. ANWIC changed its name to the Association for Multicultural Counseling and Development (AMCD) in 1984, just after APGA became known as the American Association for Counseling and Development (AACD).

The Public Offender Counselor Association (POCA, now called the International Association of Addictions and Offenders Counselors) was established in 1974. Its members focused on an increasing juvenile and probation population and the staff who worked in prison systems (Glosoff et al., 2020). That same year, what is now titled the Association for Spiritual, Ethical, and Religious Values in Counseling (ASERVIC) was established as a division (first called the National Catholic Guidance Association), beginning meaningful cultural discussions related to religious issues in counseling.

With the passage of the Community Mental Health Centers Act, discussed in the next section, there was an increase in counseling outside educational settings. Counselors were being hired in settings such as community mental health clinics, employee assistance programs, rehabilitation centers, substance abuse treatment facilities, psychiatric hospitals, and hospices. The American Mental Health Counselor Association (AMHCA) was founded as a division of AGPA in 1976 to meet the needs of community counselors working in those diverse settings. AMHCA became one of the largest divisions in APGA and remained so until its disaffiliation in 2019.

Training Standards/Accreditation

The foundation for national training standards for professional counselors began in the 1960s, addressing Caplow's second criteria. The ACES and the American School Counselor Association's (ASCA) ACA divisions formed a joint commission. The results of their work included the development of training standards, focusing on the preparation of school counselors. The "Standards for Counselor Education in the Preparation of Secondary School Counselors" were created in 1964 and adopted by ACES in 1967. ACA also established the "Standards for Preparation of Elementary School Counselors" (APGA, 1967) and *Guidelines for Programs in the Preparation of Student Personnel Workers in Higher Education* (APGA, 1969).

As counselors began to work outside of educational settings, there was a need for standards addressing the preparation of counselors who would work in other settings. The Council for Rehabilitation Education (CORE) was founded in 1972 as the first specialized accrediting body for graduate programs in counseling, establishing standards for master's programs in rehabilitation counseling. Sweeney (1991) noted that CORE was a forerunner for establishing educational standards for the preparation of professional counselors.

Regulation of Counselors

The ACA published its first Code of Ethics in 1961 to regulate the behavior of its members. This met Caplow's (1996) third criteria for professions. It was during the 1970s that state regulations for the practice of professional counseling began. Mental health professionals, similar to physicians and attorneys, are licensed by state boards. According to the ACA (2016), licensure is a credential that regulates the title, practice, or both of an occupation to protect the public by determining the training needed to practice that profession.

Before 1976, no state law defined or regulated the profession of counseling, separate from the practice of psychology. As mentioned earlier, during the 1970s, the APA began to establish state legislation that limited required a doctoral degree to practice psychology. This restriction led to the first licensure law for professional counselors. Although John Weldon advertised himself as providing guidance and career counseling services in private practice, the Virginia State Board of Psychologist Examiners served him with a cease-and-desist order, stating that he was practicing psychology without a license (Hosie, 1991). The Virginia courts found Weldon guilty of practicing outside of the law established for psychologists and noted that personnel and guidance were a profession unto itself and should be regulated separately from psychology (Hosie, 1991). After that ruling, the Virginia legislature passed the first general practice act for professional counselors in 1976. Licensure laws for professional counselors were also enacted in Arkansas and Alabama during the 1970s.

According to ACA (2016), licensure laws are granted or sanctioned by state governments. There are two different types of licensure laws. The first and most stringent form of state regulation for practitioners is a practice act, which requires practitioners, except for those who meet criteria to be exempt from the law, to be licensed to engage in the practice (ACA, 2016). There are also title acts that regulate the use of counseling-related titles (e.g., who can call themselves a professional counselor) but do not regulate the practice of counseling, meaning that someone could legally practice counseling without being licensed (ACA, 2016).

Licensure is not the only type of credential that bestows recognition of the education and skills required to be a professional counselor. Counselors are also certified by state entities to ensure they meet qualifications to hold specific jobs (and must be certified to hold the positions). For example, state boards of education certify school counselors to work in public K–12 schools, departments of vocational rehabilitation certify rehabilitation counselors to provide services, and departments of state health and human services certify substance abuse or addictions counselor. In addition to state certification, counselors are recognized by their professional peers through voluntary national certification (think of the term *certified public accountants*).

National board certification for counselors began with the certification of professional counselors specializing in rehabilitation counseling. The Commission on Rehabilitation Counselor Certification (CRCC) offered voluntary national board certification to master's-level rehabilitation counselors in 1973. The CRCC also offers certification for those with doctoral degrees in counseling or rehabilitation counseling. For more comprehensive information about becoming a certified rehabilitation counselor (CRC), go to the CRCC website (www.crccertification.com/about-crcc). AMHCA created a certification committee, and in 1978 the AMHCA board adopted procedures to certify clinical mental health counselors. In 1979, AMHCA established the National Academy of Certified Clinical Mental Health Counselors (NACCMHC), which finalized the process and guidelines for certifying clinical mental health counselors (Messina, 1985). NACCMHC would later merge with the National Board for Certified Counselors.

Examples Federal Legislation/Policies

Landmark civil rights legislation was passed during the 1960s–1970s. For example, the Civil Rights Act of 1964 ended segregation in public places and banned employment discrimination based on race, color, religion, sex, or national origin. The Title IX education amendments to that act protected people from discrimination based on sex in education programs or activities that receive federal financial assistance. In addition to the broader social justice implications of both of these laws, we encourage readers to consider the implications these acts had for counselors' work, especially (but not limited to) those working in educational (K–higher education) and career service settings.

In this section, we share a few examples of other laws relevant to the counseling profession's ongoing development, starting with the Community Mental Health Centers Act of 1963. This law established over 2,000 community mental health centers across the country and increased employment opportunities for counselors outside of educational or vocational settings. It was also significant because it provided affordable counseling services to individuals and was critical to moving large numbers of people who had been treated long-term in state psychiatric hospitals.

The Elementary and Secondary Education Act (ESEA) of 1965 expanded school counselors' services into the elementary settings. On a different front, the 1970 Hughes Act led to the creation of the National Institute of Drug Abuse (NIDA) and increased research into the prevention and treatment of alcoholism. ACA and the ARCA division were strong advocates for Public Law 94–142 in 1975, which revised and extended the Vocation Education Act of 1963. This law, "now most commonly references as the *Individuals with Disabilities Education Act* or IDEA" (Glosoff et al., 2020, p. 15), required that all children were entitled to a free, appropriate public education, regardless of their abilities. To ensure that all children could be served in public schools, each student with special needs was required to have an individualized education plan. School counselors coordinated the evaluation of students and the design and implementation of the individualized plans.

Congress also passed the Veteran's Health Care Amendments in 1979 and set up a network of vet centers across the country, separate from other VA facilities. Although this changed in the 1990s, initially the vet centers were limited to Vietnam veterans because of their special needs (Department of Veteran Affairs, n.d.).

1980s–1990s

During the 1980s and 1990s, there was an increased focus on accreditation (or credentialing of training programs), the recognition of counseling as a profession, credentialing counselors through state licensure and national certification, and an emphasis on human growth and development. There was also a continued emphasis on multiculturalism and diversity. For example, Sue et al. (1992) published Multicultural Counseling Competencies and Standards, which were endorsed by the American Counseling Association in 1992.

Professional Associations/Identity

Before becoming a national division of ACA, most groups apply for organizational affiliate status, which requires a minimum of 200 ACA members and approval by the ACA Governing Council. To become a division, groups must have at least 500 ACA members and submit an application to the ACA Governing Council along with proposed bylaws or operating rules. Reflecting the growing diversity of interests and needs of its members, the ACA underwent several changes during the latter part of the 20th century, including the addition of the Military Educators and Counselors Association (MECA) and the Association of Gay, Lesbian, and Bisexual Issues in Counseling (AGLBIC) as organizational affiliates in 1984 and 1996, respectively. Following is a list of the divisions that were added: Association for Adult Development and Aging (1986); International Association of Marriage and Family Counselors (1988); AGLBIC (1997; known as the Association for Lesbian, Gay, Bisexual, and Transgender Issues in Counseling from 2007–2020 and the Society for Sexual, Affectional, Intersex, and Gender Expansive Identities as of April 2020); and the Association for Counselors and Educators in Government (formerly MECA [1994], now known as the Military and Government Counseling Association).

As mentioned earlier in this chapter, APGA changed its name to the American Association for Counseling and Development (AACD) in 1983. This reflected shifts in professional identity away from the terms *guidance* and *personnel* while keeping a focus on the developmental nature of counseling. In 1992, "the association changed its name to the American Counseling Association (ACA) to reflect the common bond among association members and to reinforce their unity of purpose" (ACA, n.d., para. 1). During that same year, the American College Personnel Association, one of the four founding members, withdrew from ACA to become a standalone organization. The American College Counselors Association became a replacement division for ACPA, and new organizational affiliates and divisions were added.

In addition to growth in the ACA, Chi Sigma Iota (CSI) was established in 1985. CSI (2020) is an international honor society that promotes scholarship and professional excellence in counseling through its publication of the *Journal of Counselor Leadership and Advocacy*, which "provides research and evidence-based recommendations in topics that promote scholarship, research, professionalism, leadership, advocacy, and excellence in counseling" (para.1). It also provides leadership training and mentoring, professional development opportunities, grants for research and chapter development, a career center, community service events, a registry of CSI members who are licensed professional counselors, and a directory to help counselors find supervisors.

Training Standards (Accreditation)

As previously noted, the CORE was incorporated in 1972 as an accrediting body focused on setting standards for graduate programs in rehabilitation counseling. It was a forerunner to the Council for Accreditation of Counseling and Related Educational Program (CACREP). As you may recall, ACES developed *The Entry Preparation of Counselors and other*

Personnel-Service Specialists in 1973. The ACA governing council adopted the standards in 1979, and the CACREP became an organization affiliate of ACA in 1981 to accredit master's and doctoral programs in counseling. CACREP was recognized by the then U.S. Council on Postsecondary Accreditation (COPA; now known as the Council for Higher Education Accreditation, or CHEA) in 1987. CHEA (n.d.) "carries out periodic review ('recognition') of institutional and programmatic accrediting organizations" (para.1). This was significant because it put CACREP on par with other accrediting bodies such as the APA (Herr, 1985).

Although CACREP was established as an affiliate of ACA, it is important to note that CACREP is a separate entity with its own board of directors who decide on applications for accreditation. CAREP reviews and revises its accreditation standards regularly. Between 1981 and 2000, it revised the standards twice—in 1988 and 1994.

Regulation of Counselors

Broadening the specialization scopes of the CRCC and NACCMHC, the National Board for Certified Counselors (NBCC) was established in 1982. NBCC began by offering a more generic National Certified Counselor (NCC) credential to counselors with a minimum of a master's degree who passed a standardized exam, the National Counselor Exam (NCE). The exam focused on eight areas, which corresponded with the core areas of preparation required by CACREP. In 1992, NACCHMC merged with NBCC, and NBCC began to certify clinical mental health counselors and administer the National Clinical Mental Health Counseling Examination (NCMHCE), which is required to become a certified clinical mental health counselor. The NCE and NCHMHC are also the exams most frequently required by state licensing boards. In addition to the general certification of NCC, and the specialty certification in clinical mental health, NBCC currently offers national specialty certifications in school counseling (NCSC) and addictions counseling (master's addiction counselor [MAC], created in collaboration with ACA and the ACA division of IAAOC).

Earlier, we discussed how licensure for professional counselors began in the 1970s. ACA created a licensure commission in 1975 and published an action packet, drafts of model state licensure legislation, and strategies for counselors to have licensure laws enacted (APGA, 1976). There was progress in enacting state licensure laws throughout the 1980s and 1990s. Between 1981 and 1994, 36 more states enacted title or practice licensure laws for professional counselors (Glosoff et al., 2020) and, according to the ACA, by 1997, 44 states and Washington, DC, had enacted state licensure or certification laws.

In 1994, ACA endorsed a revised model licensure law to help states pass practice acts that included uniform standards for professional counselors' training or preparation (setting 60 credits of graduate counseling coursework as a requirement; Glosoff et al., 1995). The model also called for a broad scope of practice for professional counselors, including language that clearly stated that licensed counselors assess, diagnose, and treat individuals with mental disorders. If states have tiers or levels of licensure, these are those counselors at the highest level (Glosoff et al., 1994) and who have the appropriate education and supervised practice to do so.

Although tremendous strides have occurred in this area, there was, and is, variance in the laws enacted regarding the titles granted to licensed counselors, the number of graduate credits required to apply for licensure, and the requirements for post-master's supervised experience. The American Association of State Counseling Boards (AASCB, n.d.) was founded in 1985 to promote licensure and "cooperation among individuals and associations involved in providing counseling services to the public" (para. 1). AASCB has been active in working with other counseling organizations to achieve license portability.

Examples of Federal Legislation/Policies

Several federal laws were passed and policies enacted during the latter part of the 20th century that increased the counseling profession's recognition and impacted counseling services. It is beyond this chapter's scope to include all of them, so the following are only a few examples. In 1994, President Clinton signed the Elementary School Counseling Demonstration Act into law, for which ACA had strongly advocated. The act set aside $2 million in grants for states to have schools develop elementary school counseling programs. That same year was the first time that Counseling Awareness Month was celebrated.

Counseling was included as a primary mental health profession in the 1992 health care human resource statistics published by the Center for Mental Health Services and the National Institute of Mental Health (Manderscheid & Sonnenschein, 1992). This was significant because it was the first time counseling was included alongside psychology, social work, and psychiatry. Recognition by federal agencies and states was also important for counselors to be providers by managed care organizations, which had grown tremendously during the 1990s.

The Health Professions Education Partnership Act (HEPA), enacted in 1998, also put professional counseling on par with other master's-level mental health professions (e.g., social work) by including professional counselors under the health professional training programs.

With HEPA, for the first time counseling students, graduates of counseling programs, and counselor education programs were eligible for grants for curriculum and faculty development, scholarships, and loans to individuals training in recognized training programs (ACA Office of Public Policy and Information, 1998). In 1999, the Medicare, Medicaid, and SCHIP Balanced Budget Refinement Act required the Medicare Payment Advisory Commission (MedPAC) to study the possibility of including licensed professional counselors as recognized Medicare providers. This bill was important for professional counselors and consumers of counseling services because Medicare is the primary insurance provider for approximately 59 million Americans, including adults age 65 and older and younger people with long-term disabilities (Medicare Mental Health Workforce Coalition, 2020). These individuals cannot currently use Medicare to see a licensed professional counselor (LPC), limiting their access to mental health care, especially in rural communities where mental health professionals are more likely to be LPCs. Glosoff et al. (2020) noted that even though the MedPAC report did not support establishing professional counselors as provided, the act was still significant because it was "the first time that Congress and the president had enacted legislation even referencing licensed professional counselors with respect to Medicare" (p. 18). The act and ensuing report set the stage for the ongoing battle to include professional counselors as Medicare providers.

Regarding counseling services for people with disabilities, in addition to prohibiting job discrimination against people with disabilities, the Americans With Disabilities Act (ADA) required equal access to services and accommodations for people with disabilities. Also, the Rehabilitation Act of 1973 was reauthorized in 1998 and, among other things, funded training for rehabilitation counselors and upheld requirements that professionals meet state or national certification or licensure requirements to work in state agencies or for private contractors of state agencies.

We would like to highlight another of the many laws passed during the 1990s—the Higher Education Act amendments (1998). ACA members focused on multicultural issues and how societal, familial, and environmental factors impacted people's well-being and mental health. The ACA leaders advocated for this legislation because the law included lowering student loan interest rates and increasing Pell Grant awards, making college more accessible. The act also included provisions for advising and counseling regarding financial aid and college admission and counseling services for at-risk and low-income elementary, middle, and secondary students. Finally, the law provided for personal and family counseling and home visits for students with limited English proficiency (ACA Office of Public Policy and Legislation, 1998).

THE COUNSELING PROFESSION: 21ST CENTURY

The 21st century continues to bring a slew of human-made and natural disasters. The secondary trauma of these disasters is furthered by globalization and the wide use of social media to share content worldwide. Notably, September 11, 2001, and the terrorist attacks associated with this tragic day continue to be events in which mental health professionals are considered among first responders. Mental health professionals being first responders is not a new concept. Rather, it is becoming even more solidified with the American Red Cross's national efforts for training licensed professionals to become disaster mental health certified, a movement toward trauma-informed care and serving those who have been impacted. The recognition of counselors on the front lines can be seen in various contexts, including the aftermath of Hurricane Katrina, the COVID-19 response in hospitals and internationally with Red Cross, the aftermath of hate crimes, and mass shootings, to name just a few.

Professional Associations/Identity

The divisions of ACA continued to grow, with three new divisions established during the 21st century: Counselors for Social Justice (2002), the Association for Creativity in Counseling (2004), and the Association for Child and Adolescent Counseling (became the 20th division of ACA in 2014). There were also continued efforts to create a unified vision of the counseling profession.

In 2005, the ACA and the AASCB entered a cosponsored project—the 20/20: A Vision for the Future of Counseling Oversight Committee. The committee included representatives from all divisions and regions of ACA, CACREP, CORE, CRCC, and NBCC. In 2010, after two rounds of Delphi ratings and years of discussion, the delegates came to the following consensus definition of counseling: "Counseling is a professional relationship that empowers diverse individuals, families, and groups to accomplish mental health, wellness, education, and career goals" (Kaplan et al., 2014, p. 1). Twenty-nine of the 31 professional entities, including all but two ACA (ASCA and CSJ) divisions endorsed the definition. Kaplan et al. (2014) stated that "having 29 out of 31 major counseling associations agree on the definition of counseling historic" (p. 370).

Even though there was a focus on unifying the profession, ASCA and AMHCA, two of the largest divisions of ACA, disaffiliated (in 2018 and 2019, respectively), becoming independent entities. We suggest one reason for the success in passing critical federal and state law for recognizing professional counseling and affecting the provision of counseling services has been the united front presented by various ACA divisions when advocating for legislation, similar to our colleagues in psychology. Although there are many divisions in the APA, typically when members of APA lobby for legislation, they present themselves as psychologists first and specialists (e.g., clinical, counseling, forensic psychologists) second. The ACA, ASCA, and AMCHA have continued to work in alliance with the ASCA and AMHCA in advocating for public policies related to school and mental health counseling. However, it is unclear how legislators and other policy makers will react to having different groups represent themselves as counselors.

Continued Emphasis on Addressing Issues of Multiculturalism, Advocacy, and Social Justice

The counseling profession has always focused on developmental factors that might impact mental health. As our country has become increasingly diverse, counselors have become more involved in examining macro-level and systemic factors that influence how people develop—how social, economic, and cultural barriers impact well-being and contribute to people's resilience when faced with adversity and oppression. The profession's commitment to having counselors be culturally competent became more and more reflected in codes of ethics, practice guidelines, accreditation standards, documents endorsed by the ACA Governing Council, and newly established grants and scholarships.

For example, in 2012 the NBCC received a federally funded Minority Fellowship Program (MFP) grant from the Substance Abuse and Mental Health Services Administration (SAMHSA). Since then, the NBCC awards up to 24 doctoral-level minority fellowships yearly. These awards enable fellows to provide leadership to the profession through education, research, and practice benefiting vulnerable, underserved consumers. NBCC received additional federally funded MFP grants from SAMHSA. In addition to the doctoral fellowships, since 2014 the NBCC has offered up to 80 master's-level minority fellowships each year. These fellowships increase the number of culturally competent addiction counselors and mental health counselors available to underserved minority populations, focusing on transition-age youth (ages 16–25).

As previously noted, ACA endorsed the MCC in 1992. The MCC, however, was just a beginning. Leaders in the field recognized that it was not enough to simply address issues of diversity. Counselors also need to know how to advocate for changes in the theories they use, the systems throughout which people have access to counseling services, legislation, and other forms of policies that acted as systematic barriers to effective counseling for people from diverse backgrounds. To that end, the ACA Advocacy Competencies were endorsed in 2003 (Lewis et al., 2009), which were updated in 2018. The ACA also endorse several other sets of documents developed by ACA divisions to guide counselors in becoming culturally competent social justice advocates. Following are examples of those guidelines and the year that ACA endorsed them: the ALGTBIC Competencies for Counseling Transgender Clients (2009); ASERVIC Competencies for Addressing Spiritual and Religious Issues in Counseling (2009); ALGBTIC Competencies for Counseling LGBQIQA Individuals (2012); the Multicultural and Social Justice Counseling Competencies (MSJCC) (2015, see Ratts et al., 2016); the Competencies for Counseling the Multiracial Population (2015); and the ARCA Disability-Related Counseling Competencies (2019). We encourage readers to refer to the ACA website (www.counseling.org/knowledge-center/competencies) for more information about each of these.

The ACA Code of Ethics has been revised every seven to 10 years since it was first adopted in 1961. The 2005 version of the ACA Code of Ethics expanded on previous versions by including standards that reflected the profession's increased focus on cultural competence and advocacy. The preamble to the 2005 code had been revised to focus more on cultural issues, and references to diversity issues were integrated throughout the 2005 code (compared to previous editions) (Glosoff & Kocet, 2006).

For example, the code called for counselors to be aware of and attend to cultural factors that might impact confidentiality, privacy, assessment, diagnosis, treatment, and how we conceptualize families and boundaries in the counseling relationship. Also, a standard was added directing counselors to, "when appropriate, advocate at the individual, group, institutional, and societal levels to examine potential barriers and obstacles that inhibit access and/or the growth and development of clients" (ACA, 2005, A.6.). That standard was included in the most current edition of the Code of Ethics (ACA, 2014, A.7.). The 2014 code further revised the preamble to cite specific professional values that guide the work of counselors. Those values or guiding principles include the following:

1. Enhancing human development throughout the life span
2. Honoring diversity and embracing a multicultural approach in support of the worth, dignity, potential, and uniqueness of people within their social and cultural contexts
3. Promoting social justice

4. Safeguarding the integrity of the counselor–client relationship
5. Practicing in a competent and ethical manner (ACA, 2014, p. 3)

Training Standards/Accreditation

CACREP had five significant revisions to the original 1981 standards (1988, 1994, 2001, 2009, 2016) and was in the process of its seventh revision, due in 2023 when we wrote this chapter. Based on the 2016 CACREP Standards, CACREP included accreditation of doctoral programs in counselor education and supervision and master's programs in the areas of addictions counseling, mental health counseling (formerly community counseling), career counseling, clinical rehabilitation counseling, college counseling and student affairs, marriage and family counseling/therapy, and school counseling. Regardless of the area of specialization, all CACREP-accredited master's programs are expected to address the following in their curriculum: professional orientation and ethical practice, social and cultural diversity, human growth and development, career development, counseling and helping relationships, group counseling and group work, assessment and testing, and research and program evaluation (CACREP, 2016a) All programs must also include specific curricular experiences related to the area of accreditation (e.g., addictions, clinical mental health, etc.) and include 100 hours of practicum and 600 hours of field-based internship (CACREP, 2016b).

In 2015, the leaders of CORE and CACREP signed an agreement to merge, which they did in July 2017. This merger came after many years of discussion about strengthening the professional counselor identity and unifying the accreditation process. The rehabilitation counseling standards became "the eighth entry-level specialty in the 2016 CACREP Standards," with "applications to accredit programs under those standards being accepted beginning June 1, 2018" (CACREP, 2017, para. 2X).

In 2009, a group of counselor educators sought to accredit their master's counseling programs through an alternative to CACREP. They requested that the Master's in Psychology Accreditation Council (MPAC), a council established to accredit terminal master's degree programs in psychology, consider expanding their scope. The MPAC accepted the request and established the Master's in Psychology and Counseling Accreditation Council (MPCAC, n.d.). According to the MPCAC (n.d.), by 2015 there were 40 MPCAC-accredited programs. As of the end of 2020, MPCAC was under review for recognition by the Council for Higher Education Accreditation.

Regulating Counselors

As of 2009, all 50 states and the District of Columbia had passed licensure laws. As we previously mentioned, there is variance in licensure laws across states. The ACA (2016) reported that in 2015, 88.5% of the 52 counselor credentialing laws in place (all 50 states, the District of Columbia, Guam, and Puerto Rico) were practice acts. Also, various titles (e.g., professional counselor, mental health counselor, clinical professional counselor) are assigned to licensed counselors. In addition, the academic and post-academic requirements to be eligible for licensure range from a master's degree in counseling with no specified number of graduate credits to 60 master's credits in counseling (ACA, 2016).

Further, there are differences in the scopes of practice for licensed counselors. As of 2016, the ACA reported that just over 85% of the state laws specifically included that licensed counselors could assess and diagnose mental disorders. However, there are states where boards that license psychologists have claimed that most standardized tests, from career related to personality tests, require that people have a doctorate in psychology to administer and interpret the instruments effectively. Professional organizations such as ACA, AMHCA, NBCC, and CRCC have been advocating for counselors' right to administer and interpret standardized instruments based on their education and training, not based solely on the degree they earned (Peterson et al., 2014). Throughout the 21st century, the focus has been on strengthening title laws, working toward uniform scopes of practice based on the ACA model licensure legislation, and increasing licensure portability.

One of the 2020 Future of Counseling Oversight Committee goals was to establish portability by the year 2020. Currently, if counselors are licensed in one state, when they move they must apply to and be approved by the board in their new state before they can be licensed. Progress has been made in establishing interstate portability pathways for licensed counselors, and there is still work to be done. Although all organizations involved in the committee agreed on the importance of license portability, at the end of 2020, two different plans were put forward. Regardless of whether states accept recommendations from either plan, given our mobile society and increased use of virtual or remote counseling services, increasing the portability of counselor licensure is a goal shared by all professional counseling organizations.

The ACA proposed one plan with the goals of (a) making it easier to move to another state and maintain an LPC license, (b) allowing counselors to provide telehealth in multiple states without the need for multiple licenses, and (c) allowing counselors to provide services across the nearest state line while holding only a single license. The plan requires that counselors be licensed for independent practice level in their home state and have no disciplinary actions against them (Lambert, 2018). The plan also included that states may require that counselors also pass a jurisprudence examination based on the state's laws (Lambert, 2018).

The second plan is one put forth by the National Portability Taskforce, comprised of AASCB, ACES, AMHCA, and NBCC, and is titled the National Counselor Licensure Endorsement Process (NCLEP 2.0; AACSB, 2019). Like the ACA plan, the NCLEP 2.0 requires that counselors be licensed for independent practice in their home state and have no disciplinary sanctions. The difference between the plans is that the NCLEP 2.0 also notes that if counselors do not meet the standards for endorsement adopted by a state counselor licensure board, applicants must meet other requirements. Those requirements include that they be actively licensed as a mental health counselor for at least three years before applying for licensure endorsement and that they complete a jurisprudence examination and background check (if required by the state). Also, applicants must (a) have maintained a licensed to practice independently that was awarded on or before December 31, 2014 or (b) that they are credentialed as National Certified Counselors (NCCs) by the NBCC, or (c) have earned a graduate-level degree in counseling from a regionally accredited program. The plan further notes that if applicants earned their degree on or after January 1, 2025, that degree must be from a program accredited by CACREP (AACSB, 2019).

Federal Legislation/Policies

Following are some of the critical issues that professional counseling organizations advocated for at the federal level between 2000 and 2020: addressing the opioid epidemic, passage of Medicare provider recognition for professional counselors and marriage and family therapists, increased hiring of licensed counselors within the VA system, an expanded federal definition of the mental health workforce to include professional counselors, funding for school counseling programs, and the provision of telebehavioral health. Many pieces of federal legislation passed and policies were enacted that increased the counseling profession's recognition and impacted the provision of counseling services. Following are only a few examples.

In 2001, the No Child Left Behind Act included the reauthorization of the Elementary School Counseling Demonstration program (passed in 1995). What made this act significant was that it removed the word *demonstration* from the program, expanded the program to secondary schools, and required a certain dollar amount appropriated for the program to support counseling services in elementary schools. Much later in this century, the Student Support and Academic Enrichment (SSAE) grant program was included in the 2019 Labor HHS Education package. Among other things, the act included a $70 million increase over funds from the previous year. The grants fund activities expand access to, or coordinate resources for, school-based mental health services and supports, including developing critical tools such as trauma-informed practices and establishing and maintaining school counseling and bullying prevention programs.

In 2006, Congress passed the Veterans Benefits, Healthcare, and Information Technology Act (P.L. 109–461), which recognized counselors as mental health specialists within the VA system. It allowed for LPCs to be hired in clinical and supervisory positions. In 2015, the National Defense Authorization Act was reauthorized and added licensed counselors who graduated from CACREP or regionally accredited programs to the TRICARE program list of independent practitioners. The act specified that as of 2017, those providers must have passed the NCMHCE. After January of 2021, they must be graduates from CACREP-accredited programs (ACA, 2015, para. 9).

In 2016, Congress passed the 21st Century Cures Act with almost unanimous bipartisan support. One of this law's goals was to improve the integration and coordination of mental health and substance use disorder services across federal agencies. ACA and AMHCA strongly advocated for this law. The law lacked the language needed that would grant Medicare provider status to licensed counselors. However, this bill was significant in increasing a focus on prevention and early intervention, including the provision of counseling services in school and community settings. It also established a minority fellowship program to increase mental health and substance use services to people from underserved populations. Also in 2016, the Comprehensive Addiction and Recovery Act became the first legislation in 40 years that authorized $181 million to fight the opioid crisis and included provisions for education and prevention.

The Support for Patients and Communities Act, a bipartisan bill, was enacted in 2018. It included ways to increase and strengthen the mental health and addictions treatment workforce and reduce barriers to the delivery of addiction medicine via telemedicine in rural areas. The language in the Support Act and used by the Centers for Medicare and Medicaid Services expanded the definition of allowable mental health care services. It included that any LPCs or LMHCs working in opioid treatment programs (OTP) providing services to clients with opioid use disorders can provide counseling services without any disruption to bundled payments received by the OTP.

Although the Support Act's language did not expand full recognition of licensed counselors as providers for all Medicare services, that language can help in the continued fight for such recognition, as did the passage of the bipartisan Mental Health Access Improvement Act of 2019. That law amended Title XVIII of the Social Security Act to provide for the coverage of marriage and family therapist services and mental health counselor services under part B of the Medicare program.

One of the most significant advances for mental health counselors working for the federal government, especially the Department of Veteran's Affairs, was the passage of Veterans Administration (VA) Bill, S. 785, the Commander John Scott Hannon Veterans Mental Health Care Improvement Act. In addition to being a significant mental health bill for veterans, the bill directs the VA to establish an occupational series for mental health counselors with the federal Office of Personnel Management within a year of enactment. Organizations such as the ACA, AMHCA, and NBCC have been advocating for the federal government to create an employment classification for counselors for decades. Being included in the occupational series will allow professional counselors to work in federal government agencies under the title of mental health counselors. In addition to increasing our recognition as a profession and counselors' employability, this bill will allow counselors to do good by providing more services to military personnel and veterans.

CURRENT ISSUES: SOCIOCULTURAL CONSCIOUSNESS MOVEMENTS THAT IMPACT MENTAL HEALTH

In the following sections, we have attempted to highlight a few evolving sociocultural issues that impact mental health and counseling services. Although this is not an exhaustive list, these issues are ones being followed by the ACA's Government Affairs department and have caught the attention of many counselors and mental health advocates.

Advocacy in Action on Climate Change

Some may ask how climate change is an advocacy issue for professional counselors. Climate change can be described as a slow onset process that impacts humans and their ecosystems in many ways (Ferreira, 2020). As a result, psychosocial impacts might not be detected or diagnosed immediately. Mental health impacts of climate change are significant sources of stress for individuals and communities. Climate change and related disasters cause anxiety-related responses and chronic and severe mental health disorders (Ferreira, 2020). The Center for Research on the Epidemiology of Disasters (CRED, 2019) reported 10,733 lives were lost and 61.7 million people were affected by climate-induced disasters. Flooding and prolonged droughts have been associated with elevated levels of anxiety, depression, and posttraumatic stress disorders (Ursano et al., 2017). The trauma and loss from a disaster, such as losing a home or job and being disconnected from neighborhood and community, can contribute to depression and anxiety. Some people who are more vulnerable to climate change's potential impacts include children, the elderly, the chronically ill, people with cognitive or mobility impairments, pregnant and postpartum women, and people with mental illness (Hayes et al., 2018). Many potential long-term impacts of climate change, such as population migration, food scarcity, loss of employment, and loss of social support, have consequences in mental health (Hayes et al., 2018). In 2017 and 2020, the ACA published articles in their monthly *Counseling Today* magazine describing the necessity of counselors to address the associated mental health crisis that comes with climate change (Meyers, 2020; Sturm & Echterling, 2017).

Counselors need to be aware of the psychological impact of climate change, and climate change distress, which includes but is not limited to fear, loss, displacement, injury, or food and health insecurity, which are ways an individual is connected to their environment during a threat (Ingle & Mikulewicz, 2020). The concept of *solastalgia* is associated with witnessing and experiencing the pain caused by the loss and isolation of one's home and environment (Albrecht, 2005). Solastalgia can lead to adverse health effects, including mental anguish that can escalate to more mental health problems. Eco anxiety is another concept closely related to mental health. It can be described by severe and overwhelming worry about climate and environmental risks that can often result in sleeplessness, loss of appetite, and other psychosocial impacts (Ingle & Mikulewicz, 2020).

Advocacy in Action on Veterans

The members of the U.S. House committees have recognized that veterans may benefit from access to mental health services provided by the VA—including suicide prevention services—even if they were not called to active service under federal orders. Due to the growing need for mental health professionals, the VA is directed to maintain appropriate mental health staffing levels to provide veterans with timely, effective, high-quality care. The U.S. Congress proposed the Military Construction, Veterans Affairs, and Related Agencies Appropriations Act (2020), which directs the VA to prioritize the hiring of mental health professionals and to keep the appropriations committees of both Houses of Congress apprised quarterly of the way the VA is meeting its hiring goals, including actions taken to improve recruitment and retention across the country, specifically in rural areas. This report should include updates to the ratio of faculty staff to outpatient veterans being treated for mental health needs.

Advocacy in Action on Telehealth and COVID-19

Telehealth, also commonly referred to as distance counseling or telebehavioral health, is a growing industry and method of counseling in which clients and counselors use the internet that supports a video, chat, or audio stream to communicate, often through third-party HIPAA-compliant services. Technology-assisted distance supervision is not considered telebehavioral health or telehealth as there is no counseling service or mental health support provided through this platform. There are significant benefits to telehealth, including the ability to reach underserved or rural communities and bypassing obstacles that may limit or prevent individuals from accessing face-to-face therapy (CNA and Healthcare Providers Service Organization, 2019). Telehealth can be used for individuals or groups, or families. It can be synchronous (telephone, chat, or visual contact online, which occurs in real time) or asynchronous (email or texting that is not real time).

The ACA (2014) Code of Ethics outlines this topic in section H, which focuses on distance counseling, technology, and social media. According to these standards, counselors may decide whether to incorporate telehealth technology and distance counseling in their practice. Those who decide to offer telehealth in their practice should be appropriately trained to use any platform they use to provide services. Counselors must also be aware that telehealth services and electronic communications differ from state to state and consider how liability exposure may arise.

The Military Construction, Veterans Affairs, and Related Agencies Appropriations Act 2020 also included agreements for additional funding to increase telehealth capacity in rural and highly rural areas. The agreement directs the VA to develop a plan to improve veteran and provider satisfaction, increase awareness of the telehealth program, and enhance adoption of telehealth by veterans and providers. Further, due to the global pandemic, COVID-19, at the time this chapter was submitted for publication, several bills had been introduced to support broadband expansion for internet access to receive telehealth services, lower payment methods by insurance companies, and temporary lift restrictions regarding issues of jurisdiction.

Advocacy in Action on Medicare

In 2019, Representative John Katko, Republican from New York, and Representative Mike Thompson, Democrat from California, introduced HR 945, the Mental Health Improvement Act of 2019 to the House of Representatives. The American Counseling Association's Government Affairs department has made this a priority for their federal advocacy agenda. With this bipartisan legislation passed, Medicare beneficiaries will have access to mental health treatment by licensed professional counselors. According to the ACA's Government Affairs team (2019), there are more than 140,000 licensed professional counselors across the country, particularly in rural communities, who are available and accessible to help those with Medicare as their primary insurance coverage. Unfortunately, LPCs are not able to be reimbursed by Medicare, despite their credentials. Instead, most LPCs are licensed for independent practice by state and are covered independently by private-sector health plans. This piecemeal approach has detrimental impacts on the culture of receiving mental health services: LPCs are not reimbursed equitably for the quality of services they provide and become disincentivized to accept insurance. Also, consumers of these services are either unable to afford services or may go to someone who is not as qualified.

Advocacy in Action on Values-Based Practices

The ACA (2014) Code of Ethics requires that counselors respect their clients' and trainees' diversity and avoid imposing their values on them (A.4.b.). The code further directs counselors to use techniques that have a scientific foundation or are grounded in theory (ACA, 2014, C.7.a.) and to adhere to the principle of nonmaleficence, or "do no harm," which is supported by section C.7.c. These three sections relate to advocacy efforts on controversial laws introduced or passed by states on the use of conversion therapy and allowing service providers and businesses to deny services based on religious or moral beliefs.

Conversion therapy is a practice that attempts to change someone's sexual orientation identity. This practice has been discredited by mental health associations such as the ACA, APA, and the American Psychiatric Association because it is based on two assumptions. The first is that having a sexual orientation other than heterosexual is a mental disorder. Second is a priori assumption that clients should change their homosexual orientation. In 2018, Dr. Gerard Lawson, then president of the ACA, testified before the Virginia House of Delegates Committee on Health, Welfare, and Institutions. He expressed ACA's support of Virginia HB 363, which would prohibit the practice of conversion therapy on minors within the Commonwealth of Virginia. This stance aligns with the ACA Governing Council's two resolutions and an interpretation by the ACA Ethics Committee.

In 1998, the ACA Governing Council passed a resolution against portraying people who identify as lesbian, gay, or bisexual as having a mental disorder. They noted the need to disseminate accurate information based on research (Whitman et al., 2006). The next year, the Governing Council adopted a statement that opposed the use of reparative counseling (Whitman et al., 2006), and in 2006 the ACA Ethics Committee supported the interpretation that the use of reparative or conversion therapy was unethical. The committee members went beyond that to strongly discourage counselors from referring clients to anyone who engages in conversion therapy. If clients request such a referral, the committee members noted if counselors provide the referral, they do so cautiously, informing clients about the potential risks and that the treatment is not scientifically supported (Whitman et al., 2006). According to the

Human Rights Campaign (2020), the following jurisdictions had banned conversion therapy for minors as of December 2020: California, Colorado, Connecticut, Delaware, Hawaii, Illinois, Maine, Maryland, Massachusetts, Nevada, New Hampshire, New Jersey, New Mexico, New York, Oregon, Rhode Island, Utah, Virginia, Vermont, Washington, the District of Columbia, and Puerto Rico.

Conscience clause legislation refers to laws enacted by states that allow health and mental health providers and businesses to refuse to offer services based on the providers' or business owners' religious or moral beliefs. Most of the laws seem targeted at protecting professional and business owners who object to gay marriage and nonmarital sex or refuse to provide abortions. According to Rose et al. (2019), as of 2019, 14 states had enacted such laws, and another 12 states had attempted but failed. Professional counseling has not explicitly been cited in most of the laws that have been passed. However, as of 2019, Tennessee, Arkansas, and Mississippi had enacted legislation that specifically mentioned professional counselors, allowing them to "opt-out" to provide services or procedures if doing so would compromise their conscience based on firmly held beliefs (Rose et al., 2019). For counselors in those states, although it would be legal to deny services to and make referrals for clients based on the counselor's beliefs, this would conflict with the ACA (2014) Code of Ethics. Although the 2017 ACA conference was scheduled to be held in Tennessee, they moved it to another state as an act of advocacy. We anticipate that conscience laws and bills to allow or prohibit conversion therapy will be introduced in additional states. We encourage readers to think about how you might react if such bills are introduced in your state.

SUMMARY, INSIGHTS, AND ACTIONS

In addition to these global issues, in the wake of continued murder and violence against the Black community, the ACA has spoken out against racism, police brutality, systemic violence, dehumanizing forces of oppression, and White supremacy. Through their statement, the ACA took a stand with the Black Lives Matter movement and acknowledged the anti-racist work all counselors must commit to in order to be more just and culturally competent. Ongoing efforts are needed to ensure that suicide prevention legislation continues to be a priority as well as LGBTQIA+, immigrant, and students' rights. You can start by learning who your local and federal representatives are and becoming informed of the issues. By joining a national organization like the ACA, your voice will become more unified and stronger in number. You can also visit, write, and call your officials and share your story of how these laws impact you and the clients you serve. Finally, you can organize events with your communities, find your advocacy voice by practicing, and vote for people in office who align with your views.

REFLECTION AND DISCUSSION QUESTIONS

1. Suppose you had to pick up to five of the most noteworthy events (social events, pieces of legislation, actions taken by professional associations, etc.) in the 20th and 21st centuries. Which would you say most influenced the development of the counseling profession? Which of those five most demonstrate the profession's commitment to social justice?

2. In what ways has federal legislation positively influenced the recognition of the counseling profession? How does increased recognition relate to social justice across work settings?

3. What are the ways in which you can become more involved in advocating for policy change?

4. What events do you think will influence how we practice and provide counseling services in the coming years?

5. In what ways have professional counseling organizations, such as ACA, addressed issues of multiculturalism over the years?

ADDITIONAL RESOURCES

American Counseling Association: www.counseling.org

American Counseling Association competencies: https://www.counseling.org/knowledge-center/competencies

American Counseling Association government affairs information: http://www.counseling.org/government-affairs/public-policy

American Counseling Association on anti-racism: https://www.counseling.org/news/updates/2020/06/22/aca-anti-racism-statement

American Counseling Association's statements on social justice and human rights: https://www.counseling.org/about-us/social-justice

American Mental Health Counselors Association: https://www.amhca.org/hone

American School Counselor Association: https://www.schoolcounselor.org

Centers for Disease Control and Prevention: https://www.cdc.gov/rxawareness/prevent/index.html

Healthcare Providers Service Organization (HPSO) and CNA on Telebehavioral Health: http://www.hpso.com/Documents/Risk%20Education/individuals/Claim-Reports/Counselor/F-13777-619_Telebehavioral_Health_Spotlight.pdf

U.S. Congress, House of Representatives on Military Construction, Veterans Affairs, and Related Agencies Appropriations Act, 2020: https://www.congress.gov/bill/116th-congress/house-bill/2745/text

National Employment Counseling Association's endorsement of the American Counseling Association's stance on anti-racism: https://www.counseling.org/news/updates/2020/06/17/neca-statement-against-racism

Counselors for Social Justice: https://www.counseling.org/docs/default-source/announcements-and-news/csj-open-letter-call-to-action.pdf

U.S. Department of Human Services, Office of the Surgeon General: https://www.hhs.gov/surgeongeneral/priorities/opioids-and-addiction/naloxone-advisory/index.html

World Health Organization on *climate change and human health*: https://www.who.int/news-room/fact-sheets/detail/climate-change-and-health

REFERENCES

Albrecht, G. (2005). "Solastalgia": A new concept in health and identity. *Philosophy Activism Nature, 3*, 44–59.

American Association of State Counseling Boards (n.d.). *About*. http://www.aascb.org/aws/AASCB/pt/sp/about

American Association of State Counseling Boards. (2019). *Licensure and portability*. http://www.aascb.org/aws/AASCB/pt/sp/licensure

American Counseling Association. (n.d.). *Our history*. https://www.counseling.org/about-us/about-aca/our-history

American Counseling Association. (2005). *Code of ethics*. Author.

American Counseling Association. (2014). *Code of ethics*. Author.

American Counseling Association. (2015). *ACA provision in the National Defense Authorization Act signed by President Obama*. http//www.counseling.org/news/news-release-archives/by-year/2015

American Counseling Association. (2016). *Licensure requirements for professional counselors. A state-by-state report*. Author.

American Counseling Association. (2019). *Support access to mental health services for seniors, veterans, and those with disabilities*. https://www.counseling.org/docs/default-source/government-affairs/mental-health-access-improvement-act-of-2019-one-pager.pdf

American Counseling Association Office of Public Policy and Information. (1998). *Briefing paper: Congress passes bill recognizing counselors under health professional training programs*. Author.

American Personnel and Guidance Association. (1969). *Guidelines for graduate programs in the preparation of student personnel workers in higher education*. Author.

American Personnel and Guidance Association. (1976). *Model for state legislation concerning the practice of counseling, 1976, draft no. 4*. Author.

Association for Counselor Education and Supervision. (1967). Standards for counselor education preparation of secondary school counselors. *Personnel and Guidance Journal, 46*, 96–106.

Aubrey, R. F. (1977). Historical development of guidance and counseling and implications for the future. *Personnel and Guidance Journal, 61*, 288–295.

Beers, C. W. (1908). *A mind that found itself*. Doubleday.

Brewer, J. (1932). *Education as guidance*. McMillan.

Caplow, T. (1966). The sequence of professionalization. In H. M. Vollmer & D. L. Mills (Eds.), *Professionalization* (pp. 20–21). Prentice-Hall.

Center for Research on the Epidemiology of Disasters. (2019). 2018 *Review of disaster events.* https://www.cred.be/2018-review-disaster-event

Chi Sigma Iota. (2020). *JCLA.* https://www.csi-net.org/page/JCLA

CNA and Healthcare Providers Service Organization. (2019). *Counselor liability claim report: 2nd edition. Minimizing risk, achieving excellence.* http://www.hpso.com/Documents/RiskEducation/individuals/Claim-Reports/Counselor/HPSO-CNA-Counselor-Claim-Report-2019.pdf http://www.hpso.com/risk-education/individuals/Counselor-Claim-Reports

Council for Accreditation of Counseling and Related Educational Programs. (2016a). *Section 2: Professional counseling identity.* https://www.cacrep.org/section-2-professional-counseling-identity/

Council for Accreditation of Counseling and Related Educational Programs. (2016b). *Section 3: Professional practice.* https://www.cacrep.org/section-3-professional-practice/

Council for Accreditation of Counseling and Related Educational Programs. (2017). *Rehabilitation counseling standards adopted.* https://www.cacrep.org/news/rehabilitation-counseling-standards-adopted/

Council for Higher Education Accreditation. (n.d.). *Homepage.* https://www.chea.org/

Cummings, N. A. (1990). The credentialing of professional psychologists and its implication for the other mental health disciplines. *Journal of Counseling & Development, 68,* 485–490 https://doi.org/10.1002/j.1556-6676.1990.tb01395.xDepartment of Veteran Affairs. (n.d.). *VA history in brief.* https://www.va.gov/opa/publications/archives/docs/history_in_brief.pdf

Erford, B. T. (2014). *Orientation to the counseling profession: Advocacy, ethics, and essential professional foundations.* Pearson.

Ferreira, R. J. (2020). Climate change, resilience, and trauma: Course of action through research, policy, and practice [Editorial]. *Traumatology, 26*(3), 246–247. https://doi.org/10.1037/trm0000282

Gibson, R. L., & Mitchell, M. H. (2008). *Introduction to counseling and guidance.* Pearson/Merrill/Prentice Hall.

Glosoff, H. L., Benshoff, J. M., Hosie, T. W., & Maki, D. R. (1995). The 1994 ACA model legislation for licensed professional counselors. *Journal of Counseling & Development, 74,* 209–220.

Glosoff, H. L., & Kocet, M. M. (2006). Highlights of the 2005 ACA code of ethics. In G. R. Walz, J. Bleuer, & R. K. Yep (Eds.), *Vistas: Compelling perspectives on counseling 2006* (pp. 5–9). American Counseling Association.

Glosoff, H. L., Scwartz, J. E., & Shand-Lubbers, R. (2020). The counseling profession: Historical perspectives and current issues and trends. In D. Capuzzi & D. Gross (Eds.), *Introduction to the counseling profession* (8th ed.) (pp. 2–54). Cognella.

Hayes, K., Blashki, G., Wiseman, J., Burke, S., & Reifels, L. (2018). Climate change and mental health: Risks, impacts and priority actions. *International Journal of Mental Health Systems, 12,* 28. http://dx.doi.org/10.1186/s13033-018-0210-6

Herr, E. (1985). AACD: An association committed to unity through diversity. *Journal of Counseling & Development, 63*, 395–404.

Hershenson, D. B., Power, P. W., & Waldo, M. (1996). *Community counseling: Contemporary theory and practice.* Allyn & Bacon.

Hosie, T. W. (1991). Historical antecedents and current status of counselor licensure. In F. Bradley (Ed.), *Credentialing in counseling* (pp. 23–52). American Association for Counseling and Development.

Human Rights Campaign. (2020). *The lies and dangers of efforts to change sexual orientation or gender identity.* https://www.hrc.org/resources/the-lies-and-dangers-of-reparative-therapy

Ingle, H. E., & Mikulewicz, M. (2020). Mental health and climate change: Tackling invisible injustice. *The LANCET: Planetary Health, 4(4)*, e128–e130. http://dx.doi.org/10.1016/S2542-5196(20)30081-4

Kaplan, D. M., Tarvydas, V. M., & Gladding, S. T. (2014). 20/20: A vision for the future of counseling: The new consensus definition of counseling. *Journal of Counseling & Development, 92*, 366–372.

Lambert, S. (2018, November 30). From the president: Making progress toward portability. *Counseling Today.* https://ct.counseling.org/2018/11/from-the-president-making-progress-toward-portability/

Lawson, G. (2018). *Testimony of Gerard Lawson, president of the American Counseling Association, before the Virginia House of Delegates Committee on Health, Welfare, and Institutions.* https://www.counseling.org/docs/default-source/government-affairs/testimony-of-gerard-lawson-final.pdf?sfvrsn=fbd7532c_2

Lee, J. M. (1966). Issues and emphases in guidance: A historical perspective. In J. M. Lee & N. J. Pallone (Eds.), *Readings in guidance and counseling (pp. 13-XX–XX).* Sheed and Ward.

Lewis, J. A., Arnold, M. S., House, R., & Toporek, R. L. (2003). *ACA Advocacy Competencies.* https://www.counseling.org/knowledge-center/competencies

Lynch, R. K., & Maki, D. (1981). Searching for structure: A trait-factor approach to vocational rehabilitation. *Vocational Guidance Quarterly, 30*, 61–68.

Manderscheid, R. W., & Sonnenschein, M. A. (1992). *Mental health in the United Sates, 1992* (DHHS Publication No. [SMA] 92-1942). U.S. Government Printing Office.

Master's in Psychology and Counseling Accreditation Council. (n.d.). *History: How the overlap in psychology, counseling psychology, and counseling led to the development of MPCAC.* http://mpcacaccreditation.org/about-mpcac/history/

McDaniels, C. O. (1964). *The history and development of the American Personnel and Guidance Association* [Unpublished doctoral dissertation, University of Virginia].

Medicare Mental Health Workforce Coalition. (2020). *Expanding the Medicare provider workforce: A solution to the behavioral health crisis.* https://www.counseling.org/docs/default-source/default-document-library/medicare-access-coalition-handout-with-map.pdf?sfvrsn=604d572c_0

Messina, J. J. (1985). The National Academy of Certified Clinical Mental Health Counselors: Creating a new professional identity. *Journal of Counseling & Development, 63*, 607–608.

Meyers, L. (2020, September). Climate in crisis: Counselors needed. *Counseling Today, 63(3)*, 20–27.

National Institute of Mental Health. (2017). *NIMH legislative chronology.* https://www.nih.gov/about-nih/what-we-do/nih-almanac/national-institute-mental-health-nimh

Ohlsen, M. M. (1983). *Introduction to counseling.* F. E. Peacock.

Peterson, S. (2020). Celebrating the role of rehabilitation counseling. *Counseling Today, 62(8), 52–56.*

Peterson, C. H., Lomas, G. I., Neukrug, E. S., & Bonner, W. M. (2014). Assessment use by counselors in the United States: Implications for policy and practice. *Journal of Counseling & Development, 92,* 90–98.

Ratts, M. J., Singh, A. A., Nassar-McMillan, S., Butler, S. K., & McCullough, J. R. (2016). Multicultural and social justice counseling competencies: Guidelines for the counseling profession. *Journal of Multicultural Counseling and Development, 44(1),* 28–48. https://doi.org/10.1002/jmcd.12035

Reed, A. Y. (1917). Vocational guidance and educational preparedness. *Journal of Education, 86,* 152–153.

Rose, J. S., Kocet, M. M., Thompson, F. A., Flores, M., McKinney, R., & Suprima, J. S. (2019). Association for Lesbian, Gay, Bisexual, and Transgender Issues in Counseling's best practices in addressing conscience clause legislation in counselor education and supervision. *Journal of LGBT Issues in Counseling, 13,* 2–27. https://doi.org/10.1080/15538605.2019.1565800

Scull, A. (2018). Creating a new psychiatry: On the origins of non-institutional psychiatry in the USA, 1900–50. *History of Psychiatry, 29(4),* 389–408. https://doi.org/10.1177/0957154X18793596

Shertzer, B., & Stone, S. C. (1986). *Fundamentals of counseling.* Houghton Mifflin.

Snodgrass, J. (1984). William Healey (1869–1963): Pioneer child psychiatrist and criminologist. *Journal of the History of the Behavioral Sciences, 20(4),* 332–339.

Sturm, D. C., & Echterling L. G. (2017, May). Preparing for the mental health impact of climate change. *Counseling Today, 59(11),* 60–63. https://ct.counseling.org/2017/05/preparing-mental-health-impact-climate-change/

Sue, D. W., Arredondo, P., & McDavis, R. J. (1992). Multicultural counseling competencies and standards: A call to the profession. *Journal of Counseling & Development, 70(4),* 477–486. https://doi.org/10.1002/j.1556-6676.1992.tb01642.x

Sweeney, T. J. (1991). Counselor credentialing: Purpose and origin. In F. Bradley (Ed.), *Credentialing in counseling* (pp. 23–52). American Association for Counseling and Development.

Sweeney, T. J. (2001). Counseling: Historical origins and philosophical roots. In D. C. Locke, J. E. Myers, & E. L. Herr (Eds.), *The handbook of counseling* (pp. 3–26). SAGE.

Ursano, R. J. Morganstien, J. C., & Cooper, R. (2017). *Resource document on mental health and climate change.* APA.

Whitman, J. S., Glosoff, H. L., Kocet, M. M., & Tarvydas, V. (2006). Exploring ethical issues related to conversion or reparative therapy. *Counseling Today, 49(1),* 14–15.

CHAPTER 3

PROFESSIONAL IDENTITY DEVELOPMENT WITH MULTICULTURAL AND SOCIAL JUSTICE AT ITS CORE

Anna Flores Locke, Nyack College

LEARNING OBJECTIVES

1. Learn about the historical background of professional identity along with the counseling profession's journey in formulating a multicultural counseling and social justice stance.
2. Learn how professional identity development is understood for master's-level students, practicing counselors, supervisors, and counselor educators.
3. Learn an integrated perspective of professional identity development that incorporates a multicultural and social justice lens as a core component.

LEARNING OUTCOMES

1. Develop a professional identity with multiculturalism and social justice at its core.
2. Develop a more thorough understanding of what professional identity development is.
3. Through a case study, witness the development of a professional identity with multiculturalism and social justice at its center.

PROFESSIONAL IDENTITY DEVELOPMENT IN COUNSELING

As a young profession, the field of counseling has been grappling with defining a professional identity that is unique from social work, psychology, and other related fields (Gerig, 2014; Van Hesteren & Ivey, 1990). What makes professional counseling distinct is a focus on human development across the life span coupled with an emphasis on wellness and prevention. Kaplan, Tarvydas, and Gladding (2014) defines professional counseling as "a professional relationship that empowers individuals, families, and groups to accomplish mental health, wellness, education, and career goals" (p. 366). The Council for Accreditation of Counseling and Related Educational Programs (CACREP, 2016) aims to promote a unified counseling profession and includes professional identity as a standard. Hence, having a strong professional counselor identity is a highly regarded and valuable component of the counseling profession (Burkholder, 2012). Absent from this discussion, however, is language that defines professional counselor identity from a multicultural counseling and social justice perspective. Although being a culturally competent counselor has been recognized in the ACA Codes of Ethics and CACREP standards as an important feature of being a skilled clinician, it is often not associated with "who we are" as counseling professionals.

The multicultural and social justice counseling competencies (MSJCC) provide a helpful model from which to explore professional counselor identity from a multicultural counseling and social justice perspective. This model emphasizes an exploration of counselor self-awareness, client worldview, and the counseling relationship within the context of living in a society that is discriminatory toward marginalized racial, ethnic, socioeconomic class, sexual orientation, and other cultural groups (Adkison-Johnson & Johnson, 2019; Lee, 2019). Through awareness building, knowledge development, and skill acquisition during and after graduate training, multicultural and social justice competence is becoming a core component of professional counselor identity.

In this chapter, we will learn about the historical background of professional identity along with the counseling profession's journey in formulating a multicultural counseling and social justice stance. We will learn how professional identity development is understood for master's-level students, practicing counselors, supervisors, and counselor educators. By the end, we will have an integrated perspective of professional identity development that incorporates a multicultural and social justice lens as a core component.

Historical Background

In 1952, the American Counseling Association (ACA) was formed, a code of ethics was written, and credentialing and professional standards were created to legitimize our existence as a separate and unique profession (Gale & Austin, 2003). Since this time, the counseling field has been working on defining a unified definition of who a professional counselor is and how we are differentiated from other helping professions (Hanna & Bemak, 1997). Counseling as a profession has its roots in vocational or guidance counseling, education, and psychology (Glosoff & Schwarz-Whittaker, 2013). The counseling profession was birthed from a convergence of professional roles and values from these fields.

As such, professional counseling upholds certain values, such as equality; client advocacy; the importance of career and personal growth; and the influence of health, human development, and biology/neurology (Granello & Young, 2012). Counselors also believe in the benefits of science to inform practice via evidence-based treatment approaches, in addition to assessments and testing (Granello & Young, 2012). A counselor is someone who has pride in the profession and focuses on the wellness, development, prevention, and empowerment of individuals (Mellin et al., 2011; Remley & Herlihy, 2010; Van Hesteren & Ivey, 1990). As you develop your professional identity consider how these philosophical underpinnings match or do not match with your current strengths and values.

Through providing individual, family, group, and couples therapy; assessment and intervention; and consultation, counselors express these values to help others improve well-being. Additionally, counselors work across multiple levels of care to ensure the wellness of clients at various times in their lives. For example, a counselor may be involved during a crisis or psychiatric emergency, as well as during stabilization interventions in the home or in outpatient agencies. Counselors also work with all ages and apply a developmental perspective to conceptualize and treat clients in the most effective way possible.

In recent years, the counseling profession has been intentional about integrating multiculturalism and social justice into its professional identities. Diversity, inclusion, advocacy, and equity are keywords in the profession's ethical code, program and accreditation standards, and various competencies. Despite these efforts, the profession struggles with identifying multiculturalism and social justice as core values in its identity. In other words, being a social justice counselor is a newer concept, as is exploring the influence of power and privilege, oppression, and cultural variables on how we counsel, assess, and treat individuals, families, and communities.

Multiculturalism and Social Justice in Counseling

The Association for Multicultural Counseling and Development and Counselors for Social Justice emerged as divisions within ACA committed to promoting multicultural and social justice values (Ratts et al., 2010). Three major contributions came from these divisions. The first was the *Journal of Multicultural Counseling and Development* (formerly the *Journal of Non-White Concerns*) and the Multicultural Counseling Competencies (MCC) (Sue et al., 1992). The next was the Advocacy Competencies, written by Lewis et al. in 2003 and updated by Toporek and Daniels in 2018. The last was the Multicultural and Social Justice Counseling Competencies (MSJCC). Together the latter two provide invaluable frameworks from which to practice multicultural and social justice counseling.

The MCC provided a framework from which to develop the multicultural awareness, knowledge, and skills needed to effectively and ethically work with diverse clientele (Sue et al., 1992). The authors of the MCC provided a framework from which to counsel others in a multiculturally competent manner. They explained that counselors must (a) develop counselor awareness of their own assumptions, values, and biases; (b) understand the worldview of the culturally different; and (c) develop appropriate intervention strategies (Sue et al., 1992). As a call to the profession, this document spearheaded the field's commitment to developing multiculturally competent counselors.

With the creation of the advocacy competencies, social justice also took precedence in our work with clients and communities and served to revolutionize the role of the professional counselor (Ratts et al., 2010). The competencies define how to use advocacy as a mechanism for addressing clients' problems through a systemic approach that alters the oppressive social context within which clients operate. Advocacy is taking action to facilitate the removal of external and institutional barriers to clients' well-being and speaking out with and/or on behalf of a marginalized individual or group (Toporek & Daniels, 2018). The competencies describe a social justice–based intervention model for counselors to put social justice ideals into action. Specifically, the advocacy competencies provide a framework from which to advocate for students, clients, client groups, or whole populations. Based on these competencies, counselors are expected to collaborate with or act on behalf of clients or groups to facilitate empowerment and remove systemic barriers that impede well-being. Further, the competencies outline levels of advocacy intervention: (a) the individual to address issues faced by the client; (b) the school, community, or organization to address issues faced by whole groups, and (c) the public arena to facilitate social change (Toporek & Daniels, 2018).

Social justice has been central to the professional identity of counseling since its inception. Just recently, the ACA has embraced advocacy as one of three central pillars in their strategic initiatives (Toporek & Daniels, 2018). Social justice can be defined as promoting equity, access, and optimal developmental opportunities for all members of society through the elimination of systemic barriers and oppression (Kennedy & Arthur, 2014). Social justice is grounded in the belief that every person has the right to quality education, appropriate health care, and equitable employment opportunities regardless of ethnicity, race, sex, gender identity, sexual orientation, and economic status, among other characteristics (Lewis et al., 2011).

Social justice is a primary value for professional identity and should be positioned centrally in identity and practice (Kennedy & Arthur, 2014). Holding this value implies a commitment to multicultural competence and an understanding of power and privilege (in the form of systemic oppression) affecting the lives and treatment outcomes of clients (Chung et al., 2008; D'Andrea & Heckman, 2008). Thus, being a professional counselor entails being a multiculturally competent social justice advocate and change agent (Decker et al., 2016; Toporek et al., 2009).

The MSJCC provides a multicultural and social justice praxis to use when practicing multicultural and social justice counseling. These competencies added one other dimension to the MCC—power and privilege—and one additional intervention—action (Ratts et al., 2015). Now, not only do counselors have to gain awareness, knowledge, and skills to be multiculturally competent, they also must recognize the role of power and privilege and act to address social justice factors.

Further, these competencies support that multiculturalism and social justice advocacy are a "normal" and "expected counseling intervention" (Ratts & Greenleaf, 2018, p. 79) and part of "who we are" as counselors. What defines who we are as counselors is our professional identity that up to now has focused on integrating personal and professional identities. Now, the profession is moving toward integrating multiculturalism and social justice into our professional identity (Lee, 2019).

PROFESSIONAL IDENTITY DEVELOPMENT

For students, professional identity is defined as the incorporation of the activities inherent in the professional roles and obligations of that discipline with one's personal identity (Dollarhide et al., 2013). The professional aspects include expectations as a counselor, duties in the field, mentorship, educational experiences, and working with clients (Moss et al., 2014). The personal aspects consider how the student becomes more confident as a counselor over time and moves from an idealistic view of counseling to a more realistic one (Skovholt & Ronnestad, 1992). Through interpersonal (i.e., peer and faculty relationships) and intrapersonal (i.e., developing internal confidence and integration of personal and professional roles) means, students learn and adopt skills, values, roles, attitudes, ethics, and modes of thinking and problem-solving that define their professional identity (Auxier et al., 2003). The desired outcome is to develop an authentic professional identity that incorporates personal and professional aspects into one "therapeutic self" (Skovholt & Ronnestad, 1992) as a counselor and eventually a supervisor.

Developing a Professional Identity

Current research explains the process of developing a professional identity as a cyclical and developmental process. Auxier et al. (2003) reported that master's-level students engaged in a recycling identity formation process that involved conceptual learning, experiential learning, and external evaluation. Conceptual learning referred to traditional academic experiences, such as listening to lectures, reading, and writing papers (Auxier et al., 2003). Experiential learning occured when students applied conceptual learning to the practice of counseling and developed emotional and behavioral awareness, interpersonal behaviors, and skill development (Auxier et al., 2003). These experiences were linked to external evaluation or feedback from peers, supervisors, professors, and clients. Experiencing such feedback created anxiety or positive reactions from students (Auxier et al., 2003). When the feedback disconfirmed the students' perceptions of their counselor identity it led to a complex process of questioning and self re-examination (Auxier et al., 2003). When such feedback was validating, it invoked positive reactions within students. Through this complex process, students decided to accept or disregard the evaluations and struggled to define and clarify their interpersonal and counselor identity (Auxier et al., 2003). Over time, students formed a clearer personal counselor identity (Auxier et al., 2003). All of these processes interacted with each other in a cyclical manner.

Gibson et al. (2010) expanded on these findings by describing transformational tasks that master's-level students experience as they move from a reliance on external validation to self-validation. The transformational tasks included (a) defining counseling for one self, (b) being responsible for professional growth, and (c) becoming integrated into the profession (Gibson et al., 2010). This developmental process occurs over time (Prosek & Hurt, 2014), is linear, and leads to the student feeling a sense of fit within the profession and the professional community (Gibson et al., 2010).

For doctoral students, developing a professional identity as a counselor-educator entails "the paradigm shift from thinking like a counselor to thinking like an educator, supervisor, researcher, and leader" (Limberg et al., 2013, p. 41). The goal is to invest oneself in the qualities of counselor education and to be student-centered, as well as a research contributor to the field and someone who gives back to the counseling community (Adkinson-Bradley, 2013; Limberg et al., 2013). The professional expectations of teaching, research, counseling, leadership, and advocacy that doctoral students in counseling acquire gives them advanced skills in these areas and makes them future leaders in the profession of counselor education (Carlson et al., 2006; Dollarhide et al., 2013; Goodrich et al., 2011).

Dollarhide et al. (2013) developed a model that described the counselor professional identity developmental process of doctoral students. This study revealed that doctoral students in counseling experience a three-stage growth process evident in each of three specific tasks: (a) integration of multiple identities, (b) evolving legitimacy, and (c) acceptance of responsibility. The process began when the student entered the program as a student, continued throughout the doctoral student period, and ended when the student identified as a new counselor educator (Dollarhide et al., 2013).

Currently one's identity as a professional counselor encompasses someone who provides individual, family, group or couple's counseling, assessment, and consultation. Rarely does this identity as a counselor encompass multicultural and social justice principles and interventions, such as client empowerment and advocacy (Ratts & Greenleaf, 2018). Since the purpose of this chapter is to explain an integrated view of professional identity development with multiculturalism and social justice at its core, an informed case study will be provided. Through this case study, the author will describe how a student can develop a professional identity that integrates the principles explained in the MSJCC. Further, recommendations for how counselor educators and counseling programs can support the future endeavor to infuse multiculturalism and social justice into all facets of our profession will be provided.

CASE STUDY

Janet, a White American, middle-class, heterosexual, female student is entering her first semester at a CACREP-accredited graduate program in counseling. She was motivated to pursue this degree, after working in the field of behavioral health, because she wants to help people overcome life challenges and be empowered. Janet selected this program because she was intrigued by its social justice mission. She noticed that one of the required courses was counseling and social justice, and another was multicultural counseling. Janet also wanted to learn more about their social justice initiatives. From the program's website she assessed their commitment to multiculturalism and social justice as evidenced by this statement: "One of the major goals of this program is to form collaborative partnerships with local community agencies, schools, advocacy organizations, and other social service providers to address issues of marginalization and social and economic inequities that affect communities." Janet is excited to start her first semester and learn what it means to be multiculturally competent and a social justice professional counselor. Before we apply the MSJCC to Janet, an explanation of the MSJCC will be provided.

APPLYING THE MSJCC TO THE CASE STUDY

The MSJCC delineates a multicultural and social justice praxis that can be followed when developing a professional identity that infuses multicultural and social justice principles. This praxis involves four aspirational competencies that counselors must consider, (a) awareness, (b) knowledge, (c) skills, and (d) action (ASKA), when considering how institutionalized oppression (racism, sexism, etc.) manifest in counselor self-awareness, client worldview, counseling relationship, and counseling and advocacy interventions.

Because the counseling profession is predominantly White American and a microcosm of the broader U.S. society within which it is embedded, it is not immune from the effects of power and privilege (D'Andrea & Daniels, 1991). The effects of White power and privilege include (Bizumic & Duckitt, 2012; Gardiner, 2009) the following:

- White supremacy, priority, domination, and importance
- Ethnocentrism leading to an evaluation of others based on White American standards
- The oppression, control, disempowerment, and destruction of people of color

Because of power and privilege in the counseling profession, students, counselors, counselor educators, and supervisors must intentionally and actively address White supremacy, ethnocentrism, and the oppression of people of color in the work they do. In this way, they will develop a professional identity that incorporates multicultural and social justice tenets. Let's explore how this goal can be achieved for Janet.

AWARENESS/BELIEFS

From her social location as a White American, middle-class, heterosexual female, Janet's awareness would begin with an exploration of how these personal identities integrate with her professional roles to create a professional identity. As specified earlier, professional identity is the integration of personal and professional identities. Identities define how we think and behave as a person and future counselor (Wehrly, 1995); therefore, Janet would expand her awareness of the impact of her personal identities on how she thinks and behaves. This could be done through a racial self-awareness exercise, such as Green's (1982), "Cultural Awareness: Ethnicity and Identity" exercise, Hayes's ADDRESSING model, or any of the experiential activities for teaching multicultural competence in counseling (Pope et al., 2011). Further, she would engage in learning about her racial identity development and how that also influences her professional identity.

This type of activity, along with ongoing analysis and reflection in her ways of thinking, including values, assumptions, and actions that maintain oppressive economic, political, and social structures (Goodman, et al., 2004) would start during the first semester in all her courses. It would not wait until she takes the multicultural counseling or social justice in counseling courses; it would start right away. In this way, Janet would begin developing a professional identity with an awareness of how her personal identities and racial identity development influence how she interprets and makes meaning of the course material that will be taught (Toporek & Reza, 2001).

According to Helms's (1990) White racial identity developmental model, Janet's identity development could proceed through six stages:

1. Contact
2. Disintegration
3. Reintegration
4. Pseudo-independence
5. Immersion/emersion
6. Autonomy

In the contact stage, Janet would be oblivious to her own racial identity and accept the dominant narrative of meritocracy, color-blindness, and equality. In other words, Janet does not believe racism (i.e., equality) exist and believes that everyone, regardless of race or ethnicity (i.e., color-blind) can achieve what they decide by working hard at it (i.e., meritocracy). When Janet first acknowledges her White identity, the disintegration stage begins. At this time, she becomes conflicted with this new epiphany as they contradict with her current belief system that aligns with the dominant White narrative. Due to this cognitive dissonance, Janet may idealize Whites, denigrate people of color, and assume stereotypes to relieve this conflict. This is when she enters the reintegration stage. The next stage, pseudo-independence, happens when Janet intellectually accepts her own racial identity and others' race yet has not engaged in an honest appraisal of racism and the significance of being White that characterizes the immersion/emersion stage of development. Following the immersion/emersion stage is autonomy, where Janet internalizes a multicultural identity with nonracist Whiteness at its core (Helms, 1990). As a student, Janet would be given assignments, supervision, and mentorship to help her through her racial identity developmental process.

Throughout Janet's academic experience, she would participate in regular group supervision focused on processing her development of self-awareness and exploring ways that her own cultural identities are shaping her experiences (Goodman et al., 2004; Wehrly, 1995). This supervision would also help her process the emotional toll that comes with doing social justice work (Goodman et al., 2004). Supervision would also help Janet discuss the ways in which power and privilege enact in the counseling session with clients (Toporek & Reza, 2001) by applying the MSJCC competencies to her discussion of cases (Ratts et al., 2015).

KNOWLEDGE

To increase Janet's knowledge of multicultural and social justice considerations, she would engage in an immersion experience to learn about systemic factors impacting mental health, school performance, and career development. Such an experience could be volunteering a couple of hours a week at a community-based site where her role would be an interprofessional collaborator and advocate (Goodman et al., 2004). Janet would also learn the language around multiculturalism and social justice that would be used during in class and in the community discussions on systemic barriers. For example, in the research methods class, Janet would be taught nontraditional methods of collecting and analyzing data that reflect Indigenous and liberating perspectives (Goodman et al., 2004). Further, Janet would learn about her personal identities, especially related to her family's country of origin and stories of oppression faced by family members so that she can develop a more thorough understanding of her identity and history (Wehrly, 1995). By so doing, she may find points of connection with marginalized groups of people facing oppression.

SKILLS

Within the classroom, Janet would engage in critical analysis of the course content from an ecological and social justice perspective (Goodman et al., 2004). For example, in the counseling theories and techniques courses, Janet would critically analyze how the theories or techniques are culturally appropriate and applicable to various racial and ethnic groups. In counseling situations, Janet would broach her cultural identities with the client and discuss ways that power and privilege influence the counseling relationship and presenting problems.

Day-Vines et al. (2007) provided a developmental model explaining a counselor's movement between five broaching styles. Broaching is defined as the counselor's consistent and ongoing attitude of openness and genuine commitment to continually invite clients to explore issues of diversity (Day-Vines et al., 2007). There are five broaching styles:

1. Avoidant
2. Isolating
3. Continuing/incongruent
4. Integrated/congruent
5. Infusing

The authors described that a counselor who is avoidant maintains a race-neutral perspective, minimizes race, and can be naïve, resistant, and defensive when expected to consider clients' cultural context. Isolating behavior occurs when the counselor acknowledges cultural differences once but may never consider seriously how race, ethnicity, and culture shape the client's presenting problems. A counselor who is enacting a continuing/incongruent broaching style is eager to broach cultural topics in the counseling relationship but may have limited skills to fully explore issues of race in a way to empower the client. An integrated/congruent approach broaches racial, ethnic, and cultural factors and has integrated this behavior into their professional identity; an infusing counselor integrates this style into their way of being and lifestyle (Day-Vines et al., 2007). For Janet, as a White student (depending on her racial identity developmental stage; see Day-Vines et al. 2007 for more details on this aspect), may operate from an avoidant broaching style during practicum and move toward a more integrated/congruent approach as she progresses through internship and into her role as a new professional.

Additionally, Janet would develop competencies and skills to transform oppressive social structures toward a more just society by participating in an advocacy project (Wehrly, 1995). To make these changes, efforts must be directed at the micro, meso, and macro levels. The micro level is directly working with clients to increase their consciousness of how their mental well-being is rooted in larger historical and political forces, which many scholars have voiced to be limited in creating social change (Goodman et al., 2004; Toporek & Daniels, 2018). The meso level is working with families and communities, and the macro level is influencing policy at the institutional level to be social justice minded (Toporek & Daniels, 2018). Since social justice work intervenes in the social context, Janet would develop and implement a social justice advocacy project within a community. By so doing, she would be engaging in action while also exploring her personal (could be covert or unconscious) involvement in oppressive and racist behaviors (Wehrly, 1995).

ACTION

Janet would engage in a social advocacy project that is "community-centric" (University of Missouri at St Louis, 2019) and aimed at sharing power with and giving voice to community stakeholders (Goodman et al., 2004; Toporek & Daniels, 2018). When complete, Janet would leave them tools for social change that they can use to continue social justice advocacy within their communities (Goodman et al., 2004). Further, her goal would be to help them recognize themselves as competent, powerful individuals with the ability to enact solutions to problems (Goodman et al., 2004). Janet could also expand her definition of what a counselor does to include being an intercultural communicator, students' advocate, crisis intervenor, or career guide, to name a few (Wehrly, 1995).

Action can also entail advocating and lobbying for political changes to oppressive systems that negatively impact individuals' and communities' well-being and functioning (Toporek & Daniels, 2018). Within the counseling experience, action includes collaborating with clients to address oppressive systems and injustice that impacts their well-being. For example, when working with an immigrant client, Janet might work with the client to help them begin the citizenship process or connect her with legal aid to discuss her options regarding immigration status.

JANET'S PROFESSIONAL IDENTITY DEVELOPMENT

Since Janet was exposed to multicultural and social justice principles throughout her graduate program, she developed a professional identity that integrated them into how she self-identifies as a counselor. She can see the harmful consequences of oppression on human growth and development and is able to focus on addressing oppressive practices that affect clients. Janet also knows that she must use her White power and educational privilege to advocate for change in the society that oppresses others (Ratts & Pedersen, 2014; Toporek & Reza, 2001).

Janet might complete the Advocacy Competencies Self-Assessment Survey (ACSA) to reflect on how being a social change agent fits within their personal and professional identities. The ACSA will help her understand her level of advocacy competence as outlined in the Advocacy Competencies (Ratts et al., 2010). She might also complete the Multicultural Competencies Self-Assessment (MCSA) to measure her level of awareness, knowledge, and skills (Ratts, 2013).

Janet could also follow the counselor-advocate-scholar model, which explains that counselors are also advocates and seekers of knowledge as scholars (Ratts & Pedersen, 2014). Based on this model, Janet would create new scholarship ideas that promote social justice advocacy, be a critical consumer of research, and use scholarship to inform her practice. Central to this model is multiculturalism and social justice, meaning that Janet would always consider cultural variables and how power and privilege play a role in her work with others (Ratts & Pedersen, 2014). Janet's professional identity would reflect the skills, values, roles, attitudes, ethics, and modes of thinking and problem-solving that define a professional counselor. Not only will her professional identity integrate the professional attributes of a counselor, it will also embody multicultural and social justice tenets, such as (a) recognizing and challenging White power and privilege, (b) operating from a praxis that considers systemic barriers, and (c) making advocacy efforts a priority.

SUMMARY, INSIGHTS, AND ACTIONS

This chapter used an informed case study of a graduate student to describe how a student could develop a professional identity that incorporates multicultural and social justice tenets. The MSJCC, White power, and privilege, oppression, and racial identity development were explained and placed centrally in the discussion of professional identity development. A discussion was provided on how counselor educators, supervisors, and the profession have the responsibility, now, to promote professional identity development that has multiculturalism and social justice at its core, so all counselors espouse these tenets as "who we are" as helping professionals.

REFLECTION AND DISCUSSION QUESTIONS

1. For Janet, what barriers or challenges might she face developing a professional identity that includes multiculturalism and social justice at its core?
    a. How might other peers perceive this development?
    b. How might Janet react to the academic and professional tasks required of her during this development?
    c. What could Janet's professors and supervisors do to enhance her learning of multiculturalism and social justice?

2. Define three social justice tenets and describe how you will integrate them into your professional identity.
3. Why is it important to integrate multiculturalism and social justice into professional identity, and how can the counseling profession exemplify empowering counseling practices?
4. Critique a current marginalizing social event and describe three ways that this event affects a person or community's well-being.

Acknowledgements to Dr. Carla Adkison-Johnson for her support in writing this chapter.

REFERENCES

Adkison-Bradley, C. (2013). Counselor education and supervision: The development of the CACREP doctoral standards. *Journal of Counseling and Development, 91*, 44–49.

Adkison-Johnson, C. & Johnson, P. (2019). Counseling people of the African diaspora in the United States. In C. Lee (Ed.), *Multicultural Issues in Counseling: New Approaches to Diversity*. American Counseling Association.

American Counseling Association. (2009). *20/20 statement of principles advances the profession*. http://www.counseling.org/PressRoom/NewReleases.aspx?AGuid=-4d87a0ce-65c0-4074-89dc-2761cfbbe2ec https://www.counseling.org/news/updates/by-year/2009/2009/01/20/20-20-statement-of-principles-advances-the-profession

Auxier, C., Hughes, F., & Kline, W. (2003). Identity development in counselors-in-training. *Counselor Education and Supervision, 43*, 25–38.

Bizumic, B., & Duckitt, J. (2012). What is and what is not ethnocentrism? A conceptual analysis and political implications. *Political Psychology, 33*(6), 887–909.

Burkholder, D. (2012). A model of professional identity expression for mental health counselors. *Journal of Mental Health Counseling, 34*(4), 295–307.

Carlson, L., Portman, T., & Barlett, J. (2006). Self-management of career development: Intentionality for counselor educators in training. *Journal of Humanistic Counseling, Education, and Development, 45*(2), 126–137.

Chung, R., Bemale, E., Ortiz, D., & Sandoval-Perez, P. (2008). Promoting the mental health of immigrants: A multicultural/social justice perspective. *Journal of Counseling and Development, 86*(3), 310–317.

D'Andrea, M., & Daniels, J. (1991). Exploring the different levels of multicultural counseling training in counselor education. *Journal of Counseling and Development, 70*(1), 78–85. https://doi.org/10.1002/j.1556-6676.1991.tb01565.x

D'Andrea, M. & Heckman, E.F. (2011). Contributing to the ongoing evolution of the multicultural counseling movement: An introduction to the special issue. *Journal of Counseling and Development 86* (3). 259–260. https://doi.org/10.1002/j.1556-6678.2008.tb00507.x.

Day-Vines, N., Wood, S., Grothaus, T., Craigen, L., Holman, A., Dotson-Blake, K., & Douglass, M. (2007). Broaching the subjects of race, ethnicity, and culture during the counseling process. *Journal of Counseling and Development, 85,* 401–409.

Decker, K., Manis, A., & Paylo, M. (2016). Infusing social justice advocacy into counselor education: Strategies and recommendations. *The Journal of Counselor Education and Supervision, 8*(3). http://dx.doi.org/10.7729/83.1092

Dollarhide, C., Gibson, D., & Moss, J. (2013). Professional identity development of counselor education doctoral students. *Counselor Education and Supervision, 52* (2), 137–150. https://doi.org/10.1002/j.1556-6978.2013.00034.x

Gale, A., & Austin, B. (2003). Professionalism's challenges to professional counselors' collective identity. *Journal of Counseling and Development, 81,* 3–10.

Gardiner, W. (2009). *Reflections on the history of white supremacy in the United States.* Unitarian Universalist Association.

Gerig, M. (2014). *Foundation for clinical mental health counseling* (2nd ed.). Pearson.

Gibson, D., Dollarhide, C., & Moss, J. (2010). Professional identity development: A grounded theory of transformational tasks of new counselors. *Counselor Education and Supervision, 50,* 21–37.

Glosoff, H., & Schwarz-Whittaker, J. (2013). The counseling profession: Historical perspectives and current issues and trends. In D. Capuzzi & D. Gross (Eds.), *Introduction to the counseling profession* (pp. 30–76). Routledge.

Goodman, L., Liang, B., Helms, J., Latta, R., Sparks, E., & Weintraub, S. (2004). Training counseling psychologists as social justice agents: Feminist and multicultural principles in action. *The Counseling Psychologist, 32*(6), 793–837.

Goodrich, K., Shin, R., & Smith, L. (2011). The doctorate in counselor education. *International Journal of Advanced Counselling, 33,* 184–195. https://doi/org/10.1007/s10447-011-9123-7 https://doi.org/10.1007/s10447-011-9123-7

Granello, D., & Young, M. (2012). *Counseling today: Foundation of professional identity.* Pearson.

Green, J.W. (1982). *Cultural Awareness in the Human Services.* Prentice-Hall.

Hanna, F., & Bemak, F. (1997). The quest for identity in the counseling profession. *Counselor Education and Supervision, 36*(3), 194–207.

Helms, J.E. (Ed.). (1990). *Contributions in Afro-American and African studies, No. 129. Black and White racial identity: Theory, research and practice.* Greenwood Press.

Kaplan, D.M.; Tarvydas, V.M.; Gladding, S.T. (2014). 20/20: A vision for the future of counseling: The new consensus definition of counseling. *Journal of Counseling and Development. 92* (3), 366-372. https://doi.org/10.1002/j.1556-6676.2014.00164.x.

Kennedy, B., & Arthur, N. (2014). Social justice and counselling psychology: Recommitment through action. *Canadian Journal of Counselling and Psychotherapy, 48*(3), 186–205.

Lee, C. (2019). *Multicultural issues in counseling.* American Counseling Association.

Lewis, J. A., Arnold, M. S., House, R., & Toporek, R. L. (2003). *ACA advocacy competencies.* https://www.counseling.org/docs/default-source/competencies/aca-advocacy-competencies-may-2020.pdf?sfvrsn=85b242c_4

Lewis, J., Ratts, M., Paladino, D., & Toporek, R. (2011). Social justice counseling and advocacy: Developing new leadership roles and competencies. *Journal for Social Action in Counseling and Psychology, 3,* 5–16.

Limberg, D., Bell, H.; Super, J.T.; Jacobson, L., Fox, J.; DePue, M.; Christmas, C.; Young, M., & Lambie, G. (2013). Professional identity development of counselor education doctoral students: A qualitative investigation. *The Professional Counselor, 3*(1), 40–53.

Mellin, E., Hunt, B., & Nichols, L. (2011). Counselor professional identity: Implications for counseling and interprofessional collaboration. *Journal of Counseling and Development, 89*(2), 140–147. https://doi.org/10.1002/j.1556-6678.2011.tb00071.x

Moss, J., Gibson, D., & Dollarhide, C. (2014). Professional identity development: A grounded theory of transformational tasks of counselors. *Journal of Counseling and Development, 92*(1), 3–12.

Pope, M., Pangelinan, J., & Coker, A. (2011). *Experiential activities for teaching multicultural competence in counseling.* American Counseling Association.

Prosek, E., & Hurt, K. (2014). Measuring professional identity development among counselor trainees. *Counselor Education and Supervision, 53,* 284–293.

Ratts, M., & Greenleaf, A. (2018). Multicultural and social justice competencies: A leadership framework for professional school counselors. *Professional School Counseling, 21*(1b). https://doi.org/10.1177%2F2156759X18773582

Ratts, M., & Pedersen, P. (2014). *Counseling for multiculturalism and social justice.* American Counseling Association.

Ratts, M., Singh, A., Nassar-McMillan, S., Butler, S., & McCullough, J. (2015). *Multicultural and social justice counseling competencies.* American Counseling Association.

Ratts, M., Toporek, R., & Lewis, J. (2010). *ACA advocacy competencies.* American Counseling Association.

Remley, T., & Herlihy, B. (2010). *Ethical, legal, and professional issues in counseling.* Merrill.

Skovholt, T., & Ronnestad, M. (1992). Themes in therapist and counselor development. *Journal of Counseling and Development, 70,* 506–515.

Sue, D., Arredondo, P., & McDavis, R. (1992). Multicultural counseling competencies and standards: A call to the profession. *Journal of Counseling and Development, 7,* 477–486.

Sue, D., & Sue, D. (2013). *Counseling the culturally diverse: Theory and practice.* Wiley.

Toporek, R., & Daniels, J. (2018). *American Counseling Association Advocacy Competencies.* American Counseling Association.

Toporek, R., Lewis, J., & Crethar, H. (2009). Promoting systemic change through the ACA Advocacy Competencies. *Journal of Counseling and Development, 87,* 260–268.

Toporek, R., & Reza, J. (2001). Contact as a critical dimension of multicultural counseling: Articulating personal, professional, and institutional competence. *Journal of Multicultural Counseling and Development, 29*(1), 13–30.

University of Missouri at St Louis. (n.d.). *Grad cert: Social Justice in Education certificate.* https://coe.umsl.edu/mycoe/index.cfm?event=p2_pe:viewProgram&program_id=GC. SJE

Van Hesteren, F., & Ivey, A. (1990). Counseling and development: Toward a new identity for a profession in transition. *Journal of Counseling and Development, 68*(5), 524–528. https://doi.org/10.1002/j.1556-6676.1990.tb01403.x

Wehrly, B. (1995). *Pathways to multicultural counseling competence: A developmental journey.* Brooks/Cole.

CHAPTER 4

ETHICS AND ETHICAL BEHAVIOR

Perry C. Francis, Eastern Michigan University

Isabel C. Farrell, Wake Forest University

LEARNING OBJECTIVES

1. Connect the development of the American Counseling Association (ACA) Code of Ethics to the development of multiculturalism and social justice.
2. Blend the multicultural and social justice counseling competencies (MSJCC) with the professional ethics and identity of a professional counselor.
3. Apply knowledge of ethics and competencies on case studies.
4. Develop the critical thinking skills necessary to blend an ethical decision model that uses the ACA Code of Ethics with the MSJCC.

LEARNING OUTCOMES

1. Know the origin of the ACA Code of Ethics and at what time the principles of multiculturalism and social justice were introduced.
2. Understand the intersectionality of the code of ethics and how they relate to the MSJCC.
3. Process ethical questions on case studies as it pertains to each MSJCC dimension.
4. Learn about how to apply a decision model that uses ethics and multicultural competencies as frameworks for ethical decision-making.

A code of ethics for any profession is a reflection of its moral principles, commonly held values, and the expectations it has for its practitioners (Allen, 1986). It allows for the transmission of these principles, values, and expectations to those who seek to enter the profession and communicates to the public the profession's orientation of service and a commitment to protect the welfare of those it serves (Francis & Dugger, 2014; Gorman & Sandefur, 2011). While federal and state laws often set the minimum standards of acceptable care and behavior, ethical standards go beyond those set in the law and express the profession's aspirational goals to ensure the public is protected from harm and receives the best care available (Corey et al., 2018; Welfel, 2016). Those who enter the profession, as well as those who practice, pledge to abide by the profession's code of ethics and the values reflected therein.

There are several indicators that demonstrate an occupation has evolved to become a profession (American Personnel and Guidance Association [APGA], 1961; Gorman & Sandefur, 2011):

- Required training (often university based) to master specific knowledge and skills
- An established association that creates and maintains a collective identity and professional values and advocates for its members and the profession
- A body of scholarly research that is regularly disseminated to the profession and public
- Manages and regulates itself through certification, licensure, and **a code of ethics**

The occupation of counseling, by all indicators, is a profession (Francis & Dugger, 2014). The profession has come together under the American Counseling Association (ACA) and its various divisions for the purposes of sharing an identity, disseminating knowledge through research and practice, advocating for the profession, and creating and distributing of a code of ethics. Educational and program standards for those who wish to enter the field and its various specializations are created, revised, and maintained through a national accrediting body (i.e., Council for the Accreditation of Counseling and Related Educational Programs (CACREP, 2016). Finally, the profession, through various associations and organizations, advocates for the rules and laws that govern our work from state to state. Since we have established that counseling is a profession (Francis & Dugger, 2014) with a national association (ACA), we can confidently say that the ACA (2014) Code of Ethics is a reflection of the profession's moral principles, values, and expectations of its members (Allen, 1986).

A BRIEF HISTORY OF THE ACA CODE OF ETHICS

The development of the first code of ethics for the counseling profession began out of concern for the professional status and structure of a predecessor body of the ACA, the APGA (Super, 1953). As part of the process toward the professionalization of counseling, a proposed code was created to serve as a starting point ("Association Activities: Reports from divisions, officers, and committees of A.P.G.A. A Proposed Code of Ethics for A.P.G.A," 1959). Following the proposal for a code of ethics, Dugald S. Arbuckle, then president of APGA, created the Ethical Practices Committee that was tasked with the creation of a code of ethics (McDaniels, 1961). The APGA committee studied the American Psychological Association (APA) ethics code and developed its own to meet the needs of its membership. First proposed in 1959, it was adopted in 1961 (Allen, 1986), was four pages long, and contained over 3,800 words (APGA, 1961). It has been revised six times (1974, 1981, 1988, 1995, 2005, and 2014) with each revision reflecting the growth of the profession and the complexity of counselors' tasks (Francis et al., 2014). The 2014

ACA Code of Ethics is 24 pages long, contains a 50-word glossary, and has approximately 14,800 words. It is the first to contain a separate section on distance counseling, technology, and social media, which is a reflection of the times we now live in (ACA, 2014; Francis et al., 2014).

The Growth of Multicultural Sensitivity in the Code of Ethics

In Section B (Counseling) of the 1961 APGA Ethical Standards is a statement that has been maintained, using the same or similar words, in all seven versions of the counseling codes of ethics. It sets the stage for our understanding of the profession's commitment to diversity and multiculturalism. "The member's *primary* obligation is to respect the integrity and promote the welfare of the counselee or client with whom he is working" (APGA, 1961, p. 207, emphasis in original). While the meaning of this standard in 1961 was limited in scope by the culture of the time, the 2014 ACA Code of Ethics has expanded this concept. The previous statement was updated: "The primary responsibility of counselors is to respect the dignity and promote the welfare of clients" (ACA, 2014, p. 4, A.1.a.) and the preamble to the entire document now contains a list of "core professional values" (p. 3). The second core professional value is "honoring diversity and embracing a multicultural approach in support of the worth, dignity, potential, and uniqueness of people within their social and cultural contexts" (ACA, 2014, p. 3). As a core professional value, it provides the foundation for several standards in the current code of ethics that relate to the concepts set forth in the multicultural and social justice counseling competencies (MSJCC) (Ratts et al., 2015) endorsed by ACA, including the following:

- Defining diversity, multicultural/diversity competence, multicultural/diversity counseling, and discrimination in the glossary in the 2014 codes of ethics
- Awareness of one's own personal values and a prohibition on the imposition of counselor values onto the client (A.4.b.)
- An acknowledgement that multicultural counseling is a base competency required across all specialties of the profession (C.2.a.)
- The counseling professional does not engage in or condone discrimination (C.5.)
- Recognizing the impact of historical and social prejudices in assessment and diagnosis within counseling (E.5.c and E.8)

There are many more examples from the 2014 ACA Code of Ethics that will be highlighted in this chapter as they relate to the MSJCC and the profession as a whole.

The Growth of Social Justice Awareness in the Code of Ethics

The concept or ideal of social justice did not specifically appear in the counseling profession's code of ethics until the 2014 version. Yet, when it did, it appeared in one of the most prominent places in the document, the core professional values of professional counseling (p. 3). The ethics identified social justice as a foundational issue in the profession and defined it as "the promotion of equity for all people and groups for the purposes of ending oppression and injustice affecting clients, students, counselors, families, communities, schools, workplaces, governments, and other social institutional systems" (ACA, 2014, p. 21). As a foundational value, it is one of the variables that helps guide the decision-making process when counselors face ethical dilemmas. It also becomes part of the relationship with all clients as the counselor works to "actively attempt to understand the diverse cultural backgrounds of the clients they serve" (ACA, 2014, p. 4).

Closely related to social justice is the "promotion of equity for all people" (p. 21) or advocacy. This action of advocacy is the work of promoting social justice. Advocacy is defined as the "promotion of well-being of individuals, groups, and the counseling profession within systems and organizations. Advocacy seeks to remove barriers and obstacles that inhibit access, growth, and development" (ACA, 2014, p. 20). In the current code of ethics, advocacy is not only identified as an action, but also a "professional responsibility" (p. 8). The counselor is "expected to advocate to promote changes at the individual, group, institutional, and societal levels that improve the quality life" (p. 8).

As a core professional value, it also provides the foundation for standards in the current code of ethics that relate to the concepts set forth in the MSJCC (Ratts et al., 2015) and the ACA advocacy competencies (Lewis et al., 2003) endorsed by ACA, including the following:

- Promoting the growth and development of our clients by working to remove barriers to services (A.7.a)
- Advocating for change at the societal level to improve the quality of life for our clients
- Working to address bias in assessment and diagnosis (E.5.c. and E.8)
- Recruiting and retaining a diverse faculty and student body that is reflective of the diverse cultures of our society (F.11)

The values of the profession of counseling are clearly stated in the preamble of the ACA 2014 Code of Ethics. Along with the basic ethical principles (e.g., autonomy, nonmaleficence, beneficence, justice, fidelity, and veracity), these professional values provide the foundation and conceptual framework for the entire code of ethics. Central to these professional values is the belief that both clients and counselors bring something important to the counseling process, namely their many identities, statuses on the continuum of privileged to marginalized citizens of the world, values and beliefs, and ultimately themselves and all their preconceived notions about others (Ratts et al., 2016). It is required that counselors are open to their clients' experiences in the world today, and rather than impose their values effectively enter their world and empower them to find health and healing (Francis & Dugger, 2014; Kocet & Herlihy, 2014).

As we have now established that multicultural sensitivity and advocacy are foundational issues in the code of ethics, just what are these concepts? Ratts et al. (2016) have developed competencies to help professional counselors conceptualize what it looks like to be a multiculturally sensitive counselor who, when needed, can advocate for their clients, community, and society.

MULTICULTURAL AND SOCIAL JUSTICE COUNSELING COMPETENCIES AND ETHICS

The MSJCC conceptual framework (Figure 4.1) provides a structure for the exploration of the intersection of counseling ethics and the major concepts of the model. At its heart is the belief that effective counseling begins with developing an understanding of who clients are within their world (multiculturalism), how clients are situated within that world (marginalized/privileged), and what impact that makes on the clients' well-being. Counselors also need to be personally aware of all these issues and how they affect the client–counselor relationship. Additionally, counselors will want to consider what difference they can make, not only in the consultation room, but also in the broader environment where the client exists (advocacy). Finally, counselors have an obligation, according to these competencies, to move outside the consultation room and into the

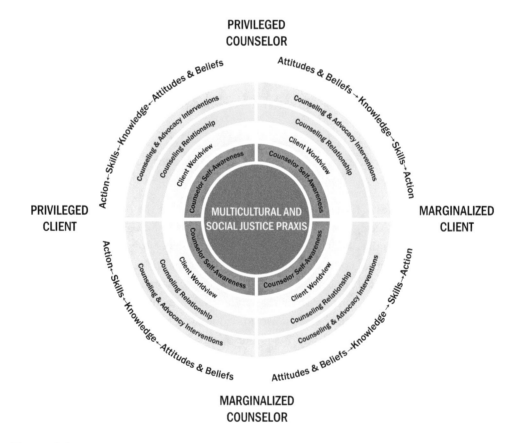

Figure 4.1

world to advocate not only for the singular client, but also for groups of people as they seek better lives (social justice) (Ratts et al., 2016). Within the four domains of awareness, worldview, relationship, and advocacy are the four aspirational competencies or tasks counselors must consider. These competencies include attitudes and beliefs, knowledge, skills, and action (ASKA). Ratts et al. (2016) breaks down the ASKA competencies as the following:

- Attitudes and beliefs involve awareness of "their social identities, social group statuses, power, privilege, oppression, strengths, limitations, assumptions, attitudes, values, beliefs, and biases" (p. 5).
- Knowledge requires "an understanding of their social identities, social group statuses, power, privilege, oppression, strengths, limitations, assumptions, attitudes, values, beliefs, and biases" (p. 5).
- Counselors must also possess skills "that enrich their understanding of their social identities, social group statuses, power, privilege, oppression, limitations, assumptions, attitudes, values, beliefs, and biases" (p. 5).
- Counselors "take action to increase self-awareness of their social identities, social group statuses, power, privilege, oppression, strengths, limitations, assumptions, attitudes, values, beliefs, and biases" (p. 6).

Reflect

Reflect on the ASKA competencies and review the professional values from the ACA 2014 Code of Ethics. How do the competencies complement the values of the profession? What personal values do you hold that complement or come into conflict with either the professional values in the Code of Ethics or the ASKA competencies in the MSJCC? Ask yourself where your own values, beliefs, and biases developed and how they impact your relationship with a client.

We will now explore each of these concepts and apply them to case studies that will allow the concept to come to life. Take your time exploring the case studies and reflection questions to explore your own thoughts, feelings, and values.

COUNSELOR SELF-AWARENESS AND ETHICS

One of the first steps in developing competence in working with a diverse client population is understanding one's own cultural development (Sue et al., 2019). This is more than exploring your family history and cultural roots, and it cannot be accomplished by analyzing your DNA to discover where your ancestors hail from. It is about identifying one's embedded cultural values, beliefs, and biases (Yoon et al., 2014) and learning how your status in your community (e.g., privileged or marginalized) affects the counseling process. This can be challenging for both the beginning counselor and the seasoned professional (Cook et al., 2012). Yet when counselors are aware of their own cultural identities and places in the world, as well as understanding the cultures that shape their clients, they are better equipped to provide competent services and fulfill several ethical mandates (e.g., A.4.b., B.1.a., C.2., etc.). This concept is illustrated in the simple act of sharing a disclosure statement with a client for the purposes of obtaining their informed consent to proceed with services. There are different considerations when the agreement to proceed is negotiated between equals (privileged counselor and privileged client), who may share the same cultural values and benefit from the same societal supports, and the client who is from an underserved or oppressed population with different cultural values and a lack of social supports (see A.2.c. & B.1.a.) or vice versa. If counselors are unaware of their personal and societal statuses in the culture and assume all clients seek counseling services with the same privileges, their cultural encapsulation will affect the relationship with clients at the very time they are trying to make a therapeutic connection. What would this look like with a client?

CASE STUDY

Dr. Frank Smith has been a member of the graduate counseling faculty at State University (SU) for 15 years, having earned the rank of full professor 3 years ago. He is well thought of at the university and has held several interim administrative positions on and off throughout the past several years. He is often seen as the "go-to guy" to get certain projects done. This often affords him a certain amount of privilege and prestige in some circles of the institution. He chalks that up to his people skills and ability to motivate others. Dr. Smith also maintains a small private practice close to the university where he gets to "practice what he teaches."

Dr. Mary Washington, a part-time instructor from the College of Arts & Sciences at SU, sought his services for depression and career counseling. Frank, as he likes to be called, agrees to see Mary for a reduced fee because SU does not offer part-time instructors health insurance. She has been an instructor at two other universities over the course of 4 years while looking for a job in her field. She landed at SU after her last position was eliminated when the department hired a tenure-track assistant professor for a position she desperately wanted and needed. She explained that as a Black woman in a field dominated by White men, she is often overlooked or shut out of faculty searches. Successful candidates in her field often have mentors or advisors who connect them to others who have openings in their departments. She has neither. Mary also pointed out that the course evaluation process was often stacked against female professors and professors of color in White-dominated universities, a fact Frank did not know.

Frank has always treated others fairly at the university. He is committed to SU and proud of the work done there to ensure racial equality, although he never really participated in any of the discussions or events on race and culture that were held on campus. He perceives himself as a progressive type of person and so was puzzled when Mary questioned him about his role as a White privileged professor at SU during the intake process. He always considered academia as a safe and egalitarian place for all people.

1. Search for the term *cultural encapsulation* and see how it can be applied to Dr. Smith.
2. Find the standards in the ACA Code of Ethics addressing competence and apply them to this case. Keep in mind that competence is not an either/or proposition but a developmental path that each person is responsible for pursuing.
3. What concrete steps can Dr. Smith take to expand his self-awareness?

COUNSELOR SELF-AWARENESS AND VALUES

Counseling is a very personal process. Its most powerful tool is the relationship between the counselor and the client and being able to connect with the client at a deeply personal level. As Skovholt and Starkey (2010) point out, "Scientific research and theory on many topics can be of use, but the practitioner, to really understand must know and feel the loss and suffering either directly or vicariously on an emotional level" (p. 129). This is why the old adage of "counselor know thyself" is so important to consider. Part of knowing oneself is knowing your values and how they affect your work and your responses to the client. It is here, at the intersection of the relationship between the counselor and client, that the counselor's personal values, the client's personal values, and counseling professional values intersect (Francis & Dugger, 2014). Being aware of one's personal values is an ethical obligation (A.4.b.). Those cultural, religious, economic, or social values help shape your attitudes, beliefs, and knowledge, as well as what skills you develop and what actions you take. Being able to bracket your personal values so to not impose them on the client as well as entering and seeking to understand the client's world are ethical obligations and cultural competencies (Kaplan et al., 2017; Kocet & Herlihy, 2014).

It is at this intersection that the counselor's competence comes into consideration. We have seen many court cases arise (e.g., *Ward v. Wilbanks*, 2009, 2011; *Keeton v. Anderson-Wiley*, 2011; *Bruff v. North Mississippi Health Services, Inc.*, 2001) where a counselor (or trainee) either refuses to see or refers a client based not on the counselor's inability to provide services but on the counselor's inability to manage their own values, take on the values of the profession, and enter the client's world and offer a safe place to share one's personal issues and journey (Kocet & Herlihy, 2014). It is important to understand the difference between an issue of competence and a values conflict. Competence is based on one's "education, training, supervised experience, state and national professional credentials, and appropriate experience" (ACA, 2014, p. 8, C.2.a.). Additionally, "whereas multicultural counseling competency is required across all counseling specialties, counselors gain knowledge, personal awareness, sensitivity, dispositions, and skills pertinent to being a culturally competent counselor in working with a diverse client population" (ACA, 2014, p. 8, C.2.a). It is also important to understand that competence is not a dichotomous state of being. Counselors continue to grow, change, and gain more experience and education the longer they are in practice (Jennings et al., 2003). Succinctly stated, "I am better today than I was yesterday *if I understand that my education and development never really ends.*" That development, from the beginning of one's career to the end of one's career, should take into account working with a diverse client population. If I am seeing a client whose issues are beyond my competence at that given moment, I am to seek continuing education, consult with colleagues, and/or seek supervision so that my client receives the best care available (ACA, 2014, p. 9X, C.2.f.). If that cannot be done in a timely fashion (i.e., where it would not adversely interfere with the client's treatment), a referral is appropriate, and the counselor should pursue additional knowledge and skills to build that competence. But, if counselors refuse to provide services to or refer clients based solely on a values conflict (e.g., the counselor does not condone the client's LGBTQ relationship), they are using their status as a privileged professional with knowledge and skills that can benefit the client and imposing their personal values onto those whose status has now been marginalized (Ford & Hendrick, 2003).

Shile (2009) proposed eight questions each counselor should ask prior to making a referral:

1. Based on both my training and professional experience, do I feel competent to work with this client?
2. Can I be respectful of my client's beliefs related to their presenting concern?
3. How might my reaction to this client differ from my reaction to a client with a similar presenting concern, but with different demographic variables?
4. Can I expand my competence regarding this issue through reading, supervision, or other professional activities?
5. Am I willing to work at expanding my competence, and if not, why?
6. Is this an area that the APA [or ACA] regards as essential for competent practice?
7. Would referring this client cause more harm than good for this client and for other clients with similar characteristics who are considering counseling?
8. Have I exhausted all other options before considering this referral? (p. 153)

Much like an ethical decision-making model, questions such as these require counselors to honestly examine their reasons for the referral, practice self-awareness, and do the necessary work called for by our ethics code to provide the best care.

AKSA Application

How does this impact the practice of counseling when viewed through the lens of multiculturalism and social justice? Blatant discrimination based on the counselor's personal values is obvious to naked eye (Ford & Hendrick, 2003) and is addressed in the ethical code (e.g., A4.b., A.11., C.2.a., C.5.). It is the more subtle or unconscious attitudes that guide the action of the counselor when seeing a client that the AKSA can address.

Awareness (Attitudes and Beliefs)

The word *aware* or *awareness* appears 21 times in the ACA (2014) Code of Ethics. Of those 21 times, 10 are directly related to the ideas that counselors are to develop and maintain self-awareness about their values (A.4.b.) and to develop and maintain their knowledge about multiculturalism and diversity (B.1.a., C.2.a.), competence (C.2.f.), appropriate use of diagnosis (E.2.b.), multiculturalism/diversity in supervision (F.2.b.), knowledge of ethics (F.4.c., F.7.e.), power differential and boundaries (F.10.f.), and multiculturalism/diversity in training (F.11.c.). Counselors who are skilled in the practice of psychotherapy continually work to develop and maintain their sense of self-awareness about their place in society, the power they hold (or lack), the assumptions they carry about others, and how all this impacts their ability to provide caring and competent services (Johnson, 2014; Ratts et al., 2016).

Knowledge

Awareness without knowledge provides no benefit to counselors or clients. With awareness, especially about the status of our own or the client's place in the world, comes the necessity to develop more in-depth understanding of the history and events that shape counselors and clients' worlds and how the world provides privilege or imposes oppression. Additionally, counselors are required to continue their education to ensure they are current with advances in the "scientific and professional information in their fields" (ACA, 2014, p. 9, C.2.f.) and to "remain informed regarding the best practices for working with diverse population" (p. 9, C.2.f.).

We have many different ways to obtain continuing education, such as graduate courses, webinars, seminars, and professional reading. Yet being immersed in another culture can have a profound impact on a counselor's ability to understand a client's lived experience and status on the continuum of privileged to marginalized (Canfield et al., 2009; Prosek & Michel, 2016). While the majority of counselors cannot afford the time and money to travel abroad for rich and comprehensive immersive experiences, that does not preclude them from finding different cultures transplanted in the many neighborhoods and events that surround them in their communities. Participating in cultural events and working with different communities to improve the lives of their citizens is one way to increase the knowledge that shapes one's worldview.

Skills

The skills necessary to put into action the awareness and knowledge one has gained include critical thinking; clear, open, and nondefensive communication with clients and their communities; the ability to explain how values and status impacts our work; and analyzing and evaluating how statuses and values influence our work with clients, communities, and the public (Ratts et al., 2015). One simple way to begin the development of these skills is by reviewing how counselors use the informed consent procedure to introduce the process of counseling to clients (Johnson-Greene, 2008). This involves more than a one-time discussion of fees, limitations of confidentiality, and potential risks and benefits. It is an ongoing process where the counselor and the client maintain the relationship through an awareness of similarities and differences and how that impacts the counseling relationship.

Action

Learning about your assumptions, worldviews, and culture through professional development opportunities is only one way to broaden your awareness of your status as a member of privileged or marginalized groups. As previously noted, exposure to and participation in your community and the community of your clients helps a counselor learn about how power and privilege influences counselors' and clients' experiences in the world. Immersion in a culture beyond your own is encouraged in the ethics through the concept *pro bono publico* (for the public good, C.6.e.). Actions that place counselors in various privileged or marginalized communities, which allows them to learn about the culture and experiences of the members of those communities, benefits counselors and the clients they serve.

CASE STUDY

Marnie is a school counselor in private K–12 Christian school and maintains a small private practice on the side. She has been a member of the large nondenominational church that owns the school since she was a child and currently serves on various committees and attends worship services weekly. She has often used her client's religious and spiritual beliefs, when appropriate, as part of her counseling interventions with much success. Debra comes to see Marnie for services because she is on a list of approved providers from her insurance company. As is her practice, Marnie asks about involvement in religious organizations and if the client's beliefs are a support to them in difficult times. Debra becomes quite agitated and shares she has just left the same church where Marine is a member due to the church's stance on a woman's place in the home and society. It seems that Debra and her husband sought pastoral counseling from the church staff for marital conflict and she was instructed to support her husband as the leader of the family. Debra always envisioned her marriage as a joint affair, with both parties having an equal say in all family decisions. Her husband continues to attend the church, and this has caused major conflict.

Debra caught Marnie off guard. Marnie had never really examined her role in the church or her church's beliefs on the role of women. She just knew that her church was where she grew up and felt safe.

- What work should Marnie do to examine her assumptions, worldviews, and beliefs in light of what Debra shared?
- How might Marnie develop her knowledge about the different beliefs on the role of women in society?
- What could Marnie do to examine how her beliefs affect her communication style with clients?

THE CLIENT'S WORLDVIEW AND ETHICS

Worldview is defined as "a comprehensive conception or apprehension of the world especially from a specific standpoint" (Merriam-Webster, n.d.). A client's worldview stems from the intersectionality of oppressed and privileged identities, systemic influences, culture, biases, values, and beliefs (Ratts et al., 2016). When working with clients of diverse worldviews, you should take into account special ethical considerations when determining a diagnosis (E.5), selecting assessment instruments (E.6 and E.8), and treatment modalities (C.7).

Most often, you will use the *Diagnostic and Statistical Manual of Mental Disorders*, fifth edition (DSM-5) (American Psychiatric Association, 2013) to diagnose. Learning to diagnose and use the DMS-5 can be overwhelming, as using a medical model instead of a wellness model for diagnosing might feel counterproductive (Remley & Herlihy, 2016). In addition, the DSM diagnosing system has a history of stigmatizing and labeling culture-bound behaviors as abnormal, especially for underrepresented populations (Rapp & Goscha, 2012). Unfortunately, many counselors will find that providing a diagnosis might be required for insurance purposes and job requirements (Comer & Comer, 2017). In cases where a diagnosis is required, you must engage in the process of ethical decision-making and multicultural exploration to ensure nonmaleficence, beneficence, and justice in the therapeutic relationship (ACA, 2014).

Ethical considerations for diagnosis are discussed in the ACA (2014) Code of Ethics and cover the following:

- Counselors must ensure that proper diagnosis, assessments, and treatment strategies are selected and utilized conscientiously (E.5.a.).
- Counselors must examine cultural influences in clients' presenting symptoms and experiences (E.5.b.).
- Counselors must understand and acknowledge biases and misdiagnosis grounded in historical and social prejudices (E.5.c.).
- Counselors must carefully consider the negative and positive impact of diagnosis. If the counselor believes a diagnosis will cause harm, the counselor must refrain from using the problematic diagnosis (E.5.d.).

Assessment is used to gather information about clients that inform and guide diagnosing, treatment planning, and interventions. Assessments can be informal or formal via observations, interviewing, or testing (Baruth & Manning, 2012). Assessments are a valuable tool for counselors, and the selection of appropriate assessments is imperative. The multicultural appropriateness of many assessments has been questioned due to concerns of cultural relevance, language appropriateness and fit, cultural norms, use of stereotypes, and misuse of cultural norms (Kress et al., 2018). Prior to administering an assessment, you should consider the needs of the client, the purpose of the assessment, if the assessment is culturally appropriate and culturally responsive, and the ethical considerations of using it (Baruth & Manning, 2012). The ethical considerations for assessment are discussed in section E of the ethical code and include the following:

- Providing an informed consent regarding the assessment, purpose, risks, and benefits (E.3)
- Providing identifiable assessment data only to qualified trained professionals (E.4)

Finally, treatment involves the selection of theory, techniques, modalities, and procedures based on clients' presenting symptoms, diagnoses, and/or goals. You need to carefully select treatment strategies to match the client's needs and culture and the counselor's training and competence. Ethical considerations for treatment are addressed in the Code of Ethics (ACA, 2014), section C.7, and include the following:

- Selected treatment must be evidenced-based or grounded in theory (C.7.a).
- If the selected treatment is innovating, through informed consent, counselors must outline to their clients the risks and benefits of such treatment and reduce any potential risks (C.7.b).
- Counselors should not use any treatment, even if requested, that has evidence of harm (C.7.c).

AKSA Application

Ethical considerations start the process for counselors to engage and process cultural aspects of diagnosing, assessing, and treating. Engaging in AKSA competencies allows further exploration of clients' worldviews and prevention of unethical behavior.

Awareness (Attitudes and Beliefs)

Clinical work is culture-bound, as each culture identifies problems, seeks help, and intervenes in specific ways (Paniagua, 2013). Therefore, you must explore how your privileged and marginalized identities view diagnosis, culture-bound syndromes (e.g., *ataque de nervios*, evil eye, etc.), pathology, and treatment. Culture-bound syndromes are defined as culturally agreed-on patterns of symptoms that are attributed to a certain causality and become historically embedded into a culture (Roldán-Chicano et al., 2017). For example, *ataque de nervios* is often described by the Latinx population as stressed-induced attacks of anger, anxiety, grief, and violent behavior that lasts for a few hours to a few days (Moitra et al., 2018). *Ataque de nervios* mirrors DSM-5 symptoms of anxiety or panic disorders. You need to examine and acknowledge your values, beliefs, and assumptions about what qualifies as "normal" behavior and how your views might differ from other cultures and identities (Ratts et al., 2016). Practicing self-awareness prevents misdiagnosis, pathologizing culture-bound behaviors, choosing incorrect assessments, or misfocusing treatment goals. You must also acknowledge that, as a clinician, providing a diagnosis and assigning assessments to a client is not only part of a privileged identity, but also creates an imbalance of power in the therapeutic relationship (Ratts et al., 2010).

Knowledge

Knowledge in diagnosis must start with the DSM-5. You must have in-depth knowledge about the DSM-5, proper diagnosis, and the relationship between diagnosis and treatment (Remley & Herlihy, 2016). After a foundation of DSM-5 knowledge is achieved, you then learn about diagnosing diverse populations, presenting symptoms, and culture-specific considerations before assigning a diagnosis. Mental health symptoms may present differently in certain populations, and it is imperative to know about diverse culture-bound syndromes and their somatic and psychological representation. For example, in some cultures, mental health symptoms might present as somatic (e.g., body aches, chest pains, etc.) and could be easily confused with physical ailments (Diller, 1999). Having knowledge about symptom manifestations and culture-bound syndromes can assist clients in properly identifying the root of their symptoms and counselors providing a correct diagnosis (Remley & Herlihy, 2016). In terms of assessments, consider your chosen instrument's validity, reliability, purpose, and biases (Ratts et al., 2010), as well as cultural appropriateness and the social and political factors that influence such instruments (Ratts et al., 2016). Ultimately, the application of this knowledge must abstain from stereotyping or generalizing (Ratts et al., 2016) and instead act as a guide for inquiry.

Skills

When assessing, diagnosing, and treating clients, awareness and knowledge sets a foundation for ethically and culturally responsive treatment. However, when awareness and knowledge are not sufficient, skills are needed to apply such information. Skills are the foundation of competence, an essential ethical consideration that protects clients from harm (Remley & Herlihy, 2016). You should not assess, diagnose, or treat without competence (ACA, 2014, p. 8X, C.2.). You must possess the skills to engage in cultural self-awareness, administer culturally appropriate assessments and interpret the results, and administer culturally and developmentally appropriate interventions (Ratts et al., 2010, 2016). Skills can be obtained via credentialing, licensure or certification, or specialization (e.g., sex therapy) (Remley & Herlihy, 2016). Skills can also be obtained or maintained through continued education, including additional degrees.

Action

The last step in the AKSA competencies is how you take action based on the acquired awareness, knowledge, and skills about your clients' worldviews and seek skills development and competency (Baruth & Manning, 2012; Ratts et al., 2016). You are not expected to know about all types of worldviews; instead, you can broach conversations with clients about worldviews, privilege and oppression dynamics, values, and beliefs to gain such knowledge (Ratts et al., 2016). Additionally, when working with diverse clientele, it is your ethical responsibility to have assessments available in the client's preferred language, have translators available if needed, and provide informed consent about assessment and treatment strategies (Baruth & Manning, 2012). If ethical concerns arise about your ability to engage in the application of AKSA, you should seek consultation.

CASE STUDY

Marian is a new client referred by a community partner. Marian is a 45-year-old Latina woman who is divorcing her husband after 23 years of marriage. She described the divorce as "messy" and hard on her and her family. She disclosed she never thought she would be divorcing and that divorce according to her family and cultural background are not acceptable. However, due to infidelity and verbal abuse, she decided to end her marriage. Marian decided to seek therapy after someone close to her shared concern over her physical appearance and "low" mood.

During the first meeting, Marian said that every night right before bed she can't breathe, feels like she is having a heart attack, and her body aches. These symptoms prevent her from going to sleep, so she hasn't been sleeping well. She believes that her husband's family gave her *mal de ojo* (evil eye) because she is the one who filed for divorce and they wish her to be ill. She is requesting for her counselor's help to heal her.

- Research *mal de ojo*, its symptoms, and its clinical implications.
- You are filing for insurance reimbursement; therefore, you must diagnose. What awareness, knowledge, and skills are needed to work with Marian in regard to assigning diagnosis and determining best treatment strategy?
- What actions might your take in order to work with Marian?
- What are your ethical responsibilities while working with Marian?

THE COUNSELING RELATIONSHIP AND ETHICS

In the introduction to Section A (The Counseling Relationship) of the *ACA 2014 Code of Ethics* are these words: "Counselors actively attempt to understand the diverse cultural backgrounds of the clients they serve. Counselors also explore their own cultural identities and how these affect their values and beliefs about the counseling process" (p. 4). This sets a tone that frames the counseling relationship as an interaction between self-aware, knowledgeable, skilled, and action-oriented counselors who are aware of their status on the continuum between privileged and marginalized and the clients who are seeking their services (Ratts et al., 2015). It is at the beginning of this relationship that both counselors and clients come into contact and develop a therapeutic bond. Therefore, it is important that as counselors enter this relationship with clients, they begin to set the boundaries that promote understanding and respect for the place where the other comes from and become aware of the effect each person in the relationship has on the other. This happens with acknowledging that the primary responsibility of the counselor is "to respect the dignity and promote the welfare of the clients" (ACA, 2014, p. 4, A.1.a).

Boundaries

Good fences make good neighbors, so the saying goes. The same is true in counseling. As the relationship begins, counselors set the boundaries to help both parties manage expectations and help define each person's role. Boundaries are created, not so much to keep people out of areas they do not belong in, although that does take place, but to introduce the counselor to the client. Beyond the concrete issues contained in many disclosure documents are the intangible issues of the clinician as a person and the clinician who is now developing a relationship with a client. As this process takes place, the ethics guide us to consider issues such as the following:

- Recognizing that clients come with various understandings of support systems that may include community members, spiritual leaders, or family members (see A.1.d.) that may be different from my own understanding of support systems.
- Understanding that the counselor's way of communicating information may need to be modified to ensure it is culturally and developmentally appropriate (see A.2.c.). This may include modifying the language to something other than the primary language of the counselor.
- Developing counseling plans and goals as a team effort between the counselor and the client. What may work with one client from a privileged community may be impossible for another client whose status is marginalized in that same community (see A.1.c.).
- Understanding that what counselors view as the need for confidentiality may have different cultural and practical meanings for clients (see B.1.a.).

These issues and others address the need for counselors to be aware of and knowledgeable about the how their worldviews, expectations, social identities, and status on the continuum of privileged or marginalized influence the counseling relationship (Ratts et al., 2015). For example, previous versions of the ACA Code of Ethics offered specific guidance on how to manage dual relationships (relationships with clients that span two or more roles). The 1995 version had a simple stricture, "Avoid When Possible" (p. 3). Recognizing that each relationship with a client is, in one way or another, unique, the 2005 and 2014 versions of the code guide counselors to consider their status in clients' lives, measure the risks and benefits to clients, and decide if extending conventional and cultural boundaries is in clients' best interest (Pope & Keith-Spiegel, 2008). Working to "respect the dignity and promote the welfare of client" involves recognizing the counselor's worldview influences and affects the relationship with the client and how boundaries are developed and drawn.

Counselor self-disclosure is used in various ways in psychotherapy. How it is used will determine if it is beneficial or detrimental to the therapeutic relationship (Herlihy & Corey, 2015). The purpose of self-disclosure is often to bring into the session what is taking place in the here and now of the consultation room. It is not to be an opportunity to share the counselor's personal life or similar story in detail. Thinking through the goal and purpose of the disclosure requires not only that the counselor consider the impact it adds to the session, but how it will be received by a client whose status is similar to or different from theirs. A sharing between equals (counselor and client) will have a different meaning than a counselor self-disclosure between a counselor and client from different parts of the privileged or oppressed spectrum. An observation (self-disclosure) from a privileged counselor to an oppressed or marginalized client may carry with it an authoritative assumption that is not intended. This is especially troublesome when the self-disclosure is more to benefit the counselor than the client and results in a boundary violation (Herlihy & Corey, 2015).

Every counselor is faced with many boundary issues day in and day out (Gitlin, 2018). From the mundane (Should I extend my session 10 minutes for a regular client who was late due to bad traffic?) to the more serious (My well-connected client insists I attend the wedding of his daughter in acknowledgment of my work to bring them back together). This is not a solitary process on the part of counselors. Similar to counseling plans that are the joint work of counselors and clients, making a decision on extending boundaries is part of the work of both persons involved in the counseling relationship. Both the counselor and the client must weigh the risks and benefits of extending boundaries, discussing the how each person's worldview, assumptions, and status affect a decision to move forward or remain with the relationship as it is (Pope & Keith-Spiegel, 2008).

AKSA Application

Counselor self-awareness is a necessary component to building a strong therapeutic relationship with a client (Gladding & Crockett, 2018). That awareness must include how the counselor's place in the world (status), cultural values, attitudes, knowledge, and beliefs affect the relationship with the client.

Awareness (Attitudes and Beliefs)

Beginning counselors often struggle with the many vagaries and complexities involved when working through difficult ethical dilemmas, preferring simple and concrete answers to complex issues (Linstrum, 2009; Lloyd-Hazlett & Foster, 2017). It is precisely at the intersection of easy ethical directives (e.g., avoid dual relationships) and culturally diverse clients and their communities where boundary *crossings* and boundary *violations* exist (Pope & Keith-Spiegel, 2008). Counselors must become aware of and acknowledge that boundary crossings (e.g., community-based interventions, redefining self-disclosure, gift-giving, bartering for services) represent a different value system held by many of our diverse cliental. These crossings and associated activities (i.e., advocacy) can positively impact the counseling relationship and be supported by the ethical and foundational principles of autonomy, nonmaleficence, beneficence, and justice (Bemak & Chung, 2015). Conversely, boundary violations (abusing or taking advantage of clients) demonstrate an awareness of counselors' privileged status and a willful disregard of the foundational ethical principles noted. Fortunately, there are few such counselors who practice in this fashion. Rather, some counselors rigidly adhere to the "letter of the law [ethics]" and demonstrate the critical thinking necessary to provide the standard of care called for in the multicultural and social justice competencies that are the foundation of this text (Linstrum, 2009).

Knowledge

The understanding of boundaries is culturally anchored (Bemak & Chung, 2015). Applying only the Western worldview of boundaries in counseling, which is often moored in legal systems and rigid guidelines, runs the risk of recreating a historical environment of oppression, racism, and discrimination. Learning about and moving beyond culturally bound or Eurocentric limitations that are often rooted in Western counseling theories can have a positive impact on the counseling relationship and expand the relationship to include support systems or resources that may have not been considered before. This also has a systemic impact on the client's community. Allowing clients to invite people of their choosing who bring a sense of community and healing into the session creates a sense of equality in a world where they may only find oppression and marginalization (Chung & Bemak, 2012).

Skills

Pope and Keith-Spiegel (2008) outline several basic assumptions about ethical awareness and decision-making that relate to the skills a competent multiculturally sensitive counselor needs. When applied to the multicultural and social justice competencies, they include the following:

1. The ability to apply what they learn with one client onto the next, continually growing along the way. Making ethical awareness an unceasing process.
2. The skill to apply the current code of ethics with an awareness and application of emerging research and theory about the practice of counseling with a diverse client population.
3. The ability to make "dauntingly complex decisions about boundaries 'on the spot'" (p. 641) while applying the ethics to interventions, techniques, and client cultural and emotional needs.

All this must be done while assessing the impact of the clients' and counselors' status on the continuum of privilege and marginalization on the counseling relationship.

Action

To limit the counseling relationship to just the counselor and the client is to miss the status each brings into the consultation room. Clients who come from diverse backgrounds or have specific issues or characteristics that cause them to stand out as the minority in the dominate culture (e.g., a person who is handicapped due to the physical environment) may, at times, need the counselor to not only be their partner in therapy, but an advocate helping to challenge the status quo of the culture. Counselors address potential or current barriers that "inhibit access and/or the growth and development or clients" (ACA, 2014, p. 5, A.7.a). This advocacy can take on many forms. From speaking to governmental authorities on behalf of a marginalized community to addressing educational inequities in K–12 schools or institutions of higher education for a family or individual (with the client's permission), counselors can move beyond the "nice counselor syndrome" (Bemak & Chung, 2008) and lend their voice to help bring about equality and equity in society.

COUNSELING AND ADVOCACY INTERVENTIONS AND ETHICS

Multiculturalism, advocacy, and ethical practices complement each other and help counselors connect concepts to real-world realities (Ratts et al., 2010). Due to the nature of their work, counselors see clients' struggles, systemic barriers, and oppressive environments (Lassiter & Barret, 2007). As a counselor, you are uniquely positioned to aid clients to overcome barriers and empower them to self-advocate. Ultimately, advocacy is a counselor's ethical responsibility (Remley & Herlihy, 2016). The ACA (2014) Code of Ethics defines advocacy as the "promotion of the well-being of individuals, groups, and the counseling profession within systems and organizations. Advocacy seeks to remove barriers and obstacles that inhibit access, growth, and development" (p. 20). The MSJCC outlines that advocacy interventions are made with or on behalf of clients and across the micro and macro continuum (Ratts et al., 2016). For example, helping a student self-advocate with the school administration to receive reading resources is working with the client at a micro level. Alternatively, speaking to government officials about reading resources for your community is working on behalf of the client and community at a macro level.

Counselors must determine what type of advocacy intervention is needed and at what level prior to advocacy engagement (Ratts et al., 2010, 2016). Ethical considerations for advocacy are discussed in the ACA (2014) Code of Ethics, section A., which covers the following:

- Acting upon an advocacy need and addressing associated clients' barriers and obstacles (A.7.a)
- Obtaining informed consent, when advocacy action engages the release of client identifiable information (A.7.b.)
- Considering the pros and cons of boundary extension and take the necessary precautions (e.g., consultation, supervision, documentation, etc.) to prevent harm (A.6.b.), when advocacy involves extending counseling boundaries (e.g., advocating for a client in court)
- Thoroughly documenting when boundary extensions occur (A.6.c)
- At times, advocacy action might elicit a change in professional relationship (e.g., counselor role to parent-teacher liaison). When role changes occur, counselors must provide informed consent outlining the change of role, risks, and notice that the client could refuse service change (A.6.d)

You might also consider engaging in case consultation during advocacy action. Ethical considerations for case consultation are discussed in the section B. Only use case consultation for professional purposes (B.7.a), and clients' confidentiality and privacy should always be protected (B.7.b).

AKSA Application

Ethical considerations start the process for counselors to engage and process cultural aspects in ethically driven advocacy. Engaging in AKSA competencies allows further exploration of counseling and advocacy interventions and prevents unethical behavior.

Awareness

Before engaging in advocacy action, as a counselor you must engage in self-awareness about your values and biases toward advocacy, the advocacy need, and the impact of historical oppression (ACA, 2014; Ratts et al., 2016). Historical oppression impacts counselors' view about themselves and their clients and shapes values and biases (Ratts et al., 2016). Values, biases, and the interaction with oppressed and privileged identities can cause counselors to not recognize a need or misuse advocacy interventions (Ratts et al., 2010). For example, if a counselor grows up in a community where political advocacy is nonexistent and their family's unspoken rule is not to involve themselves in politics, a counselor might not recognize a public policy advocacy need. You also need to engage in self-awareness on how your advocacy efforts impact clients' systems, weigh benefits and risks on advocacy intervention (Farrell, 2018), and acknowledge your privileged identity as an advocate and the influence this identity has in clients' lives and surrounding systems (Chang & Gnilka, 2010).

Knowledge

Counselors must have knowledge about their clients' worldviews prior to advocacy interventions (ACA, 2014; Ratts et al., 2016). Having an accurate understanding of clients' values, biases, and needs informs appropriate advocacy action. Advocacy also needs resources, and knowing your community resources is imperative. You can use community resources and clients' own resources to reinforce client resilience and empower self-advocacy (Ratts et al., 2010). It is important to consider that not all resources are appropriate for the client or the advocacy need and that selecting inappropriate resources could cause more harm (ACA, 2014). For example, when advocating for LGBTQ+ clients, finding resources in a noninclusive religious organization could stigmatize and isolate the client, and the client might be reluctant to seek further services. To understand what resources are appropriate, get involved into your community and have in-depth knowledge about community allies and culturally appropriate community resources (Ratts et al., 2016). In addition, community integration also helps you understand the needs and systemic barriers present and advocate at a community or political level using this knowledge (Ratts et al., 2016).

Skills

Counselors utilize awareness and knowledge as incentives to build skills that inform advocacy interventions. Advocacy is a foundation of professional identity, and counselors must build skills to include advocacy as a part of their identity and professional responsibility (Chang & Gnilka, 2010; Remley & Herlihy, 2016). As a counseling advocate, you must possess the skills to identify developmental and systemic barriers pertinent to advocacy intervention (ACA, 2014). By identifying the correct barriers, advocacy interventions are intentional, culturally sensitive, and ethically driven (ACA, 2014; Ratts et al., 2016). In addition, advocacy interventions happen within the micro and macro spectrum and require resources and partnerships. For example, if a counselor wants to provide community education about domestic violence prevention, they need to collaborate with an organization (e.g., domestic violence shelter) that can help with understanding the community's culture and how to gain trust and access to the desired target population.

Action

Using awareness, knowledge, and skills, counselors can move into advocacy action. According to the MSJCC (Ratts et al., 2016) and advocacy competencies (Lewis et al., 2002), advocacy action can occur with or on behalf of clients and can happen at three different levels: individual (intrapersonal/interpersonal), community/school or institutional, and sociopolitical (influencing public policy).

When working at an individual level, you can help clients identify systemic barriers, connect with community resources, and advocate for services on behalf of clients/students (Lewis et al., 2002; Ratts et al., 2016). You can also consult with other professionals about advocacy interventions and ethical practices around addressing advocacy needs (ACA, 2014). When working with or on behalf of a community/school or institution, advocacy action can be facilitated when you collaborate with others, build relationships with community stakeholders, and understand the community or institutional culture (Farrell, 2018). You can work with the community or institutions to promote services that they have identified as lacking (Farrell, 2018). Community education about the counseling profession or a specific need (e.g., domestic violence prevention education) as an advocacy intervention can help the community know about the work that counselors do and decrease the stigma toward seeking counseling help for diverse populations (Chang & Gnilka, 2010). Finally, if there is an advocacy need that requires public policy interventions, you must first prepare convincing data and rationale for advocacy action. Public policy interventions can happen in person, electronically, or at events organized by you or your professional organization. Prior to public-level advocacy action, you must consider the benefits and risks of such action. Advocacy action at the public policy level can cause long-term consequences for the client, surrounding systems, and the profession if not done appropriately, with consultation, or with an ethical decision model (Farrell, 2018).

CASE STUDY

Leela is a 23-year-old woman who immigrated from India 4 years ago. Originally under a student visa, she moved with her fiancé who was a U.S citizen and later became emotionally and physically abusive. Due to family expectations and pressure, she married him; however, due to the abuse and him not allowing her to go to school, she lost her student visa and is currently undocumented. Her now husband is refusing her request for residency. She comes counseling experiencing depressive and anxiety symptoms and has current suicidal ideation.

- Identify the advocacy need.
- What awareness, knowledge, and skills are needed to work with Leela in regard to advocacy needs and interventions? Consider researching laws pertaining to domestic violence survivors and immigration requests.
- What advocacy actions might your take in order to work with Leela?
- What are your ethical responsibilities while working with Leela? Consider she may be a risk of harm due to leaving an abusive relationship and reporting suicidal ideation.

ETHICAL DECISION-MAKING MODEL

Counselors "are expected to engage in a carefully considered ethical decision-making process" (ACA, 2014, p. 3). The ACA provides an ethical decision model with the foundational principles of nonmaleficence, beneficence, autonomy, fidelity, and justice. The ethical model includes the following seven steps:

1. Identify the problem; 2. Apply the *ACA Code of Ethics*; 3. Determine the nature and dimensions of the dilemma; 4. Generate potential courses of action; 5. Consider the potential consequences of all options and determine a course of action; 6. Evaluate the selected course of action; 7. Implement the course of action (Forester-Miller & Davis, 2016)

The ACA ethical decision model (Forester-Miller & Davis, 2016) provides a foundation of using the Code of Ethics as the framework in ethical decision-making. However, the model does not explore cultural considerations covered in the MSJCC (Ratts et al., 2016). Alternatively, ethical models that cover cultural consideration such as *A Model of Ethical Decision Making From a Multicultural Perspective* by Frame and Williams (2005) and *Transcultural Integrative Model For Ethical Decision Making In Counseling* by Garcia et al. (2003) do not thoroughly integrate the Code of Ethics. We designed an ethical decision model that includes the ACA ethical code and the MSJCC (Ratts et al., 2016). As demonstrated earlier in the chapter, the Code of Ethics sets a foundation for ethical responsibilities, and aspects of MSJCC dimensions and AKSA competencies provide multicultural and social justice aspects for ethical decision-making.

Step 1. Identify the Ethical Dilemma and Code of Ethics

Counselors first must identify and recognize that there is an ethical dilemma. What is the nature of the dilemma? Who is impacted? What ethical codes are relevant? Does the ethical dilemma pertain to any state or federal laws? What core principles of nonmaleficence, beneficence, autonomy, fidelity, justice, and veracity are violated?

Step 2. Engage in Counselor Awareness

After the ethical dilemma and relevant codes are identified, counselors need to engage in cultural self-awareness related to the ethical dilemma. What are my attitudes and beliefs regarding the ethical dilemma? How do privilege/oppressed identities influence the ethical dilemma and the parties involved? What biases and cultural assumptions might influence my decision-making? What knowledge do I have regarding the problem? What skills may I need to develop to engage in better self-awareness about the ethical problem? What skills may I need to develop to better understand dilemma? What actions may I need to take to develop better self-awareness, knowledge, and skills related to the ethical problem?

Step 3. Formulate Options of Addressing the Ethical Dilemma

With the information obtained through the counselor awareness process, counselors formulate a list of strategies to address the ethical dilemma. What types of interventions to the ethical dilemma are ethically and culturally sound? Who do I need to consult to be better informed about my options? Is there any existing literature regarding the dilemma that offers potential options? What are the benefits and risks of each potential option? Who are the affected parties? Do any of the options violate the core principles of nonmaleficence, beneficence, autonomy, fidelity, justice, and veracity?

Step 4. Explore Worldview Regarding Options

With a list of options, counselors engage in processing a client's worldview as it relates to the ethical dilemma and possible interventions. How does each intervention reflect the cultural worldview of the client or involved party? How does each intervention reflect my cultural worldview? How can each action be interpreted and received given the client or involved party's worldview? What knowledge do I have regarding the client or involved party's worldview as it relates to the ethical problem? What skills may I need to develop to increase my understanding about the client or involved party's worldview?

What actions may I need to take to develop better understanding of clients or involved parties' worldviews?

Step 5. Decide on a Course of Action

Exploring clients' or affected parties' worldviews helps counselors narrow down best options that are ethically and culturally sound. Using the reduced list of interventions, counselors choose the most appropriate course of action. How does this intervention best represent the core principles of nonmaleficence, beneficence, autonomy, fidelity, justice, and veracity? Why do I believe this is the best course of action? What resources do I need?

Step 6: Engage in the Counseling Relationship Exploration

After a course of action is decided, but before implementation, counselors must consider how the course of action will impact the counseling relationship. How will this course of action impact my client or the involved party in therapeutic relationship? What knowledge do I have to understand and assess such impact? What skills are needed to increase my understanding and mitigate potential consequences to the therapeutic relationship? What actions do I need to take to develop ensure core conditions and client or involved party's safety?

Step 7. Implement Course of Action With Counseling and Advocacy Interventions

Once the intervention is chosen, follow through with the course of actions. Intervention can be split into manageable steps and should be well documented. As counselors implement action plans, they should consider the integration of advocacy interventions. How can my course of action involve advocacy with or on behalf of the client or involved party, their community, or the profession? How can I assist in developing knowledge and awareness regarding the ethical problem and possible solutions? How can I empower my client or involved party?

Step 8: Conduct a Post-Intervention Evaluation

Following the intervention, counselors should evaluate the effectiveness, impact, benefits, and consequences of the intervention. In addition, if the counselor had this dilemma again, would the same choice or intervention be utilized? What changes would they make? Lastly, counselors can process any increased awareness, knowledge, and skills obtained through the ethical decision-making process.

Ethical decision-making models are not fail-proof. There is always the possibility that the chosen action has unintended consequences; this is why step 8 is imperative to the process. You must engage in evaluation of the chosen action and self-evaluation and self-reflection about your interaction with the model. Increasing your self-awareness will help you make better choices around ethical dilemmas. Additionally, by following the eight steps outlined in this chapter you can ensure that when faced with an ethical dilemma you integrate the Code of Ethics (ACA, 2014) and MSJCC (Ratts et al., 2016) and formulate solutions that engage in ethical and cultural considerations.

SUMMARY, INSIGHTS, AND ACTIONS

As we have learned, a code of ethics is more than a set of do's and don'ts. It is a statement of values about what the profession believes, practices, and aspires to be. The evolution of the ACA Code of Ethics is also a story of the development of the counseling profession. From its beginning, with one statement that is reflective of the genesis of understanding about diversity and multiculturalism ("The member's *primary* obligation is to respect the integrity and promote the welfare of the counselee or client with whom he is working" [APGA, 1961, p. 207, emphasis in original]), to the current code where it is clearly and plainly stated ("honor diversity and embrac[e] a multicultural approach in support of the worth, dignity, potential, and uniqueness of people within their social and cultural contexts [ACA, 2014, p. 3]), we have come a long way. And yet, there is much more for us to discover and learn.

A step toward that goal of being an ethically competent counselor is self-awareness—awareness of one's place in the continuum of privilege and marginalization. This awareness is not static. It rises and falls with the tides of our culture and impacts our relationships with clients whose own status affects their participation in the counseling process. A lack of awareness or an assumption that counseling is not a culture and that values bound activity risks finding the counselor encapsulated in their own world, which makes them less effective in promoting health and health. This can result in the following:

- An imposition of values onto the client
- A misdiagnosis due to a lack of understanding about the client's worldview and acceptable behaviors
- Improper treatment planning that imposes a dominant worldview onto the client rather than entering the client's world and working in partnership toward healing
- Rigid boundaries that do not take into account the many people and communities that provide care and support for the client
- Missed opportunities to move beyond the consultation room and advocate for individuals, families, communities, and populations to improve their world

Using the awareness, knowledge, skills, and actions to expand their understanding of our diverse world, the counselor becomes more effective and ultimately an agent of positive social change.

REFLECTION AND DISCUSSION QUESTIONS

1. Using any of the case studies in this chapter, work through the ethical decision-making and, citing the ACA 2014 Code of Ethics, create a plan of action that is reflective of the MSJCC (Ratts et al., 2015).

2. Choose one of the four competencies and write a self-development plan that addresses each of the AKSA areas. Note at least one concrete action you can take in each area.

3. Identify a local community in your area and plan a cultural immersion trip that takes into account social, political, economic, and religious values. Take time to reflect on what you learn about yourself as well as the members of the community you visit.

4. Reflect on your own development as a person and a counselor. Where on the continuum of privilege to marginalization would you place yourself? How will that impact your ability to interact with someone above and below your perceived status?

KEY TERMS

Advocacy: The promotion of well-being of individuals, groups, and the counseling profession within systems and organizations (ACA, 2014, p. 20)

Assessment: The process of gathering in-depth information about a client to inform treatment plan and treatment strategies

Boundary crossing: A deviation from the therapeutic relationship that does not expose the client to exploitation or further harm

Boundary violation: Harmful or potentially harmful deviation from the therapeutic relationship that exposes the client to exploitation, abuse, or physical or psychological harm

Code of ethics: Ethical obligations that professionals must follow to ensure ethical practices

Competence: Amount of knowledge and skill a counselor possesses that measures the ability to deliver treatment and achieve expected results. Multicultural competence refers to the counselor's cultural awareness and knowledge about self and others' cultural experience and impact of cultural views.

Confidentiality: Counselors' ethical duty to protect a client's identity, identifying information, and private communications. Limitations of confidentiality include cases in which the law dictates that counselors must release confidential information.

Continuing education: Education (e.g., trainings or certifications) counselors must receive after obtaining their degree and professional license. Continuing education is required for professional license renewal.

Cultural encapsulation: Lack of understanding about others' cultural background and limited understanding about one's own cultural influences

Ethical decision-making: The process of evaluating and selecting among possible actions in a manner consistent with ethical principles of the profession. An ethical decision model provides the framework for ethical decision-making.

Ethical principles: Principles set forth by the ACA that counselors must follow: Autonomy, nonmaleficence, beneficence, justice, fidelity, and veracity

Informed consent: A process of information sharing associated with possible actions clients may choose to take, aimed at assisting clients in acquiring a full appreciation and understanding of the facts and implications of a given action or actions (ACA, 2014, p. 20)

Professional identity: The integration of the values, attitudes, and behaviors set forth by the profession

Referral: Referring a client to another counselor to with a higher level of training or special expertise related to the client's presenting problem

Social justice: The promotion of equity for all people and groups for the purposes of ending oppression and injustice affecting clients, students, counselors, families, communities, schools, workplaces, governments, and other social institutional systems (ACA, 2014, p. 21)

ADDITIONAL READINGS AND RESOURCES

Barnett, J. E., & Johnson, W. B. (2015). *Ethics desk reference for counselors* (2nd ed.). American Counseling Association.

Francis, P. C. (2014). *The new 2014 Code of Ethics: An overview* [ACA podcast series]. https://www.counseling.org/knowledge-center/podcasts/docs/default-source/aca-podcasts/ht043---the-new-2014-code-of-ethics-an-overview

Forester-Miller, H., & Davis, T. E. (2016). *Practitioner's guide to ethical decision making* (rev. ed.). https://www.counseling.org/knowledge-center/podcasts/docs/default-source/aca-podcasts/ht043---the-new-2014-code-of-ethics-an-overview. https://www.counseling.org/docs/default-source/ethics/practioner-39-s-guide-to-ethical-decision-making.pdf

Herlihy, B., & Corey, G. (2015). *ACA ethical standards casebook* (7th ed.). American Counseling Association.

Herlihy, B., & Corey, G. (2015). *Boundary issues in counseling: Multiple roles and responsibilities.* American Counseling Association.

Myers, L. (2014, May 22). A living document of ethical guidance. *Counseling Today.* https://ct.counseling.org/2014/05/a-living-document-of-ethical-guidance/

REFERENCES

Allen, V. B. (1986). A historical perspective of the AACD Ethics Committee. *Journal of Counseling & Development, 64*(5), 293. http://dx.doi.org/10.1002/j.1556-6676.1986.tb01112.x

American Counseling Association. (1995). *1995 ACA Code of Ethics and standards of practice.* Author.

American Counseling Association. (2014). *2014 ACA Code of Ethics.* Author.

American Personnel and Guidance Association. (1961). Ethical standards. *Personnel & Guidance Journal, 40*(2), 206–209. https://onlinelibrary.wiley.com/doi/abs/10.1002/j.2164-4918.1961.tb02428.x. doi:10.1002/j.2164-4918.1961.tb02428.x https://onlinelibrary.wiley.com/doi/abs/10.1002/j.2164-4918.1971.tb03741.x

American Psychiatric Association. (2013). *The diagnostic and statistical manual of mental disorders* (5th ed.). Author.

Association Activities: Reports from divisions, officers, and committees of A.P.G.A. A Proposed Code of Ethics for A.P.G.A. (1959). *Personnel & Guidance Journal, 38*(2), 168–171. Retrieved from https://onlinelibrary.wiley.com/doi/abs/10.1002/j.2164-4918.1959.tb02516.x. doi:10.1002/j.2164-4918.1959.tb02516.x https://doi.org/10.1002/j.2164-4918.1959.tb02515.x

Baruth, L. G., & Manning, M. L. (2012). *Multicultural counseling and psychotherapy: A lifespan approach.* Pearson.

Bemak, F., & Chung, R. C.-Y. (2008). New professional roles and advocacy strategies for school counselors: A multicultural/social justice perspective to move beyond the nice counselor syndrome. *Journal of Counseling & Development, 86*(3), 372–381. http://dx.doi.org/10.1002/j.1556-6678.2008.tb00522.x

Bemak, F., & Chung, R. C.-Y. (2015). Cultural boundaries, cultural norms: Multicultural and social justice perspectives. In B. Herlihy & G. Corey (Eds.), *Boundary issues in counseling: Multiple roles and responsibilities* (3rd ed.) (pp. 84–90). American Counseling Association.

Canfield, B. S., Low, L., & Hovestadt, A. (2009). Cultural immersion as a learning method for expanding intercultural competencies. *The Family Journal, 17*(4), 318–322. http://dx.doi.org/10.1177/1066480709347359

Chang, C. Y., & Gnilka, P. (2010). Social advocacy: The fifth force of counseling. In D. G. Hays & B. T. Erford (Eds.), *Developing multicultural counseling competency: A systems approach* (pp. 53–71). Pearson.

Chung, R. C.-Y., & Bemak, F. (2012). *Social justice counseling: The next steps beyond multiculturalism.* SAGE.

Comer, R. J., & Comer, J. S. (2017). *Abnormal psychology* (10th ed.). Worth.

Cook, K., Lusk, A., Miller, L. C., Dodier, O. E., & Salazar, A. M. (2012). Understanding unearned privilege: An experiential activity for counseling students. *Journal of Creativity in Mental Health, 7*(3), 289–303. http://dx.doi.org/10.1080/15401383.2012.710167

Corey, G., Corey, M. S., & Corey, C. (2018). *Issues and ethics in the helping professions* (10th ed.). Cengage.

Council for the Accreditation of Counseling and Related Educational Programs (2016). *2016 CACREP standards.* https://www.cacrep.org/for-programs/2016-cacrep-standards/. https://www.cacrep.org/for-programs/2016-cacrep-standards/

Diller, J. V. (1999). *Cultural diversity: A primer for the human services.* Brooks/Cole.

Farrell, I. C. (2018). *Advocacy among counseling leaders: A constructivist grounded theory* [Doctoral Dissertation, University of Tennessee-Knoxville]. https://trace.tennessee.edu/utk_graddiss/4884/

Ford, M. P., & Hendrick, S. S. (2003). Therapists' sexual values for self and clients: Implications for practice and training. *Professional Psychology: Research and Practice, 34*(1), 80–87. http://dx.doi.org/10.1037/0735-7028.34.1.80

Forester-Miller, H., & Davis, T. E. (2016). *Practitioner's guide to ethical decision making*. American Counseling Association. www.counseling.org/docs/default-source/ethics/practioner-39-s-guide-to-ethical-decision-making.pdf?sfvrsn=f9e5482c_10

Frame, M. W., & Williams, C. B. (2005). Issues and insights: A model of ethical decision making from a multicultural perspective. *Counseling and Values, 49*(3), 165–179.http://dx.doi.org/10.1002/j.2161-007X.2005.tb01020.x

Francis, P. C., Corey, G., & Herlihy, B. (2014). An introduction to the 2014 American Counseling Association Code of Ethics revision process. In B. Herlihy & G. Corey (Eds.), *ACA ethical standards casebook* (7th ed.). American Counseling Association.

Francis, P. C., & Dugger, S. M. (2014). Professionalism, ethics, and value-based conflicts in counseling: An introduction to the special section. *Journal of Counseling & Development, 92*(2), 131–134. http://dx.doi.org/10.1002/j.1556-6676.2014.00138.x

Garcia, J. G., Cartwright, B., Winston, S. M., & Borzuchowska, B. (2003). A transcultural integrative model for ethical decision making in counseling. *Journal of Counseling & Development, 81*(3), 268–277. http://dx.doi.org/10.1002/j.1556-6678.2003.tb00253.x

Gitlin, D. (2018, September–October). In consultation: Doorknob moments, handling end-of-session bombshells. *Psychotherapy Networker, 42*(5), 17–19.

Gladding, S. T., & Crockett, J. E. (2018). Religious and spiritual issues in counseling and therapy: Overcoming clinical barriers. *Journal of Spirituality in Mental Health, 21*(2), *152–161.* http://dx.doi.org/10.1080/19349637.2018.1476947

Gorman, E. H., & Sandefur, R. L. (2011). "Golden age," quiescence, and revival: How the sociology of professions became the study of knowledge-based work. *Work and Occupations, 38*(3), 275–302. http://dx.doi.org/10.1177/0730888411417565

Herlihy, B., & Corey, G. (Eds.). (2015). *Boundary issues in counseling: Multiple roles and responsibilities* (3rd ed.). American Counseling Association.

Jennings, L., Goh, M., Skovholt, T. M., Hanson, M., & Banerjee-Stevens, D. (2003). Multiple factors in the development of the expert counselor and therapist. *Journal of Career Development, 30*(1), 59–72. doi: http://dx.doi.org/10.1023/A:1025177608990

Johnson-Greene, D. (2008). Evolving standards for informed consent: Is it time for an individualized and flexible approach? *Professional Psychological Research Practice. 38.* 183–4.

Johnson, A. J. (2014). Therapist, know thyself: Fostering cultural competence in clinical supervision. *The Behavior Therapist, 37*(5), 117–121.

Kaplan, D. M., Francis, P. C., Hermann, M. A., Baca, J. V., Goodnough, G. E., Hodges, Spurgeon, S. L., … Wade, M. E. (2017). New concepts in the 2014 ACA Code of Ethics. *Journal of Counseling & Development, 95*(1), 110–120.

Kocet, M. M., & Herlihy, B. J. (2014). Addressing value-based conflicts within the counseling relationship: A decision-making model. *Journal of Counseling & Development, 92*(2), 180–186. http://dx.doi.org/10.1002/j.1556-6676.2014.00146.x

Kress, V. E., Dixon, A., & Shannonhouse, L. R. (2018). Multicultural diagnosis and conceptualization. In D. G. Hays & B. T. Erford (Eds.), *Developing multicultural counseling competency: A systems approach* (3rd ed. (pp. 558–590). Pearson.

Lassiter, P. S., & Barret, B. (2007). Gay and lesbian social justice: Strategies for social advocacy. In C. C. Lee (Ed.), *Counseling for Social Justice* (2nd ed) (pp. 31–50). American Counseling Association.

Lewis, J. A., Arnold, M. S., House, R. M., & Toporek, R. L. (2003). *ACA advocacy competencies*. American Counseling Association. https://www.counseling.org/docs/default-source/competencies/aca-advocacy-competencies.pdf?sfvrsn=d177522c_4 https://www.counseling.org/docs/default-source/competencies/aca-advocacy-competencies-updated-may-2020.pdf?sfvrsn=f410212c_4

Linstrum, K. S. (2009). Ethical training, moral development, and ethical decision making in master's-level counseling students. *Journal of College and Character, 10*(3). https://doi.org/10.2202/1940-1639.1087

Lloyd-Hazlett, J., & Foster, V. A. (2017). Student counselors' moral, intellectual, and professional ethical identity development. *Counseling and Values, 62*(1), 90–105. http://dx.doi.org/10.1002/cvj.12051

McDaniels, C. (1961). The APGA Code of Ethics. *Journal of Counseling and Development, 40*(2), 204–205. https://doi.org/10.1002/j.2164-4918.1961.tb02427.x

Merriam-Webster. (n.d.). *Worldview.* www.m-w.com/dictionary/worldview

Moitra, E., Duarte-Velez, Y., Lewis-Fernández, R., Weisberg, R. B., & Keller, M. B. (2018). Examination of *ataque de nervios* and *ataque de nervios* like events in a diverse sample of adults with anxiety disorders. *Depression and Anxiety, 35*(12), 1190–1197. http://dx.doi.org/10.1002/da.22853

Paniagua, F. A. (2013). *Assessing and treating culturally diverse clients* (4th ed.). SAGE.

Pope, K. S., & Keith-Spiegel, P. (2008). A practical approach to boundaries in psychotherapy: Making decisions, bypassing blunders, and mending fences. *Journal of Clinical Psychology, 64*(5), 638–652. http://dx.doi.org/10.1002/jclp.20477

Prosek, E. A., & Michel, R. E. (2016). Transformative learning for counselor trainees: Implementation of the multicultural immersion experience model. *International Journal for the Advancement of Counselling, 38*(1), 61–76. http://dx.doi.org/10.1007/s10447-015-9256-1

Rapp, C. A., & Goscha, R. J. (2012). *The strengths model: A recovery-oriented approach to mental health services* (3rd ed.). Oxford University Press.

Ratts, M. J., Singh, A. A., Butler, S. K., Nassar-McMillan, S., & McCullough, J. R. (2016). Multicultural and social justice counseling competencies: Practical applications in counseling. *Counseling Today, 58*(8), 40–45.

Ratts, M. J., Singh, A. A., Nassar-McMillan, S., Butler, S. K., & McCullough, J. R. (2015). *Multicultural and social justice counseling competencies.* American Counseling Association. https://www.counseling.org/knowledge-center/competencies

Ratts, M. J., Toporek, R. L., & Lewis, J. A. (2010). *ACA advocacy competencies: A social justice framework for counselors.* American Counseling Association.

Remley, T. P., & Herlihy, B. (2016). *Ethical, legal, and professional issues in counseling* (6th ed.). Pearson.

Roldán-Chicano, M. T., Fernández-Rufete, J., Hueso-Montoro, C., García-López, M., Rodríguez-Tello, J., & Flores-Bienert, M. D. (2017). Culture-bound syndromes in migratory contexts: the case of Bolivian immigrants. *Revista Latino-Americana de Enfermagem, 25*, e2915. https://doi.org/10.1590/1518-8345.1982.2915

Shiles, M. (2009). Discriminatory referrals: Uncovering a potential ethical dilemma facing practitioners. *Ethics & Behavior, 19*(2), 142–155. http://dx.doi.org/10.1080/10508420902772777

Skovholt, T. M., & Starkey, M. T. (2010). The three legs of the practitioner's learning stool: Practice, research/theory, and personal life. *Journal of Contemporary Psychotherapy: On the Cutting Edge of Modern Developments in Psychotherapy, 40*(3), 125–130. http://dx.doi.org/10.1007/s10879-010-9137-1

Sue, D. W., Sue, D., Neville, H. A., & Smith, L. (2019). *Counseling the culturally diverse: Theory and practice* (8th ed.). Wiley.

Super, D. E. (1953). APGA: Promise and performance. *Personnel & Guidance Journal, 31*, 496–499. http://dx.doi.org/10.1002/j.2164-4918.1953.tb01934.x

Welfel, E. R. (2016). *Ethics in counseling and psychotherapy: Standards, research, and emerging issues* (6th ed.). Cengage.

Yoon, E., Jérémie-Brink, G., & Kordesh, K. (2014). Critical issues in teaching a multicultural counseling course. *International Journal for the Advancement of Counselling, 36*(4), 359–371. http://dx.doi.org/10.1007/s10447-014-9212-5

Credit

CHAPTER 5

COUNSELING THEORIES

Nathaniel O. Brown, Lewis and Clark College Graduate School of Education and Counseling

David Julius Ford, Jr., Monmouth University

James Norris, University of the Cumberlands

S. Kent Butler, University of Central Florida

Joel M. Filmore, Lighthouse Professional Counseling Center

LEARNING OBJECTIVES

1. Connect the development of the American Counseling Association (ACA) Code of Ethics to the development of a working knowledge of theories through a multicultural and social justice framework.
2. Integrate the Multicultural and Social Justice Counseling Competencies (MSJCC) with professional identity and understanding of theories as a professional counselor.
3. Apply knowledge of theories and competencies in conceptual and empirical case studies.
4. Develop critical thinking skills required to integrate theories into practice from a MSJCC framework.

LEARNING OUTCOMES

1. Know the foundation of conventional and constructivist theories in relation to MSJCC.
2. Understand the intersectionality theories and how they align with the MSJCC.
3. Process theory application to conceptual and empirical case studies pertaining to each MSJCC dimension.
4. Learn about how to apply conventional and constructivist theories that use MSJCC as a framework for application in counseling practice.

The mysterious recipe for developing a counselor identity necessitates the ingredient of clear exposure to a variety of philosophies and theories in counseling. Culturally responsive counseling is ideal as the profession continues to move toward the development of a fifth force and an expansion of the counselor role. In 2009, Ratts proffered to counselors that the counseling profession is in the midst of transformation. Specifically, Ratts acknowledged there is a growing movement within the profession that called on counselors to return to their roots by infusing a social justice perspective into counseling theories, paradigms, and practices. Kottler (2013) added,

> It's not that individual counseling or group and family modalities have become obsolete; they are just necessarily limited by the settings and context in which they take place. In most places of the world—and for that matter, within many communities in North America, traditional counseling just doesn't fit the cultural context of people's experiences. (p. 10)

The resurgence of a social justice perspective led by Ratts et al. (2004) refers to the profession's attempt to return to its roots. As a fifth force in the field, social justice is liberating and encourages student and novice counselors to rethink and expand their counseling identity. Based on this perspective, social justice counseling prominently follows the psychodynamic, cognitive behavioral, existential-humanistic, and multicultural counseling forces that exist in the profession today (Ratts, 2009).

Developing and maintaining a professional counselor identity is paramount to effective education, practice, and professional development throughout a counselor's career. Nassar-McMillan and Niles (2011) summarized that professional identity is achieved in many ways and as a result of a myriad of different influences. Professional identity is formed through continuous education, practice, and development. Students and new counselors are required to have a common base of knowledge achieved through rigorous educational standards, criteria that may change in an effort to improve the profession as a whole. Furthermore, Nassar-McMillan and Niles noted that other shared elements, such as professional associations, certification and licensure, and competency standards, add to the foundation of our professional identity.

To this end, students and novice counselors may experience curiosity and doubt about how and why they decided to become counselors. Kottler (2013) expressed, "I would be less than honest if I said that I chose this path. Rather, it chose me" (p. 10). Nevertheless, self-doubt and curiosity are part of the self-discovery process of forming a personal and professional identity. The struggle to define oneself is one of many fundamental parts of the human development process (Erikson, 1963). Analogously, achieving a professional identity is usually thought to be a vital part of becoming a mature professional (Hansen, 2010).

Unfortunately, the challenge in developing a counselor identity is based, in part, on the paradigm shift in counseling philosophy and the many choices of theories a counselor may utilize in practice and supervision. Hansen (2006) noted that theoretical understanding is an essential part of effective counseling practice. Theories help counselors organize clinical data, make complex processes coherent, and provide conceptual guidance for interventions at the micro, meso, and macro levels. In fact, moving toward a fifth force in counseling requires students and new counselors to consider the environmental factors that may contribute to individuals' mental health issues or personal challenges. Ratts (2009) promoted the need to make social justice a clearer presence in the field, primarily fueled by the continued marginalization of those who live on the fringes of society, a growing awareness that well-intentioned counselors are not adequately drawing the connection between oppression and mental health issues, and the increasing realization that counseling paradigms may be limiting when they focus solely on the individual without regard for environmental factors. Additionally, the overwhelming barrage of information with which practicing counselors are regularly confronted would be a bewildering array of random disparate happenings without the aid of organizing conceptual tools to make sense of it all (Hansen, 2006). Shallcross (2012) compiled thoughts of some of the most experienced counselors in the field on the recipe for truly great counseling and quotes Kottler:

> I've always distrusted anyone who claims they understand what counseling is all about and how it "really" works. The process is far too mysterious and complex to ever truly get a handle on all the nuances. Far too often, we don't trust ourselves when we totally buy into what supposed other 'experts' tell us is an approximation of so-called truth. Counseling is such a private enterprise that takes place behind closed doors. We rely on self-reports by counselors, and sometimes their clients, about what happened in the room, but I'm not sure those assessments are all that accurate and robust. So, I think we are all works in progress, striving to do better. I think it's reassuring to most of us to find out that we are all dealing with similar issues and that we aren't alone in the struggle. The best counselors in the field aren't necessarily those who are most well-known but rather those who are always reaching toward greatness and flat out working harder than everyone else. These counselors are constantly questioning what they do and why, being brutally honest with themselves about their work and its outcomes. They are always soliciting feedback from their clients, colleagues, begging for the most frank assessments about what is working and what is not. Most of all, they are often so humble that they don't seek attention or the limelight but just quietly go about their extraordinary commitment to helping others. (p. 26)

As students and new or seasoned professional counselors, we adhere to a code of ethics that stands to protect our clients who are members of the communities in which we serve. Nassar-McMillan and Niles (2011) reiterated that our professional identity is still growing and submit that as a result of our advocacy and legislative efforts the public will gain a more defined concept of counselors and the counseling profession. In an effort to protect our clients and utilize the most effective tools to provide support, students and new counselors are professionally required to develop a theoretical orientation for practice and supervision. Halbur and Halbur (2011) defined *theoretical orientation* as a counselor's conceptual framework to understand client therapeutic needs. Halbur and Halbur more specifically proffer that theoretical orientation provides helpers with a theory-based framework for (a) generating hypotheses about a client's experience and behavior, (b) formulating a rationale for specific treatment interventions, and (c) evaluating the ongoing therapeutic process. Having a theoretical orientation provides helpers with goals and techniques that set the stage for translating theory into practice. Tolentino (2010) concurs with Ratts that various counseling orientations are summarized into four major theoretical forces: (a) psychodynamic analytic, (b) cognitive behavioral, (c) existential humanistic, and (d) multicultural.

UNDERSTANDING THEORETICAL ORIENTATION

The idea of determining a solid theoretical orientation is complex and ever morphing based on societal change and the populations served in the 21st century and beyond.

Most helpers choose their theoretical orientation based on three considerations: the theoretical orientation of the helper's training program, the helper's life philosophy, and/or the helper's professional experience and/or client (micro, meso, and macro). Helpers also consider the evidence supporting the various therapies (Hackney, 1992; Halbur & Halbur, 2011). Since the beginning of our profession's founding, counseling has been viewed as a balance between an art and science in practice, which is not a polarizing discipline requiring a final answer but one that should evolve toward helping the client become well. New counselors should remain mindful through their educational experiences that they may need to have a clear understanding of how they view themselves, human nature, the role of the client, the counseling goals, the role of the counselor, techniques, and multicultural/social justice considerations within a pluralistic society. A counselor's theoretical orientation is based on empirically tested and formal theories of counseling (Tolentino, 2010).

Personal counseling theories provide vision, clarity, and focus that often guide practice. Tolentino (2010) emphasized additional factors that inform the personal style of a counselor: (a) professional interest and ideas that evolved from acquisition of professional experience, (b) clarification of preferred orientation as they develop counseling skills, (c) emphasis in graduate training, (d) modeling professors, (e) treatment systems advocated by internship sites or institutions where they were first employed, (f) type of clients they deal with, and (g) the counselor's personality and worldviews. While counselors may use these methods to find their theoretical orientation, each could have a pitfall. According to Halbur and Halbur (2011) initial training programs may or may not expose students to every theoretical orientation; students may be underexposed to the process of developing a personal orientation because faculties choose not to discuss their own in hopes of being unbiased in their teaching; some counselors base their theoretical orientation on their own personality and philosophy of life; helpers determine their theoretical orientation through clinical experience despite not fitting all clients in every setting; and finding an evidence-based theory that complements the counselor's personality, values, and embraces the client needs. Consequently, some theoretical orientations are grounded on underlying assumptions, personal strengths, and limitations.

USE OF THEORETICAL APPROACHES FROM A MULTICULTURAL AND SOCIAL JUSTICE LENS

> It is unfashionable, in this age of managed care and risk management to advocate for a treatment that only takes time, but also involves the possibility, on the part of the therapist, of coming to new understandings of that forgotten realm of what Buber calls the "interhuman." A treatment that does not address this level of experience risks objectifying the already wounded and creating a superficial adjustment to society which involves the risk of abuse. (Birrell & Freyd, 2006, p. 54, internal citations omitted)

It is important to begin with this quote prior to discussing different counseling theoretical approaches. It is also important to highlight that regardless of the theoretical approach a counselor utilizes, if the counselor is not engaging in a deeper understanding of the person sitting in front of them, healing will not occur. If the counselor does not challenge their assumptions and biases from the lens of an evidenced-based theoretical approach, they may do more harm than good to their client. Therefore, it is important for counselors to remember that a human being is connected to their theoretical approach and the individual(s) in front of them should drive client conceptualization and interventions.

There are many different approaches counselors can utilize when engaging in the counseling process. Some of the top 10 conventional theories used in the counseling profession include behavioral, psychodynamic, cognitive, and humanistic. While these four theories are most common in counseling, some may not be deemed the most useful when working with clients from a multicultural and social justice perspective. Theories from the humanistic school of thought, or third force, in counseling seem to be most aligned with the multicultural and social justice perspective. For example, within the humanistic school of thought are person-centered theory, developed by Carl Rogers; Gestalt theory, developed by Friedrich "Fritz" Perls; existential theory, developed from existential philosophy; and Adlerian therapy, developed by Alfred Adler. This chapter focuses on person-centered and Adlerian approaches as conventional theories that seem to be more closely aligned with the multicultural and social justice lens. Other theories of choice can be used to embrace a multicultural and social justice conceptual framework (Ratts et al., 2016), but they may not integrate as seamlessly.

PERSON-CENTERED APPROACH

The person-centered approach may be the one most aligned with the multicultural and social justice lens. Rogers (1959) understood the importance of establishing a relationship with clients to create change in their lives. Rogers believed that you could reach this pinnacle by focusing on three therapeutic conditions: empathy, unconditional positive regard, and congruence. For example, when providing interventions for Black, Indigenous People of Color (BIPOC); Other Communities of Color (OCOC); and White communities, the use of empathic understanding, unconditional positive regard, and congruence and genuineness by a culturally responsive counselor enables the formulation of relationships built on mutual respect and destined for healing. Congruence or genuineness creates an environment that is inclusive and allows everyone to align their thoughts, feelings, and experiences in a counseling space that is mirrored by the counselor. The use of unconditional positive regard provides a no judgement space and allows communities of color (COC) to freely experience their thoughts, feelings, experiences, emotions, and proclivity for acceptance.

Unconditional positive regard can be used to counter a lack of self-worth due to instability and disconnections in an individual's life. Corsini and Wedding (2010) highlighted that a counselor's counseling relationship benefits immensely when acceptance, respect, and appreciation for the client deepens. The goal of unconditional positive regard is realized when counselors are able to comprehend and learn from their client without allowing assumptions to interfere. Empathic understanding may be beneficial for BIPOC, OCOC, and White people when offered as forgiveness for current and past trauma or historical trauma they may have experienced or encountered. BIPOC, OCOC, and White people can gain an understanding through effective counseling relationships that their formative years may have largely impacted their self-conceptualization and that these influences can be overcome through internal evaluation, new experiences, and trusting oneself. Some of the ways that these counseling interventions can be implemented to facilitate the relationship and foster change are through practical skills, which include reflection of feeling, paraphrasing or rephrasing, and asking questions for clarification. These behaviors may help everyone realize the value of all voices with an understanding of their personal human context. The goal is for the counselor to model these behaviors with clients while also encouraging them to incorporate interventions into their own lives.

GOALS OF COUNSELING FROM A PERSON-CENTERED APPROACH

Corsini and Wedding (2010) assert that Rogers encourages counselors to be willing to meet the client as a human being, authentically serving them and making sure they work collaboratively. Gonçalves et al. (2012) stated that "the therapist should promote an environment of trust, empathy, attunement, and validation of what the client is experiencing at the moment" (p. 393). Therefore, from a Rogerian perspective, the goal of counseling for members of BIPOC, OCOC, and White communities is to see them as human beings, not as clients or patients, to create a safe and authentic environment where they can explore and grow in areas where they may have been unwilling to challenge themselves introspectively, or where barriers of incongruence exist within their lives. Also, focusing on building a trusted relationship, which is an important and essential factor from this perspective. Ribeiro et al. (2014), speak to the influence that the counseling relationship has on how clients experience change, because without this relationship there is not an avenue for change. To this end, the counseling process can help individuals become more open to self-evaluation, new possibilities, and trusting themselves with better context for their personal background.

ADLERIAN APPROACH

Adlerian psychology looks at individuals holistically, as beings who are creative, responsible, and always on the pursuit of fictional goals within their respective spaces. Family constellation is a very important concept when working with a client from an Adlerian perspective. Croake and Hinckle (1983) state that family constellations represent the total unit of any given household and the personal needs of anyone within this collective are considered familial issues and not individual ones. This is important when you are looking at the symptomatology of an individual in the counseling space. When you are evaluating a client, the role of their family can be contributing significantly to the behaviors they are enacting. This perspective focuses specifically on family systems with the expectation that each person or entity within the unit impacts the entire system.

From an Adlerian approach, the goal is to help members of the BIPOC, OCOC, and White communities identify and change their faulty beliefs. For example, if individuals in BIPOC, OCOC, and White communities lack self-worth or have a reliance on substance use, family can provide them with a sense of self, which can be encouraged and/ or challenged with Adlerian techniques. A part of that process is to mildly confront individuals about the underlying purpose of their substance and alcohol use as it relates to their lack of self-worth. The use of substances and alcohol to self-medicate can be a coping mechanism for dealing with the pain. The pain and feelings of inadequacy could have been developed through neglect or a lack of connection with their family of origin and unfortunately carried into adult life. Therefore, Adlerian interventions allow counselors to synthesize family history and behavior into their scope of practice, an important consideration when working with BIPOC, OCOC, and White communities.

GOAL FOR COUNSELING FROM AN ADLERIAN APPROACH

The goal for counseling includes helping individuals from BIPOC, OCOC, and White communities begin a process of working through challenges in their lives and recognizing that many of the issues experienced may stem from their upbringing. Adlerian approaches also help individuals gain a stronger and more logical perspective on how counseling heals. Utilizing the counseling relationship and family history, despite past experiences, to gain insight into personal reconciliation and healing can also benefit and restore the health of their family.

COGNITIVE BEHAVIORAL APPROACH

The cognitive behavioral therapy (CBT) approach has many tenets, which consist of different forms of applications and success rates. According to Knapp and Beck (2008), there are three major divisions when it comes to organizing cognitive-behavioral therapies:

> 1) coping skills therapies, which stress the development of a repertoire of skills designed to give the patient the instruments to cope with in a variety of problem situations, 2) problem-solving therapies, which emphasize the development of general strategies to deal with a broad range of personal difficulties, 3) restructuring therapies, which emphasize the assumption that emotional problems are a consequence of maladaptive thoughts, being the goal of treatment to reframe distorted thinking and to promote adaptive thought. (p. 55)

When looking at CBT from a multicultural and social justice lens one approach that can be utilized is Elligan's (2000) use of rap therapy. The use of this modality integrated with CBT interventions in therapeutic work with young African American men has been an effective practice. Elligan acknowledges that there are various forms of rap music that appeal to young African American men in a myriad of different ways. Eilligan (2000) states that "many youth like rap for the way its lyrical expression represents the realities of their lives and struggles" (p. 28). It is clear that rap music may be an entry point in the counseling relationship for some young African American men as they begin to discuss their lived experiences. While Eilligan (2000) does not promote nor rebuke the presence and influence of rap music, he does believe in the power of rap therapy when it "is utilized as a tool by culturally sensitive therapists who acknowledge the influence rap music has on young African American men" (p. 29). To this end, rap and other forms of music can be incorporated in counseling practices as evidenced-based techniques capable of providing effective mental health services to young individuals from BIPOC, OCOC, and White communities.

The way Eilligan (2000) integrates CBT with rap music is by utilizing a five-phase process: assessment, building alliances, reframing/restricting, role-playing with reinforcements, and action and maintenance. The first installation of the method consists of assessment, which focuses on determining if the client is significantly influenced by rap music and if the modality is appropriate for this treatment. Next, the clinician determines how much the client's self-identity is shaped by rap music. Similar to CBT, the assessment process is ongoing in an effort to moderate and change approaches based on the needs and interest of the client. Second, alliances are focused on the clinician forming strong bonds with clients. This is typically accomplished through being empathic and providing a supportive environment that embraces the client's interest in rap music. This stage is essential in order to proceed through the remaining phases. The third phrase involves reframing/restricting, which is the most difficult stage because the clinician attempts to broaden the client's appreciation of different types of rap music, promoting a further cognitive restructuring of what rap music means to the client. Fourth is role-playing with reinforcement, which focuses on facilitated written exercises. This maneuver allows the client to go through a cognitive process that begins to look at the rap lyrics they wrote as poetry. The shifting of the client's frame of mind from rap lyrics to poetry isn't to impede on the integrity of the client's constructs or rap lyrics concepts but "to determine if the reframing stage was successful through broadening the creative expression of the client" (Elligan, 2000, p. 32). The final phase incorporates action and maintenance and focuses on embracing what was learned from the previous stages; through writing about issues directly related to the treatment plan, the client's writing becomes an action through positive reinforcement.

Important takeaways for integrating CBT revolve around the clinician having mental flexibility of what counseling looks like outside of a Eurocentric framework. This allows the clinician to openly embrace forms of expression other than their own.

GOALS FOR COUNSELING FROM A COGNITIVE BEHAVIORAL APPROACH

CBT works best when it is designed to help clients learn new behaviors (i.e., coping strategies), locate new environments that promote a healthier lifestyle (whether they are physical or social), and help them replace irrational thinking with more rational thoughts. Using rap therapy in conjunction with CBT allows clients to develop new coping strategies through written form and music appreciation. Analyzing rap music during the therapeutic process and accepting the client's lyrical skills allow for new ways to connect or comprehend one's struggles, especially in relation to how they make decisions. Accomplishing these goals can allow clients to live healthier lives and reduce mental health symptoms they experience.

Power, privilege, and oppression are deeply ingrained into the fabric of our society. If counselors or counselor educators are not intentional about working from a multicultural and social justice lens, they may potentially do more harm than good to clients. This is despite their good intentions or how versed they are in a particular theoretical approach. Due to the complexity surrounding cultural responsiveness, it's going to be important for counselors and counselors-in-training to use an intersectional approach when working with clients from various theoretical frameworks. Chan et al. (2018) state that intersectionality may "address multiple cultural identities" (p. 61). This innovative viewpoint highlights that clients have multiple cultural identities when they seek counseling services, and if that isn't factored in when integrating theoretical approaches, it could lead to misdiagnosing and/or re-traumatization.

RELATIONAL CULTURAL THEORY

Relational cultural theory (RCT) posits from a social justice perspective the complexity of human relationships. According to Miller (1976) it is an approach that may successfully be paired with some of counseling's major theories. RCT alone is not capable of replacing the multicultural and social justice movement; however, it is capable of successfully working alongside the effort. Comstock et.al. (2008) purport that RCT can be used as an alternative framework in helping mental health professionals explore issues related to sex role socialization, power, dominance, and marginalization. RCT can also help determine how these areas affect the mental health and relational development of individuals. In the end, a counselor's theoretical approach should be used as an entry point when working with all clients, but to be effective it must be appropriately modified as the counselor navigates the counseling process.

UNDERLYING ASSUMPTIONS OF THEORIES FORMING THEORETICAL ORIENTATION

A professional counselor-educator and supervisor in training has underlying assumptions in developing a theoretical orientation. Those assumptions are grounded in seven theories (existential, person-centered, analytic psychology, multicultural counseling, feminist theory, narrative therapy, and solution-focused brief therapy) from three different schools of thought (humanistic, constructivist, and psychodynamic). To this end, the professional counselor in training purposefully begins exploring their theoretical orientation as a future practitioner to determine whether it will influence supervision of master's-level students. Halbur and Halbur (2011) considered the possibility that two counselors could share the same theoretical orientation or simply be different because of unique and individual roles. Therefore, they completed the Selective Theory Sorter-Revised (STS-R) based on the intentional theory selection (ITS) model. The inventory was designed to provide insight and theoretical exploration based on their beliefs, values, attitudes, assumptions, and biases related to human nature. In doing so, a worldview is conceptualized with insight into whether human beings are capable of engaging in the change process. The inventory further explores views of pathology, the counseling process, and intervention modalities. In completing the inventory, the counselor-educator and supervisor in training read statements based on a sound literature review and indicate the strength of their beliefs in a white box following the statement. A response can range from –3 to +3 depending on the extent to which you believe a statement is not at all like you (–3) to a lot like you (+3).

The counselor-educator and supervisor in training is confident that their personal life, employment experiences, education, and exposure to practicum and internship experiences influence how they respond to the inventory questions. Nevertheless, this tool serves as a roadmap to exploring their theoretical orientation. After completing the scoring portion of the STS-R, the counselor-educator and supervisor in training fluidly determines that existential (score of 13) and person-centered (score of 12) are the top two theories that resonated personally and professionally. The philosophy of these two theories guides their understanding of how they view themselves and how they view human nature in general.

MODERNISM VERSUS POSTMODERNISM

In the wake of another shift of counseling philosophy that has the potential to become a major theoretical movement in the profession, Cottone (2013) articulated that postmodernism is the movement, meaning it is more about relationships than individuals and is best represented in what has been defined as the "social constructivism" paradigm of counseling and psychotherapy. Social constructivism implies that there is no psychology of the individual and all behavior is viewed as a relationship. A paradigm is described as a set of practices that define scientific discipline (Kuhn, 1970). It further recognizes culture in human problems, which has not always been the case with earlier paradigms. As a movement in counseling, social constructivism has emerged as a framework that addresses the limits of the prior paradigms (Cottone, 2013). According to Ratts (2009), when a paradigm shifts within a discipline, its theoretical underpinnings also shift.

Before a paradigm shift occurs, an epistemological shift has to also occur. An epistemological shift includes relating to the study of nature, origin, and limits of human knowledge (Merriam-Webster, 2020), which can help practitioners better understand how humans came to be and what constitutes pathology or challenges. Modernism presumes that the singular essence of objects in the material universe can be either accurately or inaccurately represented by immaterial human minds (Hansen, 2010). Basically, modernism, an essentialist epistemology, posits that true knowledge of phenomena may be discovered through unbiased observation and presumes objects have essences or souls that can be discovered (Hansen, 2006). Hansen (2010) shared an example:

> From a modernist perspective, birds may be inaccurately portrayed in the minds of certain people as gods. Scientists, however, who use the scientific method in an attempt to discover the essence of birds, mentally represent them accurately as flying biological organisms. The scientific method is idealized by Enlightenment thought as a route to discovering true essences. (p. 102)

It may not be easy for counselors to entirely separate themselves from their observations. What if only two top theories, existentialism and person-centered, existed under modernism? In contrast, postmodernism, a nonessentialist epistemology, maintains that reality is never objectively discovered but is always, at least to some extent, created by perceivers (Hansen, 2006). Hansen (2010) shared and reaffirmed an alternative example:

> As an illustration of antiessentialism (again using birds as the object of knowing), birds might be perceived as biological entities, pets, gods to be worshipped, national symbols, nuisances, food, collections of atoms, or artistic objects. Out of all these possibilities, which one represents the correct, singular essence of birds? The postmodernist response is that there is no correct essence. Each of these perceptions of birds may be justifiable, depending on the needs of a particular community of perceivers. Postmodernism permits the coexistence of multiple perspectives, without concern for adjudicating which one is supposedly correct because there is no singular truth. The idea that one culture is closer to

the truth than another is incoherent. Various cultures are to be appreciated, not judged. Therefore, the value of diversity, and the multicultural movement that follows from it, is dependent on an overarching postmodernist framework that allows for the coexistence of multiple realities. (p. 102)

In 1963 Civil rights activist Dr. Martin Luther King Jr. eloquently and succinctly put it this way:

> In a real sense all life is interrelated. All men are caught in an inescapable network of mutuality, tied in a single garment of destiny. Whatever affects one directly affects all indirectly. I can never be what I ought to be until you are what you ought to be, and you can never be what you ought to be until I am what I ought to be. This is the inter-related structure of reality. (Loritts, 2014, p. 31)

In the field of counseling most clinicians will tell you that building a relationship with clients should be the first thing done prior to any counseling work. While this is true, the process of building a relationship with your client looks very different depending on who you are talking to and what theoretical lens the counselor is operating from. While the entry point into building a relationship with your client can happen in a variety of ways, the one common thread that will never change is a counselor's ability to connect with their clients on a human level. King's quote highlights how people share this mutuality that is deeply connected to the human race as a whole. Therefore, the counselor and client both play a significant role in the process of building the relationship, but the counselor must create an environment that encourages and gives permission to the client to engage in the mutual relationship. The understanding that the counseling relationship is a reciprocal exchange is directly connected to building and developing an authentic rapport in the counseling space.

In *Knowledge of Man*, Buber, et al., (1965) discusses the I-thou relationship. Buber highlighted that the primary word for I-thou is *relationship*. He proffers that the "I-Thou relationship is characterized by mutuality, directness, presentness, intensity, and ineffability" (Buber, et al., 1965, p. 12). Buber highlighted how human relationships consist of a shared understanding of what it means to be human; however, to gain a deeper understanding of human experience one must have a level of curiosity and intentionality. Individuals must have an authentic pursuit of the entities they are engaging with to gain understanding and build a relationship.

CULTURAL HUMILITY

Mosher et al. (2017) examined the literature to find consensus surrounding the definition of cultural humility. What emerged from their seminal work was the realization that cultural humility consisted of five content areas: (a) a lifelong motivation to learn from others, (b) a critical self-examination of cultural awareness, (c) interpersonal respect, (d) creating or developing mutual partnerships that address power imbalance, and (e) adopting other-oriented stances open to new cultural information. They also discussed the intrapersonal components of cultural humility describing the phenomena as a dynamic process of in-depth self-reflection that allows an individual to critique their cultural biases and promote cultural exploration and growth.

Mosher et al. (2017) conceptualized cultural humility in a way that integrates well into the MSJCC (Ratts et al., 2016). Both frameworks prompt counselors to engage in self-reflection, develop and improve their self-awareness of biases, develop a strong counseling relationship, and share the distribution of knowledge. When considering and developing their theoretical orientation, the first five steps are finding yourself, articulating your own values, surveying your preferences, using your personality, and capturing yourself (Halbur & Halbur, 2019). These steps instruct counselors to cultivate self-awareness, which closely aligns with the first level of the MSJCC and the concept of cultural humility.

Counselors who are culturally sensitive and exhibit cultural humility critique their own cultural biases and promote cultural exploration and self-growth (Mosher et al., 2017). Ratts et al. (2016) stated that counselor self-awareness allows for the exploration of one's attitudes and beliefs and also entails the development of knowledge, skills, and action-oriented advocacy relative to their perspective of the world. Finding yourself is akin to developing self-awareness. For a counselor to choose a theoretical orientation that is the best fit, they must authentically consider their own values, life philosophy, and worldview (Halbur & Halbur, 2019).

While developing their self-awareness counselors become more culturally attuned and aware of the impact or influence of their attitudes and beliefs, which assists them in articulating their values to their clients (Halbur & Halbur, 2019; Ratts et al., 2016). When learning how to effectively conceptualize and articulate their theoretical orientation, counselors develop a stronger sense of their counseling identity and life philosophy. A culturally attuned counselor then develops a skill set that only serves to enhance their cultural responsiveness and competence (Ratts et al., 2016). Therefore, it is important to reiterate that when counselors allow themselves to be vulnerable and open, they improve their self-awareness and set the stage for becoming culturally humble. Embracing the humbleness provides culturally responsive counselors a platform where their theoretical orientation is successfully informed and effectively integrated with the MSJCC in efforts to positively impact the lives of their clients.

SUMMARY, INSIGHTS, AND ACTIONS

W. E. B. DuBois (1903) stated,

> It is a peculiar sensation, this double-consciousness, this sense of always looking at one's self through the eyes of others, of measuring one's soul by the tape of a world that looks on in amused contempt and pity. One ever feels his twoness, an American, a Negro; two souls, two thoughts, two unreconciled strivings; two warring ideals in one dark body, whose dogged strength alone keeps it from being torn asunder. (p. 5)

This quote highlights two critical points that counselors may pull from when they are working to provide culturally relevant counseling along with understanding cultural humility. The first is that BIPOC and OCOC have been conditioned in many ways to measure themselves through a Eurocentric frame of reference, which in this quote directly speaks to members of the BIPOC and OCOC. Knowing this provides the counseling profession a unique opportunity to walk alongside BIPOC and OCOC to live through their own perspective lenses. Though there is an opportunity to help create a new reality in the counseling space, counselors must be aware of the trauma that has occurred to BIPOC and OCOC when someone else's values are forced on them.

Second, counselors can gain insight into how most BIPOC and OCOC experience society from a dual perspective; individuals experience themselves and the world around them in ways that are not congruent with their perceptions of self. Counselors can use this awareness to not impose these same values on their clients as overarching society does and create counseling spaces that allow individuals to be authentic to their cultural values. Crethar et al. (2008) quoted Arredondo and Perez (2003) in stating that

> theoretical perspectives [are] the acknowledgement that effective helping requires developing a keen awareness and knowledge of the ways that various forms of injustice, oppression, discrimination, marginalization, and social-cultural privileges adversely affect the lives of millions of people in contemporary society. (p. 269)

This speaks to the overarching theme of this chapter, which highlights how multicultural and social justice counseling must intentionally be a part of theoretical approaches if counselors want to effectively serve individuals from marginalized communities.

Therefore, this chapter provides counselors with insights from a theoretical perspective on how to utilize theories from a multicultural and social justice lens. Embracing this intentionally provides an opportunity for clients to begin a process of healing from traumas they may have experienced personally and historically. The chapter also highlights the impact discrimination and marginalization has on counseling spaces. Counselors must be aware of the inherent basis within the profession, but most importantly counselors need to be intentional in actively mitigating any biases or marginalization embedded in systems within society, counseling included. While there is an awareness to address multicultural and social justice issues, "the counseling profession has increasingly directed more time and energy in assessing and ameliorating what are viewed as individual deficits and problems rather than engaging in environmental change efforts" (Crethar et al., 2008 p. 269). This chapter provides counselors with tangible steps to take when advocating for environmental and systemic change.

This chapter was developed with the hopes that new and seasoned counselors gain new perspectives on the importance of infusing multicultural and social justice counseling into their theoretical framework. This information is intended to reinforce how cultural responsiveness and working toward change is an essential skill in the counseling profession.

REFLECTION AND DISCUSSION QUESTIONS

1. How has social justice as a fifth force in the counseling field liberated or encouraged student and novice counselors to rethink and expand their counseling identities?
2. What are the five content areas Mosher et al. (2017) identified as essential to cultivating cultural humility? In what ways are they relevant to a counselor's growth and development?
3. In what ways are a family's constellation instrumental when working with a client from an Adlerian perspective?
4. What does the code of ethics represent for counselors?
5. In what ways can a counselor utilize unconditional positive regard?
6. What criteria is necessary for a counselor's professional identity to be achieved?
7. Rap therapy can be utilized with young individuals from the BIPOC, OCOC, and White communities to provide effective mental health services. What are some other creative ways counselors can build rapport with their clients? How would you integrate these into your practice?
8. What counseling theories you would pair with RCT and why?
9. Explain the paradigm shift concept and how it impacts one's way of seeing the world.
10. Provide five takeaways from the chapter.

CASE STUDY

Andrew, a 40-year-old cisgender straight White man, is currently getting his graduate degree in clinical mental health counseling. He gravitated toward REBT and is utilizing this treatment modality in his practicum. He has gotten positive feedback from his site and faculty supervisors regarding his counseling skills and how he integrates REBT into his work. One of his clients, Darren, is a 25-year-old cisgender queer Black man. Darren has never been to counseling but believes he is open to the counseling process. He tells Andrew that he has a supportive family and network of friends that has never judged him for his affectional orientation. With the murders of George Floyd, Breonna Taylor, and countless others, Darren tells Andrew that he is angry about the killings and the lack of justice, does not trust any police officers, does not trust him as a White man and as his counselor, believes the United States is a racist nation, and believes he could end up like Jacob Blake or George Floyd. He wants to be more vocal and participate in the protests but is unsure of how he would be received because of his queer identity. He comes to counseling wearing a Black Lives Matter t-shirt with a picture of Colin Kaepernick kneeling.

Andrew, who is a retired policeman and believes strongly in "backing the blue," informs his practicum supervisor that when Darren was talking, he (Andrew) immediately felt defensive because of his stance about police, this country, his role as a counselor, and his support for BLM and Colin Kaepernick. Andrew believes that Darren's beliefs are irrational and wants to use REBT interventions to work with Darren.

QUESTIONS

1. If you were Andrew's practicum supervisor, how would you help him with developing cultural humility in his work as a counselor and using REBT?
2. What are some ways that REBT can be culturally insensitive?
3. How could Andrew implement the MSJCC into his work to become more culturally sensitive?
4. What is coming up for Andrew that led to him getting defensive?
5. What did Andrew miss in Darren's narrative?

REFERENCES

Arredondo, P., & Perez, P. (2003). Expanding multicultural competence through social justice leadership. *The Counseling Psychologist, 31*, 282–289.

Birrell, P. J., & Freyd, J. J. (2006). Betrayal and trauma: Relational models of harm and healing. *Journal of Trauma Practice, 5*, 49–63.

Buber, M., Friedman, M. S., & Smith, R. G. (1965). *The knowledge of man: Selected essays.* New York: Harper & Row.

Chan, C. D., Cor, D. N., & Band, M. P. (2018). Privilege and oppression in counselor education: An intersectionality framework. *Journal of Multicultural Counseling and Development, 46*(1), 58–73. https://doi.org/10.1002/jmcd.12092

Comstock, D. L., Hammer, T. R., Strentzsch, J., Cannon, K., Parsons, J., & Salazar, G., II. (2008). Relational-cultural theory: A framework for bridging relational, multicultural, and social justice competencies. *Journal of Counseling & Development, 86*(3), 279–287. https://doi.org/10.1002/j.1556-6678.2008.tb00510.x

Corsini, R. J., & Wedding, D. (2010). *Current psychotherapies.* Brooks/Cole.

Cottone, R. R. (September 2013). A paradigm shift in counseling philosophy, *Counseling Today.*

Crethar, H. C., Rivera, E. T., & Nash, S. (2008). In search of common threads: Linking multicultural, feminist, and social justice counseling paradigms. *Journal of Counseling & Development, 86*(3), 269–278. https://doi.org/10.1002/j.1556-6678.2008.tb00509.x

Croake, J. W., & Hinckle, D. E. (1983). Adlerian family counseling education. *Individual Psychology: Journal of Adlerian Theory, Research & Practice, 39*(3), 247–258.

DuBois, W. E. B. (1903). *The souls of Black folks.* A.C. McClurg & CO.

Elligan, D. (2000). Rap therapy: A culturally sensitive approach to psychotherapy with young African American men. *Journal of African American Men, 5*(3), 27–36. www.jstor.org/stable/41819404

Erikson, E.H. (1963). Childhood and society (2nd Ed.). Norton

Gonçalves, M. M., Mendes, I., Cruz, G., Ribeiro, A. P., Sousa, I., Angus, L., & Greenberg, L. S. (2012). Innovative moments and change in client-centered therapy. *Psychotherapy Research, 22*(4), 389–401. https://doi.org/10.1080/10503307.2012.662605

Hackney, H. (1992). Differentiating between counseling theory and process. (ERIC Digest, ED347485) https://files.eric.ed.gov/fulltext/ED347485.pdf

Hackney, H. (1992). *Differentiating between counseling theory and process* (Publication No. ED347485). ERIC. https://files.eric.ed.gov/fulltext/ED347485.pdf

Halbur, D, A. & Halbur K. V. (2019). (4th ed.) Developing your theoretical orientation in counseling and psychotherapy. Pearson.

Hansen, J. T. (2006). Counseling theories within a postmodernist epistemology: New roles for theories in counseling practice. *Journal of Counseling & Development, 84*(3), 291–297.

Hansen, J. T. (2010). Consequences of the postmodernist vision: Diversity as the guiding value for the counseling profession. *Journal of Counseling & Development, 88*(1), 101–107.

King, M. L. (1994). *Letter from Birmingham jail.* Harper.

Knapp, P., & Beck, A. T. (2008). Cognitive therapy: Foundations, conceptual models, applications and research. *Brazilian Journal of Psychiatry, 30*(2), S54–S64. https://doi.org/10.1590/S1516-44462008000600002

Kottler, J. (2013). Reenvisioning a new counselor identity. *Counseling Today, 55*(9), 10–12.

Kuhn, T. (1970). The structure of scientific revolutions. University of Chicago Press.

Loritts, B. (2014) (Ed.). Letters to a Birmingham Jail: A Response to the Words and Dreams of Dr. Martin Luther King, Jr., Moody Publishers.

Martin, B. (1975). *The knowledge of man.* Harper and Row.

Merriam-Webster. (n.d.). *Epistemological.* https://www.merriam-webster.com/dictionary/epistemological

Miller, J. B. (1976). *Towards a new psychology of women.* Beacon

Mosher, D. K., Hook, J. N., Captari, L. E., Davis, D. E., DeBlaere, C., & Owen, J. (2017). Cultural humility: A therapeutic framework for engaging diverse clients. *Practice Innovations, 2*(4), 221–233.

Nassar-McMillan, S. C., & Niles, S. G. (2011). *Developing your identity as a professional counselor.* Brooks/Cole.

Ratts, M. J. (2009). Social justice counseling: Toward the development of a fifth force among counseling paradigms. *Journal of Humanistic Counseling, Education & Development, 48*(2), 160–172.

Ratts, M. J., D'Andrea, M., & Arredondo, P. (2004). Social justice counseling: Fifth force in the field. *Counseling Today,* 28–30.

Ratts, M. J., Singh, A. A., Nassar-McMillan, S. C., Butler, S. K., & McCullough, J. R. (2016). Multicultural and social justice counseling competencies: Guidelines for the counseling profession. *Journal of Multicultural Counseling and Development, 44*(1), 28–48.

Ribeiro, E., Fernandes, C., Santos, B., Ribeiro, A., Coutinho, J., Angus, L., & Greenberg, L. (2014). The development of therapeutic collaboration in a good outcome case of person-centered therapy. *Person-Centered and Experiential Psychotherapies*, *13*(2), 150–168. https://doi.org/10.1080/14779757.2014.893250

Rogers, C. R. (1959). A theory of therapy, personality, and interpersonal relationships as developed in the client-centered framework. In S. Koch (Ed.), *Psychology: A study of science*, *Vol. 3* (pp.184–256). McGraw-Hill.

Shallcross, L. (2012). The recipe for truly great counseling. Counseling Today. https://ct.counseling.org/2012/12/the-recipe-for-truly-great-counseling/#

Tolentino, L. (2010). Filipino school counselors' explicit theory of counseling: An examination of salience. The Asia-Pacific Education Researcher, 19 (3), 539–548.

CHAPTER 6

COUNSELING RELATIONSHIPS

Amber Norman, University of Central Florida

S. Kent Butler, University of Central Florida

LEARNING OBJECTIVES

1. Understand the importance of counselor self-awareness.
2. Understand the impact of client worldviews on well-being.
3. Understand the impact of developing a strong counseling relationship.
4. Understand the importance of ethical behavior within the counseling relationship.

LEARNING OUTCOMES

1. Learn to be cognizant of how their attitudes impact the counseling relationship.
2. Learn to be self-reflective.
3. Learn how to inform clients about their theoretical orientation, competencies, and any alternatives within their counseling practice.
4. Learn how to appropriately terminate the counseling relationship.
5. Learn the value of creating empowering spaces for their clients.

Therapy is a team effort, and the process of therapeutic change hinges on the strength, care, and efficiency of interpersonal connections, working bonds, and relational networks. At times, broken relationships are at the center of the hurt that accompanies our presenting concerns in counseling (Miller, 1986). Negative experiences and interactions may have a devastating impact on how we engage with people, relate to substances, and navigate spaces. Furthermore, our societal contexts may disrupt or diminish the relational process, compounding the effects of cognitive and emotional disintegration (Kress et al., 2018). Yet amid struggle, we continue to seek compassion and understanding. As our source of vitality, comfort, and security, we look to empathetic connections to facilitate change and psychological development. Thus, the alliance formed between counselors and their clients serves as a stage to reconcile hurts, develop empathic abilities, and emerge in mutual empowerment and self-knowledge. The therapeutic interaction is an active and contextual process. Through interpersonal intentionality, counseling helps us move through connection, confront disconnection, and advance to newer and improved connections with others. The development and cultivation of the counseling relationship is arguably the cornerstone of the counseling profession (American Counseling Association [ACA], 2014; Hatchett, 2017). Carl Rogers established the central importance of the therapeutic relationship by naming interpersonal conditions necessary to facilitate change. Trust, genuineness, empathic understanding, and unconditional acceptance are therapeutic expectations that fundamentally outline the philosophical underpinnings of the profession (Rogers, 1942; Sommers-Flanagan, 2015). However, Murphy et al. (2019) insist the therapeutic connection must go beyond conditions to include the development of interpersonal relationship skills. For example, it is essential for counselors to develop proficiency in processing and recalling details of their client's narratives. This competence may also look like learning to support the client's memory systems or being patient when those systems are disrupted due to adverse or traumatizing experiences. Furthermore, counselors must adapt cognitively in order to respond to emotional expression and client disclosure. Knowledge of core pathologies, responding to contextual influences, and cultivating self-awareness are critical in communicating helpful feedback and managing the quality of relational interpretations (Fuertes et al., 2015).

During the managed care movement of the 1980s and 1990s, the complexity of counseling was challenged and systematically undermined by the advent of manualized treatments and health maintenance organizations. The mainstream emphasis on evidenced-based practice resulted in clinical trials that often minimized the role of the counselor and immoderately referenced homogenous clinical presentations with limited outcome data for diverse client populations (La Roche & Christopher, 2008; Wampold & Imel, 2015). Even so, the working alliance, congruence, empathy, appropriate self-disclosure, and collaboration consistently emerged as common factors or shared characteristics of effective counseling. Most therapy models work; however, the emphasis must be on helping clients use their own resources to change instead of overemphasizing standardized treatment packages. By the third session of counseling the client has evaluated the therapeutic bond, generated an idea about whether they are committed to the tasks of therapy, and holds a presumption of whether therapy will work for them (Duncan et al., 2010). Regardless of the counselor's theoretical approach, ratings of the therapeutic relationship continue to emerge as one of the best predictors of counseling outcomes (Lambert, 2013; Wampold et al., 2017).

CONTEXTUAL FACTORS IN COUNSELING

A contextual perspective to counseling helps build a more complete picture of the client's experience. Considerations for where counseling happens, the reason for a client's presenting concerns, and encouraging a collaborative approach to resolution are critical to the counseling relationship and client improvement (Hatchett, 2017). Ecologically speaking, a client's narrative is comprised of specific biological determinations, identity markers, and relationships and includes larger community and societal influences. Attention to cultural dynamics provides keen insight into how the client moves through the world and how they structure their interactions with others (Cook, 2015). When contextual factors are overlooked, however, misunderstandings can lead to relational disconnections, therapeutic ruptures, and client dropout. Although it is impossible for counselors to understand the idiosyncrasies of every culture, the failure to consider the context of the client's concerns diminishes trust and weakens the relationship (Hall et al., 2014).

The ACA (2014) Code of Ethics tasks counselors to actively attempt to understand the diverse cultural backgrounds of the clients they serve. Research asserts that the intersections of race, ethnicity, gender, sexuality, spirituality, socioeconomic position, age, and ability have important influences of mental health outcomes and disparities (Conron et al., 2010; Hankivsky et al., 2010). Intersectionality describes the experience of coexisting identities. Contextual thought further recognizes the compounding impact connected privileges and marginalized statuses associated with a person's social identity and disrupts the assumption that individuals are homogenous and equally positioned (Crenshaw, 1989; Shin et al., 2016). For example, an African American cisgender woman who is deaf presents a unique lived experience according to her overlapping social identities. In partnership with the client, counselors may determine how respective social identities impact an individual's development and social functioning. A contextual approach suggests counselors develop a comprehensive understanding of the client's intrapersonal (i.e., individual characteristics, attitudes, behaviors, and skills) and interpersonal (i.e., relationships and support systems) needs, with attention to the experiences of individuals who are debased along multiple axes of prejudice and inequality (McCall, 2005).

The counseling relationship is a complex space colored by the lived experiences and multidimensional struggles of both the counselor and client. In addition to the client's presentation, counselors must also be willing to explore their own identities and examine their effect on their values and beliefs about the counseling process (Ratts et al., 2016). The multicultural and social justice counseling competencies (MSJCC) (Ratts et al., 2016) were developed to acknowledge and center the complexity of diversity within the counseling relationship. Stemming from the MSJCC, counselor self-awareness and client worldview proffers counselors insight into the counseling relationship. The concept provides context to how the cultural backgrounds, social identities, and privileged and marginalized statuses of counselors and clients influence interactions, each factor vital to helping counselors circumnavigate positive interfaces with clients. Counselor self-awareness may provide counselors knowledge of how their personal biases can impact work with clients. Similarly, recognizing the client's worldview may help in understanding the influences of cultural background, which leads to appropriately selecting culturally relevant interventions and strategies.

Moreover, for counselors to understand individuals in the context of their social environment, they must also recognize the effects of oppression on mental health and well-being. For example, negative attitudes toward gay, bisexual, and other men who have sex with men may lead to rejection by friends and family, social isolation, discriminatory acts, and violence (Centers for Disease Control and Prevention [CDC], 2016). Similarly, approximately 30% of transgender persons experience poverty, with even higher rates among transgender people of color. A lack of legal protections regarding gender identity often translates into unemployment or homelessness, leading people to engage in underground economies, which may put them at increased risk for violence and arrest (Badgett et al., 2019; James et al., 2016). Whether oppression is experienced within micro-level interactions or by way of systemic inequities, the impact of invalidating systems may be devastating to the functioning and well-being of marginalized persons and groups.

CREATING EMPOWERING SPACES IN COUNSELING

In an ever-evolving society of diverse bodies and stories, counselors are tasked with creating safe, equitable, and collaborative spaces for healing to happen. The therapeutic relationship is a sensitive social interaction where the client is encouraged to share their vulnerabilities, process behaviors, and apply insights offered by the counselor. Counselors must be mindful and proactive about how underlying power dynamics may impact the therapeutic environment (Zur, 2014). There is an inherent difference in power or influence embedded in the counselor-client relationship. Interpersonal power is the ability of one person in a relationship to have influence on another person with the intention of meeting certain outcomes or objectives (Simpson et al., 2015). The counselor–client dynamic is similar to other power relationships in medicine, education, and everyday social interactions such as doctor–patient, teacher–student, or producer–consumer relationships. When a client presents a need for support, treatment, or intervention, they invest in the counselor's training and expertise as a mental health professional. The role of the counselor is to use this power to process the client's concerns, work toward agreed-on goals, and help the client empower themselves.

When working with marginalized or historically disenfranchised groups, it's important to understand how power imbalance can impede the therapeutic process. Societal power dynamics, such as race, gender, socioeconomic background, sexual orientation, religion, and ability status, must be acknowledged and explored within the counseling relationship. When neglected, counselors who are members of dominant cultural groups may intentionally or unintentionally exploit their privilege and devalue the client's values and perspectives (Ratts et al., 2016). The Western mental health system in particular is both subjective and ethnocentric, often contrasting the views and values of other cultures. Thus, a central goal of multicultural counseling is working to remedy the inequities of hierarchy and dominance inherent in asymmetrical power arrangements (Zur, 2014). By demonstrating self-awareness, care, and genuine respect for the client, the counselor positions themselves as a trusted authority equipped to validate the contextual underpinnings of the client's presenting concern.

Power can show up in the therapeutic environment through institutions, professionalism, positionality, and systems of information gathering. Mental health professionals have the ability to make judgments about which behaviors and perceptions are deemed normal, standard, or aberrant. Counselor evaluations influence recommendations that may impact a client's progress, autonomy, and well-being. For example, as mandated reporters, counselors must report abuse to legal authorities, make child and elderly dependency recommendations, and have the authority to detain a client against their will in cases of perceived harm to self or others (ACA, 2014). Additionally, counselors in correctional institutions or inpatient units make recommendations for commitment and length of treatment and monitor discharge criteria. Through the education and credentialing process, counselors are expected to apply their competence to provide equitable and appropriate care for individuals they represent. Likewise, being privy to clients' personal information is one of the most basic power positions in human relationships (Simpson et al., 2015). Counselors obtain knowledge about the history, past traumas, behavioral patterns, reactionary habits, criminal histories, and at times shameful details of a client's life. Moreover, access to clients' personal information is often accompanied by the counselor's privilege to ask but not necessarily answer questions (Zur, 2014). This power discrepancy is the primary distinction between the counseling relationship and other colloquial relationships in the client's life (i.e., friendships, romantic partnerships, etc.). The counselor's ability to propose new perspectives and ways of responding to situations requires a power-sensitive approach to helping that minimizes exploitation and promotes agency.

Power sensitivity requires the counselor to be actively engaged and attuned to the client's worldview and experiences. When a client's strengths, knowledge, and personal expertise are centered, a shared authority develops within the therapeutic dyad. The modern client views themselves more of a consumer than a "patient." Positive attitude changes toward mental health have helped reduce stigma and increased accessibility to resources and information about mental health (Thornicroft et al., 2016). Clients voluntarily commit time, emotional vulnerability, and financial resources toward the alleviation of their distress, improvement in their relationships, and changes in their behavior. Even clients mandated to outpatient, inpatient, or residential treatment facilities come to counseling with an expectation they will receive a return on their willingness to participate in therapy. A collaborative therapeutic environment is a place to explore problems, have candid conversations, brainstorm potential solutions, and reflect on alternatives (Bohart & Tallman, 1999; Duncan & Miller, 2000). Counselors must make space for tension, disagreement, and differing opinions. Counselors can also promote personal agency through curiosity about the client's perspectives. Allow the client to name their needs, ask questions, and offer ideas about the direction of counseling based on what's helpful, purposeful, missing, or not working (Deci & Ryan, 2008; Dwyer et al., 2011). Furthermore, humanistic and feminist frameworks emphasize the importance of counselors' self-disclosure as a way to create a more egalitarian relationship and level the playing field between counselors and clients.

DEMYSTIFYING THE COUNSELING PROCESS

Counseling is both an intuitive and intentional process that hinges on rapport and is guided by consent, mutual empathy, and strategies for change. Yet, illusory and mysterious procedures may result in ambivalence, especially for individuals who are seeking counseling for the first time (King, 2011). Clearly defining the process of counseling helps the client become more informed about what counseling is, what it is not, what to expect, and their rights as a consumer (ACA, 2014; King, 2011). When the client is informed, they feel more comfortable, are empowered to make their own decisions, and take ownership over the outcomes of therapy. The goal of counseling is to mobilize the client's resources to effect change at the personal and relational levels. An indicator of change is when a client actively advocates for themselves and confronts systems of oppression that contribute to their distress (Enns, 2004; Ratts et al., 2016).

THE PROCESS

Relationship building begins during the informed consent process and first meeting. Intake paperwork should be culturally inclusive in its language and structure, providing the client with opportunities to write in descriptions about their identity, values, and presenting concerns. During introductions, be cognizant of and ensure you address clients by their name and pronouns. An additional way of neutralizing perceptions of dominance is by encouraging clients to use your first name minus titles or honorifics. Clients have the freedom to choose whether to enter or remain in a counseling relationship, and their decision is often determined by how comfortable they feel with the counselor and the inclusive nature of the counseling experience (Sue & Sue, 2012). Informed consent is an active and ongoing agreement that clearly defines the purpose, goals, limitations, risks, and benefits of participating in counseling. Counselors provide their clients with information about their theoretical orientation, competencies, and alternatives to counseling so that the clients may make fully informed choices.

THE BEAUTY OF FEELING THE FEELINGS

Beyond procedure, counselors should discuss the emotional consequences associated with counseling. A successful course of therapy may result in positive feelings, reduction of symptom distress, interpersonal gains, and liberating outlooks on the world (Layard & Clark, 2014). However, the journey from hurt to healing may be taxing. The process of remembering and talking about unpleasant events, feelings, or thoughts is difficult. Disclosure may result in the client experiencing considerable discomfort, anxiety, uncertainty, or strong feelings such as anger and sadness. Likewise, the counselor may also be affected when listening to client narratives, sharing in mutual feelings of angst or discomfort. While establishing the therapeutic relationship, it is important for the counselor to express openness to discussing the contextual nature of the client's experiences, especially those involving bias, oppression, and racism. Validation is important throughout the counseling experience but is imperative early in the relationship (Fuertes et al., 2015).

A relational approach to counseling posits that empathetic responsiveness is critical to promoting therapeutic growth. Counselors are tasked with broaching topics of privilege and marginal status that have an influence on the counseling relationship (Day-Vines et al., 2020; Ratts et al., 2016). Exploring topics of oppression is complex and will require the counselor to check in with the client to confirm their understanding of the experiences and circumstances. Counselors must be diligent in managing emotional entailments that may arise from a lack of self-awareness or explicit or implicit bias, thus impairing their judgment and ability to respond with compassion. The counselor's willingness to be impacted demonstrates care, validation, and a genuine sensitivity to the cognitive, affective, and contextual experience of the client (Boysen, 2010; Jordan, 2010; Miller, 1976). Throughout the counseling process, counselors should remain cognizant that what happens during the therapy session may mimic larger societal dynamics. Social and economic tensions, inequities, interpersonal stigmas, and misunderstandings might be brought into the relationship and inform the process and outcome of counseling.

DEFINING CLOSURE

Counselors should inform clients during the initial counseling session that eventually therapy will come to an end. If the client determines the counselor is not suited to meet their needs, termination may be initiated prematurely or the client may drop out of treatment (Swift & Callahan, 2011). Ideally, termination is a collaborative experience supported by routine discussions regarding client progress throughout the relationship. The counselor must openly discuss how long it might take to achieve the goals outlined by the client in order for the client to have realistic expectations about the duration of counseling (Mueller & Pekarik, 2000; Swift & Callahan, 2008). Furthermore, it is helpful to have open discussions with the client about how they want to feel once symptoms are diminished or they have made changes in their lives. These discussions should work to enhance the therapeutic alliance and working relationship between the counselor and client, supplemented by a mutual agreement for when termination should occur. Setting a date helps both the counselor and client decide how they might best utilize their time during sessions and work intentionally toward meeting treatment goals (Goode et al., 2017).

Even when the groundwork is set for having a collaborative termination, the culmination of this process may be emotional and awkward. Saying goodbye is difficult, especially when a strong therapeutic bond was formed and maintained throughout the course of counseling. Regardless of positive treatment outcomes, termination may bring up feelings of sadness, grief, doubt, and fear as clients face the reality of navigating their futures. The termination of counseling is not simply a finish line, but a symbol of satisfaction and new meanings for the client as they carry out new perspectives and work to maintain their progress (Olivera et al., 2017). During the termination session, the client is likely to express gratitude and reflect on what they have learned in counseling. However, for the process to truly be collaborative, the counselor must also share their reflections in a way that acknowledges the client's influence in the therapeutic process. The counselor's recognition of the client's impact is supportive to the client's self-efficacy, and it helps them understand that they may impact others in a positive way (Goode et al., 2017). Further, hearing that the relationship was also meaningful for the counselor gives the client a sense of closure and equalizes the relationship (Curtis, 2002; Greenberg, 2002).

SUMMARY, INSIGHTS, AND ACTIONS

Developing multicultural and social justice competence provides counselors with self-awareness, knowledge related to power and privilege, and an understanding of client worldviews and how they impact the overall counseling relationship, ultimately leading to effective counseling and advocacy. Irrespective of setting, counseling professionals from privileged and marginalized identities must be cognizant of their status relative to the clients they come into contact with during clinical practice.

Awareness of the attitudes counseling professionals from privileged and marginalized intersectionalities possess must be relative to those they interact. Being aware of one's attitudes and beliefs relative to a client allows for meaningful understanding of how one's values and beliefs shape interactions. Moreover, awareness of one's attitudes and beliefs relative to one's client may help identify implicit bias. In a very real sense, counseling practitioners, whether they are in schools or mental health settings, must definitely be mindful of how the attitudes they hold impact clients from both privileged and marginalized communities. When counselors are cognizant of their attitudes, a vital first step to building strong relationships, they are doing so from a multicultural and social justice lens that values knowledge and skills and implores them to take action. To this end, the counseling process requires open and honest self-reflection on the part of the counseling professional, thus opening the door to fruitful counseling relationships.

REFLECTION AND DISCUSSION QUESTIONS

1. What is meant by the notion that therapy is a team effort?
2. What strategies might a counselor employ to circumvent client dropout or premature termination of counseling services by clients?
3. How might counselors' attitudes, values, and beliefs be shaped by privileged or marginalized identities?
4. What does it mean to have a contextual perspective to counseling?
5. In what tangible ways might counselors integrate advocacy practices into their work with clients who are marginalized or historically disenfranchised?
6. In what ways does the ACA Code of Ethics impact the counseling relationship?
7. How might a counselor build rapport during the intake process?
8. How might clients from marginalized communities initially perceive counselors with privileged identities?
9. List three to five values, beliefs, and biases you possess that may influence or impact your counseling relationships.
10. Where, and from whom, did you learn about your values, beliefs, biases, culture, and worldviews?

REFERENCES

American Counseling Association. (2014). *ACA Code of Ethics.* Author

Badgett, M. V. L., Choi, S. K., & Wilson, B. D. M., (2019). *LGBT poverty in the United States: A study of differences between sexual orientation and gender identity groups.* UCLA Williams Institute School of Law. https://williamsinstitute.law.ucla.edu/wp-content/uploads/National-LGBT-Poverty-Oct-2019.pdf

Bohart, A. C., & Tallman, K. (1999). *How clients make therapy work.* American Psychological Association.

Boysen, G. A. (2010). Integrating implicit bias into counselor education. *Counselor Education and Supervision, 49*(4), 210–227. https://doi.org/10.1002/j.1556-6978.2010.tb00099.x

Centers for Disease Control and Prevention. (2016, February 29). *Stigma and discrimination.* https://www.cdc.gov/MSMhealth/stigma-and-discrimination.htm

Conron, K. J., Mimiaga, M. J., & Landers, S. J. (2010). A population-based study of sexual orientation identity and gender differences in adult health. *American Journal of Public Health, 100*(10), 1953–1960.

Cook, E. P. (2015). *Understanding people in context: The ecological perspective in counseling.* Wiley.

Curtis, R. (2002). Termination from a psychoanalytic perspective. *Journal of Psychotherapy Integration, 12*(3), 350–357. http://dx.doi.org/10.1037/1053-0479.12.3.350

Crenshaw, K. (1989). Demarginalizing the intersection of race and sex: A Black feminist critique of antidiscrimination doctrine, feminist theory and antiracist politics. *University of Chicago Legal Forum, 140*, 139–167.

Day-Vines, N. L., Cluxton-Keller, F., Agorsor, C., Gubara, S., & Otabil, N. A. A. (2020). The multidimensional model of broaching behavior. *Journal of Counseling & Development, 98*(1), 107–118. https://doi.org/10.1002/jcad.12304

Deci, E. L., & Ryan, R. M. (2008). Self-determination theory: A macrotheory of human motivation, development, and health. Canadian Psychology, *49*(3), 182–185. https://doi.org/10.1037/a0012801

Duncan, B. L., & Miller, S. D. (2000). The client's theory of change: Consulting the client in the integrative process. *Journal of Psychotherapy Integration, 10*(2), 169–187.

Duncan, B. L., Miller, S. D., Wampold, B. E., & Hubble, M. A. (2010). *The heart and soul of change: Delivering what works in therapy.* American Psychological Association. https://doi.org/10.1037/12075-000

Dwyer, L. A., Hornsey, M. J., Smith, L. G., Oei, T. P., & Dingle, G. A. (2011). Participant autonomy in cognitive behavioral group therapy: An integration of self-determination and cognitive behavioral theories. *Journal of Social and Clinical Psychology, 30*(1), 24–46. https://doi.org/10.1521/jscp.2011.30.1.24

Enns, C. Z. (2004). *Feminist theories and feminist psychotherapies: Origins, themes, and diversity* (2nd ed.). Haworth.

Fuertes, J. N, Brady-Amoon, P., Thind, N., & Chang, T. (2015). The therapy relationship in multicultural psychotherapy. *Psychotherapy Bulletin, 50*(1), 41–45.

Goode, J., Park, J., Parkin, S., Tompkins, K. A., & Swift, J. K. (2017). A collaborative approach to psychotherapy termination. *Psychotherapy, 54*(1), 10–14. https://doi.org/10.1037/pst0000085

Greenberg, L. S. (2002). Termination of experiential therapy. *Journal of Psychotherapy Integration, 12*(3), 358–363. http://dx.doi.org/10.1037/1053-0479.12.3.358

Hall, K. G., Barden, S., & Conley, A. (2014). A relational-cultural framework: Emphasizing relational dynamics and multicultural skill development. *Professional Counselor, 4*(1), 71–83.

Hankivsky, O., Reid, C., Cormier, R., Varcoe, C., Clark, N., Benoit, C., & Brotman, S. (2010). Exploring the promises of intersectionality for advancing women's health research. *International Journal for Equity in Health, 9*(1), 5.

Hatchett, G. T. (2017). Monitoring the counseling relationship and client progress as alternatives to prescriptive empirically supported therapies. *Journal of Mental Health Counseling, 39*(2), 104–115.

James, S. E., Herman, J. L., Rankin, S., Keisling, M., Mottet, L., & Anafi, M. (2016). *The report of the 2015 U.S. Transgender Survey.* National Center for Transgender Equality. https://transequality.org/sites/default/files/docs/usts/USTS-Full-Report-Dec17.pdf

Jordan, J. V. (2010). *Theories of psychotherapy: Relational–cultural therapy.* American Psychological Association.

King, A. (2001). *Demystifying the counseling process: A self-help handbook for counselors.* Allyn and Bacon.

Kress, V. E., Haiyasoso, M., Zoldan, C. A., Headley, J. A., & Trepal, H. (2018). The use of relational-cultural theory in counseling clients who have traumatic stress disorders. *Journal of Counseling & Development, 96*(1), 106–114. https://doi.org/10.1002/jcad.12182

La Roche, M., & Christopher, M. S. (2008). Culture and empirically supported treatments: On the road to a collision? *Culture & Psychology, 14*(3), 333–356.

Lambert, M. J. (2013). Outcome in psychotherapy: The past and important advances. *Psychotherapy, 50*(1), 42–51. https://doi.org/10.1037/a0030682

Layard, R., & Clark, D. M. (2014). *Thrive: the power of evidence-based psychological therapies.* Penguin.

McCall, L. (2005). The complexity of intersectionality. *Signs, 30*(3), 1771–1800. https://doi.org/10.1086/426800

Miller, J. B. (1976). *Toward a new psychology of women.* Beacon.

Miller, J. B. (1986). *What do we mean by relationships?* (Vol. 22). Stone Center for Developmental Services and Studies, Wellesley College.

Mueller, M., & Pekarik, G. (2000). Treatment duration prediction: Client accuracy and its relationship to dropout, outcome, and satisfaction. *Psychotherapy, 37*, 117–123. http://dx.doi.org/10.1037/h008770 https://doi.org/10.1037/h0087701

Murphy, D., Slovak, P., Thieme, A., Jackson, D., Olivier, P., & Fitzpatrick, G. (2019). Developing technology to enhance learning interpersonal skills in counsellor education. *British Journal of Guidance & Counselling, 47*(3), 328–341.

Olivera, J., Challú, L., Gómez Penedo, J. M., & Roussos, A. (2017). Client–therapist agreement in the termination process and its association with therapeutic relationship. *Psychotherapy, 54*(1), 88–101. https://doi.org/10.1037/pst0000099

Ratts, M. J., Singh, A. A., Nassar-McMillan, S., Butler, S. K., & McCullough, J. R. (2016). Multicultural and social justice counseling competencies: Guidelines for the counseling profession. *Journal of Multicultural Counseling and Development, 44*(1), 28–48. https://doi.org/10.1002/jmcd.12035

Rogers, C. R. (1942). *Counseling and psychotherapy: Newer concepts in practice.* Houghton Mifflin

Shin, R. Q., Ezeofor, I., Smith, L. C., Welch, J. C., & Goodrich, K. M. (2016). The development and validation of the contemporary critical consciousness measure. *Journal of Counseling Psychology, 63*(2), 210–223. https://doi.10.1037/cou0000137

Simpson, J. A., Farrell, A. K., Oriña, M. M., & Rothman, A. J. (2015). *Power and social influence in relationships.* In M. Mikulincer, P. R. Shaver, J. A. Simpson, & J. F. Dovidio (Eds.), *APA handbook of personality and social psychology,* Vol. 3: Interpersonal relations (pp. 393–420). American Psychological Association. https://doi.org/10.1037/14344-015

Sommers-Flanagan, J. (2015). Evidence-based relationship practice: Enhancing counselor competence. *Journal of Mental Health Counseling, 37*(2), 95–108. https://doi.org/10.17744/mehc.37.2.g13472044600588r

Sue, D. W., & Sue, D. (2012). *Counseling the culturally diverse: Theory and practice* (6th ed.). Wiley.

Swift, J. K., & Callahan, J. L. (2008). A delay discounting measure of great expectations and the effectiveness of psychotherapy. *Professional Psychology: Research and Practice, 39*(6), 581–588. http://dx.doi.org/10.1037/0735-7028.39.6.581

Swift, J. K., & Callahan, J. L. (2011). Decreasing treatment dropout by addressing expectations for treatment length. *Psychotherapy Research, 21*(2), 193–200. http://dx.doi.org/10.1080/10503307.2010.541294

Thornicroft, G., Mehta, N., Clement, S., Evans-Lacko, S., Doherty, M., Rose, D., Koschorke, M., Shidhaye, R. O'Reilly, C, ... & Henderson, C. (2016). Evidence for effective interventions to reduce mental-health-related stigma and discrimination. *The Lancet, 387*(10023), 1123–1132.

Wampold, B. E., Baldwin, S. A., Holtforth, M. G., & Imel, Z. E. (2017). *What characterizes effective therapists?* In L. G. Castonguay & C. E. Hill (Eds.), How and why are some therapists better than others?: Understanding therapist effects (pp. 37–53). American Psychological Association. https://doi.org/10.1037/0000034-003

Wampold, B. E., & Imel, Z. E. (2015). *The great psychotherapy debate: The evidence for what makes psychotherapy work.* Routledge.

Zur, O. (2014). *Power in psychotherapy and counseling.* Zur Institute.

CHAPTER 7

INTERSECTIONALITY

Implications for Professional Counselors

Regina Finan, University of Georgia

Brean'a Parker, North Carolina State University

Michael P. Chaney, Oakland University

LEARNING OBJECTIVES

1. Understand the history and current state of intersectionality.
2. Review intersectionality within the framework of MSJCC.
3. Learn how to apply the multicultural and social justice counseling competencies (MSJCC) within a counseling context utilizing an intersectionality framework.

LEARNING OUTCOMES

1. Define and describe intersectionality.
2. Understand how intersectionality is integrated within the MSJCC.
3. Apply the MSJCC within a counseling context utilizing an intersectionality framework.

We are primed to be leaders in extending the work of intersectionality pioneered by Kimberlé Crenshaw (1989) and Patricia Hill Collins (1986). Intersectionality can be conceptualized as a field of study, an analytical strategy, and a critical praxis (Collins, 2015). It can help us to see, hear, and experience individuals as complex beings who walk through life with multiple marginalized and privileged identities. These identity categories can include ability, age, body size, class, ethnicity, gender, mental health, physical health, political affiliation, race, religion, and sexual/affectional orientation. To be clear, intersectionality does not simply focus on multiple and intersecting identities; it is an active call to dismantle sociopolitical systems and structures of oppression (Moradi & Grzanka, 2017). Ratts (2017) has criticized the counseling profession as "grossly inadequate" (p. 88) in its attention and responsiveness to the marginalization of those with multiple identity statuses and experiences.

HISTORY OF INTERSECTIONALITY

Intersectionality as a theory was coined by Black feminist and critical race theorist Kimberlé Crenshaw. Intersectionality conceptualizes the distinct ways race, gender, class, and other social identities interrelate to form a matrix of complex discrimination, stigmatization, challenges, and barriers as a result of compounding forms of oppression (e.g., racialized sexism, gendered heterosexism, etc.) for individuals and communities (Collins, 2015; Crenshaw, 1991; Love et al., 2018). This concept stems from the fundamental belief that people do not live what Audre Lorde (1984) described as "single issue lives" and, therefore, identities such as race or gender cannot be examined as exclusive or separable in understanding experiences of discrimination.

Initially, Crenshaw (1991) applied the theory of intersectionality to the experiences of Black women specifically. More recently, intersectionality as a theoretical framework has been applied in capturing the complexity of individuals who hold multiple oppressed identities, including but not limited to the LGBTQ+ community (Ferguson & Mivillie, 2017; Mustanski & Liu, 2013; Robinson, 2018), people living with disabilities (Banks, 2018; Biss, 2019; Cramer & Plummer, 2009), Indigenous populations (Gone et al., 2019), Asian diasporic populations (Gómez, 2017; Isok et al., 2012), and immigrants and undocumented folx (Fruja, 2017; Kolawole, 2017). It is important to note that while everyone has intersections of various identities (e.g., racial ethnic, gender and sexual identity, socioeconomic status, citizenship), intersectionality theory recognizes how individual social identities create a unique experience due to their overlap while simultaneously attending to the role of systemic power and oppression as a result of marginalized identities (Collins, 2015). This distinction will be important as we continue to learn how intersectionality theory can inform the way counselors are able to understand and explore the role of power and oppression with the clients and communities they serve (Chan et al., 2019).

Intersectionality theory is part of a larger branch of critical studies rooted in critical legal studies and critical race theory (Delgado & Stefanic, 2012; Solorzano, 1998). Critical studies provide a comprehensive counter analysis of how systemic forces (colonialism, migration, power, and capitalism) impact the lived realities of traditionally targeted communities. In the next few sections, we will briefly discuss the way intersectionality is discussed within different social identity categories. Please keep in mind that while these designations are separate to understand the underpinnings of intersectionality, these identities overlap, thereby creating a nuanced lived reality for individuals and communities.

INTERSECTIONALITY WITH PEOPLE OF COLOR

The term *people of color* designates the experience and racial and/or ethnic identities of community members who are not assigned the racial designation of White. People of color usually refers to Black and/or African American people, Indigenous/Native nations in the land we call the United States, Asian and Pacific islanders, Desi Americans, Latinx communities, and folx who identify as multiracial and multiethnic. Intersectionality with people of color recognizes the importance of learning the contextual histories of each cultural subgroup while also analyzing the relationship each community has with the United States. For example, TribalCrit (Brayboy, 2005), a branch of critical race theory, attends to the endemic role of colonization in the realities and relationship of Indigenous people with the United States while centering the diverse tribal philosophies, beliefs customs, traditions, and visions for the future. Traditionally, marginalized communities' values, customs, language, spiritual traditions, and experiences are compared to the values and ideology of dominant White culture. This creates a "power over" relationship, designating those with history, values, and tradition who are different from White America as deviant and inferior.

Recent literature supports that people of color oftentimes experience both overt and subtle forms of oppression daily. Overt forms of oppression can be witnessing or experiencing the mistreatment of undocumented and mixed immigrant status families, such as being detained and put in cages at the border or separating families. Overt oppression can be witnessing or experiencing Black men and women being killed or harassed by police officers without legal ramifications. In contrast, oppression can be subtle, such as microaggressions within educational and employment spaces. These forms of oppression act as sophisticated reminders that people of color do not belong in this country or should be excluded from certain spaces (Nadal et al., 2014; Sue et al., 2007). For example, the model minority myth is a subtle form of oppression that characterizes Asian Americans as socioeconomically successful, academically high achieving, talented, and thriving. It is used to counter racial dialogue about inequity and creates a wedge between other marginalized ethnic groups that experience disenfranchisement. The assumption of educational and successful proclivity cultivates extreme pressure and lack of interventions/resources for Asian American community members (Shih et al., 2019).

While racial oppression for each community looks different as a result of migration and relationships with social, political, and institutional treatment within the United States, collectively these experiences have direct mental health concerns as a result of racialized oppression (Lewis et al., 2017). People of color may experience race-based trauma, witnessing or actively experiencing harassment, violence, exploitation, and discrimination as a result of racial and ethnic identity (Carter et al., 2020). More recently, social media has provided a platform where global experiences of mistreatment and discrimination are accessible to people around the world. While this may promote international advocacy, this international platform may reinforce psychological stress for people of color who are living with the effects of race-based trauma. Mental health counselors need to be aware that these different experiences can impact the way in which clients experience anxiety, depression, posttraumatic stress disorder, dissociation, and other mental health concerns (Kapilashrami & Hankivsky, 2018).

INTERSECTIONALITY WITHIN LESBIAN, GAY, BISEXUAL, AND QUEER COMMUNITIES

Within the lesbian, gay, bisexual and queer community, intersectional experiences may differ based on one's distance from the valued norms of sexual identity (physical, emotional, affectional attraction) in the United States. It is important to understand the mechanisms of homophobia and heterosexism (i.e., discrimination and prejudice against gay and lesbian people, with the assumption that heterosexuality is the normal sexual orientation) for individuals who identity as LGBQ+. There is a significant history of violence, inequity, and hardship toward LGBQ+ individuals and communities in different institutions such as education (e.g., bullying, harassment) (Kosciw et al., 2018; Watson & Miller, 2012), employment (lack of legal protections from termination) (Resnick & Galupo, 2019), housing (e.g., denied housing due to disclosure of sexual identity) (Kattari et al., 2016), and the law (e.g., dismissal of hate crime violence) (Mogul et al., 2012). It is also important to consider the role of border groups within the LGBQ+ community; these are groups that may experience erasure from both queer and straight communities as a result of not being "gay" or "straight" enough. For example, the experiences and narratives of violence, harassment, and barriers of people who identify as bisexual, asexual, and pansexual are commonly dismissed because they may appear to belong to the dominant group (i.e., straight people). It is imperative to consider the interplay of this identity with other identities such as race/ethnicity, class, and disability when thinking about the experiences of homophobia and heterosexism among this group.

Scholarly literature informs us that young adults who identify as LGBQ+ experience mental health concerns related to major depression as a result of navigating family, social, and institutional (e.g., religion, team sports, school) dynamics that deliver and reinforce social messages that their sexual identities deviate from the norm (Johnson et al., 2019; Meyer, 2003). Additionally, news coverage on young people who commit suicide as a result of intense bullying, physical, and sexual violence in the school setting indicates the severity of how hate-based messages (overt or subtle) and treatment can be detrimental to the mental wellness of young adults who identify as LGBQ+. Further, clinicians need to be attuned to the impact of internalized homophobia and heterosexism that contribute to feelings of shame, guilt, rejection, and self-harm for clients who identify as LGBQ+.

INTERSECTIONALITY ACROSS GENDER DESIGNATIONS

Individuals who were assigned a gender at and before birth are often catapulted into social expectations and gender roles that serve to empower people who identify as men or male at center, while diminishing and subjugating those who identify as women, women at center, and nonbinary. As a result of our hierarchal society, individuals who identify as cisgender males often hold power and privilege. "Cis" from the Latin word *same*, suggests that the current gender designation you have for yourself as "male/ female" or "man/woman" aligns with the gender label prescribed by a medical doctor or family members at birth and development. *Trans* is an umbrella term for a broad range of gender experiences and stems from the Latin translation of *different*. As related to gender designations, it means that the gender assigned at birth or gestation does not reflect how someone identifies, experiences, and defines their gender currently. Additionally, some people do not identify within the gender binary of male or female and instead identify as nonbinary or gender nonconforming, while others may feel that they experience their gender along a spectrum at different times of their lives and identify as gender fluid. Moreover, some people may identify as agender and not identify with any gender characterization at all.

While the language of defining gender is ever evolving, in this chapter it is important to understand that people who do not conform to the binary gender system (male or female; man or woman) and also do not identify as male are often the recipients of unique forms of violence, discrimination, exploitation, and erasure within society. The systemic mechanisms that promote the oppression of women, trans, and nonbinary individuals are sexism, cissexism, and transphobia. All these systems serve to support the belief that there are only two genders and that men and their associated characteristics of power, logical reasoning, hierarchy, and independence are the norm. By deviating from the Western ideology of gender, gender expression and roles, and expectations, individuals within diverse gender communities are often targeted for gender-based violence like rape, physical assault, harassment, and murder; they are silenced at the individual and cultural level. At the institutional level folx who identify as women experience barriers to promotional employment opportunities. When we include the effects of race, education, experience, and disability, the "ceiling" for opportunities and access to growth in employment becomes lower. For trans and nonbinary folx who have "cis-assuming privilege," formerly known as "passing privilege," there may be access to employment, education, and resources; however, for folx who do not have cis-assuming privilege, a trans or nonbinary identity can result in institutional barriers and challenges related to basic needs for sustainability, such as shelter or housing, employment with benefits and safety, career opportunities, access to affirming health care, and matriculation through education. It is important to consider the mental health concerns around safety or security from violence, exploitation, and various forms of harassment in navigating everyday life for women, trans, and nonbinary folx (McCullough et al., 2017). Hardships associated with these multiple issues may significantly impact the mental welfare for women, trans, and nonbinary folx who support partners and spouses, caregivers, and children. Lastly, the mental health outcomes of the experience and fear of gender-based violence within relationships, school, nursing homes, workplace environments, and on the street may include depression, anxiety, complex trauma, and other common mental health diagnoses.

INTERSECTIONALITY ACROSS CLASS

While the United States does not act as a traditional caste system, wealth distribution is neither equal nor democratic in that there are few people and corporations that monopolize access to wealth over the majority of others. Class cuts across all identities; at the individual level all people need access to food, safety, adequate and sustainable health care, and quality tools and resources for educational attainment. Classism is the system of oppression that assigns prejudice or privilege to people belonging to a specific social class. For mental health counselors, there are direct implications of classism that impact the mental health concerns of clients. For instance, the opportunity to access mental health counseling at all is a class-based privilege. Individuals who live at the margins of society and experience restricted access to resources, while impacted by poverty, violence, and stress, need access to quality mental health services, yet are denied access. When addressing the intersections of class, it is important to consider the external conditions, experiences, and accessibility clients have regardless of class status.

INTERSECTIONALITY AND DISABILITY

Similar to the U.S. value of production, the value placed on the ability to perform and contribute to the labor market stems from ableism. Systemic oppression of people who have a disability often comes in the form of privileging the minds and bodies of able-bodied individuals. This is evident in employment policies, environmental structure, cultural and attitudes toward people with disabilities, and institutional accessibility for people who require medical, physical, emotional, and/or mental aids and assistive devices or resources. Intersectionality with those who have a disability acknowledges the way various forms of disability are legitimized and accommodated over others. People living with disabilities often have the burden to prove that they have one or more disabilities and that their disabilities require cultural- and institutional-level intervention and accommodation. Oftentimes, the needs and realities of people with disabilities are ignored and marginalized, even within the mental health counseling field.

In the counseling profession, we assume that both clinicians and clients have the conventionally accepted ability to engage in communication, exploration, insight, and growth in a 50-minute session. In consideration of the various forms of disability that may manifest as physical, cognitive/neurodivergent, intellectual and mental, clinicians practicing within an intersectional framework must be attuned to the way institutions and practices exclude accessibility to counseling for folx who live with disabilities. We must scrutinize the deficiencies and deliberate on effective and appropriate accommodations to support the mental well-being of individuals with disabilities, especially those who also have other marginalized identities.

INTERSECTIONALITY IN COUNSELING

While the counseling profession embraces social justice as the fifth force (Ratts, 2009), there is a growing call to imbue the field with a deeper action-based form of social justice: intersectionality (Chan et al., 2018; Ratts, 2017). The American Counseling Association (ACA) has endorsed a definition of counseling as "a professional relationship that empowers diverse individuals, families, and groups to accomplish mental health, well-ness, education, and career goals" (Kaplan et al., 2014, p. 368). Our profession calls on us to develop our capacity as culturally sensitive and social justice–oriented practitioners, scholars, and educators. This is evidenced by guiding principles embedded in our ethical code, standards, and professional competencies. However, very little exists to help guide counselors and counselor-educators to use intersectionality to effectively explore the complexity of multiple marginalized identities (Ratts, 2017). Yet, with an investment in social justice advocacy, this work can be intentionally and thoughtfully integrated into clinical practice, supervision, training programs, and research.

CLINICAL PRACTICE

If we conceptualize our clients as intersectional beings, with multiple identities experiencing complex interactions of privilege and oppression, we may be better equipped to hear and see their authentic selves. We do not live compartmentalized lives, where only one identity matters at any given time. Thus, it is important for clinicians to understand intersections of both privileged and marginalized identities (Ratts, 2017) and how they interact with an individual's circumstances, lived experiences, available resources, and so on. However, clinicians may have been trained using single identity frameworks (e.g., working with women, working with men, working with Asian Americans, working with children, etc.). If we cannot attend to this richness of human diversity, we risk rendering clients with multiple marginalized identities invisible (Ratts, 2017).

It is especially important to have an awareness of assumptions we bring into the counseling space that are attributed to power and privilege (Chan et al., 2017). When an affluent, straight, White, cisgender, able-bodied man occupies space, he must do so with the recognition that he represents multiple identities that benefit from power and privilege. There need not be shame and guilt associated with these identities, yet it is appropriate and necessary to consider how they shape one's view of the world and others in it. Particularly, it is imperative that we assess ourselves for biases and blind spots. How does one's access to and relationship with wealth and resources shape how they attend to the needs and concerns of a client who is poor and lacks access to basic resources such as food, shelter, and health care? Further, what biases may come up related to that client's race, gender, and mental health? Do we find ourselves thinking that their circumstances are simply a result of their own poor choices when the client is a person of color? Do we experience them as less capable and shamefully irresponsible if the client is also a single mother with multiple children? These are the insidious ways that we are socialized to conceptualize human beings with multiple marginalized identities.

It is also important to attend to our blind spots, or the issues that we may overlook. For example, much literature fails to include issues related to body size as a social identity, despite the fact anti-fat bias exists, even within counseling (Kinavey & Cool, 2019). While we may not immediately consider this social identity and the related impact, it is a lived reality for many individuals. A counselor who works from an intersectional framework and is attuned to diverse social identities is better equipped to self-monitor for anti-fat bias and to more expansively support a client experiencing the deleterious effects of oppression related to fat phobia and sizeism (Smith, 2019). One way counselors can look for blind spots is to make a comprehensive list of issues a client may experience. Then, the counselor can briefly assess whether they believe they have adequate knowledge and experience with the issues listed. Next, they determine which gaps are most significant and begin to seek more knowledge and resources in an effort to reduce their blind spots and increase their aptitude as a counselor. This is not to suggest that counselors must have expertise in every area; however, as a commitment to professionalism and lifelong learning, it is essential for practitioners to continue to broaden their knowledge and to have a sense of what they do not know.

When we use our power and privilege to avoid addressing a client's identities and do not offer an exploration of how those intersecting identities may experience privilege and oppression, we can contribute to rendering a person as unseen. Even when we discuss identity categories, if we focus on a single analytic framework (Ratts, 2017) by addressing identities as separate, we can miss an opportunity to attend to the compounding and unique effects of intersecting marginalization. In taking an intersectional approach to clinical work, practitioners can disrupt harmful experiences by providing a space and relationship characterized by warmth, positive regard, and an active stance to promote diversity and social justice. The counseling experience can become a place of critically conscious growth and empowerment. Critical consciousness, conceptualized by Paulo Freire (2000), refers to understanding the oppressive forces in one's life and the sense of self-efficacy to engage in action to resist those forces. Ratts (2017) created the Multicultural and Social Justice Counseling Competencies Assessment Form (MSJCC-AF) as a tool grounded in the MSJCC for interventions, teaching, and research. This tool can be introduced during intake and utilized throughout the counseling process to help the client explore the ways in which their identities and dynamics of power, privilege, and marginalization impact the way they experience the world, including the counseling relationship.

It is important to be mindful that clients with multiple marginalized identities may not be in counseling to specifically address issues associated with their identities (Smith, 2019). However, as counselors operating from an intersectionality framework, we know that any issue can be impacted by various social identities. Additionally, all interventions or resources identified to support a specific social identity (e.g., LGBTQ+, Black women, etc.) may not be appropriate (a conservative religious organization may not be a supportive resource for a gay Asian man) (Heard Harvey & Ricard, 2018).

CLINICAL SUPERVISION

Clinical supervision is a specific intervention relationship whereby an experienced counselor provides oversight, assistance, and support to a less-experienced counselor (Bernard & Goodyear, 2014). This relationship is an evaluative and hierarchical process that occurs over a period of time with the goal of strengthening the quality and effectiveness of a practitioner (Bernard & Goodyear, 2014). There is often a power differential in relationships, and this is true for the supervisory relationship in counseling. Although there is a healthy availability of literature addressing multicultural clinical supervision (Tohidian & Quek, 2017), there is considerably less related to intersectionality in clinical supervision (Garcia et al., 2009; Gutierrez, 2018).

Hernández and McDowell (2010) suggested that a multicultural lens is insufficient to critically analyze the intersections of identity, privilege, oppression, and related power dynamics. Rather, an intersectional approach is more appropriate to capture the discrete complexity within these experiences. However, as with teaching in counselor education programs, clinical supervision creates opportunities for difficult dialogues, which may be challenging for students. Individuals who are resistant to reflexive practices in examining their own social identities in relation to power, privilege, and oppression may experience exceptional difficulty in engaging in clinical and personal growth and development (Hernández & McDowell, 2010). When practitioners are able to embrace an intersectionality approach in clinical supervision, there is an opportunity to develop critical consciousness (Freire, 2000; Garcia et al., 2009) and relational safety (Hernández & McDowell, 2010; Hernandez & Rankin, 2003). Relational safety refers to coconstructed discourse whereby questioning, challenging, exploration, and expressing feelings are practiced (Hernandez & Rankin, 2003). The MSJCC and the MSJCC-AF (Ratts, 2017) can be utilized as a guide for engaging in relational safety in supervision (Ratts, 2017). It would support efforts to engage in an intersectionality approach in that the supervisor and supervisee(s) can engage in an intentional process to identify and discuss social identities they possess and how those identities intersect within the context of privilege and oppression.

TRAINING PROGRAMS

Counselor education programs are well situated to infuse intersectionality theory and practices throughout the curriculum and within operational aspects, including advising and program development. Yet scholars argue that graduate programs do not adequately educate students on how to conceptualize individuals with mutually interdependent identities (Cheshire, 2013; Ratts, 2017; Ratts et al., 2016). This can result in practitioners who feel underprepared to work with clients with multiple marginalized identities and to navigate the unique intersections of privilege and oppression with these clients (Ratts, 2017). Programs can infuse multicultural content via a single class, across curriculum, or both (Celinska & Swazo, 2016).

In order to prepare counselors-in-training to practice from an intersectionality framework, there must be various opportunities across the curriculum and within a specific course to learn about, discuss, and process conversations about social identities, privilege, and marginalization. While these conversations can be both transformative and challenging for students (Chan et al., 2018; Heard Harvey & Ricard, 2018; Watt et al.,

2009), facilitating learning in this way can provide salient context and enhance our capacity to support clients (Heard Harvey & Ricard, 2018). Further, intersectionality can be promoted through pedagogy and not just through inclusion within the curriculum (Thompson & Bridges, 2019).

There are multiple ways to engage in these efforts. During program interviews, faculty and current students can introduce themselves by sharing salient social identities. While this does not truly represent intersectionality (intersectionality is not simply about multiple identities, but about the unique interaction of how multiple identities experience marginalization), it can be a way to softly introduce applicants to identity awareness. As an activity for orientation, students can use the MSJCC to explore their own intersecting identities in a way that allows them to identify possible identity conflicts arising from identity-based marginalization and privilege. For example, a queer, Christian, light-skinned Black woman may experience privilege as a member of a widely accepted and accessible faith in this country while also feeling rejected by that same faith due to her identity as a queer woman; she may experience light-skinned privilege due to colorism (discrimination based on skin color), while also feeling guilt for having that privilege; and she may experience racism and anti-Blackness as well. All of this is inextricably linked to her walk through life as a woman. Intersectionality captures the complexity of these interconnections (Heard Harvey & Ricard, 2018).

Counselors-in-training can explore intersectionality in various ways. One suggestion is to use creativity (Ali & Lee, 2019). Using a creative approach may help counseling students to explore their own identities and how they related to the concept of intersectionality (Ali & Lee, 2019). This can be accomplished through using interactive, experiential, and arts-based activities. Intersectionality can also be included as an ethical responsibility for consideration in a program's ethics course. One specific way to address this is to discuss the relevance of intersectionality within core professional values cited in the ACA Code of Ethics (American Counseling Association, 2014). For example, the code includes "2. Honoring diversity and embracing a multicultural approach in support of the worth, dignity, potential, and uniqueness of people within their social and cultural contexts." (ACA, 2014, p. 3). Students can engage in small group discussions to explore intersectionality considerations of their clients through an ethical lens.

COUNSELING RESEARCH

While still limited, intersectionality research in counseling is a growing area of interest and exploration (Chan et al., 2019). There is a tension in the social sciences regarding how to approach intersectionality research related to methodology and intersectionality theory (Chan et al., 2019; Cole, 2009; Else-Quest & Hyde, 2015; Parent et al., 2013). Ultimately, there are multiple ways to engage in intersectionality research, however scholars caution that research should adhere to the fundamental spirit of intersectionality as an applied framework that does not reduce itself to intersecting singular identities (Cole, 2009; Grzanka et al., 2017; Moradi & Grzanka, 2017; Parent et al., 2013; Shin et al., 2017). These efforts should reflect individuals who exist in multiple social categories that are impacted by sociopolitical systems of stratification and oppression (Marecek, 2015; Shields, 2008). Practitioners can use this research to inform their clinical work in meaningful ways.

It is important to recognize that individuals with multiple marginalized identities who encounter privilege and oppression subject to various contextual factors, may have distinctly nuanced experiences. Heard Harvey and Ricard (2018) considered race, sexual orientation, and religion through the lens of intersectionality. In this conceptual article, the authors discussed how exploring intersectionality can deepen and contextualize multicultural conversations. They suggested that practitioners use the MSJCCs as a guide and seek relevant intersectionality literature in an effort to increase awareness and skills to work with client to process dynamics unique to intersectional concerns and experiences.

Gangamma & Shipman (2018) provided a conceptualization of considerations in their study related to transnational intersectionality, or intersectionality within the context of the ways power, oppression, and marginalization impact the lives of refugees and migrant families. Salient considerations for therapists working with these families included (a) critical awareness of transnational contexts, (b) understanding differences of social identity experiences in various contexts, (c) acknowledging the postmigration factors of oppression that affect refugee resettlement, and (d) critically reflecting on the intersectional identity experiences of the client, therapist, and interpreter. A unique aspect of their conceptualization is considering the ways in which client and counselor identities may intersect. Counselors and counselor educators can use the MSJCC to explore privileged and marginalized identities with clients or students.

We can also consider the ways in which intersectional identities and experiences may impact faculty in counselor education programs who are training future counselors. In a study conducted by Haskins et al., (2016) participants who identified as African American mothers in counselor education reported that they both felt supported as mothers in family-friendly work environments while also experiencing marginalization professionally. This qualitative study illuminated the contradictory ways in which these women had positive and negative experiences related to their identities as Black women mothers who are counselor educators. The authors recommended infusing intersectionality discussions throughout the counseling curriculum and also modeling support that is inclusive of individuals' identities (such as parents). These examples highlight some of the complexities embedded within intersectionality and ways in which they may manifest in counseling-related research. They also bring to light how counselors and counselor educators can use intersectionality research to inform their work.

MULTICULTURAL AND SOCIAL JUSTICE COUNSELING COMPETENCIES (MSJCC) AND INTERSECTIONALITY

The MSJCC are an ideal framework to help counselors and counselor-educators to conceptualize identity, privilege, and marginalization within the realm of our work as clinicians and educators (Ratts, 2017; Ratts et al., 2016). These competencies extended the work by Sue et al. (1992) on the multicultural counseling competencies (MCC). More than a framework to help conceptualize theory, practice, and research through a multicultural and social justice lens, the MSJCC promotes understanding of the intersections of identities as they are influenced by power, privilege, and oppression for both counselors and their clients (Ratts et al., 2016). Ratts and colleagues intentionally incorporated intersections of identity through use of quadrants, which exhibit the relational interactions between privileged and oppressed identities and experiences unique to both counselor and client (Ratts, 2017). It includes four domains within which the counseling relationship can be processed: (a) counselor self-awareness, (b) client worldview, (c) counseling relationship, and (d) counseling and advocacy interventions. The first three domains can be developed by attending to attitudes and beliefs, knowledge, skills, and action. The final domain (counseling and advocacy interventions) involves interventions at multiple levels, including intrapersonal, interpersonal, institutional, community, public policy, and international/global. The MSJCC serve as a guide in our work as counseling professionals to advance multicultural and social justice actions and initiatives in ways that attend to intersectionality as necessary practice.

COUNSELOR SELF-AWARENESS AND INTERSECTIONALITY

A foundational and required characteristic of a counselor is self-awareness. Counselors must be able to acknowledge and deconstruct their values, beliefs, and biases—as they are situated within both privileged and marginalized social identities and contexts—in an effort to function ethically and with care and compassion. A counselor who operates within an intersectionality framework can engage in the self-awareness process promoted by the MSJCC (attitudes and beliefs, knowledge, skills, and action).

Attitudes and Beliefs

Multicultural and social justice competent counselors invest time and effort to gain awareness of and connection with their salient social identities and statuses. They recognize that these identities do not exist within silos but are inextricably connected to and influenced by other salient identities. Through deep reflection, they are able to examine ways in which they benefit from and are marginalized by oppressive sociopolitical systems and structures. Further, they engage in reflective and reflexive practices to become more self-aware of their strengths and limitations as a counselor, as well as their personal assumptions, attitudes, values, beliefs, and biases. As counselors committed to multicultural and social justice competence, they will acknowledge these interlocking experiences and lean into them as they continue to learn and grow. Counselors can utilize self-exploration activities and tools as a way to gain awareness. One tool that can be effective is a cultural genogram. A traditional genogram is a graphic depiction of family history and relationships. A cultural genogram promotes the exploration of cultural learning, understanding, and practices within a family that inform an individual's concept of power, privilege, and marginalization.

Knowledge

Multicultural and social justice–competent counselors seek knowledge and training in an effort to more deeply understand and conceptualize their salient social identities and statuses. They understand that they will never know all there is to know because we are dynamic beings in a society that is constantly changing; thus, new knowledge is created for our consumption. They learn how society has created social inequity and injustice and how their assumptions, attitudes, values, beliefs, and biases have been influenced by these constructed sociopolitical systems and structures. These counselors know how to apply their strengths and leverage their limitations to dismantle these systems and structures. As counselors committed to multicultural and social justice competence, they will work to develop resources and knowledge that deepen their understanding and capacity to engage in action to promote equity and justice. Counselors can research and request recommendations for salient resources to help broaden and deepen their knowledge related to identities within various social locations and contexts. The internet and the library are useful places to begin a search for relevant content. Counselors can also turn to professional organizations, local counseling programs, and community groups for assistance in identifying resources.

Skills

Multicultural and social justice–competent counselors develop and maintain skills to intentionally foster insight of their salient social identities and statuses. They cultivate the skills necessary to promote their understanding of the complex reality of interlocking systems of power and privilege that oppress individuals with multiple marginalized identities. These counselors utilize skills necessary for analyzing how they have been complicit in oppressive systems and practices within various contexts; they also critically reflect on ways they have been oppressed. As counselors committed to multicultural and social justice competence, they will learn, develop, and pass along skills that promote healing and liberation within themselves as well as for others. Counselors can attend workshops or identify activities that focus on skills related to self-awareness and critical reflection. One way individuals can develop critical reflection skills is through journaling. Through writing about one's experiences of privilege and marginalization, people can more deeply reflect on and understand themselves as intersectional beings. This understanding and awareness can develop deeper understanding and empathy for others.

Action

Multicultural and social justice–competent counselors are actively engaged in the work required to deepen their understanding of and connection to their salient social identities and statuses. They follow through with actions identified to enhance their attitudes and beliefs, knowledge, and skills related to self-awareness as it is related to intersectionality. These counselors actively use this self-awareness to promote understanding for others in ways that can cultivate healing and well-being. As counselors committed to multicultural and social justice competence, they recognize that all action (whether big or small) can be impactful and meaningful.

CLIENT WORLDVIEW AND INTERSECTIONALITY

For a counseling professional to adequately attend to the needs of a client, they must be able to recognize how their client views the world. To do this, a counselor needs to reflect on how experiences of marginalization and privilege impact the intersectional identities of an individual; they must understand that these experiences will shape how a client views the world and their place in it. A counselor who operates within an intersectionality framework can recognize how their social identities and experiences influence how they understand their client's worldview; commit to do the work necessary to center their client's way of perceiving and understanding the world; and use their knowledge and skills to foster awareness of how marginalization and privilege impact the client's worldview.

Attitudes and Beliefs

Multicultural and social justice–competent counselors seek to understand the rich and nuanced ways that identity, marginalization, and privilege uniquely impact the way individuals perceive and experience the world. These counselors recognize that each individual has their own distinct experience and worldview. They do not assume that others see and feel things in the same way. As counselors committed to multicultural and social justice competence, they embrace as truth that they cannot fully know and understand a client's worldview; they strive to always learn more. Further, they acknowledge the significant ways in which sociopolitical systems and structures impact clients' lived experiences. Counselors can create space to learn more about their clients' lived experiences. One tool that can be utilized is a modified Adlerian lifestyle assessment. This assessment, based on Alfred Adler's individual psychology (Ansbacher & Ansbacher, 1956), includes questions that collect information about a client's early life experiences, family members, and their perceived role in their family (Carlson & Englar-Carlson, 2013). The counselor should mindfully develop the assessment with questions that reflect multicultural and social justice considerations.

Knowledge

Multicultural and social justice–competent counselors work diligently to increase their knowledge related to the multifaceted contexts that influence client worldview, including sociopolitical realities, discrimination and oppression, privilege, and identity development. They examine and explore their own abilities, gaps, attitudes, and beliefs and critically reflect on how those things impact how they conceptualize the client worldview. As counselors committed to multicultural and social justice competence, they recognize that obtaining and enhancing their knowledge is a lifelong investment. Counselors can read historical accounts of the lived experiences of oppressed peoples and reflect on how those histories impact the experiences of those peoples today. They can meet with representatives from advocacy groups to discuss the various ways that colonization, discrimination, oppression, and marginalization hurt individuals and communities. These actions can help deepen the basic understanding of factors that can influence a client's worldview. Further, counselors can coconstruct new knowledge with clients by examining the complex impact on and outcome of identity-based experiences of privilege and marginalization.

Skills

Multicultural and social justice–competent counselors seek, develop, and practice skills that enable them to be more attuned to the perspectives and experiences of their clients and how clients' complicated intersectionality of privileged and marginalized statuses influence how they experience the world. These counselors also use their skills to reflect on and analyze their own intersecting identities and how they influence the counselor's attitudes and beliefs about clients. As counselors committed to multicultural and social justice competence, they are able to acknowledge, honor, and support the multifaceted ways that clients perceive and experience the world based on those client's unique identities. Counselors can invest time and resources to work on developing and enhancing their culturally responsive communication and interviewing skills. These skills are essential to a counselor's ability to engage in nuanced and reflective dialogue with clients, so as to facilitate a client's capacity to explore and acknowledge the effects and influence of power, privilege, and oppression.

Action

Multicultural and social justice–competent counselors intentionally explore opportunities to broaden and deepen their own awareness of how their clients experience the world based on their social identities, historical context, mental health strengths and challenges, and sociopolitical realities. Counselors committed to this work can engage in ongoing supervision and consultation with individuals who are culturally responsive and multiculturally oriented and who operate within an intersectionality framework. This structure of accountability can help a counselor address their own blind spots and biases. As counselors committed to multicultural and social justice competence they are willing to embrace the discomfort that comes with growth so that they are better prepared to engage in action to address inequity and oppression.

COUNSELING RELATIONSHIP AND INTERSECTIONALITY

A foundational element to the delivery of mental health counseling involves the counseling relationship. When counselors are able to attend to their own self-awareness and the worldview or perspectives of their clients, they are able to better understand the way privilege and marginalized identities impact the counseling relationship. A counselor who operates within an intersectionality framework can more critically examine and gain insight into the role of power, privilege, and oppression as they build or harm the counseling relationship.

Attitudes and Beliefs

Multicultural and social justice–competent counselors are aware of the presence of privileged and marginalized statuses within the counseling relationship. In their counselor sessions they are able to name and conceptualize the ways power, privilege, and oppression are reinforced through the counseling relationship by way of utilization of theory; they are able to develop client conceptualization through exploration, diagnosis, and interventions. As counselors committed to multicultural and social justice competence, they acknowledge that power, privilege, and oppression can be perpetuated within the counseling relationship and find opportunities to shift the role of power to better support the client's goals and mental wellness. Utilizing narrative techniques in counseling and taking on a collaborative role in addressing counseling issues can be advantageous in addressing the dynamic of power and oppression that manifest in counseling relationships while modeling a different dynamic for the client and their future relationships.

Knowledge

Multicultural and social justice–competent counselors are knowledgeable on intersectionality frameworks, critical theories, and concepts that examine how privileged and marginalized identities impact the counseling relationship. They recognize that the impact can vary, depending on the intersections of social identity (race/ethnicity, religious beliefs, sexual and gender identity, citizenship) within and between the clinician and client. Additionally, counselors know that issues related to historical experiences, values, culture, and identity development can impact one's ability to connect, trust, engage, and authentically participate in counseling. As counselors committed to multicultural and social justice, they will work to examine the way worldviews, attitudes, beliefs, historical narratives, and values strengthen or harm the counseling relationship. Counselors can utilize knowledge of the way intersectional identities create a unique inner world and reality to build rapport, understanding, and a healthy therapeutic alliance.

Skills

Multicultural and social justice–competent counselors utilize their knowledge of personal, cultural, and institutional privilege and oppression dynamics to effectively broach conversations about stereotypes, discrimination, prejudice, and identity development with their clients. Counselors will incorporate information from intersectionality theory and other critical theories to better apply interventions that acknowledge, center, and maintain alignment with creating a more equitable, affirming, and healthy relationship. They understand that this is possible, despite differences in identity and worldviews in the counseling relationship. As counselors committed to multicultural and social justice competence, they can consider the ways the different perspectives, values, and lived realities of having both similar and different marginalized and privileged identities impact the counselor–client relationship. These counselors can combine knowledge of basic interpersonal skills with an understanding of how systems of oppression affect the individual lives of both counselor and client as well as the counseling relationship. This will equip counselors with the ability to evaluate how privilege and oppression impact the counseling relationship.

Action

Multicultural and social justice–competent counselors are able to combine their knowledge and skills of oppression, power, and privilege to foster a strong and affirming counseling relationship. Additionally, clinicians can use information from their sessions to participate in professional and community action to create a more affirming, responsive therapeutic alliance and environment for all clients. These actions can be workshops or webinars that discuss ways to engage in culturally affirming relationships. Counselors might also engage in research and information-gathering to identify diverse and nontraditional intervention models that can be relevant for working with various client populations. As counselors committed to multicultural and social justice competence, they will use culturally relevant techniques in counseling to facilitate and support client change. They can share these techniques and approaches with colleagues, peers, and supervisors to help broaden culturally affirming counseling and training practices.

COUNSELING AND ADVOCACY INTERVENTIONS WITH INTERSECTIONALITY

Utilizing an intersectionality framework as a multicultural and social justice–competent counselor provides language and awareness about the impact of systems of power, privilege, and marginalized identities on the individual client and counseling experiences; it also highlights how those experiences converge in the counseling relationship. As counselors become more attuned to their own worldview, values, and cultural experiences as intersectional beings, they are better able to understand their client's experiences and how those experiences create a power dynamic in the counselor–client relationship. With this understanding, counselors can appropriately explore issues in the counseling relationship while initiating culturally affirming strategies to shift the dynamic of power and decrease the manifestation of oppression or marginalization. Thus, through critical reflection, multicultural and social justice–competent counselors can use interventions and strategies that address individual, communal, and larger social change and awareness to benefit clients in counseling. Counseling advocacy, embedded in intersectionality, can involve helping clients reflect on the impact of early life socialization and promote exploring opportunities to resolve issues through groups, organizations, or their own advocacy efforts. An example is a queer cisgender man who was socialized with heterosexism and now experiences internalized heterosexism, guilt, and shame. This client might benefit from a group for men with similar experiences, which may lead to advocacy efforts that benefit queer adolescents. In this way, advocacy can move out of the individual counseling office, and through this collaborative relationship can support incremental sociopolitical change concerning inequity for certain groups in the community.

CASE STUDY

Patel is a 55-year-old Southeast Asian man who was diagnosed with stomach cancer over a year ago. Patel is currently experiencing depression and distress related to his diagnosis and accessibility issues in acquiring the expensive medications and treatment required to treat his condition. Patel was referred to counseling as a result of his symptoms and lack of adherence to medication and attendance to office visits.

How can we use our knowledge of intersectionality and the multicultural and social justice counseling competencies to support and respond to Patel's needs? Following we offer some considerations in working with Patel and some reflective questions to further support a clinician's intervention and treatment plan.

APPLYING INTERSECTIONALITY AND MSJCC TO PATEL

The MSJCC requires that we reflect on our own attitudes and beliefs towards our client, our client's worldview, assess our knowledge and skills in supporting and addressing our client's concerns, and engage in action to support our client. We must also consider the inextricable intersections that our clients occupy and how that influences how they maneuver their world. The first step may be to consider the identities salient for Patel and consider the role of these identities in influencing Patel's behavior, attitude, and mental health concerns related to depression and distress. This can be a part of the intake process and include a demographic questionnaire that you discuss with Patel. As you review this information, you can quickly scan yourself for any bias you may have been socialized to hold related to Patel's various identities. Patel is an older Southeast Asian man who lives alone. You may realize that you have been socialized to have a specific belief about Asian American and Pacific Islanders (AAPI). A popular stereotype about the Asian American and Pacific Islander (AAPI) diaspora is the Model Minority Myth. This myth assumes that AAPI are inherently more successful, healthy, and well-adjusted than any other minoritized group within the United States. However, this myth and stereotype can be detrimental to AAPI individuals, possibly resulting in a misdiagnosis by physicians who assume that Southeast Asians are healthier than other groups. Additionally, this myth assumes that Patel must be financially secure because he is Southeast Asian, when in reality he may be one of many Southeast Asians who live in poverty. He may struggle to afford food, medicine, and doctor's visits. You acknowledge that you have limited knowledge about Patel's needs and experiences, so you invite him to tell you what he feels is important for you to know.

While it is important to explore how Patel feels about his diagnosis, it may also be culturally relevant to talk about his support system. Patel's experience if he lives in a community with access to Southeast Asian doctors, community centers, and neighbors would be markedly different than if he lives in a community where he may experience racism, xenophobia, and/or limited community support. It is also important to consider your knowledge on the relationship between the Eurocentric-based medical field and the Southeast Asian community. Does Patel trust his oncologist? Does he belong to a religious or spiritual community that offers alternative practices for healing? Is this something that is relevant for him or is he comfortable with Western medicine? These are some of the considerations that may be important to explore with Patel within the counseling session.

You can also reflect on what knowledge and skills are necessary to engage in culturally responsive work with Patel, and how to access and integrate them into your clinical treatment. There may be some discomfort if you are unsure what is necessary. It might be appropriate to acknowledge that as a counselor with your specific identity, you realize there may be differences in perspectives and understanding and that you trust Patel as the expert in the room on his experiences and perspectives. For example, if Patel identifies as Sikh, then consideration for dietary needs, suitability of medicines, clinical examination and procedures, beliefs attached to mental and physical illness, and even the importance of the Five Kakkars or articles of faith may be important to discuss. These are cultural elements that may impact the distress associated with his stomach cancer diagnosis. It will be important to not place the burden of explaining these cultural elements; rather, as a counselor committed to multicultural and social justice competence, you would engage in your own research to better understand these factors in context to Patel's unique circumstances.

You could also utilize a counseling theory that provides opportunities to center Patel's value systems and contextual experiences (e.g., Acceptance and Commitment Therapy, Relational Cultural Theory). Other considerations might include any additional disability or chronic illness, gender, age, sexual orientation, and immigration status. How might your identities as Patel's counselor impact and be impacted by his identities? How might his identities impact and be impacted by yours? In what ways do you experience a marginalized identity in relation to his privileged identity? In what ways does he experience a marginalized identity in relation to your privileged identity?

Lastly, the MSJCC requires that counselors take action to support their clients and their communities. Working with Patel, a counselor could help identify a healthcare provider who is knowledgeable and able to work with Sikh patients. This may help Patel feel more comfortable with medical visits and procedures. Another action could include adapting or creating a healthcare handbook for working with Sikh clients and patients, especially if that population is prominent in your community. Counselors can also connect with local religious leaders and community agencies that provide food, utility relief, and host communal engagement for Sikh or Southeast Asian community members. The range of actions done with and/or on behalf of clients are varied, however utilizing an intersectional lens along with the MSJCC when working with clients will provide a more individualized and affirming experience of mental health counseling.

Below are some reflective questions that may be important for clinicians to consider when applying both intersectionality and the MSJCC in working with clients like Patel.

SUMMARY, INSIGHTS, AND ACTIONS

The application of the MSJCC in counseling practice is becoming a widely accepted and practiced concept within the mental health counseling field. In this chapter we briefly discussed the history of intersectionality theory as coined by Black feminists and its use in understanding the overlapping and complex experiences of folx who experience compounding forms of oppression as a result of their identities. The MSJCC inherently considers the interaction and relationship between the counselor and client as contextual beings and the counselor's role in integrating both multiculturalism and social justice within their clinical practice. This chapter reviewed the way components of intersectionality are integrated into the MSJCC in considering the minoritized and privileged identities within and between clients and counselors and how those components influence attitudes and beliefs, knowledge, skills, and action for counseling professionals. Moreover, we utilized a case study to demonstrate considerations that may need be addressed in conducting counseling from a MSJCC and intersectionality approach.

The MSJCC is becoming a standard approach and practice for counseling professionals. By approaching counseling treatment from the MSJCC and intersectionality framework, we ensure we are mindful of the distinct ways that clients who hold distinct constellations of oppressed and privileged identities experience different forms of equity, access, treatment, and barriers in both their individual lives and within our society. Counseling practitioners must consider the way identities such as race/ethnicity, citizenship, gender and sexual identity, ability and body size, and class conjure differential treatment and mistreatment by individuals and institutions, which directly impacts client mental health wellness. It is our hope that you continue your educational knowledge on intersectionality by reviewing our suggested reading list.

REFLECTION AND DISCUSSION QUESTIONS

1. How well are you connected or knowledgeable about community service and organizations that could work to address at least one of your client's concerns?
2. Are there areas of your counseling practice (e.g., theory, conceptualization, treatment plans) that can unintentionally harm or invalidate my client's concerns or experiences?
3. Which of your intersecting identities are most salient for you and why?
4. Thinking about your most salient identity, how does it impact your other identities?
5. What counseling strategies will you utilize to assist clients and/or students to explore their intersecting identities?
6. When working with clients from the dominant culture, how will you help them understand the influence of privileged and oppressed identities on mental health and well-being?
7. How will your multiple identities influence your work as a professional counselor? How will these identities influence your counseling relationships?
8. What issues and cultural identities have been historically left out of discussions related to multicultural and social justice counseling?

9. How do systemic policies, practices, and laws influence individuals' intersecting identities?
10. What social, political, and environmental contexts affect individuals' multiple identities?

ADDITIONAL READINGS AND RESOURCES

Collins, P. H. (2015). Intersectionality's definitional dilemmas. *Annual Review of Sociology*, *41*(1), 1–20. doi:10.1146/annurev-soc-073014-112142.

Collins, P. H. (2019). *Intersectionality as critical social theory*. Duke University Press.

Collins, P. H., & Bilge, S. (2016). *Intersectionality*. Polity.

Crenshaw, K. (1989). Demarginalizing the intersection of race and sex: A Black feminist critique of antidiscrimination doctrine, feminist theory and antiracist politics. *University of Chicago Legal Forum*, 139–168. https://chicagounbound.uchicago.edu/cgi/viewcontent.cgi?article=1052&context=uclf.

Crenshaw, K. (1991). Mapping the margins: Intersectionality, identity politics, and violence against women of color. *Stanford Law Review*, *43*(6), 1241–1299. https://doi.org/10.2307/1229039

Crenshaw, K. (2016, October). *The urgency of intersectionality* [Video]. TED. https://www.ted.com/talks/kimberle_crenshaw_the_urgency_of_intersectionality?language=en

National Conference for Community and Justice. (n.d.). *Intersectionality*. https://www.nccj.org/intersectionality

Ratts, M. J., Singh, A. A., Nassar-Mcmillan, S., Butler, S. K., & McCullough, J. R. (2016). Multicultural and social justice counseling competencies: Guidelines for the counseling profession. *Journal of Multicultural Counseling and Development*, *44*(1), 28–48. https://doi.org/10.1002/jmcd.12035.

Shin, R. Q., Welch, J. C., Kaya, A. E., Yeung, J. G., Obana, C., Sharma, R., Vernay, C. Collin, N., & Yee, S. (2017). The intersectionality framework and identity intersections in the *Journal of Counseling Psychology and the Counseling Psychologist*: A content analysis. *Journal of Counseling Psychology*, *64*(5), 458–474. https://doi.org/10.1037/cou0000204

REFERENCES

Ali, S., & Lee, C. C. (2019). Using creativity to explore intersectionality in counseling. *Journal of Creativity in Mental Health*, *14*(4), 510–518. https://doi.org/10.1080/15401383.2019.1632767

American Counseling Association. (2014). *2014 ACA code of ethics*. Author.

Ansbacher, H. L., & Ansbacher, R. R. (Eds.). (1956). *The individual psychology of Alfred Adler: A systematic presentation in selections from his writings*. Basic Books.

Banks, J. (2018). Invisible man: Examining the intersectionality of disability, race, and gender in an urban community. *Disability & Society*, *33*(6), 894–908. https://doi.org/10.1080/09687599.2018.1456912

Bernard, J. M., & Goodyear, R. K. (2014). *Fundamentals of clinical supervision* (5th ed.). Allyn & Bacon.

Biss, D. C. (2019). Getting "woke" on intersectionality: Illuminating the rhetorical significance of disability discourse in feminist activist spaces. *Kaleidoscope: A Graduate Journal of Qualitative Communication Research, 18*, 41–59.

Brayboy, J. & McKinley, B. (2005). Toward a tribal critical race theory in education. *Urban Review: Issues and Ideas in Public Education 37* (5). 425–446.

Carlson, J. D., & Englar-Carlson, M. (2013). Adlerian Therapy. In M. D. Spiegler & J. Frew, (Eds.) *Contemporary psychotherapies for a diverse world.* (87–130). Routledge.

Carter, R. T., Kirkinis, K., & Johnson, V. E. (2020). Relationships between trauma symptoms and race-based traumatic stress. *Traumatology, 26*(1), 11–18. https://doi.org/10.1037/trm0000217

Celinska, D., & Swazo, R. (2016). Multicultural curriculum designs in counselor education programs: Enhancing counselors-in-training openness to diversity. *The Journal of Counselor Preparation and Supervision, 8*(3), 288–310. https://doi.org/10.7729/83.1124

Centers for Disease Control and Prevention. (2018). *HUS 2018 trend tables.* https://www.cdc.gov/nchs/data/hus/2018/021.pdf

Chan, C. D., Cor, D. N., & Band, M. P. (2018). Privilege and oppression in counselor education: An intersectionality framework. *Journal of Multicultural Counseling and Development, 46*(1), 58–73. https://doi.org/10.1002/jmcd.12092

Chan, C. D., Henesy, R. K., & Erby, A. N. (2019). Toward praxis, promise, and futures of intersectionality in multimethod counseling research. *Counseling Outcome Research and Evaluation, 10*(1), 12–18. https://doi.org/10.1080/21501378.2018.1562845

Cheshire, L. C. (2013). Reconsidering sexual identities-Intersectionality theory and the implications for educating counsellors. *Canadian Journal of Counselling and Psychotherapy, 47*(1), 4–13.

Cole, E. R. (2009). Intersectionality and research in psychology. *American Psychologist, 64*(3), 170–180. https://doi.org/10.1037/a0014564

Collins, P. H. (1986). Learning from the outsider within: The sociological significance of Black feminist thought. *Social Problems, 33*(6), S14–S32. https://academic.oup.com/socpro/article-abstract/33/6/s14/1610242

Collins, P. H. (2015). Intersectionality's definitional dilemmas. *Annual Review of Sociology, 41*(1), 1–20. https://doi.org/10.1146/annurev-soc-073014-112142

Cramer, E. P., & Plummer, S.-B. (2009). People of color with disabilities: Intersectionality as a framework for analyzing intimate partner violence in social, historical, and political contexts. *Journal of Aggression, Maltreatment & Trauma, 18*(2), 162–181. https://doi.org/10.1080/10926770802675635

Crenshaw, K. (1989). Demarginalizing the intersection of race and sex: A Black feminist critique of antidiscrimination doctrine, feminist theory and antiracist politics. *University of Chicago Legal Forum*, 139–168. https://chicagounbound.uchicago.edu/cgi/viewcontent.cgi?article=1052&context=uclf.

Crenshaw, K. (1991). Mapping the margins: Intersectionality, identity politics, and violence against women of color. *Stanford Law Review, 43*(6), 1241–1299. https://doi.org/10.2307/1229039

Delgado, R., & Stefancic, J. (2012). *Critical race theory: An Introduction* (2nd ed.). New York, NY: New York University Press.

Else-Quest, N. M., & Hyde, J. S. (2015). Intersectionality in quantitative psychological research: Theoretical and epistemological issues. *Psychology of Women Quarterly, 40*(2), 155–170. https://doi.org/10.1177/0361684316629797

Ferguson, A. D., & Miville, M. L. (2017). It's complicated: Navigating multiple identities in small town America. *Journal of Clinical Psychology, 73*(8), 975–984. https://doi.org/10.1002/jclp.22507

Freire, P. (2000). *Pedagogy of the oppressed* (30th anniversary ed.). Continuum.

Fruja A. R. (2017). "If only I did not have that label attached to me": Foregrounding self-positioning and intersectionality in the experiences of immigrant and refugee youth. *Multicultural Perspectives, 19*(4), 193–206. https://doi.org/10.1080/15210960.2017.1366862

Gangamma, R., & Shipman, D. (2018). Transnational intersectionality in family therapy with resettled refugees. *Journal of Marital and Family Therapy, 44*(2), 206–219. https://doi.org/10.1111/jmft.12267

Garcia, M., Kosutic, I., McDowell, T., & Anderson, S. (2009). Raising critical consciousness in family therapy supervision. *Journal of Feminist Family Therapy, 21*(1), 18–38. https://doi.org/10.1080/08952830802683673

Gómez, J. M. (2017). Does ethno-cultural betrayal in trauma affect Asian American/Pacific Islander college students' mental health outcomes? An exploratory study. *Journal of American College Health, 65*(6), 432–436.

Gone, J. P., Hartmann, W. E., Pomerville, A., Wendt, D. C., Klem, S. H., & Burrage, R. L. (2019). The impact of historical trauma on health outcomes for Indigenous populations in the USA and Canada: A systematic review. *American Psychologist, 74*(1), 20–35.

Grzanka, P. R., Santos, C. E., & Moradi, B. (2017). Intersectionality research in counseling psychology. *Journal of Counseling Psychology, 64*(5), 453–457. https://doi.org/10.1037/cou0000237

Gutierrez, D. (2018). The role of intersectionality in marriage and family therapy multicultural supervision. *American Journal of Family Therapy, 46*(1), 14–26. https://doi.org/10.1080/01926187.2018.1437573

Haskins, N. H., Ziomek-Daigle, J., Sewell, C., Crumb, L., Appling, B., & Trepal, H. (2016). The intersectionality of African American mothers in counselor education: A phenomenological examination. *Counselor Education and Supervision, 55*(1), 60–75. https://doi.org/10.1002/ceas.12033

Hayes, S. C., Strosahl, K. D., & Wilson, K. G. (2012). Acceptance and commitment therapy: An experiential approach to behavior change, New York NY: Guilford Press.

Heard Harvey, C. C. C., & Ricard, R. J. (2018). Contextualizing the concept of intersectionality: Layered identities of African American women and gay men in the Black church. *Journal of Multicultural Counseling and Development, 46*(3), 206–218. https://doi.org/10.1002/jmcd.12102

Hernández, P., & McDowell, T. (2010). Intersectionality, power, and relational safety in context: Key concepts in clinical supervision. *Training and Education in Professional Psychology, 4*(1), 29–35. https://doi.org/10.1037/a0017064

Hernandez, P., & Rankin, P. (2003). Relational safety and liberating training spaces: An application with a focus on sexual orientation issues. *Journal of Marital and Family, 34*(2), 251–264.

Johnson, B., Leibowitz, S., Chavez, A., & Herbert, S. E. (2019). Risk versus resiliency: Addressing depression in lesbian, gay, bisexual, and transgender youth. *Child and Adolescent Psychiatric Clinics of North America, 28*(3), 509–521. https://doi.org/10.1016/j.chc.2019.02.016

Jordan, J. V. (2001). A relational-cultural model: Healing through mutual empathy. Bulletin of the Menninger Clinic, 65, 92–103.doi:10.1521/bumc.65.1.92.18707

Kapilashrami, A., & Hankivsky, O. (2018). Intersectionality and why it matters to global health. *The Lancet, 391*(10140), 2589–2591. https://doi.org/10.1016/S0140-6736(18)31431-4

Kaplan, D. M., Tarvydas, V. M., & Gladding, S. T. (2014). 20/20: A vision for the future of counseling: The new consensus definition of counseling. *Journal of Counseling and Development, 92*(3), 366–372. https://doi.org/10.1002/j.1556-6676.2014.00164.x

Kattari, S. K., Whitfield, D. L., Walls, N. E., Langenderfer-Magruder, L., & Ramos, D. (2016). Policing gender through housing and employment discrimination: Comparison of discrimination experiences of transgender and cisgender LGBQ individuals. *Journal of the Society for Social Work & Research, 7*(3), 427–447.

Kim, I., Chen, J., & Spencer, M.S. (2012). Social determinants of health and mental health among Asian Americans in the united states. *Journal of the Society for Social Work and Research, 3*(4), 346. https://doi.org/10.5243/jsswr.2012.21

Kinavey, H., & Cool, C. (2019). The broken lens: How anti-fat bias in psychotherapy is harming our clients and what to do about it. *Women and Therapy, 42*(1–2), 116–130. https://doi.org/10.1080/02703149.2018.1524070

Kolawole, B. (2017). African immigrants, intersectionality, and the increasing need for visibility in the current immigration debate. *Columbia Journal of Race & Law, 7*(2), 373–409.

Kosciw, J. G., Greytak, E. A., Zongrone, A. D., Clark, C. M., & Truong, N. L. (2018). *The 2017 national school climate survey: The experiences of lesbian, gay, bisexual, transgender, and queer youth in our nation's schools.* GLSEN.

Lorde, A. (1984). Learning from the 60s. In A. Lorde & C. Clarke (Eds.), *Sister outsider: Essays and speeches* (pp. 134–144). Crown.

Love, C. D., Booysen, L. A. E., & Essed, P. (2018). An exploration of the intersection of race, gender and generation in African American women doing social justice work. *Gender, Work & Organization, 25*(5), 475–494. https://doi.org/10.1111/gwao.12095

Marecek, J. (2015). Invited reflection: Intersectionality theory and feminist psychology. *Psychology of Women Quarterly, 40*(2), 177–181. https://doi.org/10.1177/0361684316641090

McCullough, R., Dispenza, F., Parker, L.K., Viehl, C.J., Chang, C.Y., & Murphy, T.M. (2017). The counseling experiences of transgender and gender nonconforming clients. *Journal of Counseling & Development, 95*(4), 423–434. https://doi.org/10.1002/jcad.12157

Meyer, I. H. (2003). Prejudice, social stress, and mental health in lesbian, gay, and bisexual populations: Conceptual issues and research evidence. *Psychological Bulletin, 129*(5), 674–697. https://doi.org/10.1037/0033-2909.129.5.674

Mogul, J., Ritchie, A. J., & Whitlock, A. K. (2012). *Queer (in)justice: The criminalization of LGBT people in the United States.* Beacon.

Moradi, B., & Grzanka, P. R. (2017). Using intersectionality responsibly: Toward critical epistemology, structural analysis, and social justice activism. *Journal of Counseling Psychology, 64*(5), 500–513. https://doi.org/10.1037/cou0000203

Mustanski, B., & Liu, R. T. (2013). A longitudinal study of predictors of suicide attempts among lesbian, gay, bisexual, and transgender youth. *Archives of Sexual Behavior, 42*(3), 437–448. https://doi.org/10.1007/s10508-012-0013-9

Nadal, K. L., Griffin, K. E., Wong, Y., Hamit, S., & Rasmus, M. (2014). The impact of racial microaggressions on mental health: Counseling implications for clients of color. *Journal of Counseling & Development, 92*(1), 57–66. https://doi.org/10.1002/j.1556-6676.2014.00130.x

Nadal, K. L., & Haynes, K. (2012). The effects of sexism, gender microaggressions, and other forms of discrimination on women's mental health and development. In P. K. Lundberg-Love, K. L. Nadal, & M. A. Paludi (Eds.), *Women and mental disorders*, Vols. 1–4. (pp. 87–101). ABC-CLIO.

Nadal, K. L., & Haynes, K. (2012). The effects of sexism, gender microaggressions, and other forms of discrimination on women's mental health and development. In P. K. Lundberg-Love, K. L. Nadal, & M. A. Paludi (Eds.), Women's psychology. Women and mental disorders (p. 87–101). Praeger/ABC-CLIO.

Parent, M. C., DeBlaere, C., & Moradi, B. (2013). Approaches to research on intersectionality: Perspectives on gender, LGBT, and racial/ethnic identities. *Sex Roles, 68*(11–12), 639–645. https://doi.org/10.1007/s11199-013-0283-2

Ratts, M. J. (2009). Social justice counseling: Toward the development of a fifth force among counseling paradigms. *Journal of Humanistic Counseling, Education & Development, 42*(2), 160–172. https://doi.org/10.1002/j.2161-1939.2009.tb00076.x

Ratts, M. J. (2017). Charting the center and the margins: Addressing identity, marginalization, and privilege in counseling. *Journal of Mental Health Counseling, 39*(2), 87–103. https://doi.org/10.17744

Ratts, M. J., Singh, A. A., Nassar-Mcmillan, S., Butler, S. K., & McCullough, J. R. (2016). Multicultural and social justice counseling competencies: Guidelines for the counseling profession. *Journal of Multicultural Counseling and Development, 44*(1), 28–48. https://doi.org/10.1002/jmcd.12035

Resnick, C. A., & Galupo, M. P. (2019). Assessing experiences with LGBT microaggressions in the workplace: Development and validation of the microaggression experiences at work scale. *Journal of Homosexuality, 66*(10), 1380–1403. https://doi.org/10.1080/00918 369.2018.1542207

Robinson, B. A. (2018). Conditional families and lesbian, gay, bisexual, transgender, and queer youth homelessness: Gender, sexuality, family instability, and rejection. *Journal of Marriage and Family, 80*(2), 383–397. https://doi.org/10.1111/jomf.12466

Shields, S. A. (2008, September). Gender: An intersectionality perspective. *Sex Roles. 59*(5–6), 301–311. https://doi.org/10.1007/s11199-008-9501-8

Shih, K. Y., Chang, T. F., & Chen, S. Y. (2019). Impacts of the model minority myth on Asian American individuals and families: Social justice and critical feminist perspectives. *Journal of Family Theory & Review, 11*(3), 412–428.

Shin, R. Q., Welch, J. C., Kaya, A. E., Yeung, J. G., Obana, C., Sharma, R., Vernay, C.N.; Yee, S. (2017). The intersectionality framework and identity intersections in the journal of counseling psychology and the counseling psychologist: A content analysis. *Journal of Counseling Psychology, 64*(5), 458–474. https://doi.org/10.1037/cou0000204

Smith, C. A. (2019). Intersectionality and sizeism: Implications for mental health practitioners. *Women and Therapy, 42*(1–2), 59–78. https://doi.org/10.1080/02703149.2018.1 524076

Solorzano, D. G. (1998) Critical race theory, race and gender microaggressions, and the experience of Chicana and Chicano scholars, International Journal of Qualitative Studies in Education, 11:1, 121-136, DOI: 10.1080/095183998236926

Sue, D. W., Arredondo, P., & McDavis, J., R. (1992). Multicultural counseling competencies: A call to the profession. *Journal of Multicultural Counseling and Development, 70*(4), 477–486. https://doi.org/10.1037/0003-066X.59.8.761

Sue, D. W., Capodilupo, C. M., Torino, G. C., Bucceri, J. M., Holder, A. M., Nadal, K. L., & Esquilin, M. (2007). Racial microaggressions in everyday life: Implications for clinical practice. *American Journal of Psychology, 62*(4), 271–286. https://doi. org/10.1037/0003-066X.62.4.271

Thompson, J. D., & Bridges, C. W. (2019). Intersectionality pedagogy in the classroom: Experiences of counselor educators. *Teaching and Supervision in Counseling, 1*(2). https://doi.org/10.7290/tsc010207

Tohidian, N. B., & Quek, K. M. T. (2017). Processes that inform multicultural supervision: A qualitative meta-analysis. *Journal of Marital and Family Therapy, 43*(4), 573–590. https://doi.org/10.1111/jmft.12219.

Watson, S., & Miller, T. (2012). LGBT oppression. *Multicultural Education, 19*(4), 2–7.

Watt, S. K., Curtis, G. C., Drummond, J., Kellogg, A. H., Lozano, A., Nicoli, G. T., & Rosas, M. (2009). Privileged identity exploration: Examining counselor trainees' reactions to difficult dialogues. *Counselor Education & Supervision, 49*(2), 86–105. https://doi. org/10.1002/j.1556-6978.2009.tb00090.x

CHAPTER 8

PROFESSIONAL SETTINGS IN COUNSELING

Dawnette Cigrand, Winona State University

Matthew Beck, Western Illinois University-Quad Cities

Erin Lane, Western Illinois University-Quad Cities

LEARNING OBJECTIVES

1. Understand the specific settings in which counselors work and the unique role of each counselor specialization within those settings.
2. Learn the multicultural and social justice (MSJCC) issues that clients typically present in each counseling setting.
3. Identify MSJCC skills and competencies necessary to advocate for and with marginalized client populations within and across each setting.
4. Recognize counselors' training needs to be effective with specific populations within settings.

LEARNING OUTCOMES

1. Identify the values, knowledge, and beliefs relative to working with clients across various counseling settings using a social justice framework.
2. Discuss the MSJCC issues typical in each setting and consider courses of action to support clients in each setting using a case study example.
3. Describe how each role aligns or does not align with one's developing professional counseling identity.
4. Differentiate the roles of multicultural social justice counselors within educational settings, clinical mental health settings, and specialized settings.

Counselors work in a variety of settings to meet the varied needs of their clients. Counselors work in educational settings, from early childhood centers, daycares, and preschools to primary and secondary public and nonpublic schools and institutes of higher education. Counselors also work in community settings, such as hospitals, behavioral health clinics, career centers, residential settings, and treatment centers for addiction (U.S.

Bureau of Labor Statistics, 2020). Some counselors open their own businesses and deliver services through private practice, while others are employed by agencies and hospitals or government entities such as military or correctional facilities. The setting in which a counselor provides services determines the clientele with whom they work as well as the counselor's roles and day-to-day tasks.

Most counselors acquire a common core set of counseling competencies in their graduate training, which are typically aligned to standards set by the Council for the Accreditation of Counseling and Related Educational Programs (CACREP, 2016) and include the multicultural and social justice counseling competencies (MSJCC; Ratts et al., 2016). Additionally, each professional counseling setting requires specialized training and understanding of the counselor's specific role and responsibilities.

While it is important for aspiring counselors to understand the specific roles and responsibilities of the counseling profession they choose to enter to be effective in their role, it is also important to align their professional goals and values to their work setting to increase the likelihood that they will have higher career satisfaction (Rehfuss et al., 2012) and remain in the profession. Thus, counseling students should take ample time to review the variations across counseling settings and contemplate how those differences impact work with clients and the professional tasks required for each area of practice.

To this aim, this chapter describes the role of the counselor and the services provided in each counseling setting as well as the multicultural social justice counseling considerations particular to each of them. In addition, we suggest specific action steps counselors-in-training can take to learn more about counseling settings, to develop a counseling identity, and to guide professional decision-making in choosing a counseling specialty.

CASE STUDY

Applications of this case study will be considered in the discussion of each setting and counselor roles within those settings.

After a 4-year tour of active duty, a Latinx veteran, Marlon, returns to his home in a rural Midwestern community. He is reunited with his wife, Christina, and two children, son Daniel, age 15, and daughter Isabelle, age 10. Marlon has met with the clinical mental health provider three times at the regional Veteran's Administration (VA), where he was diagnosed with posttraumatic stress disorder (PTSD). Marlon is also struggling with re-entering the workforce in light of his disability as well as his hiatus from his place of employment. The changes associated with Marlon's return home have also impacted his family, specifically his wife who is trying to redefine her place in the home as a military spouse pursuing an associate's degree, and their son, who has not yet disclosed his sexual identity to his family.

EDUCATIONAL SETTINGS

Counselors in educational settings support the intersections of academic, career, social, and emotional development for children, adolescents, and young adults within primary, secondary, and postsecondary institutions (American School Counselor Association [ASCA], 2019; Hodges, 2016). Though the overarching goals of the counselors are similar, the methods of counseling facilitation may look different for each developmental level. Similarly, the understanding of multicultural concerns and social justice advocacy may vary based on the developmental level of individuals in each setting.

PK–12 Educational Setting

In primary and secondary settings, school counselors work directly with students, as well as indirectly, through consultation or collaboration with teachers, school administrators, or parents. Large caseloads, on average 482 students to every school counselor (National Association of College Access Counselors [NACAAC] & ASCA, n.d.), often affect how school counseling services are delivered to students. Using national, research-based standards developed by the ASCA (2014), school counselors provide curriculum through large-group or classroom lessons, small group counseling, and individual counseling sessions. Tiered models, such as the MTSS model (Goodman-Scott et al., 2019; Hatch, 2017) can aid school counselors in deciding the most effective avenues to present systemic and student-focused interventions.

Classroom counseling curriculum delivery is designed to help all students achieve academic success indicators, prepare for college and career futures, and develop social/emotional competencies based on the ASCA (2019) standards. Through analysis of system-wide data and classroom lesson outcomes, the school counselor may find that some students need more specialized interventions to achieve growth toward a mind-set or behavior standard (ASCA, 2019). These interventions may come directly from the counselor, or the counselor may arrange to put other supports in place, such as work experience programs or Gay–Straight Alliance (GSA) clubs. School counselors also collaborate and consult with other educators in the school setting, parents/guardians, and various community resources to systemically support the development of all students in and out of school.

When student concerns are outside the school counselor's scope of practice or cannot be addressed within the time limitations of the school counseling program, school counselors are ethically mandated to refer students for more intensive and ongoing counseling services (ASCA, 2019). Referrals may be made to clinical mental health professionals working in an agency or school. Benefits of school-based mental health services have been documented, including increased access to mental health support and reduced transportation issues for families (Burnett-Zeigler & Lyons, 2010; Kaffenberger & O'Rourke-Trigiani, 2013).

School-based mental health counselors are employed by counseling agencies or schools and provide individual counseling, and sometimes small group counseling, to selected students (Doll et al., 2017). These counselors may be assigned to one large school district and serve students in multiple buildings or may have multiple districts to serve; therefore, travel and flexibility to work in various locations is usually part of the position. Counselors in this role must understand the unique needs of each school or district they serve in order to best meet the differing needs of that setting and those students. It is also important for all mental health supports in schools to be coordinated to maximize resources and broaden efforts to support students by building on the expertise and perspectives of multiple professions who provide a continuum of services (Adelman & Taylor, 2010).

Culture of PK–12 Educational Setting

As a major component of their role and function, school counselors are charged with serving all students as advocates and leaders in their schools and districts, as well as systemic change agents (ASCA, 2019). In particular, multiculturally and social justice conscious school counselors must not only understand the culture, worldview, and biases of themselves and their students, but also be adept at understanding, reading, and responding to the culture inherent in school settings. The counselor must be aware of how these intersecting cultures can impact interventions and services within the academic, career, and social/emotional domains.

From analyzing disparities in discipline referrals in grade-level team meetings to planning positive school climate activities that celebrate cultural diversity (Ziomek-Daigle et al., 2016), school counselors work to provide all students with opportunity equity. Additionally, school counselors support students with disabilities to ensure their rights under the Individuals With Disabilities Act (IDEA, 1984) and Section 504 of Rehabilitation Act (1973).

Secondary school counselors in particular, often balance the role of empowering students to speak about their concerns and using their power and leadership in the school to provide greater advocacy. The latter approach is often necessary when addressing systemic change and social justice concerns. School counselors using a social justice lens may find it essential to not only speak about issues occurring in their school or district, but also larger concerns impacting students across the state or even the nation (Cigrand et al., 2015).

CASE STUDY APPLICATION

Using the case study as an example, Marlon's return into the home environment would be a cause for the school counselor to check in with Isabelle and Daniel in the counseling office. Before meeting with them, it would be important for the school counselor to examine their own biases about military families as well as check their understanding of the role of the father and oldest male child in the Latinx family.

The elementary school counselor may provide direct intervention through small group counseling or individual counseling to Isabelle, who may have anxiety surrounding her father's deployment. A small group setting can provide a supportive space for Isabelle to explore her experiences of being a military child with other students as well as identify coping strategies in her family, school, and cultural community.

From a high school perspective, Daniel may be struggling with some role changes as his father returns home considering he may have felt it was his job to be the "head of the house" while his father was away. Once a strong and trusting relationship is formed, Daniel may feel comfortable talking with his school counselor about his sexual orientation and how his identity as a gay individual may be received by his family, his father's military community, and his extended cultural community.

The school counselor may also support Isabelle and Daniel indirectly through consultation with parent figures, like Marlon and Christina, or their teachers to monitor the effects of familial changes on their academics and life at home. The school counselor may also provide a referral to the school-based mental health program or a family therapist if intensive and/or ongoing needs are identified.

MSJCC QUESTIONS

1. In working with elementary or secondary students who are minors in small group counseling, parents/guardians are informed and give consent for counseling. How do cultures differ in their response to and support of counseling for their children? As a school counselor, how might your approaches to gain consent be modified to align to cultural differences of parents/guardians?
2. What are some additional MSJCC issues in this case study that pertain to school counseling with Isabelle and Daniel?
3. What further advocacy actions might you engage in to support Isabelle and Daniel?

Postsecondary Institutions

Postsecondary counseling services are found in a wide variety of settings, including vocational-technical schools, community colleges, and colleges and universities. The literature suggests that the role and function of postsecondary counselors and student affairs personnel vary due to institutional settings (small liberal arts college versus large research university), location, fiscal constraints, as well as variations with student needs (Stone & Archer, 1990). For example, postsecondary counselors who work in small community/college settings may find their roles engaged in a wider, comprehensive variety of services offered to students, including recruitment, advising, and outreach, whereas postsecondary counselors who practice in larger departments may provide more specialized service to clients with particular presenting issues such as depression or student adjustment.

In efforts to meet student caseloads and maximize resources, individual counseling in postsecondary settings tends to be short-term in nature. In addition, postsecondary counselors provide referral resources for students with needs that require more long-term support and/or a certain specialization that is not available in the setting. Postsecondary student concerns can also be effectively and efficiently addressed through group counseling. Group counseling can strengthen support, provide alternatives to postsecondary student concerns, as well as connect members with others who may have worked through similar concerns. Because students come to postsecondary institutions from various cultures and countries, it is imperative for postsecondary counselors and student affairs personnel to have strong MSJCC to navigate student differences that are certain to permeate student interactions and subsequent counseling sessions (Reynolds & Pope, 2003).

Postsecondary counselors also consult and provide outreach advocacy services with faculty, residence hall staff, and stakeholders in their settings. Postsecondary counselors may also hold teaching/adjunct positions in counseling-related programs as well as assist in training and provide supervision of field-based counseling experiences (i.e., practicum and internship experiences). Conducting research on social justice campus initiatives and evaluating the effectiveness of the services provided at the postsecondary counseling setting may also be common practices for counselors who work in this particular setting. Lastly, it also is common for postsecondary counselors and student affairs personnel to assist with crisis management teams and campus resource/policy development. Examples of issues that may require advocacy include domestic abuse, sexual assault, personal safety, and suicide prevention.

Postsecondary Institutions' Culture

The MSJCC framework can be an important tool to assist postsecondary counselors when exploring the broad intersections of academic, career, and personal/social student experiences. The framework is especially important when postsecondary counselors are working to meet the needs of those students from marginalized backgrounds with multiple identities (e.g., African American gay men; Ratts et al., 2016). Given the large and diverse pool of students, acknowledging and exploring one's privileged attitudes and beliefs (i.e., counselor self-awareness, professional development, critical analysis) and how your beliefs might differ from other identities found within the postsecondary setting would be an important beginning place for counselors (Ratts et al., 2010, 2016). With regard to knowledge, postsecondary counselors understand the importance of combining social justice advocacy with campus counseling interventions. This knowledge may lead to enhanced counselor insights about the different ways that power, privilege, and discrimination impact postsecondary students' experiences (Ratts et al., 2016).

Unique situations may warrant intrapersonal and direct counselor advocacy interventions with postsecondary students (Ratts et al., 2016). Examples may include but are not limited to assisting first-generation African American male college students (Owens et al., 2010), exploring ethnic minority student experiences at predominantly White institutions, and supporting victims of violence and sexual assault (Kress et al., 2003). For example, postsecondary group counselors might offer a transgender inclusive group, which can be especially helpful for individuals who need a safe and supportive location to explore gender variance, gender identity, gender expression, and sexuality (Schmitz & Tyler, 2018). Advocacy interventions within the group setting can occur across multiple campus levels, including interpersonal (e.g., family, friends), institutional (e.g., combating discrimination), and public policy (e.g., advocating for gender inclusive housing).

Further, with respect to action, postsecondary counselors are mindful that their advocacy work extends beyond the campus counseling center (Ratts et al., 2016). An example includes creating and delivering a presentation and/or workshop on multicultural/diversity topics to stakeholders. Partnering and collaborating with other multicultural campus and community centers (e.g., Latino Native American, Asian Pacific, African American) can strengthen ways to address issues of power, privilege, and oppression across the campus. Counselors may also consult with student groups such as the fraternity and sorority community to enhance communication and impart knowledge of how stereotypes, prejudice, discrimination, and power influence the experiences of marginalized students.

CASE STUDY APPLICATION

The aforementioned case example acknowledges the importance of multicultural and social justice competence for postsecondary counselors, specifically the development of awareness, knowledge, and advocacy skills for counselors who work directly with and/or advocate on behalf of Christina. As a Latinx military spouse, Christina is trying to redefine her place in the home while pursuing an associate's degree at a community college. One MSJCC competence concern to consider in this example is for the postsecondary counselor to gain knowledge of and understand the implications of Christina's family structure, particularly the challenges associated with military spouse employment and education (e.g., frequent moves, parenting responsibilities) as well as her cultural identity. When working directly with Christina, the counselor might encourage Christina to reflect on the ways in which her family's military lifestyle has impacted her education and her own views toward counseling. Other MSJCC considerations that may impact Christina include issues related to gender and entering college as a nontraditional student.

MSJCC QUESTIONS

1. What counselor beliefs and attitudes could interfere with the services pro-vided to Christina in this case study? How would you navigate these poten-tial issues as a postsecondary counselor?
2. As you conceptualize Christina's case, how might the MCSJ counselor broach the various issues that could present themselves without stereotyp-ing her situation?
3. What further advocacy actions might you engage in to work with Christina?

CLINICAL MENTAL HEALTH SETTINGS

Clinical mental health counselors work in varied settings, including private practice, community settings, and mental health centers. In clinical and community settings, counselors provide services to a broader range of clients, including individuals, couples, families, adolescents, and children. Their clients present with a range of therapeutic needs, from basic problems in living (e.g., career issues, stress, life transitions and relationship issues) to more moderate to severe mental health disorders that require in-patient and/or long-term treatment.

Private Practice

Counselors who work in private practice may be the sole practitioner or serve as a member of an established group practice that includes other mental health counselors. Private practice may appeal to counselors who seek flexibility with their schedules and/or desire to work with a specialized population or with therapeutic techniques (Meyers, 2019). Counselors who enter private practice also need an understanding of management and marketing skills that will enable them to start and sustain an effective business in coun-seling (Reynolds, 2010). Unique business considerations pertaining to private practice may include licensure regulations and costs in several states, liability and business insur-ance rates, billing for services (e.g., managed care, preferred provider) as well as financial investments to make the counseling business successful and profitable (Reynolds, 2010).

Private Practice Culture

Counselors in private practice need to recognize the complexities of multiculturalism and understand how social justice barriers inhibit clients' ability to seek counseling services (Ratts et al., 2016). By using the MJSCC framework, counselors in private practice can be more attuned to the unique experiences and needs of their clients. For example, one important consideration is exploring the strengths and limitations in where a counselor chooses to hold their office space. Some clients may feel reluctant to seek services in their counselor's home, while some may find the impersonal nature of a large office building intimidating. This awareness also requires counselors to learn more about themselves (e.g., values, biases, power, privilege, assumptions) as members of privileged groups and how this can impact their work with underserved populations (Ratts et al., 2016). In addition, counselors in private practice are encouraged to learn about the communication styles and overall experiences of marginalized groups in the communities surrounding their practice (Ratts et al., 2016). Through attending cultural events and "immersing themselves in the communities," private practice counselors are able to deepen their understanding of how discrimination, privilege, and power can impact client experiences (Ratts et al., 2016, p. 40).

More specifically, private practice in rural settings can pose unique barriers for both counselors and clients from underrepresented groups. Community members in rural settings may hold more stigmatizing views about counseling, so fewer mental health resources related to meeting clients' cultural needs may be available (Cohn & Hastings, 2013). Additionally, individuals in rural areas, compared to urban areas, tend to foster traditional gender roles as well as heteronormativity, which may impact gender beliefs toward education and careers across the life span (Cohn & Hastings, 2013). These multicultural and social justice barriers must be addressed by private practitioners in order to meet the unique cultural needs of clients and families within rural settings.

CASE STUDY APPLICATION

When providing couples counseling to Marlon and Christina, private practice counselors need to acknowledge the importance of multicultural and social justice competence. Seeking knowledge about the unique implications of military marriages would be an important starting point. Furthermore, developing self-awareness about personal values and attitudes regarding levels of commitment in a marital relationship would be advantageous to explore. For example, Marlon and Christina may hold traditional values regarding the sanctity of marriage as practicing Catholics, but they may also feel conflicted given the prolonged separation of military couples.

Additionally, Marlon's homecoming may create marital friction at times as Christina transitions from being the sole parent and authority figure to sharing duties, or even "being overruled," as Marlon attempts to resume his head of household position in the family. Others in their rural community may notice and comment on this tension when Marlon and Christina attend community or school events.

The counselor could encourage the couple to identify various individuals within their community who will support them both personally and as a couple, as well as interventions that are culturally relevant and span intrapersonal, interpersonal, and institutional levels.

MSJCC QUESTIONS

1. What you are your beliefs about marriage? How might they impact your work with couples like Marlon and Christina in counseling?
2. How can you mitigate imposing your beliefs in counseling work with clients?
3. What advocacy actions might you engage in to work with Marlon and Christina?

Community Settings

In 1963, federal legislation known as the Community Mental Health Act (CMHA; 1963) was enacted to promote local community-based mental health initiatives. As early as the 1970s, the focus of these community mental health centers moved from prevention, education and consultation to treatment due primarily to deinstitutionalization (Dixon & Goldman, 2003). Today, the primary goal of community-based mental health centers is to provide the mental health portion of integrated services that address clients' holistic needs. Mental health centers often work with hospitals or other treatment facilities to provide systems of care for a range of mental health issues, from chronic to acute, focusing on the delivery of five services: short-term inpatient treatment, outpatient treatment, partial hospitalization, crisis intervention, and education/consultation.

While definitions for integrated health care vary, it is commonly defined as efforts to systematically and intentionally coordinate physical and mental health care in the same setting (Soltis-Jarrett et al., 2017). Integrated health care is often coordinated by consumer-operated service organizations (COSOs), which are independent, nonprofit entities that provide peer support and other nonclinical services to clients. The purpose of COSOs is ultimately to support the autonomy and self-determination of clients as they work to achieve their goals within their community setting (Tanenbaum, 2011).

Another setting for integrated care is home-based mental health services. In particular, this counseling setting is appropriate for individuals who live in rural environments (Bowen & Carson, 2016) as well as children and individuals who have limited access to outside resources and/or feel more at ease in their own homes (Tate et al., 2014). Clients may have legitimate concerns about maintenance of confidentiality that cannot be assured in public settings. Additionally, the uncertainty of the home environment can present a safety risk to counselors (Mattek et al., 2010; Tate et al., 2014). There is also a concern about crossing relational boundaries as a counselor becomes more comfortable in such an informal setting (Tate et al., 2014). However, the benefit of in-home counseling provided to those from disadvantaged backgrounds has been shown in limited research to outweigh the concerns (Annamalai et al., 2018); nonetheless, these concerns should be addressed through proper training and counselor supervision (Mattek et al., 2010; Tate et al., 2014).

Community Settings' Culture

Community mental health centers often serve clients who tend to be low-income and have unmet behavioral health needs (Shin et al., 2013). Within this population, transportation and the ability to pay for services, including issues with private insurance or poor coverage, often prevent individuals from receiving services. However, even when clients are able to receive services, some may prematurely terminate treatment due to counselors' lack of multicultural competence (Stevens et al., 2006). Understanding personal bias and identifying barriers for clients is important in order to maintain treatment continuity. In rural settings in particular, community mental health centers struggle with insufficient fiscal support and mental health providers shortages (Jameson et al., 2009).

Social justice issues associated with integrated health care include varied availability by geographic region of and lack of behavioral health services or substance abuse treatment accessibility (Jones & Ku, 2015). Even so, benefits of integrated health continue to mount. One recent longitudinal study found significantly higher positive health outcomes for individuals with serious mental illnesses when using integrated services, including fewer hospitalizations and shorter hospital stays (Wells et al., 2018). Rural mental health providers are needed and must have a broad scope of knowledge to meet clients' varied needs (Hastings & Cohn, 2013). Inter-professional collaboration in integrated health centers is also essential to the successful outcomes of integrated care (Annamalai et al., 2018).

CASE STUDY APPLICATION

For clients with multifaceted needs like Marlon, integrated health care may be a good option. Using this type of service, Marlon would be able to receive mental and physical health support in the same location. Integrated services would allow a psychiatrist, physician, and clinical mental health counselor to collaborate to provide coordinated services for Marlon, while potentially reducing Marlon's missed time at work for appointments. Although using a holistic approach might be beneficial, there are cultural considerations that the counselor would want to acknowledge and address. The counselor will want to support Marlon's autonomy and self-determination in making his health care decisions while also recognizing that Marlon may be experiencing a conflict between his mental health diagnosis and his cultural expectation as a self-sufficient and prideful male. For example, Marlon may not feel comfortable expressing what he perceives as mental and physical weakness.

MSJCC QUESTIONS

1. To expand your worldview of Marlon, research the following Latinx concepts: *machismo and marianismo, familismo, personalismo, individualismo, fatalismo.*

   - Discuss how these concepts may present themselves in the counseling setting.
   - How might you as a MSJCC counselor help Marlon maintain his autonomy and self-determination as well as ensure he is receiving adequate integrated mental and physical health care?

2. Discuss your perspective of the various settings where clients access clinical mental health counselors (in home, hospitals, community clinics) with classmates. What are multicultural social justice issues that may present themselves in each of these settings? What is important to you in determination of your preferred counseling setting?

COUNSELING IN OTHER SPECIALIZED SETTINGS

Career opportunities exist for counselors who desire to specialize by working in a distinct setting or with a particular population of clients. From a multicultural and social justice perspective, counselors may choose to follow their passions to work with a particular marginalized group. Likewise, counselors who identify as a member of a marginalized population may be drawn toward developing a counseling specialty based on firsthand life experiences. The next sections will describe the role of multicultural and social justice counselors who specialize in the legal and correctional systems, military/government settings, as well as career and employment agencies.

The Legal and Correctional System

Deinstitutionalization has had the unintended effect of moving individuals with acute mental illness from mental health institutions to prisons (Tartaro, 2016; Torrey et al., 2010). Similar to providers in other settings, mental health counselors provide services in correctional institutions to juvenile and adult clients with criminal histories and deliver interventions through individual (Abracen et al., 2016) and group counseling modalities (Zielinski et al., 2016) to attend to the varied needs of clients, from previous trauma (Laux et al., 2011) to co-occurring disorders (Balyakina et al., 2014). Correctional facilities also contract with clinical mental health counselors to assess inmates' readiness for jobs, program placements, and return to the community (Braxton-Mintz & Pinson, 2000).

In addition, clinical mental health counselors contract with specialty courts such as domestic violence courts (Tutty & Babins-Wagner, 2019), mental health courts, drug courts, and veteran treatment courts to provide mental health services, such as addictions treatment, which reduce recidivism (Phillips, 2010) and improve outcomes for clients involved with the legal system (Davis & Cates, 2017). Mental health therapists may also work with the court to provide expert testimony (Patel & Choate, 2014). It is important to consider the ethical implications of multiple roles that emerge as being both a court expert and a therapist in the assessment and treatment of incarcerated and adjudicated individuals (Shapiro & Walker, 2017).

Legal and Correctional System Culture

Counselors working in correctional systems must be able to navigate the political and social issues that permeate them. Disparities in the criminal system exist in the identification and adjudication of individuals based on gender, race, ethnicity, sexual identity (Borysova et al., 2012), and gender identity (Whitman, 2017). Thus, advocacy efforts are paramount to counseling work with clients facing legal consequences. Counselors can be an allied voice to ensure clients' proper placement in settings that support mental health treatment, with consideration for security risks (Braxton-Mintz & Pinson, 2000). The maltreatment of prison inmates has also been documented (Torrey et al., 2010). Counselors can provide expertise to decrease harm to incarcerated individuals (e.g., suicide; Cummings & Thompson, 2009) and model advocacy to maintain humane treatment of all persons regardless of setting, mental health, or criminal history.

Government and Military Systems

Counselors who work with members of the military or government service acknowledge the unique roles they play within a hierarchical setting (Westwood et al., 2012). The counselor may hold a military rank at a level above or below their client, which may have a distinct impact on the counselor–client relationship (Johnson, 2015). In addition, the counselor and client are part of a larger system requiring informed consent measures that extend what is common in the counseling field (Prosek & Holm, 2014). For example, the counselor may be required to reveal a diagnosis or treatment plan or be called on to share what is discussed in session to determine promotion, demotion, or discharge from active service. Counselors in this setting should be aware that common topics explored in counseling, such as sexual orientation or gender identity, may be masked by service members due to the hyper-masculine culture of military and government work (Westwood et al., 2012). Counselors and their clients must contemplate the personal and professional consequences to the individual should such topics in counseling sessions be revealed. Cultural competence about military life and expectations is essential, and counselors must understand their unique role within that culture in order to advocate in the best interest of their clients (Prosek & Holm, 2014). Counselors working in government or military settings may need to learn to navigate incongruences between military culture and their legal and ethical responsibilities that emerge. Examples include the repealed "Don't Ask, Don't Tell" policy on disclosure of sexual identity (Johnson et al., 2015) and the ongoing debate around "enhanced interrogation techniques" in military situations (Eisenhower, 2017).

Military System Culture

Military or government workers have a culture unto themselves, with their own language, rules, and insular community (Westwood et al., 2012). Counseling in a military or government setting may create unique social justice concerns, including lack of flexibility to choose a mental health provider or refer clients, especially while deployed (Johnson, 2015), and fluctuating government regulations. Counselors must be cognizant of professional ethics as well as personal biases when counseling in military or government settings as counseling diagnosis and treatment in this setting may have profound implications on the service members' future (Johnson, 2015; Prosek & Holm, 2014).

Career, Employment, and Vocational Rehabilitation Agencies

Career and employment service counselors may work in community agencies, schools, and postsecondary settings, employee assistance programs (EAPs), or vocational rehabilitation programs. Services provided by these counselors may include but are not limited to assisting clients with career development, helping veterans with disabilities reintegrate into the workplace, navigating employee rights, and developing strategies to overcome personal work-related concerns (Moran et al., 2013; Savickas, 2012; Swanson & Fouad, 2015). In addition, the National Employment Counseling Association (NECA) and the National Career Development Association (NCDA; both divisions of the American Counseling Association) represent the unique interests and development of counselors who desire to work in the growing field of career and employment counseling.

Clients from oppressed groups face unique barriers in the workplace and in utilizing career service centers (Fickling et al., 2018). These internal and external barriers may impact a client's career decision-making attitudes, beliefs, and aspirations (Fickling et al., 2018). Employment practices and environmental conditions (e.g., policies and guidelines, fair and inclusive practices) can either support or inhibit career and employment decision-making for clients from diverse backgrounds (Giannantonio & Hurley-Hanson, 2006). Thus, clients may eliminate career choices and even compromise for less desirable career and employment options (Gottfredson, 1981) as a result of discrimination and limited exposure to inclusive workplace environments. Examples include the lack of celebrated female icons in science, engineering, and building trade vocations and identifiable Native American politicians.

Career Counseling Settings' Culture

Career counselors must stay abreast of current federal and state law, which affect the rights of their clients in the workplace. Additionally, career opportunities are also always evolving with the advancement of new technologies and society's changing needs. Thus, career counselors must seek professional development to stay current for the sake of their clientele. Additionally, career counselors recognize when the intersection of client identities and workplace environments may be harmful to clients, especially those from marginalized backgrounds. Counselors help clients become aware of unequal social structures inconsistent with social justice (Fickling, 2016), which may foster stigma and hinder the ability for workers to feel safe. Thus, career and employment service counselors need to work closely with their clients and collaboratively discuss where advocacy interventions need to occur at intrapersonal, interpersonal, institutional, community, and public policy levels (Ratts et al., 2016). To promote acceptance and inclusion in the workplace, counselors may rally with clients to challenge public policy at the local, state, and federal levels on topics such as same-sex benefits, gender equality, and accommodation for physical/mental disabilities. Interventions at this level may include advocating for client/employee rights (Ratts et al., 2016).

CASE STUDY APPLICATION

The aforementioned case example illustrates multiple barriers that may persist for Marlon. In particular, his reintegration and transition to the workplace while navigating a disability indicates a clear need for advocacy and intervention. The counselor in this setting is encouraged to seek knowledge that pertains to public policy (e.g., legislative mandates) that work to increase opportunities for underserved veterans within the vocational rehabilitation process at the local, state, and national levels. Collaborating with local mental health organizations and advocating on Marlon's behalf to receive specific services that help address his PTSD would also be warranted.

MSJCC QUESTIONS

1. What are some additional MSJCC issues in this case study that pertain to Marlon?
2. What further advocacy actions might you engage in to work with Marlon?

Religious Organizations

Assisting, supporting, and preparing counselors to work with clients from diverse religious and spiritual backgrounds and traditions is clearly noted in the literature (ACA, 2014; Association for Spiritual, Ethical, and Religious Values in Counseling [ASERVIC], 2009; Reiner & Dobmeier, 2014). Counselors who desire to specialize in pastoral clinical mental health counseling (PCMHC) can take courses that address spiritual and religious issues in counseling. PCMHC combines traditional individual and group counseling services (similar to clinical mental health counseling) with an emphasis on the client's religious and/or spiritual context, as outlined by the ASERVIC (2009), as a part of the overall client's wellness (Myers & Williard, 2003). Faith-based agencies, organizations, and institutions often employ counselors who desire a specialization in PCMHC. It is important for counselors within this setting to be aware of the often interchangeable terminology used to describe spiritual counseling. For example, an individual may choose to see their clergy/church staff for what they believe are counseling services, but the person whom they work with may not have the credentials of a licensed counselor. Therefore, certain situations may call on those counseling in this setting to discuss their role and credentials to multiple stakeholders, both inside and outside of the setting.

Religious Counseling Settings' Culture

Counselors, specifically those who choose to work within religious organizations, should practice from a multicultural perspective, understanding that varying values and belief systems exist across religions and within various religious settings. Religious clients who experience distress may seek assistance from clergy/church staff who may not be adequately trained to address mental health concerns (Polson & Rogers, 2007). For example, Polson and Rogers (2007) explored the counseling and referral practices of 51 Protestant congregations in Waco, Texas, and found referral rates for mental health counseling of church staff were low (Polson & Rogers, 2007). Maintaining respect for religious leaders and advocating for the needs of clients, then, may be a challenge. To help with this issue, counselors must learn about clients' cultural perspectives and maintain professionalism yet demonstrate their effectiveness. Thus, Plunkett (2014) asserted that "mental health professionals must have a clear understanding of how black American churchgoers use religion and spirituality to address mental health issues" (p. 218). Counselors should also be aware of the competencies outlined by ASERVIC to assist with best-practice approaches to religious counseling.

SUMMARY, INSIGHTS, AND ACTIONS

Development of one's professional identity is an important process for counseling students as they grow into counseling professionals. To develop a counseling identity, it is imperative for counselors to gain cultural knowledge of the setting where they intend to work, to understand the specialized language of the workplace, and to consider how the values of the setting align or do not align with their own. Additionally, counselors must also develop the skills and professional behaviors needed for their setting through appropriate training in graduate programs and continued professional development after entrance into the field as a professional. While there are common competencies and practices across settings for practicing counselors, such as the MSJCC, each counseling setting has contextual factors and specific competencies that counselors must develop to be proficient in their area of expertise. Even after counselors work in their chosen field, sometimes counselors decide they would fit better in a different counseling setting, or even decide to become counselor educators. Making a professional change is not uncommon and is always an option as you embark on your professional journey.

REFLECTION AND DISCUSSION QUESTIONS

1. What are the advantages and disadvantages of working in each counselor setting?
2. Describe the social justice issues in each counselor setting and the role of the counselor in terms of advocacy.
3. Job shadowing or conducting counselor interviews in counseling fields can be helpful for students just entering their program of study. Based on information you have learned in this chapter, develop three questions related to a counseling setting or specialty you want to learn more about to add to your own professional learning goals.
4. Which counselor setting do you feel most drawn to and why? Create three action steps you can take to develop MSJCC aligned to your preferred professional setting.
5. What experiences, personal qualities, values, and interests have you already acquired that may be beneficial in counseling work with clients in one or more settings described in this chapter?

REFERENCES

Abracen, J., Gallo, A., Looman, J., & Goodwill, A. (2016). Individual community-based treatment of offenders with mental illness. *Journal of Interpersonal Violence, 31*(10), 1842–1858.

Adelman, H. S., & Taylor, L. (2010). *Mental health in schools: Engaging learners, prevention problems, and improving schools.* Corwin.

American Counseling Association. (2014). *Code of ethics and standards of practice.* https://www.counseling.org/resources/aca-code-of-ethics.pdf

American School Counselor Association. (2014). *Mindsets and behaviors for student success: K–12 college- and career-readiness standards for every student.* Author.

American School Counselor Association. (2019). *ASCA national model: A framework for school counseling programs* (4th ed.). Author.

Annamalai, A., Staeheli, M., Cole, R. A., & Steiner, J. L. (2018). Establishing an integrated health care clinic in a community mental health center: Lessons learned. *Psychiatric Quarterly, 89*(1), 169–181. https://doi.org/10.1007/s11126-017-9523-x

Association for Spiritual, Ethical, and Religious Values in Counseling. (2009). *Competencies for addressing spiritual and religious issues in counseling.* https://www.counseling.org/docs/default-source/competencies/competencies-for-addressing-spiritual-and-religious-issues-in-counseling.pdf?sfvrsn=8./

Balyakina, E., Mann, C., Ellison, M., Sivernell, R., Fulda, K., Sarai, S., & Cardarelli, R. (2014). Risk of future offense among probationers with co-occurring substance use and mental health disorders. *Community Mental Health Journal, 50*(3), 288–295. https://doi.org/10.1007/s10597-013-9624-4

Borysova, M. E., Mitchell, O., Sultan, D. H., & Williams, A. R. (2012). Racial and ethnic health disparities in incarcerated populations. *Journal of Health Disparities Research and Practice, 5*(2), 92–100.

Bowen, J. M., & Carson, S. L. (2016). A qualitative analysis of home-based counselors' experiences in rural settings. *Journal of Counseling & Development, 94*(2), 129–140.

Braxton-Mintz, R., & Pinson, M. (2000, October). Personnel: Your most important resource. *Corrections Today*, 96–98.

Burnett-Zeigler, I., & Lyons, J. S. (2010). Caregiver factors predicting service utilization among youth participating in a school-based mental health intervention. *Journal of Child and Family Studies, 19*(5), 572–578. https://doi.org/10.1007/s10826-009-9331-5

Cigrand, D., Havlik, S. G., Malott, K. M., & Jones, S. G. (2015). School counselors united in professional advocacy: A systems model. *Journal of School Counseling, 13*(8), 1–48.

Cohn, T. J., & Hastings, S. L. (2013). Building a practice in rural settings: Special considerations. *Journal of Mental Health Counseling, 35*(3), 228–244. https://doi.org/10.17744/mehc.35.3.12171572424wxhll

Council for the Accreditation of Counseling and Related Educational Programs. (2016). *2016 CACREP standards.* http://www.cacrep.org/wp-content/uploads/2017/08/2016-Standards-with-citations.pdf

Cummings, D. L., & Thompson, M. N. (2009). Suicidal or manipulative? The role of mental health counselors in overcoming a false dichotomy in identifying and treating self-harming inmates. *Journal of Mental Health Counseling, 31*(3), 201–212.

Davis, T. O., & Cates, K. A. (2017). Mental health counseling and specialty courts. *Professional Counselor, 7*(3), 251–258.

Dixon, L. B., & Goldman, H. H. (2003). Forty years of progress in community mental health: The role of evidence-based practices. *Australian and New Zealand Journal of Psychiatry, 37*, 668–673. https://doi.org/10.1111/j.1440-1614.2003.01274.x

Doll, B., Nastasi, B. K., Cornell, L., & Song, S. Y. (2017). School-based mental health services: Definitions and models of effective practice. *Journal of Applied School Psychology, 33*(3), 179–194. https://doi.org/10.1080/15377903.2017.1317143

Eisenhower, W. D. (2017). Torture in the naked public square. *Ethics & Behavior, 27*(5), 423–435. https://doi.org/10.1080/10508422.2016.1172313

Fickling, M. J. (2016). An exploration of career counselors' perspectives on advocacy. *Professional Counselor, 6*(2), 174–188. https://doi.org/10.15241/mf.6.2.174

Fickling, M. J., Lancaster, C., & Neal, A. V. (2018). Social justice in career services: Perspectives of university career center directors. *Career Development Quarterly*, 66(1), 64–76. https://doi.org/10.1002/cdq.12122

Giannantonio, C. M., & Hurley-Hanson, A. E. (2006). Applying image norms across Super's career development stages. *Career Development Quarterly*, 54(4), 318–330. https://doi.org/10.1002/j.2161-0045.2006.tb00197.x

Goodman-Scott, E., Betters-Bubon, J., & Donohue, P. (Eds.). (2019). *The school counselor's guide to multi-tiered systems of support*. Routledge.

Gottfredson, L. S. (1981). Circumscription and compromise: A developmental theory of occupational aspirations. *Journal of Counseling Psychology*, 28(6). 545–579. https://doi.org/10.1037/0022-0167.28.6.545

Hastings, S. L., & Cohn, T. J. (2013). Challenges and opportunities associated with rural mental health practice. *Journal of Rural Mental Health*, 37(1), 37–49. https://doi.org/10.1037/rmh0000002

Hatch, T., Duarte, D., & De Gregario, L. K. (2018). *Hatching results for elementary school counseling: Implementing core curriculum and other tier one activities*. Corwin.

Hodges, S. J. (2016). College counseling: Past, present, and future. *The College and University Counseling Manual: Integrating Essential Services Across the Campus*. Springer.

Jameson, J. P., Chambless, D. L., & Blank, M. B. (2009). Empirically supported treatments in rural community mental health centers: A preliminary report on current utilization and attitudes toward adoption. *Community Mental Health Journal*, 45(6), 463–467. https://doi.org/10.1007/s10597-009-9230-7

Johnson, W. B. (2015). Multiple relationships in military mental health counseling. In B. Herlihy & G. Corey (Eds.), *Boundary issues in counseling: Multiple roles and responsibilities* (3rd ed.) (pp. 254–259). American Counseling Association.

Johnson, W. B., Rosenstein, J. E., Buhrke, R. A., & Haldeman, D. C. (2015). After "Don't ask don't tell": Competent care of lesbian, gay and bisexual military personnel during the DoD policy transition. *Professional Psychology: Research and Practice*, 46(2), 107–115. https://doi.org/10.1037/a0033051

Jones, E. B., & Ku, L. (2015). Sharing a playbook: Integrated care in community health centers in the United States. *American Journal of Public Health*, 105(10), 2028–2034.

Kaffenberger, C. J., & O'Rourke-Trigiani, J. (2013). Addressing student mental health needs by providing direct and indirect services and building alliances in the community. *Professional School Counseling*, 16(5), 323–332.

Kress, V. E. W., Trippany, R. L., & Nolan, J. M. (2003). Responding to sexual assault victims: Considerations for college counselors. *Journal of College Counseling*, 6(2), 124–133.

Laux, J. M., Calmes, S., Moe, J. L., Dupuy, P. J., Cox, J. A., Ventura, L. A., Williamson, C.; Barbaranne, B. J., & Lambert, E. (2011). The clinical mental health counseling needs of mothers in the criminal justice system. *Family Journal*, 19(3), 291–298.

Mattek, R. J., Jorgenson, E. T., & Fox, R. A. (2010). Home-based therapy for young children in low-income families: A student training program. *The Family Journal: Counseling and Therapy for Couples and Families*, 18(2), 189–194.

Meyers, L. (2019, March 22). Establishing a private practice. *Counseling Today.* https://ct.counseling.org/2019/03/establishing-a-private-practice/

Moran, S., Schmidt, J., & Burker, E. J. (2013). Posttraumatic growth and posttraumatic stress disorder in veterans. *Journal of Rehabilitation, 79*(2), 34–43.

Myers, J. E., & Williard, K. (2003). Integrating spirituality into counselor preparation: A developmental, wellness approach. *Counseling and Values, 47*(2), 142–155.

National Association of College Access Counselors & American School Counselor Association. (n.d.). *State-by-state student-to-counselor ratio report.* Author.

Owens, D., Lacey, K., Rawls, G., & Holbert-Quince, J. A. (2010). First-generation African American male college students: Implications for career counselors. *Career Development Quarterly, 58*(4), 291–300.

Patel, S. H., & Choate, L. H. (2014). Conducting child custody evaluations: Best practices for mental health counselors who are court-appointed as child custody evaluators. *Journal of Mental Health Counseling, 36*(1), 18–30. https://doi.org/10.17744/mehc.36.1.e00401wv7134w505

Phillips, L. A. (2010). Substance abuse and prison recidivism: Themes from qualitative interviews. *Journal of Addictions & Offender Counseling, 31*(1), 10–24. https://doi.org/10.1002/j.2161-1874.2010.tb00063.x

Plunkett, D. P. (2014). The Black church, values, and secular counseling: Implications for counselor education and practice. *Counseling and Values, 59*(2), 208–221.

Polson, L. M., & Rogers, R. K. (2007). Counseling and mental health referral practices of church staff. *Social Work & Christianity, 34*(1, 72–87.

Prosek, E., & Holm, J. (2014). Counselors and the military: When protocol and ethics conflict. *The Professional Counselor, 4*(2), 93–102.

Ratts, M. J., Singh, A. A., Nassar-McMillan, S., Butler, S. K., & McCullough, J. R. (2016). Multicultural and social justice counseling competencies: Guidelines for the counseling profession. *Journal of Multicultural Counseling and Development, 44*(1), 28–48. https://doi.org/10.1002/jmcd.12035

Ratts, M. J., Toporek, R. L., & Lewis, J. A. (2010). *ACA advocacy competencies: A social justice framework for counselors.* American Counseling Association.

Rehfuss, M. C., Gambrell, C. E., & Meyer, D. (2012). Counselors' perceived person–environment fit and career satisfaction. *Career Development Quarterly, 60*(2), 145–151. https://doi.org/10.1002/j.2161-0045.2012.00012.x

Reiner, S. M., & Dobmeier, R. A. (2014). Counselor preparation and the association for spiritual, ethical, and religious values in counseling competencies: An exploratory study. *Counseling and Values, 59*(2), 192–207.

Reynolds, A. L., & Pope, R. L. (2003). Multicultural competence in counseling centers. In D. B. Pope-Davis, H. L. K. Coleman, W. M. Liu, & R. L. Toporek (Eds.), *Handbook of multicultural competencies: In counseling & psychology* (pp. 365–382). SAGE. https://doi.org/10.4135/9781452231693.n23

Reynolds, G. P. (2010). *Private practice: Business considerations.* http://counselingoutfitters.com/vistas/vistas10/Article_36.pdf

Savickas, M. L. (2012). Life design: A paradigm for career intervention in the 21st century. *Journal of Counseling & Development, 90*(1), 13–19.

Schmitz, R. M., & Tyler, K. A. (2018). LGBTQ+ young adults on the street and on campus: Identity as a product of social context. *Journal of homosexuality, 65*(2), 197–223.

Shapiro, D. L., & Walker, L. E. A. (2017). Multiple relationships in forensic settings. In O. Zur (Ed.), *Multiple relationships in psychotherapy and counseling: Unavoidable, common, and mandatory dual relations in therapy* (pp. 82–91). Routledge.

Shin, P., Sharac, J., & Mauery, D. R. (2013). The role of community health centers in providing behavioral health care. *The Journal of Behavioral Health Services & Research, 40*(4), 488–496. https://doi.org/10.1007/s11414-013-9353-z

Stevens, J., Kelleher, K. J., Ward-Estes, J. & Hayes, J. (2006). Perceived barriers to treatment and psychotherapy attendance in child community mental health centers. *Community Mental Health Journal, 42*(5), 449–458.

Soltis-Jarrett, V., Shea, J., Ragaisis, K. M., Shell, L. P., & Newton, M. (2017). Integrated behavioral healthcare: Assumptions, definition and roles: Position paper from the international society of psychiatric-mental health nurses. *Archives of Psychiatric Nursing, 31*(5), 433–439. https://doi.org/10.1016/j.apnu.2017.06.002

Stone, G. L., & Archer Jr, J. (1990). College and university counseling centers in the 1990s: Challenges and limits. *The Counseling Psychologist, 18*(4), 539–607.

Swanson, J. L., & Fouad, N. A. (2015). *Career theory and practice: Learning through case study* (3rd ed.). SAGE.

Tanenbaum, S. J. (2011). Mental health consumer-operated services organizations in the US: Citizenship as a core function and strategy for growth. *Health Care Analysis, 19*(2), 192–205. https://doi.org/10.1007/s10728-010-0151-y

Tartaro, C. (2016). Keeping mentally ill offenders out of jail: Evaluation results. *American Jails, 30*(1), 20.

Tate, K. A., Lopez, C., Fox, R., Love, J. R., & McKinney, E. (2014). In-home counseling for young children living in poverty: An exploration of counseling competencies. *The Family Journal, 22*(4), 371–381.

Torrey, E. E., Kennard, A. D., Eslinger, D., Lamb, R., & Pavle, J. (2010). *More mentally ill persons are in jails and prisons than hospitals: A survey of the states.* Treatment Advocacy Center.

Tutty, L. M., & Babins-Wagner, R. (2019). Outcomes and recidivism in mandated batterer intervention before and after introducing a specialized domestic violence court. *Journal of Interpersonal Violence, 34*(5), 1039–1062. https://doi.org/10.1177/0886260516647005

U.S. Bureau of Labor Statistics. (2020). *Substance abuse, behavioral disorder, and mental health counselors. Occupational outlook handbook.* https://www.bls.gov/ooh/community-and-social-service/substance-abuse-behavioral-disorder-and-mental-health-counselors.htm

Wells, R., Kite, B., Breckenridge, E., & Sunbury, T. (2018). Community mental health center integrated care outcomes. *Psychiatric Quarterly, 89*, 969–982. https://doi.org/10.1007/s11126-018-9594-3

Westwood, M., Kuhl, D., & Shields, D. (2012). Counseling military clients: Multicultural competence, challenges, and opportunities. In C. C. Lee (Ed.) *Multicultural issues in counseling: New approaches to diversity. American Counseling Association.* (pp. 275–294).

Whitman, C. N. (2017). Transgender criminal justice: Ethical and constitutional perspectives. *Ethics & Behavior, 27*(6), 445–457. https://doi.org/10.1080/10508422.2016.1183490

Zielinski, M. J., Karlsson, M. E., & Bridges, A. J. (2016). Adapting evidence-based trauma treatment for incarcerated women: A model for implementing exposure-based group therapy and considerations for practitioners. *The Behavior Therapist, 39*(6), 205–210.

Ziomek-Daigle, J., Goodman-Scott, E., Cavin, J., & Donohue, P. (2016). Integrating multi-tiered system of supports with comprehensive school counseling programs. *Professional Counselor, 6*(3), 320–332. https://doi.org/10.15241/jzd.6.3.220

CHAPTER 9

MULTICULTURAL TECHNIQUES IN COUNSELING

Michelle D. Mitchell, Wake Forest University

Michael Brooks, North Carolina Agricultural and Technology University

LEARNING OBJECTIVES

1. Assess one's ability to engage in an ongoing self-awareness when maintaining a multicultural counseling relationship.
2. Understand the importance of therapeutic approaches and behaviors related to engaging in a multicultural counseling relationship.
3. Better understand various forms of cultural communication as they are relevant in establishing a multicultural counseling relationship.
4. Gain a working knowledge of cultural presentation that is necessary to implement the respective techniques properly.

LEARNING OUTCOMES

1. Assess ability to engage in ongoing self-awareness to maintain the multicultural counseling relationship.
2. Become familiar with the necessary influence of a therapeutic approach and how it needs to be rooted in multicultural counseling philosophies.
3. Better understand the various forms of communication.
4. Learn multicultural values necessary for proper technique implementation.

Since **multiculturalism** and **social justice** are considered the fourth and fifth forces of counseling (Pedersen, 1988; Ratts, 2009), it is by no surprise that counselors are establishing and maintaining more of an ethical commitment to embrace a multicultural approach throughout clinical practice (American Counseling Association [ACA], 2014; Assembly, 2008; American Psychological Association [APA], 2002). With this newly found focus of multicultural counseling, competencies relating to work with culturally diverse clients have adapted with society's growing conceptualization of culture (Wong et al., 2006). Thus, highlighting concepts of privilege, oppression, and marginalization are helpful in understanding the complex dynamics taking place in counseling sessions. Furthermore, contemporary aspects of multiculturalism have been intentional to integrate a variety of cultural identity statuses, including sexual orientation, gender identification, socio-economic status, spiritual and/or religious beliefs, and racial/ethnic diversity, which was the focus of the original multicultural definition (Ratts et al., 2016; Robinson, 1999).

As we explore the ever-expanding conceptualization of culture, we must understand that definitions of culture are vast. Specifically, culture is a "a complex collection of components that a group of people share to help them adapt to their social and physical world" (Yamamoto et al., 1997, p. 34). However, other scholars have defined culture as

> a set of denotative (what is or beliefs), connotative (what should be, or attitudes, norms, and values), and pragmatic (how things are done or procedural roles) knowledge, shared by a group of individuals who have a shared history and who participate in a social structure. (Basabe et al., 2002, p. 104)

While the definitions, as mentioned earlier, provide a framework for the similarities we find among groups of people, they fail to recognize the specific and targeted aspects of culture, incorporating elements of surface culture deep culture. Therefore, to address those elements, **culture** will be defined and understood as

> an integrated pattern of human behavior which includes but is not limited to—thought, communication, languages, beliefs, values, practices, customs, courtesies, rituals, manners of interacting, roles, relationships, and expected behaviors of an ethnic group or social groups whose members are uniquely identifiable by that pattern of human behavior. (Gilbert et al., 2007, p. 14)

With this definition of culture in mind, the remainder of this chapter addresses various aspects of culture, including metacognition, behavior, communication, image, and pop culture influences.

METACOGNITION

Metacognition is the awareness of one's thinking and thought processes (Gredler, 2009) and is associated with more significant problem-solving and goal development skills (Wilkinson, 2011). Given the independent nature of the clinical practice and the intimate nature of counseling work, the field of counseling (multicultural counseling) requires the development of metacognitive skills. Thus, counselors who intend to work with diverse populations should establish this ongoing self-reflective skill set. Without the ability to utilize metacognition in preparation for and actual work with clients, counselors may have difficulty identifying techniques required to understand and interpret client information (Stewart, 2002).

To ensure clinicians can engage in metacognitive skills, individuals should retain a growth mind-set, which believes that intelligence can be developed, not fixed over time (Claro et al., 2016). It is imperative that counselors attempting to increase their multicultural knowledge and self-efficacy understand a lack of understanding is not a permanent state of being. The core belief that one can change and grow is a foundational building block in engaging in multicultural counseling.

Furthermore, clinicians must regularly establish goals and create pathways for goal-monitoring. For these goals to assist in the use of metacognition, the goals must be **SMART**, which are *specific* and narrow for achievability; *measurable* to describe the evidence required to assess progress and outcomes; *attainable* to ensure resources, skills, talents, and abilities are present to achieve the goal; *relevant* to ensure they align with your long-term goals and objectives; and *time-based* to provide a realistic end date (Kiresuk & Sherman, 1968). Goal establishment is vital in the creation and maintenance of metacognitive skills. At the same time, counselors-in-training and novice counselors will require assistance in the development of goals. In this way, students and early career counselors should utilize counselor educators and supervisors to aid in these goals' creation and monitoring.

Lastly, clinicians must evaluate their performance and make adjustments when needed. The process of self-evaluation is gradual and progressive over time; therefore, as a counselor develops, this skill set will require less supervision and prompting. Once a counselor develops adequate metacognitive skills, continual maintenance of these skills is imperative.

BEHAVIOR

Integrating multicultural skills and behaviors in work with clients is essential in service delivery to diverse populations. **Multicultural skills** refer to recognizing that helping styles may be culture-bound (Sue et al., 1992). Research has shown a positive association between artistic skills and behaviors identified as part of the process of care (e.g., listening, understanding, confidentiality, respect, decision, plan, trust) to have functional outcomes in the areas of life problem management, career/academic improvement, and improved social interactions (Michalopoulou et al., 2014). In this way, multicultural skills are critical in relationship development and outcome achievement among clients of diversity.

Moreover, an essential element of multicultural skill development is utilizing culturally relevant interventions and strategies within the counseling session (Ratts et al., 2016). Employing multicultural skills requires the ability to interpret and evaluate how power, privilege, and oppression influence client experiences. Thus, multicultural skill development necessitates the recognition and integration of social justice advocacy (Ratts et al., 2016).

The development of multicultural skills requires the examination of several cultural concepts, identity statuses, and intersectionality. Taking a holistic perspective toward clients entails that counselors engage in behaviors that go beyond the primary focus on culturally specific values and traditions.

To identify salient aspects of one's culture as a counselor, broaching is a highly useful skill. **Broaching** refers to the counselor's deliberate and intentional efforts to discuss those racial, ethnic, and cultural (REC) concerns that may impact the client's presenting concerns (Day-Vines et al., 2007). As counselors assess their ability to broach, five styles of this skill may apply: (a) avoidant, (b) isolating, (c) continuing/incongruent, (d) integrated/congruent, and (e) infusing. When considering the integration of multicultural skills, infusing counselors are best able to engage with clients by maintaining a social justice focus while integrating multicultural techniques at large. An integrated/congruent counselor only provides surface assistance by helping clients connect their presenting problems and REC issues, as needed. Continuing/incongruent counselors provide broaching mechanically. This form of broaching can lack the nuanced skills needed to allow for explicit discussions about the client's REC concerns. Lastly, isolating counselors broach minimally. More specifically, counselors providing this form of broaching do so in an obligatory style, while avoidant counselors fail to broach altogether (Day-Vines et al., 2007). Unfortunately, all of these broaching styles do not display multicultural skills and behaviors, which may not appropriately engage diverse clients. A failure to effectively broach (or not) REC concerns with clients is harmful considering both actions (or inactions) preserve the dominant culture's cultural paradigms (Day-Vines et al., 2020).

COMMUNICATION

Communication is the act of sending and receiving meaning from one person/group to another through mutually understood signs, symbols, and semiotic rules. The relationship between communication and culture is a very complex and intimate one. First, communication creates culture; that is, communication is the means of human interaction through which cultural characteristics—whether customs, roles, rules, rituals, laws, or other patterns—are created and shared. It is not so much that individuals make a culture when interacting in relationships, groups, organizations, or societies. Instead, cultures are a natural by-product of social interaction. In a sense, cultures are the "residue" of social communication. Without communication and communication media, it would be impossible to preserve and pass along cultural characteristics from one place and time to another. One can say, therefore, that culture is created, shaped, transmitted, and learned through communication. The reverse is also the case: Communication practices are created, shaped, and shared by culture.

MULTICULTURAL (CROSS-CULTURAL) COMMUNICATION

When people from multiple backgrounds with different communication methods coexist without really interacting deeply, that's a multicultural communication situation. There are numerous cultures present, but there isn't much crossover or integration between the groups, who remain mostly separate. Often, there is one group (or maybe a few) that has the most prestige relative to the others. This doesn't have to be the case; instead, think of **multicultural communication** as the prerequisite for the other two types. There must be more than one culture to have moments produced by intercultural or cross-cultural communication. But sometimes it takes resources (such as language services) or a shift in attitudes to move beyond this starting point. When interactions between people in different cultures occur in a solely multicultural context, they are rarely rich learning experiences for anyone involved.

Multicultural communication focuses on the dynamics relating to sending/receiving messages across cultures. It is not limited to the happenings when people of different cultures meet. Still, it is also inclusive of what happens when people of other diverse groups come together in an organization, community, or country. Successful multicultural communication is more than just translating existing material from English. Instead, it must embrace the social nuance of different markets. That entails culturally sensitive imagery, appropriate interpersonal communication dynamics, and the right jargon or slang. Language differences, dialects, slang, colloquialisms, nonverbal (facial) cues, and power distances are all examples of multicultural communication as well as factors that can affect its effectiveness.

IMAGE

Culture has a significant impact on how we feel about ourselves and how we think about our bodies. Many cultural traditions also contribute to body image and influence either negative or positive body image and self-esteem.

The way one represents themself by their **image**. One is perceived (and sometimes inaccurately judged) based on their appearance. A picture can project values or a particular purpose. Some businesses/agencies have professional images and qualities they'd like promoted to attract and retain customers. These images, however, are dependent on the nature of the company.

Image quality is not a single factor but is a composite of early environmental factors, cognitive vulnerabilities, and cultural influences. Environment can include how one is raised and introduced to how physical appearance impacts self-perceptions. Body image demurs or exertions are dependent on how one judges themself. Personalities who tend to focus on flaws rather than strengths have body image challenges.

POP CULTURE INFLUENCES

Social media and even mobile phone apps (such as Plump&Skinny Booth) are capable of altering one's view of self. Cyberbullying is another contributor to negative body image and performance pressures (e.g., sports). New websites are popping up instructing people on "how to get an eating disorder" to control weight (see "Additional Resources"). Counter knowledge can help increase a more accurate view of oneself and others.

CASE STUDY

Rachel identifies as a 35-year-old White female and is an internship student in a counseling program. She has had four sessions with her client Jessie who identifies as a 25-year-old Black man. During their counseling sessions with one another, Jessie has discussed the recent loss of his grandmother from COVID-19. Jessie has expressed how important his grandmother was in his life since she helped raise him. Each time he begins to discuss the recent loss of his grandmother Jessie begins to fidget within his seat.

During Rachel's next supervision session, she mentioned these dynamics in her multicultural case presentation. Toward the conclusion of her presentation, she asked her supervisor for feedback concerning her preliminary diagnosis of attention deficit hyperactivity disorder (ADHD) based on Jessie's inability to sit still during the majority of their counseling sessions. The supervisor inquired about ADHD-specific symptomatology of inattention and hyperactivity impulsivity, to which Rachel was able to indicate that Jessie either did not display the listed *Diagnostic and Statistical Manual* (DSM-5) symptoms or she hadn't worked with him long enough to decide. Since this was ruled out, Rachel's supervisor inquired if she had broached the topic of race and gender differences between herself and her client in any of their sessions. Rachel informed her supervisor that she only broached the issues of race and gender in their first counseling session during their intake as verification of how he identified; however, she hadn't mentioned it since.

QUESTIONS

1. What style of broaching has Rachel implemented with her client?
2. What style of broaching would be most appropriate and beneficial for Jessie as he continues to attend counseling sessions?
3. What communication pattern was misidentified and used to justify the preliminary diagnosis of ADHD?
4. What are a few clinical repercussions of Rachel's minimal competence and understanding concerning Jessie's communication patterns?
5. Based on the intersectional identities presented, how would Rachel be categorized as a counselor (e.g., marginalized, privileged) and why?
6. Based on the intersectional identities presented, how would Jessie be categorized as a client (e.g., marginalized, privileged) and why?
7. Based on the multicultural and social justice counseling competencies (MSJCC), what self-reflective questions may the counselor want to ask herself concerning her values, beliefs, and potential biases in her work with Jessie?
8. In what ways do you believe power and privilege may have impacted the growth and development of the presented client?
9. Which multicultural technique(s) can the counselor use (e.g., broaching, communication, image) to enhance the counseling relationship?
10. What are some institutional, community, public policy and/or internationally based counseling and advocacy interventions that can be implemented for this case study?

CHAPTER HIGHLIGHTS

Throughout this chapter, several key terms and concepts were reviewed:

- **Multiculturalism** relates to work with culturally diverse clients, integrating concepts of privilege, oppression, and marginalization.
- **Culture** refers to an integrated pattern of human behavior and expected behaviors of an ethnic group or social group whose members are uniquely identifiable by that pattern of human behavior.
- **Metacognition** is the awareness of one's thinking and thought processes.
- **SMART goals** refer to goals that are *specific, attainable, relevant,* and *time-based.*
- **Multicultural skills** refer to the recognition that helping styles may be culture-bound.
- **Broaching** refers to the counselor's deliberate and intentional efforts to discuss those racial, ethnic, and cultural (REC) concerns that may impact the client's presenting concerns.
- **Communication** is the act of sending and receiving meaning from one person/group to another through mutually understood signs, symbols, and semiotic rules.
- **Multicultural communication** focuses on the dynamics relating to sending/receiving messages across cultures.
- **Image** refers to the way one represents themself.

SUMMARY, INSIGHTS, AND ACTIONS

Given the integration of multiculturalism and social justice within and throughout the counseling field, it has become even more critical that counselors comprehend and utilize multicultural techniques. First, processing and gaining awareness of one's thought process is foundational to the pursuit of engaging with clients in a manner that promotes diversity and culture. Second, counselors must implement and discuss racial, ethnic, and other cultural issues as they present themselves within sessions.

As expressed earlier in the chapter, the integration of metacognition, behavior, communication, image, and pop culture influences is vital in counselors' understanding and use of multicultural counseling techniques. The establishment and help of empirically sound multicultural counseling strategies are needed to ensure counselors are providing culturally informed plans for their clients. The continual application of multiculturally based techniques, alongside the ongoing pursuit of knowledge concerning culture, supports the aspirational model of counselor cultural competence.

REFLECTION AND DISCUSSION QUESTIONS

1. Name a few essential concepts that are integrated into multicultural counseling.
2. Name two strategies a counselor could use to enhance the development of their metacognition.
3. What broaching style might a continuing/incongruent counselor utilize to address racial, ethnic, and cultural concerns within a counseling session?

4. When considering multicultural communication, what are a few techniques or considerations that may be involved?

5. How might culture and cultural influences impact self-image?

ADDITIONAL RESOURCES

Ratts, M.J.; Toporek, R.L. & Lewis, J.A. (2010). ACA advocacy competencies: A social justice framework for counselors. American Counseling Association.

Association for Multicultural Counseling and Development: http://www.multiculturalcounseling.org/

Cash, T. (1998). Body Image Workbook

Center for Change: www.centerforchange.com

Chung, R. C., & Bemak, F. P. (2012). *Social justice counseling: The next steps beyond multiculturalism*. SAGE.

Mitchell, Michelle. (2018). The development and validation of the Multicultural Competency Assessment. Electronic Theses and Dissertations. 6375. https://stars.library.ucf.edu/etd/6375

Oh, S., & Shillingford-Butler, A. (2020). The client assessment of multicultural competent behavior (CAMCB): Development and validation. *Measurement and Evaluation in Counseling and Development*, 1–19.

Wasatch Family Therapy: https://wasatchfamilytherapy.com/archives/29985

REFERENCES

American Counseling Association (2014). *ACA Code of Ethics*. Author.

American Psychological Association. (2002). Ethical principles of psychologists and code of conduct. *American Psychologist, 57*(12), 1060–1073.

Basabe, N., Paez, D., Valencia, J., González, J., Rimé, B., & Diener, E. (2002). Cultural dimensions, socioeconomic development, climate and emotional hedonic level. In A. S. R. Manstead & A. H. Fischer (Eds.), *Culture and emotion* (pp. 103–125). Taylor & Francis.

Byars-Winston, A. M., & Fouad, N. A. (2006). Metacognition and multicultural competence: Expanding the culturally appropriate career counseling model. *Career Development Quarterly, 54*(3), 187–201.

Claro, S., Paunesku, D., & Dweck, C. S. (2016). Growth mindset tempers the effects of poverty on academic achievement. *Proceedings of the National Academy of Sciences, 113*(31), 8664–8668.

Day-Vines, N. L., Cluxton-Keller, F., Agorsor, C., Gubara, S., & Otabil, N. A. A. (2020). The multidimensional model of broaching behavior. *Journal of Counseling & Development, 98*(1), 107–118.

Day-Vines, N. L., Wood, S. M., Grothaus, T., Craigen, L., Holman, A., Dotson-Blake, K., & Douglass, M. J. (2007). Broaching the subjects of race, ethnicity, and culture during the counseling process. *Journal of Counseling & Development, 85*(4), 401–409.

Gilbert, J., Goode, T., & Dunne, C. (2007). Cultural awareness: Curricula enhancement module series. National Center for Cultural Competence, Georgetown University Center for Child and Human Development. https://nccc.georgetown.edu/curricula/awareness/index.html.

Gredler, M.E. (2009). *Learning and Instruction: Theory into Practice.* Pearson.

Kiresuk, T. J., & Sherman, R. E. (1968). Goal attainment scaling: A general method for evaluating comprehensive community mental health programs. *Community Mental Health Journal, 4*(6), 443–453.

Michalopoulou, G., Falzarano, P., Butkus, M., Zeman, L., Vershave, J., & Arfken, C. (2014). Linking cultural competence to functional life outcomes in mental health care settings. *Journal of the National Medical Association, 106,* 42–49.

Pedersen, P. (1988). *A handbook for developing multicultural awareness.* American Association for Counseling and Development.

Ratts, M. J. (2009). Social justice counseling: Toward the development of a fifth force among counseling paradigms. *Journal of Humanistic Counseling, Education and Development, 48*(2), 160–172.

Ratts, M. J., Singh, A. A., Nassar-McMillan, S., Butler, S. K., & McCullough, J. R. (2016). Multicultural and social justice counseling competencies: Guidelines for the counseling profession. *Journal of Multicultural Counseling and Development, 44*(1), 28–48.

Robinson, T. L. (1999). The intersections of dominant discourses across race, gender, and other identities. *Journal of Counseling & Development, 77*(1), 77–79.

Stewart, J. B. (2002). Developing a multicultural career mindset. Unpublished manuscript, University of New Brunswick, Fredericton, Canada.

Sue, D. W., Arredondo, P., & McDavis, R. J. (1992). Multicultural counseling competencies and standards: A call to the profession. *Journal of Multicultural Counseling and Development, 20*(2), 64–88. https://doi.org/10.1002/j.2161-1912.1992.tb00563.x

Wilkinson, R.T. (2011). Increasing counselor self-awareness: The role of cognitive complexity and metacognition in counselor training programs. *Alabama Counseling Association Journal, 37* (1), 24–32.

Wong, P. T. P., Wong, L. C. J., & Scott, C. (2006). Beyond stress and coping: The positive psychology of transformation. In P. T. P. Wong & L. C. J. Wong (Eds.), *Handbook of multicultural perspectives on stress and coping* (pp. 1–28). Springer.

Yamamoto, J., Silva, A., Ferrari, M., & Nukariya, K. (1997). Culture and psychopathology. In G. Johnson-Powell, & J. Yamamoto (Eds.), *Transcultural child development: Psychological assessment and treatment* (pp. 34–60). Wiley.

CHAPTER 10

CAREER COUNSELING

Spencer G. Niles, William & Mary

Okenna Egwu, William & Mary

Jennifer K. Niles, William & Mary

LEARNING OBJECTIVES

1. Explore the roles, activities, and responsibilities of culturally competent career counselors.
2. Examine the intersection of social justice, client advocacy, and career counseling.
3. Build strategies for developing a hope-action orientation for supporting clients' career development across the life span.

LEARNING OUTCOMES

1. Learn skills for exploring clients' culture and its influence on life-role salience.
2. Understand the skills, behaviors, and attitudes of career self-management.
3. Understand the relevance of hope-action theory in culturally competent career counseling.

Today, one would be hard-pressed to identify a counseling setting in which knowledge and skills related to career counseling are not relevant. Children, adolescents, and adults experience career development challenges regularly. Niles and Harris-Bowlsbey (in press) note that children must learn about themselves and the world of work in ways that are not influenced by bias and discrimination related to gender, race/ethnicity, heterosexism, and so on. Adolescents must develop clear, comprehensive, and accurate pictures of who they are and what educational and career options exist for them. They must also learn how to access the options they choose to pursue. Adults must cope with unstable employment situations while they also live their lives as partners and parents. They must learn skills and acquire knowledge that will allow them to remain viable to current and prospective employers. They must also deal with the stress that exists due to job security being nearly nonexistent. Finally, we also know that when employment experiences become negative, incidents of partner abuse, substance abuse, depression, and suicide increase. Thus, virtually every professional counselor will encounter either directly or indirectly clients/students attempting to cope with career concerns (Niles & Bowlsbey, in press).

The prevalence of career concerns stands alongside the fact that many in the counseling profession diminish the centrality of career counseling within the work they do (Lindo et al., 2019). Some may view career development interventions as separate from more general counseling interventions and hold the view that the skills required for effective career intervention are less than the skill required for more "advanced" therapeutic interventions. We know from longstanding research that people do not live lives in compartmentalized silos (Super, 1980). While busy making a living, people are busy living lives that include a multiplicity of life role engagements. When adults present for career counseling, they express their concerns holistically. That is, they discuss topics related to self-esteem, relationship issues, family-of-origin struggles, and sometimes depression and an overall sense of meaninglessness in their lives. Thus, we find two things particularly perplexing concerning the diminishment of career counseling within the counseling profession: (a) How do those without counselor training provide career interventions that address the full range of concerns career counseling clients express? and (b) How is it that professional counselors themselves diminish the role of career interventions in the work they do with their clients when career concerns are so inextricably linked to other life concerns?

We contend that such notions are rooted in ignorance relative to the importance and challenges involved in career counseling. Moreover, we pose these questions at a time when the number of CACREP-accredited career counseling specialty programs is decreasing. Something is awry when an area so central to the history of the counseling profession and so central to life receives such little advocacy from the profession (Heppner et al., 1996; Lindo et al., 2019; Multon et al., 2001). Readers should feel free to read this particular critique as a challenge to the profession to awaken to the fact that the need for counseling-based career interventions is increasing while the commitment within the profession to prepare counselors who can help their clients address these core issues of living is decreasing (Savickas et al., 2011). Thus, we challenge the privileged view that career counseling competencies are basic, simple, and/or irrelevant to any counseling setting.

A partial, and defensive, response to this challenge is that the primary career counseling theories are themselves privileged and have largely been developed by White males for White males. There is no denying this fact. Most career theories were developed between 1950 and 1990. They often ignore crucial issues about prejudice, discrimination, and privilege. More recent theories seek to address these gaps (e.g., the psychology of working theory and hope-action theory).

That the history of career counseling theory is limited in these ways should not provide an excuse for researchers and practitioners to ignore their clients' career concerns and/or minimize the importance of these concerns in their clients' lives. Both researchers and practitioners share a responsibility to fill in the gaps to address the career needs people experience in the 21st century. Career counselors are called to adapt old theories to current contexts when possible; engage in theory innovation; create theories informed by cultural context, cultural relevance, and cultural humility; and develop the skills and knowledge to help their clients address their career challenges effectively. To us, this is a professional ethical obligation.

That being the case, in this chapter we identify key roles and activities of career counselors and the centrality of cultural influences in career development, describe a model that can be used to help clients address their career concerns in the 21st century, and provide an illustrative case example in which this model (hope-action theory; Niles et al., 2011) is applied.

CAREER COUNSELORS' ROLES AND ACTIVITIES

Given the need to innovate and respond to current theoretical inadequacies, what knowledge, skills, and awareness are needed to provide competent career counseling? The knowledge and skills required for providing culturally career counseling encompass and go beyond those required in more general counseling (National Career Development Association, 2003; Spokane, 1991). For example, career counseling competencies include having knowledge and skills in counseling theory; knowledge of career development theory and the skills to apply theories effectively to address diverse client concerns; individual and group counseling skills; individual/group assessment skills that embrace standardized and nonstandardized assessments; possessing a knowledge of unbiased career information/resources and the skills to effectively engage clients in accessing this information; possessing the skills to engage clients in stress-reduction interventions; having the capacity to understand career concerns systemically and to integrate family interventions in the career intervention process when that is appropriate; being able to integrate cognitive behavioral interventions in career counseling when that is necessary; having the capacity to use advanced multicultural counseling skills and a keen awareness of how dominant and personal cultural influences impact the career development experience; being able to develop a deep understanding of ethical/legal issues and how they intertwine with the career intervention process; being able to translate a sensitivity to social power imbalances that impact career options into career practice; having the capacity to use technology, especially social media, effectively in the career intervention process; demonstrating the commitment to developing a high level of self-awareness to understand how one's own assumptions and biases and how they can influence the career intervention process; and having an abiding commitment to cultural competencies and cultural humility, to name just some (Niles & Harris-Bowlsbey, in press).

This partial list of the knowledge, skills, and awareness needed to provide culturally competent career counseling offers a clear counter to those who maintain the view that career intervention is simplistic, solely information-based, and heavily reliant on standardized career assessments.

Essentially, culturally competent career counselors help people consider how they will develop and use their talents as they live their lives (Lee, 1989). It is, however, much more complex than that simple statement suggests. We know, for instance, that people develop and evolve throughout their lifetimes. Their perspectives at one life stage can be very different from their perspectives at another. We each have countless interactions with our environments that shape our understanding of the world and our perceptions of our place within the world. Herr (1997) and Super (1980) noted that the self-concept evolves, making choice and adjustment continuous processes. There are few things that are static in the human development process. Thus, having the capacity to adapt to change and to integrate information acquired as a result of our continuous environmental interactions is crucial for positive career development. Furthermore, we know that the world of work continues to evolve, making the need for choosing and adjusting to the evolutionary changes in work continuous requirements (Niles & Harris-Bowlsby, in press). There is, therefore, no avoiding the need for being vigilant about maintaining self-understanding and occupational awareness. These facts make complacency a major risk factor in the career development process. The natural human tendency for eliminating ambiguity runs counter to this fact. The truth is that we are always on a continuum between knowing and not knowing relative to career certainty (Niles, 2018). A person may have high confidence about their career choice today, but work is not static and, as we have pointed out, neither are people. Ignoring change places the person at peril for experiencing significant career challenges.

These realities point to the need for career counselors to empower their clients to construct meaning out of their unique life experiences and then translate that derived meaning into appropriate occupational and other life-role choices.

Culturally competent career counselors provide interventions that help clients clarify and articulate their self-concepts. These interventions can include formal, standardized assessments as well as informal, nonstandardized assessment activities that actively and creatively engage clients in the career intervention process (Amundson, 2018). Culturally competent career counseling practice also requires counselors to be skilled at developing effective working alliances with clients from various backgrounds (Anderson & Niles, 2000). As is typically the case in counseling intervention, the relationship matters and holds center stage relative to the career counseling process. Thus, a key to effective career counseling is understanding each client.

Clients inherit many perspectives, demands, and expectations from family, friends, community members, and society. It is not uncommon for these to be conflictual. One parent may take the view that their adolescent should do whatever they want. Another may expect the same child to follow in the parent's occupational footsteps, society may take the view that particular occupations are less desirable than others, and friends my apply pressure to attend a particular college or pursue a different career path. When we also consider the fact that work decisions play out within a life context that intertwines with other life roles and responsibilities, the challenging and often stressful nature of career development becomes abundantly clear (Vondracek et al., 1986). Therefore, it should not be surprising that many clients present for career counseling experiencing substantial distress.

Career counseling is further complicated when clients are marginalized. Exclusion from the contextual affordances provided to more privileged people leads many marginalized clients to disengage from school and work. They often and not surprisingly lack hope for the future (Niles et al., 2020). In such instances, counselors and teachers often blame marginalized students for their lack of engagement in school activities and career planning processes. Some people who experience this type of "one-down" discriminatory circumstance created by a racist, sexist, homophobic, heterosexist, and ableist society can rise above and demonstrate remarkable resilience and perseverance. The counseling profession needs to learn more about those who demonstrate these capacities. Often, however, people exposed to discrimination struggle and experience challenges related to self-esteem, self-efficacy, and developing a sense of hope that the future can be more satisfying than the past. Clients coping with such challenges require more assistance in resolving their career dilemmas than a standardized test battery can provide. Given this fact, it is not surprising that career counseling clients describe the support of an effective therapeutic alliance with their career counselors as one of the most helpful aspects of their career counseling experience (Anderson & Niles, 2000).

Further, how clients understand life experiences is critical to how they engage with the career counseling process. Lent et al. (1994) draw connections between exposure to diverse positive experiences and the development of vocational interests. Self-efficacy is a large part of this relationship and factors into the client's anticipation of positive outcomes. People from marginalized backgrounds have less access to opportunities and greater difficulty imagining themselves being successful in various occupations. Limited exposure can cause individuals from underresourced communities to become hemmed in by self-deprecating beliefs. For example, despite a national demand for a larger STEM (science, technology, engineering, and mathematics) workforces, females and minority groups face systemic barriers in their pursuits of STEM careers (Falco, 2017). Unfortunately, underrepresented groups frequently internalize cultural narratives that they are unable, uninterested, or not cut out to be successful in these jobs. Career counselors do the important work of helping their clients see diverse possibilities for themselves and visualize the different ways that their strengths can contribute to their achievement. Skills found to be crucial counseling skills (e.g., establishing rapport, reflective listening, expressing empathic understanding) are also crucial career counseling skills. Moreover, knowledge and skills related to advocacy and social justice become core to career intervention processes.

Working collaboratively and effectively with clients therefore requires career counseling practitioners to possess multicultural competencies at an advanced level (Leong, 1995). This starts with career counselors having a clear understanding of their own biases, assumptions, and perspectives related to work and career development. However, many individuals lack an awareness of how contextual factors (e.g., the dominant culture, culture of origin or orientation) interact with identity development to shape life-role salience (Niles & Harris-Bowlsbey, 2021). Addressing this lack of awareness can begin with an in-depth multigenerational personal history review.

Dominant Culture

Often persons simply inherit patterns related to the values they embed in the life roles that they play. These values are passed on from the dominant or popular culture. Such inheritances can be problematic when they are embedded in beliefs based on gender, race, and other stereotypes. For example, gender bias is a persistent factor that shapes life-role salience, and occupational sex-role stereotyping continues to influence career aspirations, especially for young people. Antiquated and oppressive perceptions of life-role participation place women who have high salience for the worker role at an obvious disadvantage in the workforce. Also, such biased perceptions lead men to limit their opportunities for participating in the home and family roles where their presence is needed and where their absence is harmful. Raising client awareness regarding the influence of the dominant culture on patterns of life-role salience helps clients minimize the influence of racist beliefs and sexist attitudes in their career decision-making.

Culture of Orientation

Discussions related to the influence of the dominant culture on life-role salience can also lead to discussions focusing on how the person's immediate cultural background influences their career development. Exploring how one's culture of orientation influences the values expressed in life roles (e.g., seeking to express self-actualization in work for the individual from an individualistic cultural background or seeking to express cultural identity in work for the individual from a collectivistic background) is also a vital component. When these discussions occur in small groups, they stimulate increased awareness of, and sensitivity to, cultural diversity in career development and can foster a sense of cultural humility.

This type of exploration can also lead to exploring the various cultural prescriptions (e.g., Eurocentric men are expected to be good providers and upwardly mobile in their occupations) that are generally assigned to specific life roles. In these discussions, counselors can encourage clients to identify how they perceive and interpret the role expectations emanating from their cultures of origin and how these expectations influence their career decisions. Special attention can be paid to exploring how these expectations influence the client's understanding of the behaviors required for effective role performance (e.g., men who define their parenting role primarily as being a good provider can consider whether this behavior is sufficient for good parenting).

A family genogram offers one specific activity for discussing these topics (Storlie et al., 2019). Storlie and colleagues found the family genogram to be a useful tool for exploring the interaction between family background and cultural prescriptions in the process of life design. Additionally, a family genogram provides a tool for tracking career decisions across generations and identifying sources of important career beliefs and life themes that people have acquired. These beliefs can be examined as to whether they are facilitating or problematic in career decision-making.

This technique can be expanded to address the same topics for other life roles. That is, by using the genogram, counselors can encourage clients to identify the beliefs and life themes pertaining to specific life roles (e.g., parent, and citizen) that they have acquired from members of their immediate and extended families. Counselors can also use the information provided by clients to contrast the influences on life-role salience emanating from group-oriented cultures with influences from more individualistic cultures. Terms such as *cultural assimilation* and *cultural accommodation* can be introduced in these discussions. The effects of sex-role stereotyping on life-role salience can also be examined in these discussions. The goal of these interventions is to increase client awareness as to the factors influencing their beliefs about the primary roles of life so they can make informed decisions about their future life-role participation.

Many people have little awareness related to the ways that culture influences career choice, goals, and expectations. Culturally competent career counselors cannot ignore this fact. Engaging clients in the exploration of cultural influences (immediate and distal) stimulates deeper awareness regarding career development processes. Culturally competent career counselors integrate this understanding into their career interventions. For instance, clients operating from a collectivistic orientation engage in the career planning process in important ways that differ from clients operating from an individualistic orientation. Working with the client's cultural context is essential to providing culturally sensitive career assistance. The client's cultural context shapes their perceptions of career and should also inform the career intervention process. For example, Conkel-Ziebell et al. (2019) found that anticipation of a racially hostile work climate is negatively related to career decision self-efficacy for urban youths of color. Conkel-Ziebell et al. suggest that for underrepresented youth, career goals must include the development of a plan for addressing racism to be viable. Gibbons et al. (2019) advocate for the development of culturally sensitive career education plans built from an ecological contextual understanding rather than traditional implementation of standard programming. Specifically, they describe how the use of emic values and a strengths-based approach can uniquely meet the needs of rural Appalachian communities as well as those of other underserved groups. Further, Fan and Leong (2016) discuss the unique barriers Chinese immigrants often face when attempting to enter the workforce in Western countries. Lack of culturally normalized interventions, assessments, and Indigenous models of practice creates challenges for clinicians working with Chinese people in these contexts. Gomez et al. (2001) found that Latina career development is strongly influenced by sociopolitical, cultural, contextual, and personal variables. Specifically, factors such as socioeconomic status, family, cultural identity, and the existence of a support network all helped to shape the course of career development for the Latinas participating in the Gomez et al. study. The client's constellation of cultural/contextual variables matters in the career intervention process. Additionally, researchers have been able to demonstrate that an individual's sense of belonging to their ethnic group can also impact the trajectory of their career development. Bounds (2017) found that African American high school students with a stronger sense of ethnic identity demonstrated higher career decision-making self-efficacy and academic self-concept. Thus, similar to general counseling interventions, the career development intervention process is a dynamic, complex, and challenging one that requires career counselors to draw on multicultural counseling skills to effectively help their clients move forward in their career development (and all career counseling is multicultural counseling). Indications are that the career development process will become more, not less, complex soon.

The current work context requires workers to demonstrate an extensive set of skills, behaviors, and attitudes to manage their careers effectively. Among other things, effective career self-management today requires the ability to (a) continuously learn new skills, (b) cope with change and tolerate ambiguity, (c) acquire and use occupational information effectively, (d) interact competently with diverse coworkers, (e) adjust quickly to changing work demands, (f) and use technology effectively (Niles & Harris-Bowlsbey, in press). To help people acquire these competencies, career development interventions must be holistic, comprehensive, and systematic. Moreover, because career development is an essential aspect of human development, career practitioners must be skilled at helping their clients cope with their career concerns within a developmental context. Because children, adolescents, and adults are presented with career development tasks, professional counselors must be skilled at providing career interventions and understanding the career development process, regardless of their work setting (Niles & Pate, 1989).

The need for providing systematic assistance to individuals attempting to deal more effectively with the influence of work in their lives is tremendous. The young, the elderly, the unemployed, the underemployed, the displaced homemaker, the displaced worker, and members of diverse racial, ethnic, and socioeconomic groups are each confronted with work-related issues that have significant implications for their lives. How well they can cope with these issues may well be the difference between living a life that is meaningful and productive and one that is largely void of meaning and satisfaction.

Professional counselors provide career assistance to their clients in several ways. For example, counselors in high school, postsecondary, and community settings can teach clients the types of skills (e.g., self-assessment, job search, and career information acquisition) that are necessary for effective career planning and career decision-making. Professional counselors in all settings can also help their students/clients realize that decisions about work influence one's total life. Correspondingly, counselors can help clients develop realistic expectations for what work can provide in terms of personal satisfaction. When work is lacking in personal satisfaction, meaningful participation in other life roles helps offset this lack of satisfaction. Given the extreme emphasis we place on intra-individual variables in career development, a major task confronting counselors involves helping people realize that self-worth is not defined by one's work situation. Self-worth relates more to how one lives rather than where one works. These are important lessons, especially in traditional Western cultures, that professional counselors in school, postsecondary, and community settings can teach and reinforce in their students/clients.

DEFINITION OF TERMS

Niles and Harris-Bowlsbey (2021) provide useful definitions of essential career-related terms. Having a common language is important because career development interventions are shaped, in part, by how we define key terms (Herr et al., 2004). A major issue within the area of career development interventions is the misuse of terminology among career practitioners as well as clients. For example, it is not uncommon for professional counselors to use the terms *career* and *work* interchangeably. It is also not unusual to hear professionals talk about "doing career development" as if career development were an intervention rather than the object of intervention. Similarly, counselors often confuse terms such as *career guidance* and *career counseling*. This lack of precision confuses practitioners, students, clients, and policy makers and therefore is a barrier to advancing the efficacy of, and legislative support for, career development interventions. When language lacks precision, the implication is that terminology does not matter. Words have power, however, in that career counselors are "engaged in a verbal profession in which words and symbols frequently become the content of the interactions they have with clients" (Herr, 1997, p. 241). Thus, the need exists for greater clarity and specificity about the key terms related to career development interventions. Such specificity enhances the credibility of our profession and provides a common ground for devising, implementing, and evaluating career development interventions. We define key terms in the following sections.

Career

Rather than limiting the definition of career to work, Niles and Harris-Bowlsbey (2021) advocate viewing career as a lifestyle concept. Herr et al. (2004) propose the notion of career as the total constellation of roles played throughout a lifetime. This definition provides more holistic definitions of career. Broader definitions highlight the multiple life roles people play and acknowledge differences across people regarding life-role salience generally and provide flexibility regarding the areas in one's life where work is located. For example, broad definitions of career apply to those locating work in the life role of homemaker or volunteer activities.

Career Development

Career development refers to the lifelong psychological and behavioral processes as well as contextual influences shaping one's career over the life span. As such, career development involves the person's creation of a career pattern, decision-making style, integration of life roles, values expression, and life-role self-concepts (Niles & Harris-Bowlsbey, 2021)

Career Development Interventions

Career development interventions, defined broadly, involve any activities that empower people to cope effectively with career development tasks (Spokane, 1991). For example, activities that help people develop self-awareness, develop occupational awareness, learn decision-making skills, acquire job-search skills, adjust to occupational choices after they have been implemented, and cope with job stress can each be labeled as career development interventions. Specifically, these activities include individual and group career counseling, career development programs, career education, computer-assisted career development programs, and computer information delivery systems, as well as other forms of delivering career information to clients.

Career Counseling

Career counseling involves a formal relationship in which a professional counselor assists a client, or group of clients, to cope more effectively with career concerns (e.g., making a career choice, coping with career transitions, coping with job-related stress or job searching). Typically, career counselors seek to establish rapport with their clients, assess their clients' career concerns, establish goals for the career counseling relationship, intervene in ways that help clients cope more effectively with career concerns, evaluate clients' progress, and, depending on clients' progress, either offer additional interventions or terminate career counseling (Niles & Harris-Bowlsbey, 2021).

CAREER COUNSELING AND SOCIAL JUSTICE

Interestingly, acknowledging the multiple ways in which the societal context artificially limits career development for many people has led commentators to remind career theorists and practitioners of the importance of addressing social justice in career development interventions in the 21st century (Niles & Harris-Bowlsbey, 2021), although the reality is that striving for social justice through career interventions commenced with the work of Frank Parsons and his outreach to immigrant populations in Boston the nature of social justice within career interventions has evolved significantly since the early 1900s. Herr and Niles (1998) noted that over the years career counseling and assessment have become "sociopolitical instruments, identified by legislation at the federal level, to deal with emerging social concerns such as equity and excellence in educational and occupational opportunities, unemployment, human capital development, persons with disabilities, child abuse, AIDS, teenage pregnancy, and substance abuse" (p. 121). As such, the use of career interventions to address social justice concerns rests largely on the work of advocacy groups who apply pressure to policy makers to provide funding and opportunities for career services provision—especially to marginalized populations.

In addition to the career counseling competencies mentioned previously, culturally competent career counselors engaged in social action use community resources to provide clients access to information and opportunities (e.g., employment offices, "one-stop career shops," support groups). Career counselors engaging in social action play the role of facilitator by providing information, referrals, and encouragement to clients. Having a thorough knowledge of community resources also allows career counselors to identify gaps in career services. In these instances, counselors once again take on a strong advocacy role and seek to rectify service deficiencies in their communities.

Advocacy is also important when clients' career concerns are the result of external factors such as large-scale downsizing, wage stagnation, and salary inequities experienced by women, persons of color, and persons with disabilities. More often than many care to acknowledge, workers struggle to earn a living. On average, women are paid $.79 for every $1.00 men are paid (U.S. Bureau of Labor Statistics, 2019). As a group, full-time, year-round workers with a disability earn 87 cents for every dollar earned by those with no disability (U.S. Census Bureau, 2019). African American workers have made no progress in closing earnings gaps with White men since 2000. In each of these instances, career counselors concerned with social action address not only the career concerns of individual clients but also the political aspects of career and pay inequities. This is accomplished by integrating individual career counseling skills with community counseling skills. Community career counseling builds on the strength of individual career counseling and offers assistance to people in their struggle to maintain their communities as they create opportunities for career development and strive for equity in their earnings.

CREATING AND SUSTAINING HOPE IN CAREER DEVELOPMENT

For many, especially those experiencing marginalization and discrimination, having a sense of hope for the future is difficult. Yet, without hope, it is unreasonable to expect individuals to construct career plans and/or engage constructively in the educational process. Thus, the need for helping clients be hopeful is substantial. Essentially, career counselors who instill hope in their clients and empower them to manage their careers are multiculturally competent, act as facilitators of information and referrals, advocate for their clients when employment practices and community traditions stand in the way of equity in the workplace, and integrate individual career counseling skills with community counseling skills to assist people in their struggle to maintain their communities and create opportunities for career development.

Hope-action theory (Amundson et al., 2018; Niles et al., 2011; Yoon, 2015) provides an example of recent career theory that acknowledges basic and essential 21st-century career development facts. Niles and Harris-Bowelsby (2021) identified these facts as the following:

1. Constant environmental interactions continually influence self-clarity and our perceptions of career possibilities.
2. Without intentional self-reflection, it is difficult to understand the implications our environmental interactions have relative to our emerging self-clarity.
3. When there is intentional and regular engagement in self-reflection, the individual is better positioned for developing the level of self-clarity necessary for creating a vision of one's potential future.
4. Goals and plans should emerge from consideration of future possibilities emerging from self-clarity that is grounded in self-reflection.

5. Implementing goals and plans requires a leap of faith because there is always a gap between what we think any particular career option will be like and what any particular career option is actually like.

6. Due to the gaps between what we know and what is relative to a career option, adapting is a crucial step in the career development process.

7. Adapting involves the capacity to learn from your actions and use that learning to inform your subsequent career choices (e.g., What do I know now about this option and myself that I didn't know before I implemented this choice? How does this new learning inform my sense of whether this is an appropriate career choice? How does what I have learned from implementing my career choice shape my sense of who I am and what I need relative to my career choice?).

8. Hope emerges from having clear and meaningful goals, pathways for achieving your goals, the motivation to take the steps necessary to achieve your goals, and the confidence that if you take those steps you will be able to use the information you have acquired about yourself and your world to inform your subsequent goals.

These career development facts represent the essential components of hope-action theory (Niles et al., 2010). Hope-action theory (HAT) is an innovative, adaptive, hope-centered framework for effectively identifying and navigating career challenges across the life span. Grounded in the work of Bandura (2001), Hall (1996), and Snyder (2002), the HAT framework outlines important attitudes and behaviors for constructing careers with hope (Niles et al., 2011). Specifically, HAT attitudes and behaviors include (a) hope, (b) self-reflection, (c) self-clarity, (d) visioning, (e) goal-setting/planning, and (f) implementing/adapting (Niles et al., 2011). The robust nature of the HAT framework has been demonstrated in its use with recent immigrants to Saskatchewan, Syrian refugees, unemployed adults, adults with disabilities in Italy, human resource professionals in China, long-term unemployed adults in British Columbia, and others (e.g., Yoon, Amundson, & Niles, in press; Yoon, Bailey et al., in press)

Hope empowers one to consider the possibilities within a situation and propels them toward enacting change (Niles et al., 2011). When one demonstrates the capacity to create meaningful goals and the belief that specific actions will result in positive outcomes, hope emerges. Hopeful, goal-oriented thinking requires an individual to have the ability to identify steps toward achieving the goal, be confident those steps are feasible, and desire the outcome. When confronted with obstacles to goal achievement, a person with hope remains adaptable and evolves with the constant change experienced. Adaptable individuals adjust and advance when confronted with obstacles. Rather than simply giving up, hope provides the strength people need to make adaptations and implement the change needed to reach their goals.

The capacity to explore one's feelings, thoughts, behaviors, beliefs, and circumstances through a process of self-reflection is crucial. This willingness to question and examine ongoing experiences leads an individual to consider larger questions related to their purpose and meaning in life. Regular self-reflection encourages self-clarity and provides a solid foundation of understanding related to one's evolving self-concept, thus increasing the likelihood new information will be considered in decision-making (Niles et al., 2011). Asking questions of oneself encourages reflection; answering those questions leads to self-clarity. Empowered by a sense of hope, skillful self-reflection, and a reasonably developed sense of self-clarity positions one to create a hopeful personal vision of the future (Niles et al., 2014).

Hope provides the ability to engage in possibility thinking. Brainstorming conceivable future possibilities (visioning) focuses on generating a quantity of ideas over quality of ideas (Clarke et al., 2018; Niles et al., 2011; Yoon, Bailey et al., in press). When a sufficient and diverse list of options are developed through visioning, then one begins using their recently formed self-clarity to identify those options that are most desirable. Exploration of those most desirable options allows for additional information-gathering and exploration to determine the feasibility of the options. Specific goals are selected and strategies to achieve the goals are identified. Once this has occurred, goal implementation begins. Professional counselors working with clients who are implementing their goals often provide "support, encouragement, and guidance" (Niles et al., 2011, p. 175). As clients work toward achieving goals, new information is gathered. Reflecting on this information will lead to additional self-clarity, which will help inform subsequent goals. The willingness to revise previously set goals requires personal adaptability. As one adapts to changes, they must also work to maintain self-clarity. Throughout this process, the clinician must monitor the client's level of hope. The degree to which the client has hope for managing each of these tasks successfully is imperative to positive forward momentum (Niles et al., 2011).

The Hope Action Inventory (HAI; Niles et al., 2010) is used to assess a person's degree of hope as it relates to the hope-action competencies. The HAI specifically measures the six hope-centered competencies of hope, self-reflection, self-clarity, visioning, goal-setting and planning, and implementing and adapting. The HAI can be used with adults aged 18 years and older. The HAI is a 28-item measure with response options based on a four-point Likert scale (1 = *definitely false* to 4 = *definitely true*).

A HOPE-ACTION THEORY CASE STUDY: JASON

Jason was a 39-year-old African American man with a college degree in management when he presented for career counseling. He and his family lived in a large city in the northeastern United States. His son was 2 years old, and his partner was a middle school teacher. Jason had recently worked as a human resource manager in an IT company that had about 500 employees. Before moving to that company, he had worked in human resources for three Fortune 500 companies for 14 years. Jason had diverse experience in HR planning, compensation and benefit, recruiting, and staffing. Although he had a broad range of experience in HR, he never felt he was an expert. He had recently lost his job at his last company during company downsizing. Reflecting on his career at the time, he reported he was not satisfied with his previous jobs and that he just tried to do what he was told to do. He often felt anger and resentment due to the discrimination he observed and experienced in his last position. Jason had developed rather significant expertise in the areas of diversity, equity, and inclusion. At first, his supervisor supported this. At time went on, however, his supervisor seemed less eager for Jason to do work in these areas. When he tried to advocate for employees, his supervisors were not supportive. This lack of support was demoralizing and also contributed to Jason's job dissatisfaction.

Jason was seeking a new job that could provide him with long-term employment and greater satisfaction, especially in the area of diversity, equity, and inclusion. He was unsure about how to proceed, however. He reported feeling very anxious, staying up late each night watching TV and not sleeping well. Jason noted that sustainable employment was very important to him because his son was very young and Jason felt immense pressure to support his family. Also, the cost of living was high in the city where he lived, and his wife's salary was not enough to support the family and allow them to save money for his son's education. Last but not least Jason wanted to work in an environment that supports opportunity for all workers and where discrimination at any level is not tolerated.

Jason decided to meet with a career counselor and agreed to take the HAI to assess his career competencies. (His results are listed in Table 10.1.) Jason's career counselor used HAT to explore Jason's degree of hope-action competencies. Immediately, the counselor was drawn to Jason's HAI score. This score indicated he needs some assistance generating a sense of hope. Jason's career counselor decided to start with a goal he was fairly confident Jason could achieve. When they explored the possibilities, Jason expressed the need to feel more relaxed and developing a greater understanding of what was important to him. Jason noted he had always wanted to learn meditation but had never taken the time to do so. Thus, learning meditation became his initial goal in career counseling. When Jason and his counselor discussed this goal, Jason indicated that learning meditation was something he thought he could do and something he would do (two requirements for a hope-action goal). Jason's career counselor began by teaching Jason some basic breathing and visualization techniques. This provided Jason with a beginning sense of relaxed control over his emotions as he considered his career transition. Jason also expressed a desire for greater clarity regarding his core values and wondered how they might connect to career options. Because he was already engaged in self-reflection (as evidenced by his self-reflection score of 3.75), Jason's career counselor recommended that he keep a journal in which he recorded thoughts regarding what was important to him. Also, Jason's career counselor took him through a Sophie's choice values sort activity (Niles & Harris-Bowlsbey, 2017). Jason's top values were good health, a good family relationship, helping others, and living in a world free of discrimination.

Table 10.1   Jason's HAI Results

	SUBSCALE	YOUR SCORE	GROUP 25%	GROUP 75%	MAX SCORE
1	Hope	2.50	3.00	3.50	4.00
2	Self-reflection	3.75	3.00	3.25	4.00
3	Self-clarity	2.50	3.00	3.25	4.00
4	Visioning	3.25	3.00	3.25	4.00
5	Goal-setting and planning	3.00	2.75	3.00	4.00
6	Implementing	3.50	3.00	3.25	4.00
7	Adapting	2.75	3.00	3.25	4.00
Overall		3.04	3.00	3.29	4.00

* 4 = definitely true, 3 = somewhat true, 2 = somewhat false, 1 = definitely false

To provide clarity in Jason's worldview and better understand the nature in which his values have been shaped by his background, his counselor asked him to complete a family career genogram and then asked specific questions about family values. Through this activity, Jason discovered his life-long focus on structure came from his father who was a construction manager and constantly stressed following directions when Jason was growing up. Through discussing his family history, Jason realized he always hoped to promote more creativity and flexibility in his household but didn't feel that he was setting that type of example for his young son. This activity caused Jason to reflect on the ways that he's pursued his interests in the past. He remarked how through most of his career he had worked hard at whatever was asked of him because he felt that was what was necessary to get the next promotion. Discussing his genogram also boosted Jason's sense of self-clarity by helping him distinguish and balance his values with those that come from his family of origin.

To further explore self-clarity, Jason was directed to complete an online interest self-assessment on the U.S. Department of Labor website. The results of his assessment described his personality type as enterprising and conventional according to Holland's codes. Several occupations that matched Jason's personality code were particularly interesting to him. Among these were travel agent, human resource consultant, and higher education administrator. Jason and his counselor discussed the different tasks, levels of training required, skills, and work environments associated with several positions from the website. They also reviewed these occupations in light of Jason's expressed values. Jason's counselor helped him identify occupations that could combine his interests and values. Jason ultimately decided he would be able to best encapsulate his values, skills, and interests in human resource consultation working within an organization that valued diversity. Jason further clarified that his attention to detail and his creative nature could help him be successful in solving corporate problems without the restrictions and regimentation common in corporate environments. Jason's counselor reminded him of his years of experience in large companies and the wealth of information he had amassed as a result. Uplifted by a sense of direction, Jason revealed he had envisioned the possibility of opening his own consulting firm in the past but was never confident enough because he didn't "feel like an expert." Entries from Jason's journal were consistent with this goal, however. On at least three occasions, he had written about being able to "break out of a box" and "be his own boss" with the freedom to prioritize social justice in his work. Jason's career counselor reminded him that the step of visioning in HAT emphasizes possibilities, not probabilities. When putting the probability of "success" aside, Jason remained enthusiastic about starting his own firm.

When talking with his counselor about this possibility further, Jason expressed anxiety about potentially starting his own business with a young child at home. He had a clear idea of how his own consulting firm would operate and even had extant relationships with a couple of potential clients. Moreover, Jason shared that he had always been a good planner and had demonstrated the skill of being able to identify specific steps he would have to take to accomplish a goal—in this case getting a business off the ground, but he worried about failing and not being able to support his family. Looking back at his HAI results, Jason's counselor pointed out his relatively high scores in visioning and implementing. Together, they recounted instances in Jason's life where he demonstrated both skills associated with developing an idea and seeing it through. Jason recalled a particularly challenging experience that involved a major overhaul of his company's training and hiring systems. He led a team that oversaw the design and implementation of new company-wide systems that incorporated new policies, requirements, and computer software systems. He described feeling confident while working on that project and receiving lots of positive feedback at the end of the process.

With help from his counselor, Jason identified several other major accomplishments he achieved in his corporate experiences and began to feel more confident in his knowledge and skill base. He reported seeing his dream of starting a business as an avenue for self-expression and a good use of his insights and experience. Finding a career path where he could exercise more of his skills gave Jason an increased sense of hope. He was excited about moving toward an occupation that utilized more of his values, interests, and abilities and one that he thought would help him feel less like a cog in a machine. Jason reported a stronger sense of clarity, deciding to focus on what excited him rather than allow extrinsic motivators and fear to drive his decision-making. With an increased sense of identity and his skills and knowledge, he felt hopeful about his options and began to create his plan. He reported enjoying using the HAI and thought it was helpful in focusing his work in career counseling.

SUMMARY, INSIGHTS, AND ACTIONS

Careers are person-specific and created by the choices we make throughout our lives. Careers emerge from the constant interplay between the person and the environment. They are influenced by distal and proximal cultural influences as well as genetic propensities and contextual affordances. Careers are the manifestations of our attempts at making sense out of our lived experiences as we evolve and as the world of work continues to change. Teaching clients a theory they can use throughout their lifetimes to manage these processes and maintain a sense of hope is essential in the 21st century. Hope-action theory delineates competencies that are central to these processes. Finally, regardless of which theoretical perspectives career counselors draw on, they have an ethical obligation to be prepared to help their clients cope with their career challenges. All clients experience such challenges and managing them effectively is crucial to experiencing a life that is purposeful and meaningful.

REFLECTION AND DISCUSSION QUESTIONS

1. What are the six elements of effective career self-management?
2. Name three strategies for exploring clients' culture of orientation. How might you utilize these strategies to understand the ways culture influences a client's career choice, goals, and expectations?
3. Define the following: career, career development, career development interventions, career counseling.
4. In what ways do culturally competent career counselors engage in social action?
5. What are the eight essential facts of career development as identified by Niles and Harris-Bowlsbey?

6. List the essential components of hope-action theory.
7. Imagine you are working with a client who has experienced significant marginalization and systemic oppression. How might you utilize the hope-action theoretical approach to instill hope and support positive outcomes for your client?

REFERENCES

Amundson, N. E. (2018). *Active engagement* (2nd ed.). Ergon.

Amundson, N. E., Goddard, T., Yoon, H. J., & Niles, S. G. (2018). Hope-centered interventions with unemployed clients. *Canadian Journal of Career Development, 17*(2), 87–98.

Anderson, W. P., & Niles, S. G. (1995). Career and personal concerns expressed by career counseling clients. *Career Development Quarterly, 43*(3), 240–245.

Anderson, W. P., Jr., & Niles, S. G. (2000). Important events in career counseling: Client and counselor descriptions. *Career Development Quarterly, 48*(3), 251–263.

Bounds, P. S. (2017). Contextual factors related to African American adolescent career development. *Career Development Quarterly, 65*(2), 131–144.

Clarke, A., Amundson, N. E., Niles, S. G., & Yoon, H. J. (2018). Hope: An agent of change for internationally educated professionals. *Journal of Employment Counseling* (4), *55*, 155–165.

Conkel-Ziebell, J. L., Gushue, G. V., & Turner, S. L. (2019). Anticipation of racism and sexism: Factors related to setting career goals for urban youth of color. *Journal of Counseling Psychology, 66*(5), 588–599.

Day, J.C. & Taylor, D. (2019). *In most occupations, workers with or without disabilities earn about the same.* U.S. Census Bureau. https://www.census.gov/library/stories/2019/03/do-people-with-disabilities-earn-equal-pay.html.

Falco, L. D. (2017). The school counselor and STEM career development. *Journal of Career Development, 44*(4), 359–374.

Fan, W., & Leong, F. T. L. (2016). Introduction to the special issue: Career development and intervention in Chinese contexts. *Career Development Quarterly, 64*(3), 192–202.

Gibbons, M. M., Brown, E. C., Daniels, S., Rosecrance, P., Hardin, E. E., & Farrell, I. (2019). Building on strengths while addressing barriers: Career interventions in rural Appalachian communities. *Journal of Career Development, 46*(6), 637–650.

Gibbons, M. M., Hughes, A., & Woodside, M. (2015). Exploring the influence of culture on career through the Career-in-Culture interview. *Adultspan, 14*(2), 77–89.

Gomez, M.J., Fassinger, R., Prosser, J., Cooke, K., Mejia, B., & Luna, J. (2001). Voces abriendo caminos (voice forging paths): A qualitative study of the career development of notable Latinas. *Journal of Counseling Psychology, 48* (3), 286–300.

Heppner, M. J., O'Brien, K. M., Hinkelman, J. M., & Flores, L. Y. (1996). Training counseling psychologists in career development: Are we our own worst enemies? *The Counseling Psychologist, 24*(1), 105–125.

Herr, E. L. (1997). Super's life-span, life-space approach and its outlook for refinement. *Career Development Quarterly, 45*(3), 238–246.

Herr, E. L., Cramer, S. H., & Niles, S. G. (2004). *Career guidance and counseling through the lifespan: Systemic approaches* (6th ed.). Allyn & Bacon.

Lee, C. C. (1989). Needed: A career development advocate. *Career Development Quarterly, 37*(3), 218–220.

Lent, R. W., Brown, S. D., Hackett, G. (1994). Toward a unifying social cognitive theory of career and academic interest, choice, and performance. *Journal of Vocational Behavior, 45*(1), 79–122.

Leong, F.T.L. (1995). *Career Development and Vocational Behavior of Racial and Ethnic Minorities.* Routledge.

Lindo, N. A, Ceballos, P., Blalock, S., Conner, C., Edwards, J., Spellings, M., Webster, L., & Opiala, K. (2019). Student perceptions of career counseling: an examination of a graduate curriculum in the United States. *British Journal of Guidance & Counselling, 48*(6), 803–814. https://doi.org/10.1080/03069885.2019.1679350

Multon, K. D., Heppner, M. J., Gysbers, N. C., Zook, C., & Ellis-Katton, C. A. (2001). Client psychological distress: An important factor in career counseling. *Career Development Quarterly, 49*(4), 324–335.

National Career Development Association. (2003). *Career counseling competencies.* Author.

Niles, S. G. (2018, January). *Reclaiming your soul from work* [Keynote speech, Cannexus Conference, Ottawa, Canada].

Niles, S. G., Amundson, N. E., & Yoon, H. J. (2010). *Hope-action inventory.* Hope Centered Career.

Niles, S. G., & Anderson, W. P. (1993). Career development and adjustment: The relation between concerns and stress. *Journal of Employment Counseling, 30*(2), 79–87.

Niles, S. G., & Harris-Bowlsbey, J. (2021). *Career development interventions* (6th ed.). Pearson.

Niles, S. G., & Harris-Bowlsbey, J. (2017). *Career development interventions* (5th ed.). Pearson.

Niles, S. G., In, H., & Amundson, N. (2014). Using an action-oriented hope-centered model of career development. *Journal of Asia Pacific Counseling, 4*(1), 1–13.

Niles, S.G., Amundson, N.E., Neault, R. A., Yoon, H.J. (2020). Career recovery: Creating hopeful careers in difficult times. Cognella Press.

Niles, S. G., & Pate, P. H., Jr. (1989). Competency and training issues related to the integration of career counseling and mental health counseling. *Journal of Career Development, 16*(1), 63–71.

Niles, S. G., Yoon, H., Balin, E., & Amundson, N. E. (2010). Using a hope-centered model of career development in challenging times. *Turkish Psychological Counseling and Guidance Journal, 4*(34), 101–108.

Savickas, M. L., Pope, M., & Niles, S. G. (2011). The Career Development Quarterly: A centennial retrospective. *The Career Development Quarterly, 59*(6), 528–538.

Spokane, A. R. (1991). *Career interventions.* Prentice Hall.

Storlie, C. A., Hilton, T. M. L., McKinney, R., & Unger, D. (2019). Family career genograms: Beginning life designs with exploratory students. *The Family Journal: Counseling and Therapy for Couples and Families, 27*(1), 84–91.

Super, D. E. (1980). A life-span, life-space approach to career development. *Journal of Vocational Behavior, 16*(3), 282–298.

U.S. Bureau of Labor Statistics (2019, March 22). *Women had higher median earnings than men in relatively few occupations in 2018.* https://www.bls.gov/opub/ted/2019/women-had-higher-median-earnings-than-men-in-relatively-few-occupations-in-2018.htm

Vondracek, F. W., Lerner, R. M., & Schulenberg, J. E. (1986). *Career development: A life-span developmental approach.* Erlbaum.

Yoon, H. J., Bailey, N., Amundson, N., & Niles, S. (2018). The effect of a career development program based on the hope-action theory: Hope to work for refugees in British Columbia. *British Journal of Guidance and Counselling 47* (1), 6–19. https://doi.org/10.1080/03069885.2018.1544827.

Yoon, H. J., In, H., Niles, S.G., Amundson, N.E., Smith, B.A. & Mills, L. (2015). The effects of hope on student engagement, academic performance, and vocational identity. *Canadian Journal of Career Development, 14*(1), 34–45.

CHAPTER 11

INTRODUCTION TO CRISIS, TRAUMA, AND DISASTER MENTAL HEALTH COUNSELING

Cirecie A. West-Olatunji, Xavier University of Louisiana

Kalesha Jenkins, University of Cincinnati

LEARNING OBJECTIVES

1. Understand the trauma/disaster intervention models, with a focus on reactions and symptoms and provide additional resources.
2. Learn the cultural considerations necessary for examining our own attitudes and biases about diverse traumatic responses and reactions among diverse clients.
3. Learn the assessment tools available for PTSD, complex and simple trauma, traumatic stress, and historical trauma for children, adolescents, and adults.
4. Learn evidence-based interventions when working with culturally diverse clients who have experienced direct, vicarious, or historical trauma.

LEARNING OUTCOMES

1. Examine your worldview of how crisis and trauma influence cultural responses as well as therapeutic interventions.
2. Enhance your ability to conceptualize clinical cases involving culturally diverse clients, particularly those who have experienced interpersonal or mass violence, sexual or historical trauma, grief and loss, and human-made or natural disasters.
3. Better position yourself to develop rapport with culturally diverse clients and establish more authentic relationships with reduced bias about culturally and socially marginalized clients, particularly those evidencing trauma symptoms.
4. Articulate and apply culturally sensitive practices with individuals facing traumatic experiences.

CASE ILLUSTRATION: ANTOINETTE

Antoinette is a 38-year-old African American high school English teacher from New Orleans, Louisiana. Her family has lived in the Lower Ninth Ward for three generations, since the early 1900s. Antoinette's husband, also African American, works in the construction field. Antoinette and her husband are homeowners with two daughters, ages 14 and 10. The family evacuated New Orleans just prior to onset of Hurricane Katrina. Following the disaster, they resided in Houston, Texas for 9 months where Antoinette and her husband were able to find comparable work and send their children to school.

Upon returning to New Orleans and learning that their home was significantly damaged, they secured a FEMA trailer as temporary housing while they attempted to rebuild their home. Antoinette was able to secure a job at a public secondary school teaching English, and her husband found plenty of work due to the need for construction. In session, Antoinette noted that her husband's career also gives them access to resources for rebuilding and thus accelerates their pace of renovations compared to that of other homeowners who have returned to the city. Antoinette's family members, many of whom used to live in her neighborhood, have not returned to New Orleans. She reports that some of her neighbors have come back, including the pastor of her church who has started impromptu services in his front yard beside his own FEMA trailer. Due to reports of frequent headaches and disrupted sleep patterns, Antoinette sought counseling services. She states that she wakes up sometimes with nightmares about flood waters seeping underneath her bedroom door or into her children's room. Using resilience theory, the clinician assessed for relevant risk factors and facilitated the use of culture-centered protective factors. Notably, with an awareness of Antoinette's background, it is critical to assess for multiple layers of traumatic stress.

CRISIS, TRAUMA, AND DISASTER MENTAL HEALTH COUNSELING

In this chapter we will provide an overview of crisis, trauma, and disaster mental health intervention models to help provide a foundation for further discussion on the key elements of service provision. A necessary aspect of providing competent care for trauma-affected clients is multicultural competence. Thus, it is imperative we offer an overview of the cultural considerations in trauma-informed care by focusing on historical trauma experienced by members of culturally and socially marginalized groups. In addition, we provide an overview of useful assessments to aid in conceptualizing clients' needs. Finally, we introduce evidence-based practices for conceptualizing, assessing, intervening, and evaluating clinical activity with individuals, groups, and organizations.

Crisis, Trauma, and Disaster Mental Health Theories

Paramount in service delivery is professional counselors' role in expediently and effectively facilitating clients' recovery and return to normal day-to-day life. In this section, we begin with definitions of the three key concepts: crisis, trauma, and disaster mental health counseling. Following the key concepts discussion, we provide an exposition of the goals and mission of crisis, trauma, and disaster mental health counseling with a focus on (a) the various types of individuals most affected, (b) the most vulnerable populations, (c) best practices for interventions, and (d) key issues professional counselors face. Most importantly, we share three models that serve as frameworks for disaster mental health service delivery. Finally, we outline the limitations of crisis and trauma counseling practices in an ethical context.

Definitions

Although there is some commonality in definition, the terms *crisis*, *trauma*, and *disaster* all have distinct definitions. A *crisis* has two main considerations: First, it must connote a critical juncture that causes instability, and second it must task the individual beyond their normal coping capacity (Halpern & Tramontin, 2007). Trauma has typically been defined as a direct personal experience in which an individual feels threatened or witnesses an event involving danger, threat, violence, or other serious harm (Briere & Scott, 2013). A *disaster* is a sudden event, such as a natural occurrence or an uncontrollable accident, that causes significant damage and/or near-death experience. Although disasters are not planned, emotional and psychological reactions to the disaster can be expected. And, as disasters can affect anyone at any given time in one's life, providing disaster mental health workers with developmentally appropriate protocols for evaluating disaster reactions is imperative. Of note, it is necessary to critically evaluate distress related to the disaster because often times the reactions do not have a lasting effect. Counselors should remember that people are resilient, and they can recover from adversity if immediate distress is treated appropriately (Shelby & Tredinnick, 1995).

Goals and Roles

The goals of crisis, trauma, and disaster mental health counseling are to (a) provide relief to affected individuals and communities, (b) assist in the recovery of individuals and communities, (c) conduct triage in identifying vulnerable populations, and (d) collaborate with other professionals in defining effective disaster response interventions and preparation. Clinical practice involves providing service in chaotic environments, offering short-term interventions, focusing on pragmatic concerns, being "flexible, mobile and responsive," assessing for trauma responses, and conducting triage (West-Olatunji et al., 2014, p. 50). It should be noted that counselors and other mental health workers experience secondary trauma when treating trauma-affected individuals. This form of secondary trauma has been termed *compassion fatigue* and can be defined as a function of bearing witness to the suffering of others and an occupational hazard of psychological work with trauma survivors (Figley, 2002). This can result in counselors experiencing reduced empathy and associated emotional and behavioral issues. Personal prevention strategies focus on exercising, engaging in meditation, stretching, and drinking water frequently. Professional strategies emphasize developing peer support, scheduled debriefings, having mental health days to recuperate, and engaging in open discussion about the stressors while providing service.

Models

Several models are available for counselors who provide crisis, trauma, or disaster mental health service delivery. Most notable are psychological first aid (PFA) and critical incident stress debriefing (CISD). However, an emerging model, culture-centered disaster mental health counseling (CDMHC), provides culturally responsive tools for aiding trauma-affected clients. PFA is an evidence-based approach employed in disaster response to aid those impacted in the hours and early days following a crisis or disaster (Uhernik & Husson, 2009). PFA primarily includes developing contact and engaging with victims and survivors, establishing safety and stabilization, gathering information, identifying social supports, providing information about coping, and referring to collaborative services (U.S. Department of Veterans Affairs, 2016).

Critical incident stress debriefing (CISD) interventions are also useful immediately following a disaster (Pender, & Anderton, 2015) and involves a multi-intervention approach for crisis stabilization. One approach of the CISD model is the seven-step Mitchell model (Mitchell, 2009) that involves introduction; fact gathering; the exploration of thoughts and then emotions, symptoms and reactions; normalizing through teaching about stress reactions; summarizing; handouts; and follow-up. However, over the last decade, counselors have sought to explore alternative paradigms for disaster mental health service delivery that incorporate a more humanistic philosophy.

One emergent model of disaster mental health service delivery is the culture-centered model that expanded the psychosocial approach (Miller & Rasmussen, 2010) that focused attention on the mediating contribution of daily stressors. The culture-centered disaster mental health counseling (CDMHC) model relies on community stakeholders to serve as self-actualization agents for their communities (West-Olatunji et al., 2014; West-Olatunji & Yoon, 2013). Such an approach is grounded in the needs of the affected community. Culture-centered interventions are inherently developed by community members and provide expedient services to affected individuals, families, and communities.

Limitations

There are some limitations to providing crisis, trauma, and disaster mental health counseling. First, disasters can serve as triggers for counselors' prior traumatic experiences. Additionally, compassion fatigue can occur without proper self-care. Both of these concerns can compromise counselors' ability to provide effective clinical services. Also, the lack of appropriate interdisciplinary team skills can sometimes aggravate clients' emotional and psychological dispositions. Finally, altruism without proper disaster training can exacerbate client symptoms. Ethical concerns go beyond general standards of service delivery. Counselors should be aware of their preconceived notions about the individuals, families, and communities they serve following a crisis, traumatic event, or disaster. Additionally, counselors need to acquire community engagement skills in order to effectively partner with community stakeholders. This allows for sustainability of interventions and expedites recovery.

Reactions/Signs and Symptoms

After the individual is safe from immediate harm and danger, there are various physiological, cognitive, and emotional reactions to the disaster. Common physiological and emotional responses to crises, trauma, and disasters are reactions to the perceived danger and function as a control center to the acute stress. Common physiological reactions to acute stress often stem from a series of autonomic nervous system responses that trigger the sympathetic and parasympathetic nervous systems. These physiological responses produce energy triggers within the brain that creates fight-or-flight processing located in the amygdala, hypothalamus, and cerebral cortex (Briere & Scott, 2013). As the brain responds to the burst of energy, the emotional and cognitive processing takes over and continues to respond to the perceived danger.

Common emotional responses to danger are anger, sadness, anxiety, and numbness (Graham, 2010; Shelby & Tredinnick, 1995). Common cognitive responses to stress are both voluntary and involuntary (Connor-Smith et al., 2000). Voluntary cognitive efforts can be described as one's attempt to regulate behavioral, cognitive, emotional, and physiological responses. Involuntary responses include conditioned reactions that an individual may or may not be consciously aware of, such as intrusive thoughts or rumination and emotional numbing. Even when immediate danger has been eliminated, these emotional and cognitive responses can often last for a significant period of time. After an extended period of time, survivors of disasters may exhibit symptomology related to DSM-5 anxiety disorders, chronic stress, and posttraumatic stress disorders (Graham, 2010).

Though understanding and addressing the acute stress symptomatology can assist in crisis and disaster exchanges, using culturally appropriate interventions is necessary for emphasizing self-preservation and resiliency within the individual and community (Goodman & West-Olatunji, 2008). Counselors must pay close attention to the cultural beliefs, values, and traditions of individuals affected by trauma (West-Olatunji & Goodman, 2011).

A multicultural lens is imperative when evaluating an individual's response to the disaster (Mattar, 2010). Culture is intertwined in an individual's cognitive and emotional responses. Cultural considerations such as race, gender, and community must be taken into account when evaluating such reactions. For example, cognitive and emotional reactions can be intersected with oppression in disenfranchised communities, creating multilayer distress responses (West-Olatunji & Goodman, 2011).

SUMMARY, INSIGHTS, AND ACTIONS

Cultural Considerations

Recognizing and understanding how culture influences every aspect of human nature can assist counselors working with individuals suffering from trauma-related distresses. Culture not only provides a foundation for how we think, act, and understand the world, culture distributes how power and privilege are reconciled in everyday behavior. Traumatic responses are intertwined with other ecosystemic factors that compound behavioral, cognitive, and emotional expressions (Goodman & West-Olatunji, 2010). The systemic and immediate structures in which individuals reside provide both protective and hindering factors, influencing how an individual expresses trauma. Counselors must consider the systemic, collective, and individual effects to become culturally informed about trauma-related distresses (Marsella & Christopher, 2004). For example, women suffering from intimate partner violence may have been socialized to not discuss these kinds of incidents outside the household. Thus, how clients express these events to their counselor and how they process these experiences are laden with cultural values. Subtle facial expressions and physiological manifestations may not always be easily identified, yet they may be critical cultural components when assisting with trauma-related treatment and alleviating distress.

Equally important, culturally competent counselors must develop a heightened level of awareness about their own biases. In particular, culturally competent counselors need to consider their social positioning or positionality when working with diverse clients. Without this self-awareness, they can further exacerbate clients' distress. A culture-centered framework for conceptualizing trauma-related concerns enhances clinical effectiveness (Wynn & West-Olatunji, 2008).

Trauma and Oppression

Micro- and macroaggressions continue to impact the mental well-being of members of marginalized groups in the United States. First termed by African American counseling psychologist Dr. Chester Pierce (1970), the concept of *microaggressions* connotes the subtle, covert often daily acts of racism that plague people of color regardless of socio-economic status. Sue and colleagues (2007) expanded on the concept of microaggressions to include any marginalized group, referring to the conscious and unconscious slights and underhanded messages that (a) reinforce stereotypes and (b) enhance cognitive dissonance among targeted victims. Macroaggressions are overt acts by members of privileged groups intended to distract and create distress among individuals of marginalized communities. Macroaggressions can be targeted hate crimes and other outright acts against historically marginalized groups that perpetuate the status quo, resulting in poor mental health, including low self-esteem and compromised self-actualization (Kira et al., 2013). Both micro- and macroaggressions can be viewed as immediate encounters that create physiological and psychological stress responses for victims. These types of encounters can lead to chronic or traumatic stress.

Traumatic stress can be evident among marginalized individuals acutely (micro- and macroaggressions), generationally (slavery) or systemically (police shootings). Traumatic stress can afflict mental anguish among marginalized groups with fear and wound them with emotional and psychological distress. Moreover, the impact of traumatic stress influences every aspect of these individuals' lives and can lead to overarching negative reactions in their environment. When individuals are tormented with the mental burdens of trauma and oppression across multiple generations, the impact can often be vast and life encompassing. Individuals suffering at the hands of institutional racism and historical trauma can feel trapped by the difficulties that encompass their very existence. Historical attacks are often distal to their immediate contacts and inter-actions but can lead to hypervigilance and anxiety within an individual's everyday environment (Kirmayer et al., 2014). For example, in a recent epigenetic study, Vukoje-vic et al. (2014) found that a glucocorticoid receptor gene was modified (often linked to traumatic memory expression) in men of genocide survivors, increasing their risk for posttraumatic stress disorder.

Finally, the effects of historical trauma and oppression create societal power differentials among privileged and marginalized groups. Young (2014) stated that for every oppressed group there is a group privileged in relation to that group. Power and privilege may not necessarily suggest one may oppress (unjust control of a social group), yet an individual in a more substantial position of power over another has the contextual dominance to oppress marginalized individuals. Oppression highlights the inequities within systems that hinder some and benefit others. Oppression in and of itself is traumatizing to those who are in subordinate positions from its inequities. Scholars believe that the effects of oppression provide a significant layer of mental health distress that embodies feelings of defeat and unworthiness (Goodman & West-Olatunji, 2008b; Young, 2014). Such defeating and unworthy feelings can intensify an individual's suffering, causing traumatic rage (Dutton, 1999). Traumatic rage is defined as the behavioral expression from systemic maltreatment that highlights the mental wellness of the marginalized individual and/or social group.

With multiculturalism and social justice being the fourth and fifth forces (respectively) of counseling theories, the counseling profession seeks to understand how culture and diversity influence counseling practices (Ratts et al., 2016). According to the 2010 U. S Census, of the total U.S. population, Latinos comprise 16.3%, African Americans 12.6%, Asian Americans 4.8%, Native American Indians/Alaska Natives 0.9%, and individuals consisting of two or more racial cultural groups 2.9%. (U.S. Census, 2014). As racial and ethnic diversity increases in the United States, counselors need to be aware of the cultural implications that are placed in their work to ensure all individuals are effectively served. Embracing cultural competency in clinical practice means developing a working knowledge of how one's own assumptions are manifested in clinical work.

Evidence-Based Practices

The dimensions of power and privilege are intervened within the counselor's own self-awareness. Counselors need to be aware that power and privilege influence the therapeutic roles that both the counselor and client take part in. Counselors must address their own attitudes and biases about power and privilege. Thus, self-awareness and self-understanding is critical and foundational to selecting culturally appropriate interventions.

Culture-Centered DMHC Interventions

In cases where clients present with affect regulation and memory intensity issues, they may experience hyper-emotionality and increased avoidance. Additionally, relational schemas can cause sudden intense thoughts and feelings that may have been encoded during the traumatic event. Thus, clinical interventions should be customized to the needs of individual clients based on the counselor's assessment of the client's current level of functioning. In considering sociocultural context, women are typically socialized to internalize their feelings and are more likely to express fear and sadness, whereas men are typically socialized to externalize their feelings and are more likely to express anger; males are more apt to present themselves as strong and able to defend themselves. Counselors are to encourage their clients to express the full range of emotions and thoughts associated with the traumatic event. Of significance, social, sexual, and racial discrimination have direct negative psychological effects that are traumatic. Such traumas are typically associated with environmental conditions and are repeated. In conceptualizing trauma-affected clients, counselors should be aware that transgenerational traumas are also common. Further, individuals experiencing social maltreatment often have reduced access to mental health services. Also, refugees to the United States often bring with them trauma experienced in their countries of origin that may have lasting effects.

Psychoeducation can be helpful during the intervention phase of individual and family counseling. Other forms of psychoeducational activities include support groups, print media (magazines, flyers, posters), digital media (Facebook, Twitter, websites), and public service announcements (PSAs) on the radio and television. Advocacy and social justice are a developmental progression of counselor efficacy (West-Olatunji, 2010). Thus, social empathy and social action are socio-communal acts, allowing counselors to develop insight about clients' lives, circumstances, and realities (Segal, 2007). Social action is the mechanism by which human beings counter artificial limitations imposed on them by external forces. Thus, advocacy and social justice counseling must include (a) an understanding of the ecosystemic and contextual barriers to clients' self-actualization and (b) clinical skill sets that facilitate the creation of limit acts (i.e., micro acts of liberation that reflect empowerment and voice) (Freire, 2000).

To reflect culture-centered practices, counselors can use Indigenous and culturally informed healing practices that promote empowerment and voice as well as develop community-wide interventions. Systemic interventions promote sustainable resilience by restoring a sense of community, facilitating existing strengths of the community, and focusing on empowerment. They also aid in healing the various types of trauma symptomology by giving voice to the experiences. Community-wide interventions are culturally informed because they incorporate the historical coping and transgenerational resilience of the community members through various forms of testifying (or *testimonios*). For example, counselors can engage in dialogue with community stakeholders to determine appropriate creative projects, consider both cognitive and expressive mediums, employ both written and verbal expression, and facilitate the presentation of creative projects (while deferring to the community to select the presentation venue).

Now that you have increased your knowledge about crisis, trauma, and disaster counseling, we hope you feel more confident about working with trauma-affected clients. With the additional information on working with culturally diverse clients and issues of systemic oppression, you may feel the need to read further about traumatic stress, historical trauma, and intergenerational trauma. Critical in developing cultural competence when working with traumatized clients is the need for enhanced self-awareness about the biases we each bring to our clinical interactions. Finally, it is important to adapt culturally informed practices when working with diverse clients that aid in our ability to expediently resolve presenting problems and in clients' ability to positively influence their social support networks.

Standardized and Informal Assessments

Trauma-informed screening refers to a brief, focused inquiry to determine whether an individual has experienced specific traumatic events. Trauma screening is usually limited to several questions, exploring a range of events that may include natural disasters, serious accidents, deaths, and physical and sexual abuse. Probes need to be clear and explicit, particularly following an incident of physical and sexual abuse. It is advisable to not only screen during the initial meeting but periodically repeat probes, as clients may be more willing to disclose with the development of rapport. Trauma assessment consists of a more in-depth exploration of the nature and severity of the traumatic events, the sequelae of those events, and current trauma-related symptoms. Assessment should also look for less obvious connections, such as trauma sequelae seen in a wide range of life domains that affect the client in ways not apparently related to abuse or violence (Harris & Fallot, 2001). Trauma assessments are needed to (a) identify current triggers or stressors, (b) identify coping resources and strengths, (c) incorporate multiple perspectives on the presenting issues, and (d) employ a range of assessment tools. Assessments are usually conducted in a three-stage process that begins with stage 1: ensuring safety, exploring past experiences, and educating the client (Ford, 2005). In stage 2 the counselor utilizes very targeted assessment tools to examine the impact of current and past trauma exposure, discusses healthy self-protective reactions to trauma, and aids the client in gaining more organized and self-regulated schemas for comprehending current or past trauma-related experiences, Finally, in stage 3, the counselor monitors the client's continued growth.

Suggested List of Trauma Assessment Tools

- Life Stressor Checklist–Revised (LSC-R) (Wolfe & Kimmerling, 1997)
- PDS-Modified; comprehensive (Rosenberg, 2004)
- Trauma Assessment for Adults (TAA) (Resnick, 1993)
- PTSD Checklist for Adults (Weathers, 1994)
- Traumatic Events Screening Inventory (TESI) (Ford et al., 2000)
- Trauma Symptom Inventory (TSI) (Briere, 1997)
- Diagnostic Interview Schedule for adults (DIS) (Helzer & Robins, 1988)
- Schedule for Affective Disorders and Schizophrenia Present and Lifetime Version (SADS-PL) (Kaufman et al., 1997)
- Inventory of Interpersonal Problems-Short Form (IIP-32) (Barkham et al., 1996)
- Post-Traumatic Cognitions Inventory (PTCI) (Foa et al., 1999)
- Generalized Expectancies for Negative Mood Regulation (NMR) (Cantanzaro & Mearns, 1990)
- Meta-Experience of Mood Scales (Meta-Scales) (Mayer & Stevens, 1994)
- Positive Affect Negative Affect Scales (PANAS) (Watson et al., 1988)
- Parenting Stress Index Short Form (PSI) (Abidin, 1995)
- Historical Trauma (Gone, 2013)
- Historical Losses Associated Symptoms Scale (Whitbeck et al., 2004)
- Historical Losses Scale (Whitbeck et al., 2004)
- Race-Based Traumatic Stress Symptom Scale (Carter et al., 2013)
- The Perceived Racism Scale for Latina/os (Collado-Proctor, 1999)
- The Racial Microaggressions Scale (RMAS) (Torres-Harding et al., 2012)

REFLECTION AND DISCUSSION QUESTIONS

1. Given the relatively new literature on traumatic stress that refers to the chronic and persistent experiences with macro- and microaggressions that culturally marginalized people experience, how can counselors better assess and treat historical trauma and intergenerational trauma?
2. In a racialized society such as the United States, it sometimes is difficult to focus on cultural and ethnic values and characteristics for culturally diverse clients. What are some ways counselors can become more knowledgeable about the strengths of culturally diverse individuals, families, and communities? What are some evidence-based culture-centered interventions counselors can use with diverse client populations?
3. Imagine you are working in a community agency with an adult male Vietnamese American client (35 years old) who is severely depressed and previously had been admitted to a residential substance abuse rehabilitation facility. When discussing his concerns, he starts wringing his hands, appearing to be in emotional distress, and relating to the residential facility as "nothing but a concentration camp." From a crisis and trauma perspective, how do you perceive this client's thoughts and feelings about the previous residential facility experiences?

4. You are a community mental health counselor working with a first-generation Latina client who has developed anxiety attacks over the past several months. She discloses that she has nightmares about having to leave the United States, though she was born there. How do you, a culturally competent counselor, assess this client's concerns?

5. After being deployed in a city following a hurricane, you have been working with residents who are living in shelters and in FEMA trailers. Day after day, individuals are sharing stories about how they were able to escape harm and the challenges the experienced in evacuating. Many of them have no idea about the status of their homes or when they might be able to return to their jobs or schools. You have heard many stories about the loss of loved ones and the terror of possibly drowning in their own homes. By the fifth day, you are starting to feel emotional and psychological fatigue. On day 6, your clinical supervisor comes to you and tells you to take the day off. You are very annoyed by this and challenge your supervisor, who is resolute and says that you must not report to work that day. How would you handle this situation as the disaster mental health counselor?

ADDITIONAL READINGS AND RESOURCES

Resources

West-Olatunji, C., & Yoon, E. (2014). *Ferry boat disaster in South Korea.* American Counseling Association Podcast Series. Retrieved from https://www.counseling.org/knowledge-center/podcasts/docs/default-source/aca-podcasts/ht045.

West-Olatunji, C., & St Juste, S. (2010). *Stress and Haitian Americans, after the earthquake.* American Counseling Association Podcast Series. Retrieved from: https://www.counseling.org/knowledge-center/podcasts/docs/default-source/aca-podcasts/ht016-stress-and-haitian-americans-after-the-earthquake.

Useful Websites

Trauma and Mental Health Report: http://trauma.blog.yorku.ca/
Child Trauma Academy: http://childtrauma.org/
National Child Traumatic Stress Network: http://www.nctsn.org/
National Center for PTSD: http://www.ptsd.va.gov/
National Disaster Preparedness Training Center: https://ndptc.hawaii.edu/
Trauma.Org: http://www.trauma.org/
Psychological Trauma Resources: https://resource4trauma.wordpress.com/
Trauma-Informed Practices and Expressive Arts Therapy Institute:
 http://www.trauma-informedpractice.com/
National Library of Medicine, Disaster Information Management Research Center:
 https://disasterinfo.nlm.nih.gov/
American Counseling Association Disaster Mental Health Resources:

http://www.counseling.org/knowledge-center/trauma-disaster
Society of Trauma Nurses: http://www.traumanurses.org/
Boston Trauma: http://www.bmc.org/trauma-emergency-care.htm
American Red Cross: http://www.redcross.org/
London Trauma Conference: http://www.londontraumaconference.com/
Humanity Road: http://humanityroad.org/

REFERENCES

Abidin, R. R. (1990). *Parenting stress index-short form* (p. 118). Charlottesville, VA: Pediatric psychology press.

Barkham, M., Hardy, G. E., & Startup, M. (1996). The IIP-32: A short version of the Inventory of Interpersonal Problems. *British Journal of Clinical Psychology, 35*(1), 21–35. doi: **https://doi.org/10.1111/j.2044-8260.1996.tb01159.x**

Brave Heart, M. Y. H. (1998). The return to the sacred path: Healing the historical trauma and historical unresolved grief response among the Lakota through a psychoeducational group intervention. *Smith College Studies in Social Work, 68*(3), 287–305.

Brave Heart, M. Y. H., Chase, J., Elkins, J., & Altschul, D. B. (2011). Historical trauma among indigenous peoples of the Americas: Concepts, research, and clinical considerations. *Journal of Psychoactive Drugs, 43*(4), 282–290.

Breslau, N., Kessler, R. C., Chilcoat, H. D., Schultz, L. R., Davis, G. C., & Andreski, P. (1998). Trauma and posttraumatic stress disorder in the community: The 1996 Detroit Area Survey of Trauma. *Archives of General Psychiatry, 55,* 626–632.

Briere, J. (1995). Trauma Symptom Inventory (TSI) Professional Manual, Psychological Assessment Resources, Inc.

Briere, J. N., & Scott, C. (2013). *Principles of trauma therapy: A guide to symptoms, evaluation, and treatment.* SAGE.

Bryant-Davis, T., & Ocampo, C. (2005). The trauma of racism: Implications for counseling, research, and education. *The Counseling Psychologist, 33,* 574–578.

Burstow, B. (2003). Toward a radical understanding of trauma and trauma work. *Violence Against Women, 9,* 1293–1317.

Carlson, E. B. (1997). *Trauma assessments: A clinician's guide.* Guilford.

Carter, R. T. (2007). Racism and psychological and emotional injury: Recognizing and assessing race-based traumatic stress. *The Counseling Psychologist, 35,* 13–105.

Carter, R. T., Mazzula, S., Victoria, R., Vazquez, R., Hall, S., Smith, S., ... & Williams, B. (2013). Initial development of the Race-Based Traumatic Stress Symptom Scale: Assessing the emotional impact of racism. *Psychological Trauma: Theory, Research, Practice, and Policy, 5*(1), 1. Doi: 10.1037/a0025911

Catanzaro, S. J., & Mearns, J. (1990). Measuring generalized expectancies for negative mood regulation: Initial scale development and implications. *Journal of personality assessment, 54*(3–4), 546–563.

Choi, H., Meininger, J. C., & Roberts, R. E. (2006). Ethnic differences in adolescent mental distress, social stress, and resources. *Adolescence, 41*, 263–283.

Cholewa, B., & West-Olatunji, C. (2008). Exploring the relationship among cultural discontinuity, psychological distress, and academic achievement outcomes for low-income, culturally diverse students. *Professional School Counseling, 12*, 54–61.

Collado-Proctor, S. M. (1999). The Perceived Racism Scale for Latina/os: A multidimensional assessment of the experience of racism among latina/os. *Dissertation Abstracts International: Section B: The Sciences and Engineering, 60*(1-B), 0361.

Connor-Smith, J. K., Compas, B. E., Wadsworth, M. E., Thomsen, A. H., & Saltzman, H. (2000). Responses to stress in adolescence: measurement of coping and involuntary stress responses. *Journal of consulting and clinical psychology, 68*(6), 976. doi: 10.1037//0022-006X.68.6.976

Dadlani, M. B., Overtree, C., & Perry-Jenkins, M. (2012). Culture at the center: A reformulation of diagnostic assessment. *Professional Psychology: Research and Practice, 43*(3), 175–182.

Danieli, Y. (1998). Introduction: History and conceptual foundations. In Y. Danieli (Ed.), *International handbook of multigenerational legacies of trauma* (pp. 1–20). Plenum.

Danieli, Y. (2007). Assessing trauma across cultures from a multigenerational perspective. In J. P. Wilson & C. S-K. Tang (Eds.), *Cross-cultural assessment of psychological trauma and PTSD* (pp. 65–89). Springer.

Dass-Brailsford, P. (2007). *A practical approach to trauma.* SAGE.

De Young, A. C., Kenardy, J. A., & Cobham, V. E. (2011a). Diagnosis of posttraumatic stress disorder in preschool children. *Journal of Clinical Child & Adolescent Psychology, 40*(3), 375–384. https://doi.org/10.1080/15374416.2011.563474

De Young, A. C., Kenardy, J. A., & Cobham, V. E. (2011b). Trauma in early childhood: A neglected population. *Clinical Child & Family Psychology Review, 14*(3), 231–250. https://doi.org/10.1007/s10567-011-0094-3

Din-Dzietham, R., Nembhard, W. N., Collins, R., & Davis, S. K. (2004). Perceived stress following race-based discrimination at work is associated with hypertension in African Americans: The Metro Atlanta Heart Disease Study, 1999–2001. *Social Science and Medicine, 58*, 449–461.

Dutton, D. G. (1999). Traumatic origins of intimate rage. *Aggression and Violent Behavior, 4*(4), 431–447.

Elliot, D. M. (1997). Traumatic events: Prevalence and delayed recall in the general population. *Journal of Consulting and Clinical Psychology, 65*, 811–820.

Fang, C. Y., & Myers, H. F. (2001). The effects of racial stressors and hostility on cardiovascular reactivity in African American and Caucasian men. *Health Psychology, 20*, 64–70.

Figley, C. R. (2002). Compassion fatigue: Psychotherapists' chronic lack of self-care. *Journal of Clinical Psychology, 58*(11), 1433–1441.

Foa, E. B., Ehlers, A., Clark, D. M., Tolin, D. F., & Orsillo, S. M. (1999). The posttraumatic cognitions inventory (PTCI): Development and validation. *Psychological assessment, 11*(3), 303.

Ford, J. (2000). Traumatic Events Screening Inventory–Parent Report Revised (TESI). *Unpublished manuscript. Storrs, CT: University of Connecticut.*

Frazier, K. N., West-Olatunji, C., St Juste, S., & Goodman, R. (2009). Transgenerational trauma & CSA: Reconceptualizing cases involving young survivors of child sexual abuse. *Journal of Mental Health Counseling, 31*, 22–33.

Freire, P. (2000). *Pedagogy of freedom: Ethics, democracy, and civic courage.* Rowman & Littlefield Publishers.

Gone, J. P. (2013). A Community-Based Treatment for Native American Historical Trauma: Prospects for Evidence-Based Practice. *Journal of Consulting & Clinical Psychology, 77*(4), 751–762. doi: 10.1037/a0015390

Goodman, R. D., Miller, M. D., & West-Olatunji, C. A. (2012). Traumatic stress, socioeconomic status, and academic achievement among primary school students. *Psychological Trauma: Theory, Research, Practice, and Policy, 4*(3), 252–259. https://doi.org/10.1037/a0024912

Goodman, R. D., & West-Olatunji, C. A. (2008a). Traumatic stress, systemic oppression, and resilience in post-Katrina New Orleans. *Spaces for Difference: An Interdisciplinary Journal, 1*(2), 51–68.

Goodman, R. D., & West-Olatunji, C. A. (2008b). Transgenerational trauma and resilience: Improving mental health counseling for survivors on Hurricane Katrina. *Journal of Mental Health Counseling, 30*, 121–136.

Goodman, R., & West-Olatunji, C. (2009). Cultural competency and disaster response. *Journal of Counseling & Development, 87*, 458–465.

Goodman, R. D., & West-Olatunji, C. A. (2010). Educational hegemony, traumatic stress, and African American and Latino American students. *Journal of Multicultural Counseling & Development, 38*(3), 176–186.

Graham-Bermann, S. A., & Levendosky, A. A. (1998). Traumatic stress symptoms in children of battered women. *Journal of Interpersonal Violence, 13*, 111–129.

Graham, L. B. (2010). Implementing CACREP disaster/crisis standards for counseling students. Retrieved from http://counselingoutfitters.com/vistas/vistas10/Article_90.pdf.

Halpern, J., & Tramontin, M. (2007). *Disaster mental health: Theory and practice.* Brooks/Cole.

Harrell, J. P., Hall, S., & Taliaferro, J. (2003). Physiological responses to racism and discrimination. *American Journal of Public Health, 93*, 243–248.

Harris, M., & Fallot, R. (2001). Creating cultures of trauma-informed care (CCTIC): A self-assessment and planning protocol.

Harvey, M. R. (1996). An ecological view of psychological trauma and trauma recovery. *Journal of Traumatic Stress, 9*(1), 3–23.

Helzer, J.E., & Robins, L.N. (1988). The diagnostic interview schedule: Its development, evolution, and use. *Social Psychiatry and Psychiatric Epidemiology.* 23, 6–16 https://doi.org/10.1007/BF01788437

Kaufman, J., Birmaher, B., Brent, D., Rao, U., Flynn, C., Moreci, P., Williamson, D., & Ryan, N. (1997). Schedule for Affective Disorders and Schizophrenia for School-Age Children-Present and Lifetime Version (K-SADS-PL): initial reliability and validity data. *Journal of the American Academy of Child and Adolescent Psychiatry, 36*(7), 980–988. doi: https://doi.org/10.1097/00004583-199707000-00021

Kira, I.A., Fawzi, M.H., Fawzi, M.M. (2013). The dynamics of cumulative trauma and trauma types in adult patients with psychiatric disorders: Two cross-cultural studies. *Traumatology, 19* (3), 179-195. https://doi.org/10.1177/1534765612459892.

Kirmayer, L. J., Gone, J. P., & Moses, J. (2014). Rethinking historical trauma. *Transcultural Psychiatry, 5*(3), 299–319.

Lau, B. W. K. (2002). Does the stress in childhood and adolescence matter? A psychological perspective. *The Journal of the Royal Society for the Promotion of Health, 122*(4), 238–244. https://doi.org/10.1177/146642400212200411

Levine, P. A., & Kline, M. (2007). *Trauma through a child's eyes: Awakening the ordinary miracle of healing.* North Atlantic Books.

Lieberman, A. F. (2004). Traumatic stress and quality of attachment: Reality and internalization in disorders of infant mental health. *Infant Mental Health Journal, 25*(4), 336–351. https://doi.org/10.1002/imhj.20009

Lieberman, A. F., & Van Horn, P. (2008). *Psychotherapy with infants and young children: Repairing the effects of stress and trauma on early attachment.* Guilford.

Litz, B. T., Gray, M. J., Bryant, R. A., & Adler, A. B. (2002). Early intervention for trauma: Current status and future directions. *Clinical Psychology: Science and Practice, 9*(2), 112–134. https://doi.org/10.1093/clipsy.9.2.112

Marsella, A.J. & Christopher, M.A. (2004). Ethnocultural considerations in disasters: an overview of research, issues, and directions. *Psychiatric Clinics of North America 27*, 521–539. https: doi: 10.1016/j.psc.2004.03.011.

Masten, A. S., & Coatsworth, J. D. (1998). The development of competence in favorable and unfavorable environments. *American Psychologist, 53*, 205–220.

Mattar, S. (2010). Cultural considerations in trauma psychology education, research, and training. *Traumatology, 16* (4), 48-52. https://doi.org/10.1177/1534765610388305.

Mayer, J. D., & Stevens, A. A. (1994). An emerging understanding of the reflective (meta-) experience of mood. *Journal of research in personality, 28*(3), 351–373.

McKnight, A. N. (2004). Historical trauma, the persistence of memory and the pedagogical problems of forgiveness, justice and peace. *Educational Studies, 36*(2), 140–158.

Miller, K. E., & Rasmussen, A. (2010). War exposure, daily stressors and mental health in conflict and post-conflict settings: Bridging the divide between trauma-focused and psychosocial frameworks. *Social Science & Medicine, 70*, 7–16. https://doi.org/10.1016/j.socscimed.2009.09.029

Modrowski, C. A., Miller, L. E., Howell, K. H., & Graham-Bermann, S. A. (2013). Consistency of trauma symptoms at home and in therapy for preschool children exposed to intimate partner violence. *Psychological Trauma: Theory, Research, Practice, and Policy, 5*(3), 251–258. https://doi.org/10.1037/a0027167

Nagata, D. K. (1990). The Japanese American internment: Exploring the transgenerational consequences of traumatic stress. *Journal of Traumatic Stress, 3,* 47–69.

Paradies, Y. (2006). A systematic review of empirical research on self-reported racism and health. *International Journal of Epidemiology, 35,* 888–901.

Pender, D. A., & Anderton, C. (2016). Exploring the process: A narrative analysis of group facilitators' reports on critical incident stress debriefing. *The Journal for Specialists in Group Work, 41*(1), 19–43. doi: https://doi.org/10.1080/01933922.2015.1111485

Pierce, C. (1970). Offensive mechanisms. *The black seventies, 265,* 82.

Ratts, M. J., Singh, A. A., Nassar-McMillan, S., Butler, S. K., & McCullough, J. R. (2016). Multicultural and social justice counseling competencies: Guidelines for the counseling profession. *Journal of Counseling & Development, 44*(1), 28–48.

Resnick, H. S. (1993). Psychometric review of trauma assessment for adults (TAA). *Measurement of stress, trauma, and adaptation,* 362–365.

Schuster, M. A., Stein, B. D., Jaycox, L. H., Collins, R. L., Marshall, G. N., Elliot, M. N., Zhou, A. J., Kanouse, D. E., Morrison, J. L., & Berry, S. H. (2001). A national survey of stress reactions after the September 11, 2001, terrorist attacks. *New England Journal of Medicine, 345,* 1507–1512.

Segal, E. A. (2007). Social empathy: A new paradigm to address poverty. *Journal of Poverty, 11*(3), 65–81.

Shelby, J. S., & Tredinnick, M. G. (1995). Crisis intervention with survivors of natural disaster: Lessons from Hurricane Andrew. *Journal of Counseling and Development: JCD, 73*(5), 491. doi: http://10.1002/j.1556-6676.1995.tb01784.x

Sotero, M. (2006). A conceptual model of historical trauma: Implications for public health practice and research. *Journal of Health Disparities Research and Practice, 1*(1), 93–108.

Streeck-Fischer, A., & van der Kolk, B. A. (2000). Down will come baby, cradle and all: Diagnostic and therapeutic implications of chronic trauma on child development. *Australian and New Zealand Journal of Psychiatry, 34,* 903–918.

Torres-Harding, S. R., Andrade, A. L., & Romero Diaz, C. E. (2012). The Racial Microaggressions Scale (RMAS): a new scale to measure experiences of racial microaggressions in people of color. *Cultural diversity & ethnic minority psychology, 18*(2), 153–164. doi: https://doi.org/10.1037/a0027658

Uhernik, J. A., & Husson, M. A. (2009). Psychological first aid: An evidence informed approach for acute disaster behavioral health response. In G. R. Waltz, J.C. Bleuer, & R. K. Yep (Eds.), *Compelling counseling interventions: VISTAS, 200*(9), 271–280. Alexandria, VA: American Counseling Association.

U.S. Census Bureau (2014). Data Profiles. Retrieved from: https://www.census.gov/acs/www/data/data-tables-and-tools/data-profiles/2014/.

Utsey, S. O. (1998). Assessing the stressful effects of racism: A review of instrumentation. *Journal of Black Psychology, 24,* 269–288.

Vernberg, E. A., La Greca, A. M., Silverman, W. K, & Prinstein, M. J. (1996). Prediction of posttraumatic stress symptoms in children after Hurricane Andrew. *Journal of Abnormal Psychology, 105,* 237–248.

Vukojevic, V., Kolassa, I. T., Fastenrath, M., Gschwind, L., Spalek, K., Milnik, A., Heck, A., Vogler, C., Wilker, S., Demougin, P., Peter, F., Atucha, E., Stetak, A., Roozendaal, B., Elbert, T., Papassotiropoulos, A. & Dominique, J. F. (2014). Epigenetic modification of the glucocorticoid receptor gene is linked to traumatic memory and post-traumatic stress disorder risk in genocide survivors. *Journal of Neuroscience, 34*(31), 10274–10284.

Walker, R. L. (2007). Acculturation and acculturative stress as indicators for suicide risk among African Americans. *American Journal of Orthopsychiatry, 77,* 386–391.

Watson, D., Clark, L. A., & Tellegen, A. (1988). Development and validation of brief measures of positive and negative affect: the PANAS scales. *Journal of personality and social psychology, 54*(6), 1063.

Weathers, F. W. (1994). The PTSD Checklist: Reliability, validity and diagnostic utility. In *Presented at the Annual Meeting of the International Society for Traumatic Stress Studies. San Antonio, TX, October, 1993.*

West-Olatunji, C. A. (2019). The importance of incorporating knowledge of trauma remediation modalities into counselor education and practice. In M. O. Adekson (Ed.), *Handbook of counseling and counselor education.,* pp. 223–237. Routledge.

West-Olatunji, C., Henesy, R., & Varney, M. (2014). Group work during international disaster outreach projects: A model to advance cultural competence. *Journal for Specialists in Group Work, 40* (1), 38–54.

West-Olatunji, C., & Wolfgang, J. D. (April 2018). 10 interventions for attachment and traumatic stress issues for young children (birth-5 years). *Counseling Today.*

West-Olatunji, C., & Yoon, E. (2013). Culture-centered perspectives on disaster and crisis counseling. *Journal of Asia Pacific Counseling, 3*(1), 35–43.

Whitbeck, L. B., Adams, G. W., Hoyt, D. R., & Chen, X. (2004). Conceptualizing and measuring historical trauma among American Indian people. *American journal of community psychology, 33*(3–4), 119–130. doi: https://doi.org/10.1023/b:ajcp.0000027000.77357.31

Williams, D. R., Neighbors, H. W., & Jackson, J. S. (2003). Racial/ethnic discrimination and health: Findings from community studies. *American Journal of Public Health, 93,* 200–208.

Wolfe, J., Kimerling, R., Brown, P., Chrestman, K., & Levin, K. (1997). Life Stressor Checklist-Revised (LSC-R). *Measurement instrument. Retrieved from: http://www. ptsd. gov.*

Wozniak, J., Crawford, M. H., Biederman, J., Faraone, S. V., Spencer, T. J., Taylor, Blier, H. K. (1999). Antecedents of complications of trauma in boys with ADHD: Findings from a longitudinal study. *Journal of the American Academy of Child & Adolescent Psychiatry, 38,* 48–55. https://doi.org/10.1097/00004583-199901000-00019.

Wynn, R.D. & West-Olatunji-C. (2009). Use of culture-centered counseling theory with ethnically diverse LGBT clients. *Journal of LGBT Issues in Counseling, 3* (3–4), 198-214. https:// DOI: 10.1080/15538600903317218.

Young, A. (2004). When traumatic memory was a problem: On the historical antecedents of PTSD. *Posttraumatic stress disorder: Issues and controversies,* 127–146. doi: **https://doi. org/10.1002/9780470713570.ch7**

CHAPTER 12

CREATIVITY

Jacqueline M. Swank, University of Florida

Jo Lauren Weaver, University of Florida

Patrice Leopold, University of Florida

LEARNING OBJECTIVES

1. Examine the use of creativity to foster multicultural social justice counseling competency within the four domains of awareness, knowledge, skills, and action.
2. Explore the integration of creativity within the counseling process to work with diverse clients.
3. Discuss ethical and other considerations when integrating creativity within counseling.

LEARNING OUTCOMES

1. Learn creative strategies to enhance counselor self-awareness.
2. Learn to use creative interventions to explore the client's worldview.
3. Learn creative techniques to foster the counseling relationship.
4. Learn creative interventions to apply within the multicultural social justice counseling competencies framework.

Counselors can infuse creativity in their work with diverse clients to foster the development of the counseling relationship and enhance the counseling process. This chapter focuses on exploring the concept of creativity, the history of its use in counseling, and the importance of using creativity in counseling. Additionally, the authors discuss the use of eight creativity interventions with diverse clients, cautions and considerations related to using the interventions, and the use of creativity to develop multicultural social justice counseling competencies. Finally, the chapter concludes with the presentation of two case studies related to infusing creativity in counseling that align with the development of multicultural social justice counseling competency.

DEFINING CREATIVITY

The integration of creativity in counseling has become more prevalent in literature, research, and practice over the last several decades (McCarthy, 2017). According to McCarthy (2017), creativity in counseling is a skill that nurtures change by shifting thoughts, attitudes, behaviors, and emotions in a clinician's work with clients. It is not limited to applying an experiential intervention, but also provides a safe space for relational and emotional healing. Creating safe spaces is also at the foundation of the multicultural competencies, as safety creates an atmosphere for exploring and understanding intersectionality.

In counseling, creativity is coconstructed with the client. Kottler and Hecker (2002) reported that creativity is often fostered through a clinician's frustrations in feeling stuck in their work with clients. These frustrations typically serve as the catalyst for developing a creative intervention. Therefore, when counselors are intentional about being creative, they may not be as efficient, partially because the attempt is unnatural and objective of the client's process.

There are three constructs in establishing creativity, which include considering person, process, and product (Carson & Becker, 2004). The person involves awareness of intersectionality of the client, counselor, and alliance; the process is the method for cultivating growth in an imaginative way; and the product is the relational and individual outcomes at termination. Thus, implementing the same creative interventions creates a unique experience and outcome for every client and the clinician due to unique personalities and alliances. Nonetheless, a clinician should not desire nor expect the same encounter with every client. Safety also involves the counselor being nonjudgmental, to allow the client the space to engage in self-expression without feeling judged by the counselor. Channeling creativity in counseling facilitates expression in multiple forms that extend beyond talk therapy. Thus, clients are provided with diverse, flexible opportunities of experiencing counseling.

HISTORY OF CREATIVITY IN COUNSELING

Counseling professionals have infused creativity in counseling throughout the history of the profession. Specifically, theorists from various theoretical orientations have emphasized the importance of creativity in counseling. Carl Rogers (1959) in his person-centered approach asserted that creativity is one of the outcomes of therapy. His daughter, Natalie Rogers, expanded this view of creativity in counseling by integrating creativity in counseling sessions through expressive arts therapy, referred to as creative connection (Rogers, 1993). Additionally, Virginia Axline (1964), a student of Rogers, created a person-centered approach to counseling children through play.

Carl Jung (1973) used visual arts, specifically drawing and painting mandalas, in analytic psychotherapy as a symbolic representation of oneness or wholeness. In family therapy, Virginia Satir (1972) used a form of psychodrama called "family sculpting" for members to visually represent experiences from the viewpoint of "the sculptor." Additionally,

Rollo May (1975) devoted a book to creativity in existential therapy entitled *The Courage to Create*. Furthermore, Laura Perls, one of the developers of Gestalt therapy, described using poetry to communicate with clients and asserted that a background and continuation to experience the arts broadens a therapist's ability to effectively communicate with clients (Amendt-Lyon, 2001). Through the foundation laid by these scholars for the use of creativity in counseling, counselors can now use creativity as a gateway for promoting self-awareness, understanding the client's worldview, and fostering the therapeutic relationship.

WHY CREATIVITY IS IMPORTANT IN COUNSELING

Creativity in the counseling room provides an outlet for expression and a space for discovery of both self and others. Creative interventions can equip the client with a new outlet to voice their experiences without verbalization (Binkley, 2013). The rediscovery of their voice can be especially beneficial for individuals who have been silenced through abuse, neglect, oppression, and marginalization. Additionally, creativity provides an opportunity to explore emotions, such as anxiety and fear, by providing a space to reflect and examine them symbolically and from a safe distance (Rappaport, 2011). This may result in integrating these emotions with their thoughts and physical experiences (Huss et al., 2012), thus inspiring a sense of healing and synthesis.

Through creative interventions, clients are able to focus inward, augmenting their self-connection. Creativity provides an opportunity for self-exploration where words are not always necessary, and silence is promoted. The idea of creating something can also provide clients with a sense of accomplishment, increased self-worth, and awareness of their own strengths and resources (Malchiodi & Miller, 2003). Additionally, creative techniques can aid in the understanding and regulation of coping responses to emotionally difficult situations (Armstrong & Ricard, 2016). Emotional intelligence and vocabulary can also be built through creative interventions, especially for younger clients (Ali, 2017).

Relationally, counselors can facilitate creative interventions within groups to foster social support and reduce isolation (Huss et al., 2012). In session, the sense of trust and safety built through sharing the experience of creating can foster the therapeutic alliance and enhance self-awareness for both the client and the counselor. The client gains insight into their own experiences, while the counselor can further evaluate their own position in the relationship; the multicultural and social justice counseling competencies (MSJCC) framework can provide a structured guide for this examination (Ratts et al., 2015). Thus, creativity can be an integral part of the therapeutic process as it provides a unique opportunity to cultivate exploration, connection, and healing for the client.

CREATIVE INTERVENTIONS

Counselors can integrate a variety of creative interventions in the counseling process. We describe a variety of counseling interventions, including (a) animals, (b) bibliotherapy, (c) dance and movement, (d) drama, (e) literature, (f) music, (g) nature, (h) play, (i) visual arts, and (j) writing. We are not presenting these are specialized forms of therapy (i.e., music therapy, art therapy), but instead are discussing the use of the intervention in counseling sessions as one of many.

Animals in Counseling

In 1919, Franklin Lane recommended using dogs with psychiatric patients at St. Elizabeth Hospital in Washington, DC. Then, in 1942, staff used dogs in a military hospital to help recovering veterans. Finally, in 1962, Boris Levinson began using his dog Jingles as his cotherapist in providing counseling to children. He was the first clinician to document the effect of integrating animals in counseling. When involving animals in the counseling process, the counselor often refers to the animal as a cotherapist. The animal, client, and clinician interact with the intent of achieving positive clinical outcomes. Therapeutic sessions typically occur in the counseling room but can also occur in different settings that accommodate the animal.

The presence of an animal in the counseling session can help soothe clients as they explore their concerns with the therapist. The counselor can provide cues as needed to guide the client on how to interact with the animal during the session through petting, grooming, holding, hugging, and staring at the animal. The benefits of integrating animals in counseling sessions include a reduction in heart rate, stress, rapid breathing, anxiety, depression, and loneliness, while also leading to enhancement in relaxation, relationship building, self-esteem, mood, trust, acceptance, and assertiveness (Beetz et al., 2012; Morrison, 2007).

There are a variety of animals counselors can integrate in the counseling process, and there is no single breed considered most effective. However, there are several areas to consider in selecting an animal to use in counseling. The animal should be obedient, easy to train and control, calm, social with different age groups and ability levels, tolerant of varying levels of noise and activity, tolerable of touch, and comfortable in the clinician's choice of work setting. Dogs are the most common animals used in counseling because of their ease in responding to training and ability to communicate effectively with humans. Researchers have examined the effectiveness of integrating dogs in counseling to treat depression, substance abuse, trauma, dementia, and schizophrenia and found significant improvements compared to the absence of a dog (Canadian Agency for Drugs and Technologies in Health [CADTH], 2012). Counselors also use horses often in counseling, known as equine therapy, which may include interacting with the horse on the ground, riding, and grooming. The presence of the horse helps to elicit communication between the therapist and client. Researchers report positive outcomes in using horses to help clients experiencing trauma, schizophrenia, and other conditions (CADTH, 2012).

Professionals can also integrate dolphins in their work with clients by using dolphin-assisted therapy (DAT), which clinicians have used to treat individuals with both psychological and physical conditions, including depression, attention-deficit/

hyperactivity disorder (ADHD), autism, down syndrome, posttraumatic stress disorder, cancer, and hearing impairments (Whale and Dolphin Conservation Society [WDCS], 2007). Interactions with dolphins is associated with more relaxing and calming brain waves (WDCS, 2007). Presence in the water can also be calming for clients. Finally, farm animals are also useful for counseling due to their domestic nature. These animals are often easy to work with and train. Some clients experience comfort interacting with these animals, including pigs, goats, and cows.

Animals are used in counseling with diverse populations. Animals are not stained with the same premonitions, stereotypes, and discriminants that people have about one another. Animals are uniquely able to work with people of all ages, races, and abilities in various settings. Clients who are unable to communicate due to delays can experience isolation and often find comfort in having an animal present because they don't have the pressure to talk. Other populations that experience feelings of isolation also find solace in the presence of an animal, such as veterans who suffer from PTSD, survivors of sexual trauma, children who are bullied, and clients with substance abuse.

Clinicians may also recommend a client having a pet in the home. Although the pet is not trained to help improve behavior, researchers have found that the bond between humans and their pets can help to improve attachment, with the pet serving as an attachment figure (Zilcha-Mano et al., 2011). There are also animals trained to help clients with their clinical needs, which are typically cats and dogs. Emotional support animals (ESA) and therapy animals are companion animals that are trained to tend to the emotional needs of their owner. When the owner is visibly upset or agitated, an ESA or therapy animal will soothe the owner by licking and nudging them. Researchers have found that the presence of ESA and therapy animals reduces anxiety and loneliness and improves self-esteem (Beetz et al., 2012).

In using animals in counseling, it is important that the clinician has training on how to integrate the animal effectively in sessions. Additionally, animals must have training to ensure their appropriateness for use in counseling. Furthermore, clinicians must avoid using animals in counseling with people with reduced immunity, allergies, and fear of animals.

Bibliotherapy

Bibliotherapy uses literature to address client concerns. These literary works can be prescriptive or creative in nature. Prescriptively, a counselor can recommend a book (e.g., self-help book) as supplemental to counseling, also referred to as cognitive bibliotherapy. Creatively, counselors use literature to facilitate difficult concepts or conversations with clients, especially with children and adolescents (e.g., Arruda et al., 2017). Literature can also promote cultural awareness and be a tool to explore diversity (Gilmore & Howard, 2016). In using literature, the counselor should be aware of the client's developmental level, including literacy level. The counselor should also be mindful of culturally representative and diverse literacy in selecting literature to use in counseling.

Researchers support the use of bibliotherapy in counseling for example, when using superhero stories to treat anxiety and aggression, and to encourage forward, goal-oriented thinking for children with parental absence, researchers found that participants reported a decline in symptoms of anxiety and aggressive behavior, and they set goals successfully (Betzalel & Shechtman, 2017). Additionally, Theron et al. (2017) examined the use of African American folktales with orphaned and vulnerable children. The children who listened to resilience-themed folktales reported an increase in awareness of personal and community-based protective resources, thus enhancing their own resilience. While less research is available on creative bibliotherapy with adults, in one systematic review of creative bibliotherapy for PTSD, researchers found overall positive effects with addressing clients' symptoms (Glavin & Montgomery, 2017). In session, creative bibliotherapy provides an opportunity for the client and counselor to collaborate, explore, and connect with greater depth through works of literature.

Literary characters provide a point of reference for the counselor and the client. Clients can compare themselves and others to fictional characters, which facilitates metaphoric exploration of these figures. With their literary counterpart, clients can safely express their self-perception and worldview. This can create a sense of universality for clients having someone, even fictitious, who has the same struggles. The character can also be a source of inspiration for the client. Thus, the counselor can use a question prompt, such as "What would (insert character) do in this situation?" (Shectman, 2017). Additionally, the counselor can promote self-exploration through the guise of the character. Therefore, bibliotherapy gives clients a means to navigate their world with the help of literature.

Dance and Movement

There are several techniques in this creativity intervention category, including dance/movement therapy (DMT), therapeutic dance, and yoga, to name a few. Counselors can integrate dance and movement in counseling to help clients connect with their mind, body, and spirit, as movement is communicative and expressive (American Dance Therapy Association [ADTA], 2016). Capello (2016) stated that movement promotes self-awareness. Then, as we make contact with others, they learn about us and offer us new knowledge that further promotes insight and self-awareness. As a form of self-expression, movement and dance can represent an individual's own unique identity, cultural group, or spiritual group or connection.

One approach in this category is dance/movement therapy (DMT), which is a formalized treatment with specified training requirements and practice parameters. Therefore, an individual must meet the training requirements to be identified as a registered dance and movement therapist (R-DMT); however, counselors can use dance and/or movement in counseling by stating that they are counselors who use dance and/or movement and ensuring that they integrate these inventions ethically in their work with clients. Research supports the use of DMT with various populations. Specifically, in a review of 23 studies with 15 different populations, Koch et al. (2014) found that DMT and dance were effective for decreasing symptoms of mental illness (e.g., depression, anxiety) and increasing well-being and quality of life.

Yoga focuses on connecting the five layers of human existence that include the physical body, breath, mind, astral realm, and bliss or pure consciousness (Rybak & Deuskar, 2010). A disturbance in any layer affects all layers, and, conversely, healing in any layer affects all layers, as they operate together as one unit, not as separate systems (Rybak & Deuskar, 2010). Counselors can use yoga, including stretching and breathing exercises, in counseling to help clients develop greater self-awareness, as well as use it in group to help clients make connections with others. Researchers have found that yoga shows promising results for addressing mental health concerns, such as depression (Pilkington et al., 2005), and stress (Hunt et al., 2018).

Counselors can also integrate dance and movement with music. This may involve clients moving their bodies to express the feelings they experience when hearing music, instead of relying solely on verbal descriptions of their feeling. This may also involve witnessing and responding to the movements of others made in response to the music.

Drama

The purpose of using drama in therapy is to help clients gain new perspective by understanding the way they communicate with others, are perceived by others, express strong emotions and feelings, and may be creating a barrier to change in their lives (Orkibi, 2018). There are two primary ways in which drama is used for therapeutic outcomes: psychodrama and drama therapy. Both experiential interventions have similar constructs with important distinctions. Psychodrama is usually when clients role-play as either themselves or significant people in their actual lives, whereas drama therapy is mainly metaphorical and fantasy oriented where clients role-play fictional and symbolic roles (Orkibi, 2018). Drama therapy involves story making, storytelling, puppetry, masks, miniature objects, and rituals. This creates an indirect distance from clients' presenting concerns. In contrast, psychodrama involves mirroring, role reversal, doubling, and soliloquy to allow clients to work directly on their concerns.

In the early 1920s, psychiatrist Jacob Levy Moreno created psychodrama spontaneously while experimenting in a theatre (Kedem-Tahar & Kellerman, 1996). Moreno became curious about the therapeutic potential of acting without a script and with less division between the actors and audience. With time, psychodrama became a recognized form of group therapy with an established organization in 1942. Then, in the 1960s clinicians began using drama therapy with students, prisoners, and hospital patients to enact relatable emotional and social issues. Clinicians then began using the approach with other populations.

Although clinicians can use drama in individual, family, and group counseling, it is most often used where it originated, in group counseling. In group counseling, psychodrama typically has three stages: (a) warm-up, client chosen and provided scenario with a pertinent, difficult situation; (b) enactment, the group role-plays events from the past, present, and future of the client's story; and (c) sharing, the group and the client share their perspectives based on their roles. Although the steps in drama therapy are not as succinct as psychodrama, warming up the group, enacting the given activity, and sharing or debriefing are all necessary components. One difference is that in psychodrama the focus is on one particular client and their issue, whereas in drama therapy all members relate to the presented issue. The enactment involves the counselor and the client during individual counseling, the couple in couples counseling, and all or select family members during family counseling. Similar to group counseling, warming up the client(s), enacting the given activity, and sharing or debriefing are necessary during individual, couple, and family counseling. It is important that in using drama in any counseling modality that the client is willing to participate in this engaging, imaginary process instead of being forced to participate.

Drama therapy can be more effective than psychodrama in working with clients who are more nonverbal, such as clients with developmental disorders, learning disabilities, autism, and conduct disorders (Kedem-Tahar & Kellerman, 1996). Drama therapy is preferable because it provides more flexibility to accommodate various ways of communicating and levels of awareness with adaptable activities such as movement and play. In contrast, psychodrama can be more useful for clients who present with issues that may require confrontation, such as substance abuse and personality disorders, due to the direct focus on the specific client (Kedem-Tahar & Kellerman, 1996). However, a counselor can use drama therapy and psychodrama with various ages, settings, and concerns, including PTSD, sexual abuse history, substance abuse issues, eating disorders, depression, and anxiety (Kedem-Tahar & Kellerman, 1996).

Music

Music has the ability to mollify, incite, conjure, augment, and unite people, perhaps within the same arrangement. The complex stimulus composed of various characteristics creates a whole, mellifluous unit open to interpretation. As multisensory beings, humans uniquely experience music, and thus a specific response cannot be simply assured. Music can reach feelings and thoughts difficult to verbalize or that are long suppressed; it provides an anchor in universality and a sanctuary for exploration. In counseling, music can be multifunctional as a means of rapport building, catharsis, intervention, or coping.

In rapport building, music can connect the client and counselor through a shared affinity, or an opportunity for the client to educate the counselor on their favorite type of music. Music may offer a less intimidating connection to one's identity, life events, and feelings. Clients can cathartically convey their emotions through song lyrics or rhythms, and even disclose parallel experiences that evoke these responses. Through the universality of music, clients can find themes (e.g., hope, empowerment, sadness, peace, happiness) embedded in the composition. Using existing music or creating original music provides an avenue for expression and insight into the client's cognitions, feelings, and life events (Amir & Bodner, 2013). The integration of music may evoke dormant or unvisited emotions, thoughts, or experiences, and therefore counselors should use it with forethought and intentionality.

In session, musical interventions can include lyric analysis, original songwriting, editing existing songs, improvisation, or drumming. Lyrics help clients create an enriched narrative by accessing memoires, emotions, longings, and thoughts often left unspoken in traditional talk therapy. In lyric analysis, a client and counselor identify symbolism, emotions, and themes in the lyrics of the song and explore how this relates to the client (Gladding et al., 2008). The counselor can prompt the activity by asking the client to select a song that describes their current state, or a song the client has frequently listened to. A song frequently listened to may evoke less pressure for clients who appear disconnected from their thoughts and emotions. Lyric revision may follow the analysis process to empower the client to convey their own message after processing. The lyrical changes often reflect the client's own personal experience with incisive word choices and descriptions (Kimbel & Protivnak, 2010). Counselors can also use songwriting as an intervention to encourage self-expression, which may involve recording the client performing the song and then having the client listen to it.

Improvisation is a free form, in-the-moment expression and creation of music that includes writing lyrics, playing musical instruments, or creating a beat through tapping or clapping. Improvisation can build the therapeutic alliance by inviting and providing space for clients to express themselves freely without judgment (Gold et al., 2007). However, the counselor should be attuned to any severe block or insecurity in client creativity, as improvisation can be intimidating for some clients.

Although counselors can use multiple types of instruments in counseling, percussive instruments require little music knowledge to produce the desired sound, thus making clients more inclined to use them. Drumming is especially useful for releasing suppressed emotions, such as anger or sadness (Krüger, 2010). In group settings, clients can express their feelings on the drum, while other members interpret their playing and/or add to the rhythm (Silverman, 2009).

As a coping mechanism, music can aid in managing various presenting problems. Music assists clients in learning to self-regulate and placate their reactions to stressful situations (McIntyre, 2009). The counselor and client can compile a calming playlist for the client to access in stress- or anxiety-inducing situations. In addition, music can serve as a reminder of the coping mechanism they learned in session. The counselor and client can explore the client's accessible music catalog and designate specific songs or artists as reminders for specific coping skills.

Nature

The use of nature in counseling may involve various senses and occur inside or outside. Integrating nature in an indoor environment can encompass using an electronic device to view a picture of nature or listen to sounds from nature. Counselors can also integrate nature in their counseling office through the use of windows, photographs and murals, water features, sounds from nature, and plants.

Counselors can also facilitate counseling sessions in an outdoor environment. This can involve sitting outside or engaging in outdoor activities during counseling, such as taking a walk or playing an outdoor game, sport, or activity. This can also include the integration of specialized therapeutic interventions that involve nature, such as horticultural therapy/therapeutic gardening, adventure-based counseling, and wilderness therapy. Some of these traditional outdoor activities can also be modified to use inside, such as using pots to engage in therapeutic gardening inside.

There are specific cautions and considerations related to using nature in counseling because the counselor has less control over the outside environment. This includes concerns related to confidentiality, weather, and critters (Swank & Shin, 2015b). Regarding confidentiality, it is more difficult to ensure that someone will not overhear the session or see the client during session when the session occurs outside, depending on the outdoor space. Additionally, the temperature and the presence of precipitation can affect the session. There are also a variety of critters in the outdoor environment that may be present during a counseling session held in the outdoor setting. It is also crucial for the counselor to be comfortable in nature before facilitating a counseling session in that environment.

Researchers report that the more people are connected to nature, the happier they are in life (Zelenski & Nisbet, 2014). Additionally, the natural environment is therapeutic and promotes wellness and development, including social and emotional development (Robinson & Zajicek, 2005), self-understanding (Robinson & Zajicek, 2005), self-esteem (Swank & Shin, 2015a), improved mood (Swank & Shin, 2015a), and physical health (McCurdy et al., 2010).

Play

Counselors can integrate play into their work with a variety of age groups; however, in working with younger children (ages 3–12), it is best practice to use play because it is the language of children. Therefore, children are able to express thoughts and feelings in play that they may not be able to verbalize.

There are a several different theoretical approaches to play therapy that range from nondirective to directive. For example, cognitive behavioral play therapy is directive, while client-centered (child-centered) is nondirective. In a child-centered play therapy approach, the counselor allows the child to take the lead during session and the counselor sets limits only as needed. In contrast, a counselor can use a more directive approach where the counselor leads the session by structuring activities.

There are a variety of play materials counselors can integrate in sessions when using play in counseling. In setting up a playroom, Landreth (2012) recommends the use of toys/materials in a variety of categories to help facilitate self-expression, reenact situations and events, foster self-control, and address a variety of concerns. Categories of toys include nurturing toys, aggressive toys, expressive toys/materials, pretend/fantasy toys, and scary toys. Nurturing toys include dolls, dollhouses, and baby bottles and can help with building a relationship with the counselor and exploring family dynamics. Aggressive toys include bop bags, toy guns, swords, and miniature army figures that help facilitate the expression of anger and the need for control in situations. Expressive toys and materials include a variety of art materials, including paint, markers, crayons, construction paper, and Play-Doh that facilitate self-expression. Pretend/fantasy toys include kitchen playsets, blocks, dress-up clothes, puppets, miniature figurines, doctor kits, and telephones that help facilitate the reenactment of situations and experimenting with a variety of roles. Finally, scary toys include plastic animals and puppets of scary or fierce animals and creatures, such as dinosaurs, monsters, sharks, and snakes, that help children express their fears and develop strategies to cope with them. Sandtray therapy is a specialized area of play therapy that involves clients creating their world in a tray of sand using miniatures.

Researchers have also examined the efficacy of play. Ray and McCullough (2016) reported four meta-analyses that have focused on examining the outcomes of play therapy interventions, with favorable results in addressing behavior problems (Bratton et al., 2005; LeBlanc & Ritchie, 2001; Lin & Bratton, 2015; Ray et al., 2015), academic concerns (LeBlanc & Ritchie, 2001; Ray et al., 2015), adjustment concerns (Bratton et al., 2005; LeBlanc & Ritchie, 2001), relationships (Lin & Bratton, 2015), trauma (LeBlanc & Ritchie, 2001), and self-efficacy (Lin & Bratton, 2015; Ray et al., 2015). Thus, research supports the use of play therapy in counseling.

Visual Arts

Counselors can use a variety of visual methods in the counseling session to provide a mechanism for self-expression. This includes painting, drawing, sculpture, crafts, videography, and photography. There are various types of material used in each method. With painting, the counselor can choose to integrate various types of painting including watercolor, acrylic, or finger paint. The drawing category also encompasses different materials including pencils, colored pencils, pens, markers, and crayons. Additionally, sculpture can involve Play-Doh or clay. Crafts is a large category that can include construction paper, glitter, feathers, craft sticks, magazines, pipe cleaners, tissue paper, yarn, beads, and many other materials. Videography and photography can involve videos and/or photographs or the development of them.

In selecting visual methods and materials with these methods, it is important to consider the goals of the session, as well as the materials most appropriate for the client. For example, counselors can use finger paint and Play-Doh with younger children, while adolescents and adults may prefer acrylic paint or clay. However, it is important for the counselor not to assume that just because a client is older that they will prefer clay over Play-Doh or acrylic paint over finger paint. Older clients may enjoy the opportunity to be able to use a variety of materials without fear of being judged by what they choose to use for self-expression.

Researchers have examined the effectiveness of using visual arts with a variety of client populations to address various concerns. For example, Duong et al. (2018) found that coloring a blank sheet of paper or a mandala was effective in reducing situational anxiety among counseling students. Additionally, researchers found a significant decline in anxiety symptoms for college students who participated in sessions of free-form painting (Sandmire et al., 2016). Furthermore, when using visual arts with adults with depressive disorders, researchers found that clients had a greater ability to explore and express emotions, address their problems, communicate, achieve a greater understanding of self, and make overall progress in counseling (Lee et al., 2017).

Writing

In counseling, writing can aid in the client's exploration of their thoughts and feelings and provide a vessel to tell their story. Journaling, free writing, and re-authoring are some examples of this creative medium. Regarding journaling, counselors can encourage clients to reflect, process, evaluate, and plan through journaling outside of session and can recommend this as homework between sessions. The client can use journaling to reflect and process daily events, which can facilitate curiosity, self-development, and empowerment (Lasater & Nielsen, 2009). An entry can also follow the use of a coping mechanism learned in counseling, as the writing process, due to being reflective, allows the client to process their thoughts and feelings and evaluate the effectiveness of the intervention (Coulson & Homewood, 2016). Clients can also use gratitude journals, which may enhance feelings of gratitude, life satisfaction, and positive affect (Işık & Ergüner-Tekinalp, 2017). Counselors can also encourage online journals or blogs, when appropriate, which can be more accessible than traditional journals. However, counselors should also remind clients to check the security and accessibility of their online entries by other users. Clients can bring their journals to counseling sessions to discuss them with the counselor. The counselor can also create space for a client to further explore their prose through an exercise called free writing.

In free writing, the counselor invites the client to uninhibitedly release their thoughts and feelings onto the page. The counselor explains that the client can use this time to write whatever and however they wish. Not having a writing prompt can be intimidating for both the counselor and client; therefore, the counselor should be confident in their execution of the intervention, and mindful of the client's capacity to engage in it. Free writing can also uncover topics of a sensitive nature. Clients should have the freedom to decide if and what they share with the counselor. Free writing allows clients to safely express themselves and better navigate their own process. Researchers report that it helps clients find their voice, shifts perceptions, and serves as an outlet for traumatic events (Pinhasi-Vittorio, 2018).

Re-authoring is narrative therapy technique that allows the client to regain a sense of agency over their life, their story. During session, clients write about specific events in their lives and process the event(s) with their counselors. The narration can focus on re-telling and editing past events, as well as present and future events. Clients can construct their trajectory of how their future will be or how they want it to be in life. This provides clients with a space to safely compose, process, and develop their stories. Similar to free writing, the counselor should encourage clients to write their stories in a way that is fitting for them instead of the counselor providing structure in how a story should be written. Clients can present their stories creatively as a poem, rap, or movie script. Clients can also write their stories in another setting, such as a video game (Graham, 2014). The client can frame, or reframe, and learn to manage their life circumstances in a new or more meaningful way (Hutto & Gallagher, 2017). The counselor can also introduce clients to other literary works as a means of discussing difficult topics, expressing themselves, and having a sense of universality. In using writing modalities, the counselor should be conscientious of the client's developmental level. Furthermore, written accounts can be more detailed and cathartic than verbal retellings; therefore, it is imperative for the counselor to establish a safe environment and rapport with the client.

Cautions and Considerations

In choosing to integrate creative approaches in counseling, it is important that the counselor clearly communicates they are using the intervention in the counseling process, not that the counselor is a credentialed therapist in that area (e.g., dance and movement therapist), unless they have the required training and credentials for the specific area. If a counselor refers to oneself as an art therapist without having the credential, then the counselor is misrepresenting oneself. A counselor should also ensure they have adequate training and supervision when integrating new creative techniques within the counseling process.

When integrating creative activities in the counseling process, it is important to focus on the process instead of the product. The client's ability to draw, write a story, or develop a song is not the focus, similar to the client's use of proper grammar not being the focus of counseling when using talk therapy. The counselor instead emphasizes self-expression and what occurs during the intervention. Because the focus is on the process and not the product, the counselor is also careful in how the creative product is interpreted and how the counselor describes the product. Counselors can offer clients the opportunity to discuss the product and process during the intervention. Counselors should refrain from praising the client about the product or judging the quality of the product. For example, counselors should refrain from referring to the product as "pretty" or sharing with the client they are an amazing artist, but instead focus on encouraging language, such as "You worked hard on that drawing" and "The song evoked a lot of anger related to the event."

Product confidentiality is also important. For example, a client may produce a really "cool" drawing that you want to display in your office. However, similar to it not being appropriate to audio record a counseling session and play it for others, it is not appropriate to display a product a client creates during session as part of the therapeutic process. This is different than a client bringing you a thank-you card they made and asking you to hang it up in your office; however, even with the card, you want to make sure that the client's name is not visible.

CREATIVITY AND MULTICULTURAL SOCIAL JUSTICE COUNSELING COMPETENCY

Awareness

Creativity can help foster awareness and develop insight by viewing something from a different perspective (thinking out of the box). This can occur through a variety of mechanisms, such as through the use of a metaphor or visual representation. A visual provides something to look at, which can prompt and enhance discussions. Sandtray is a powerful technique to increase awareness because it brings things that are in the subconscious to the conscious awareness. Counselors can gain valuable insight through the use of miniatures to represent their own statuses, values, beliefs, and values as well as those of the client, and also how both of these influence the counseling relationship. Following participation in a sandtray group, adolescent participants reported that the sandtray intervention facilitated self-expression and the development of insight (Swank & Lenes, 2013). As with other creative interventions, it is crucial that counselors receive training in sandtray before using this technique.

Writing, such as journaling, is another creative intervention that counselors can use to help promote awareness. Writing allows an individual to put thoughts and feelings on paper and then reread them to promote reflection. Counselors and counseling students can use this to reflect on their experiences, as well as reflect on readings and lectures (Jones et al., 2013). Thus, creative interventions can enhance verbal discussions about awareness by providing mechanisms that offer further opportunities to pause and reflect.

Knowledge

Awareness can help foster knowledge by creating a desire to learn and know more. Reading is one of the most fundamental ways to enhance knowledge, and counselors can use creativity in this process by challenging themselves to go beyond reading basic textbooks to read writings by diverse authors from diverse perspectives, as well as different formats of writing, such as short stories, poems, case studies, and personal accounts. Counselors can also enhance their knowledge through experiences, such as observations and interactions with diverse groups, and experiencing how worldviews, beliefs, values, and biases affect self, clients, and relationships. This can also include observation of counseling sessions to witness relationship dynamics. Researchers also found that self-reported multicultural counseling competence increased among counseling students after taking a multicultural counseling course that emphasized the use of film to increase multicultural knowledge (Greene et al., 2014). Jones et al. (2013) provide a list of films to use in fostering multicultural competence. Counselors can also use games to help increase their knowledge competency (Jones et al., 2013). This may include a quiz or matching format or include acting, which would also relate to developing skill competency. Furthermore, counselors can engage in teaching to further develop knowledge. Through these creative mechanisms, learning extends beyond traditional textbook knowledge.

A clinician should also possess knowledge of how their and a client's privileged or marginalized identities inform their overall perspective of creativity in counseling. A clinician or client who was raised in an environment that supported and allowed creativity may be privileged to exploring their creative side from their privileged experience. Therefore, the privileged clinician may find solace in facilitating creative interventions and the privileged client may expect them in session. However, a clinician or client who may not have been as creatively enriched or as able-bodied would be marginalized in this area. Nonetheless, the marginalized clinician can refrain from the use of creative interventions and the marginalized client may be resistant to acknowledging the potential of creative interventions. A clinician should be aware of their and the client's stance in this regard. Hence, a marginalized clinician should consider the expectations of privileged clients for using creativity and a privileged counselor should consider the resistance of a marginalized client and show compassion for these differences. This shows that the clinician is considering the clients attitudes and beliefs surrounding creative interventions in general and the intervention specifically chosen.

Skills

As a counselor develops awareness and knowledge of diversity and multicultural considerations, the next step in the process is to acquire skills of both a creative and inclusive nature. Counselors can gain skill sets of various creative interventions through specified trainings and supervised experiences. During trainings, counselors should be mindful of their own privilege and status alongside modifications and considerations when executing these with clients of various backgrounds.

With the development of skills, counselors can make cultural adaptions of interventions to be compatible with the client's cultural patterns, meanings, and values. For example, a counselor training to interpret a child's play should be aware of their own ethnocentric beliefs, especially when the client is of a different background than the counselor's background (Chang et al., 2005). Another example is learning to use dance or movement in session. The skill of mirroring—the imitation of the client's movements, emotions, or intentions by the therapist—is extremely useful when working with marginalized clients (Carmichael, 2012). Clients embody cultural messages that can be relayed through mirroring. This type of explicit nonverbal connection can foster a kinesthetic empathy for both parties and an increased sense of safety for the mover. The skill uniquely reveals the client's worldview and fosters the relationship between the counselor and client. When a counselor begins to acquire these skills involving creativity, one should be cognizant of their clientele and their status (i.e., privileged or marginalized) in comparison by referring to the quadrants of the MSJCC model (Ratts et al., 2015). With these considerations, the counselors can be intentional and purposeful with their pursuit of certain creative skill sets to best meet the needs of their clients.

Action

The counselor and client may identify differently between privileged and marginalized identities, and it is crucial to consider this in the counseling process (Chan et al., 2018). For example, a client may feel uncomfortable with an intervention, and instead of perceiving the client's discomfort as resistance, from a multicultural social justice lens the counselor recognizes the need to creatively modify the intervention and takes action in doing this to help the client feel more comfortable.

Client and counselor statuses, both privileged and marginalized, also influence the counseling relationship, and counselors use creativity in the counseling process to foster the counseling relationship (Haskins & Singh, 2015). Through the use of creative modalities, the counselor can help encourage the client to express their thoughts, feelings, and beliefs that the client may struggle with finding the words to express, instead of ignoring it when the client struggles with verbally expressing these areas (Molina et al., 2005). Counselors can use visual arts to facilitate expression and conversation about how statuses influence the counseling relationship. For example, the counselor can use drawing or sculpting to portray the counseling relationship and how the client and counselor statuses are affecting the relationship, which may help facilitate a conversation with the client. It is also crucial that counselors use language that the client will understand and that is respectful of the client's privileged and marginalized identities, demonstrating cross-cultural communication (Kim & Park, 2015).

CASE STUDY 1: MARGINALIZED CLIENT (FABIOLA) & PRIVILEGED COUNSELOR (LISA)

Fabiola is a 21-year-old Hispanic female client. She has attended four counseling sessions with her 30-year-old White female counselor Lisa. Fabiola entered counseling to seek help with her ongoing depression that she "can't seem to shake." Lisa has tried to engage Fabiola to talk about the issues that could be surrounding and/or continuing to exacerbate her depression, but this has not been successful. As a counselor with an identity grounded in cognitive behavioral therapy (CBT), Lisa tried various CBT interventions (i.e., disputing irrational beliefs, shame-attacking exercises). However, Fabiola reported she didn't feel any better. Lisa sought support from her supervisor and reported the difficulty she has experienced with developing a relationship with Fabiola.

Lisa's supervisor challenged her to consider possible barriers to forming a relationship with Fabiola. Lisa was encouraged to reflect on her privileged identity in comparison to her client's marginalized identity. As a result, Lisa recalled that Fabiola had never been to counseling before and that her family had been against her attending counseling due to stigma related to seeking mental health assistance and sharing personal information with someone in the secular world. At the next session, Lisa asks Fabiola some of the ways she copes with stress, as well as strategies her family uses. Fabiola stated, "I guess music. My grandma loves her church hymns, my mom loves salsa music, and my dad and brother love to jam out to reggaeton. I love a little bit of everything." Lisa then encouraged Fabiola to identify a song she enjoyed that closely resonated with her desire to "overcome her depression." Fabiola brought in Demi Lovato's "**Warrior**" to the next session and reported loving the artist because she is also of Hispanic descent. Lisa printed the lyrics for each of them and as they listened to the song, each of them underlined lyrics they believed to be salient for Fabiola. After listening to the song, each of them shared their thoughts line by line.

In sessions that followed, the song and term *warrior* were used to help Fabiola share more with Lisa. Fabiola began to share the areas of her life that were stopping her from becoming the warrior she wanted to be, and Lisa was then able to dispute those irrational beliefs by relating back to the song. Fabiola continued to attend sessions with Lisa over the next few months. At termination, Fabiola told Lisa that she felt misunderstood by her, had started to believe her family's views that counseling was a waste of time, and contemplated not continuing counseling after the first couple of sessions. However, she reported that after sharing the song in session, she felt a breakthrough. Fabiola stated, "It's like we shared the same language with the song. I finally felt understood."

CASE STUDY 2: PRIVILEGED CLIENT (CHAD) AND MARGINALIZED COUNSELOR (MICHAEL)

Chad is a middle-aged White male client who has had six sessions with his middle-aged Black male counselor Michael. Chad is in the Army and returned from serving in combat 8 months ago. He reported he has struggled with readjusting to living back home. In counseling, Chad has proudly shared several war stories but is dismissive with Michael's attempts to explore Chad's emotions surrounding them and PTSD symptoms. Michael has used his own identity as a man to try to relate to Chad, get him to talk about his emotions, and provide psychoeducation related to PTSD for war veterans; however, Chad continues to be reluctant to share at a deeper level during sessions.

At the seventh session, Michael checked in with Chad on how he was experiencing counseling thus far. Chad stated, "To be honest, I am growing bored with the idea of coming here just to talk about how I feel each week. I was actually wondering when I can be done because this isn't going anywhere." Michael consulted with another counselor, John, about his difficulties. John explored Michael's use of creativity in counseling and out-of-the-box thinking to enhance the relationship with Chad. Michael admitted his reluctance with using creativity due to not considering himself a creative person and having limited exposure to creative experiences and forms of expression throughout his life. John reminded Michael that although his experiences with creative expression were limited, this might not be true for his client. He shared with Michael that it is the counselor's responsibility to be aware of how his own statuses and experiences affect the counseling process and be open to consult about and integrate adapted and creative inventions into counseling to meet the needs of the client. After this consultation, Michael was determined to explore his "creative juices."

Michael remembered Chad sharing that he enjoyed drawing and that he kept a sketchbook while overseas, so Michael decided to introduce art and drawing in sessions and encouraged Chad to bring his sketchbook. During the next session, Michael and Chad processed his art from overseas and what they meant for him. Chad admitted that he had not drawn since being back. During session, Michael encouraged Chad to draw a picture of his life being back in the States. Drawing became a consistent component of Chad's counseling sessions and a healthy coping skill to use between sessions. During the final session, Chad reflected on the session where he expressed not wanting to continue counseling. He stated, "I knew I wasn't ready to end counseling, but I also knew that things were not improving for me. When you let me bring in my drawing, I finally felt alive in here."

SUMMARY, INSIGHTS, AND ACTIONS

This chapter provided an overview of how counselors can use creativity in their practice with clients of various backgrounds. The authors briefly described the history and significance of creativity in counseling, along with eight creative interventions. Additionally, they discussed the application of creativity in accordance with the MSJCC. Finally, the case studies provide readers with multiple vantages (e.g., the marginalized counselor/ privileged client; the privileged counselor/marginalized client) and an opportunity to apply the MSJCC framework when incorporating creativity into counseling. Readers are encouraged to explore the additional resources to learn more about these creative interventions and to continually develop their MSJCC throughout their development as professional counselors.

REFLECTION AND DISCUSSION QUESTIONS

1. In what ways do you see yourself as a creative person?
2. Think about a creative intervention discussed in this chapter that you feel connected to; how might you use this intervention to develop a relationship with a client who is different than you?
3. How might you use creativity to foster your multicultural social justice counseling competency in the following areas: (a) awareness, (b) knowledge, (c) skills, and (d) action?
4. How might you introduce a creative intervention to clients who do not consider themselves "creative"?
5. How might Lisa have used other creative interventions to connect with Fabiola?
6. How might Michael use other forms of art in his sessions with Chad?

ADDITIONAL READINGS AND RESOURCES

Association for Creativity in Counseling: www.creativecounselor.org/
Animal Assisted Intervention International: aai-int.org/
International Society for Animal Assisted Therapy: www.aat-isaat.org/
American Library Association: www.ala.org/tools/atoz/bibliotherapy
American Dance Therapy Association: adta.org/
North American Drama Therapy Association: www.nadta.org/
American Society of Group Psychotherapy and Psychodrama: www.asgpp.org
American Music Therapy Association: www.musictherapy.org/
Children and Nature Network: www.childrenandnature.org/
Association for Play Therapy: www.a4pt.org
Evidence-based Child Therapy: evidencebasedchildtherapy.com/
American Art Therapy Association: arttherapy.org/about-art-therapy/

REFERENCES

Ali, S. (2017). *Inside Out* and counseling: Creative interventions to facilitate emotional intelligence. *Journal of Creativity in Mental Health, 12*(3), 377–387. https://doi.org/10.10 80/15401383.2016.1275995

Amendt-Lyon, N. (2001). Art and creativity in Gestalt therapy. *Gestalt Review, 5*, 225–248.

American Dance Therapy Association. (2016). *Home page.* https://adta.org/

Amir, D., & Bodner, E. (2013). Music therapy students' reflections on their participation in a music therapy group. *Nordic Journal of Music Therapy, 22*(3), 243–273. https://doi.org/10.1080/08098131.2012.762035

Armstrong, S. N., & Ricard, R. J. (2016). Integrating rap music into counseling with adolescents in a disciplinary alternative education program. *Journal of Creativity in Mental Health, 11*(3), 423–435.

Arruda-Colli, M. N. F., Weaver, M. S., & Wiener, L. (2017). Communication about dying, death, and bereavement: A systematic review of children's literature. *Journal of Palliative Medicine, 20,* 548–559. https://doi.org/10.1089/jpm.2016.0494

Axline, V. M. (1964) *Dibs in search of self: personality development in play therapy* Boston: Houghton Mifflin

Beetz, A., Uvnäs-Moberg, K., Julius, H., & Kotrschal, K. (2012). Psychosocial and psychophysiological effects of human-animal interactions: The possible role of oxytocin. *Frontiers in Psychology, 3.* https://doi.org/10.3389/fpsyg.2012.00234

Betzalel, N., & Shechtman, Z. (2017). The impact of bibliotherapy superheroes on youth who experience parental absence. *School Psychology International, 38*(5), 473–490. https://doi.org/10.1177/0143034317719943

Binkley, E. (2013). Creative strategies for treating victims of domestic violence. *Journal of Creativity in Mental Health, 8,* 305–313. https://doi.org/10.1080/15401383.2013.821932.

Bratton, S., Ray, D., Rhine, T., & Jones, L. (2005). The efficacy of play therapy with children: A meta-analytic review of treatment outcomes. *Professional Psychology: Research and Practice, 36,* 376–390.

Canadian Agency for Drugs and Technologies in Health. (2012). *Therapy dogs and horses for mental health: A review of the clinical effectiveness.* Author.

Capello, P. P. (2016). Basics: An intra/interactional model of DMT with the adult psychiatric patient. In S. Chaiklin & H. Wengrower (Eds.), *The art and science of dance/movement therapy: Life is dance* (pp. 77–101). Routledge.

Carmichael, N. (2012). Turning towards multicultural diversity competence in dance/movement therapy. *American Journal of Dance Therapy, 34*(2), 99–113. https://doi.org/10.1007/s10465-012-9140-z

Carson, D. K., & Becker, K. W. (2004). When lightning strikes: Reexamining creativity in psychotherapy. *Journal of Counseling & Development, 82,* 111–115.

Chan, C. D., Cor, D. N., & Band, M. P. (2018). Privilege and oppression in counselor education: An intersectionality framework. *Journal of Multicultural Counseling & Development, 46*(1), 58–73. https://doi.org/10.1002/jmcd.12092

Chang, C. Y., Ritter, K. B., & Hays, D. G. (2005). Multicultural trends and toys in play therapy. *International Journal of Play Therapy, 14*(2), 69–85. https://doi.org/10.1037/h0088903

Coulson, D., & Homewood, J. (2016). Developing psychological literacy: Is there a role for reflective practice? *Journal of University Teaching & Learning Practice, 13*(2). http://ro.uow.edu.au/jutlp/vol13/iss2/5

Duong, K., Stargell, N. A., & Mauk, G. W. (2018) Effectiveness of coloring mandala designs to reduce anxiety in graduate counseling students. *Journal of Creativity in Mental Health, 13*(3), 318–330. https://doi.org/10.1080/15401383.2018.1437001

Gilmore, L., & Howard, G. (2016). Children's books that promote understanding of difference, diversity, and disability. *Journal of Psychologists and Counsellors in Schools, 26,* 218–251. https://doi.org/10.1017/jgc.2016.26

Gladding, S. T., Newsome, D., Binkley, E., & Henderson, D. A. (2008). The lyrics of hurting and healing: Finding words that are revealing. *Journal of Creativity in Mental Health*, 3(3), 212–219. https://doi.org/10.1080/15401380802385210

Glavin, C. E. Y., & Montgomery, P. (2017). Creative bibliotherapy for post-traumatic stress disorder (PTSD): A systematic review. *Journal of Poetry Therapy*, 30(2), 95–107. https://doi.org/10.1080/08893675.2017.1266190

Gold, C., Wilgram, T., & Voracek, M. (2007). Predictors of change in music therapy with children and adolescents: The role of therapeutic techniques. *Psychology and Psychotherapy: Theory, Research, and Practice*, 80(4), 577–589. https://doi.org/10.1348/147608307X204396

Graham, J. (2014). Narrative therapy for treating video game addiction. *International Journal of Mental Health and Addiction*, 12, 701–707. https://doi.org/10.1007/s11469-014-9491-4

Greene, J. H., Barden, S. M., Richardson, E. D., & Hall, K. G. (2014). The influence of film and experiential pedagogy on multicultural counseling self-efficacy and multicultural counseling competence. *Journal of the Scholarship of Teaching and Learning*, 14(5), 63–78. https://doi.org/10.14434/josotlv14i5.12656

Haskins, N. H., & Singh, A. (2015). Critical race theory and counselor education pedagogy: Creating equitable training. *Counselor Education & Supervision*, 54(4), 288–301. https://doi.org/10.1002/ceas.12027

Hunt, M., Al-Braiki, F., Dailey, S., Russell, R., & Simon, K. (2018). Mindfulness training, yoga, or both? Dismantling the active components of a mindfulness-based stress reduction intervention. *Mindfulness*, 9, 512–520. https://doi.org/10.1007/s12671-017-0793-z

Huss, E., Elhozayel, E., & Marcus, E. (2012). Art in group work as an anchor for integrating the micro and macro levels of intervention with incest survivors. *Clinical Social Work Journal*, 40, 401–411. https://doi.org/10.1007/s10615-012-0393-2

Hutto, D. D., & Gallagher, S. (2017). Re-authoring narrative therapy: Improving our self-management tools. *Philosophy, Psychiatry, & Psychology*, 24, 157–167. https://doi.org/10.1353/ppp.2017.0020

Işık, Ş., & Ergüner-Tekinalp, B. (2017). The effects of gratitude journaling on Turkish first year college students' college adjustment, life satisfaction and positive affect. *International Journal for the Advancement of Counselling*, 39, 164–175. https://doi.org/10.1007/s10447-017-9289-8

Jones, J. M., Sander, J. B., & Booker, K. W. (2013). Multicultural competency building: Practical solutions for training and evaluating student progress. *Training and Education in Professional Psychology*, 7(1), 12–22. https://doi.org/10.1037/a0030880

Jung, C. G. (1973). *Mandala symbolism*. R. F. C. Hull, Trans. Princeton University Press.

Kedem-Tahar, E., & Kellerman, P. F. (1996). Psychodrama and drama therapy: A comparison. *The Arts in Psychotherapy*, 23, 27–36.

Kim, B. S. K., & Park, Y. S. (2015). Communication styles, cultural values, and counseling effectiveness with Asian Americans. *Journal of Counseling & Development*, 93(3), 269–279. https://doi.org/10.1002/jcad.12025

Kimbel, T. M., & Protivnak, J. J. (2010). For those about to rock (with your high school students), we salute you: School counselors using music interventions. *Journal of Creativity in Mental Health, 5*(1), 25–38. https://doi.org/10.1080/15401381003626857

Koch, S., Kunz, T., Lykou, S., & Cruz, R. (2014). Effects of dance movement therapy and dance on health-related psychological outcomes: A meta-analysis. *The Arts in Psychotherapy, 41*(1), 46–64. https://doi.org/10.1016/j.aip.2013.10.004

Kottler, J. A., & Hecker, L. L. (2002). Creativity *in therapy: Being struck by lightning and guided by thunderstorms. Journal of Clinical Activities, Assignments, & Handouts in Psychotherapy Practice, 2,* 5–21.

Krüger, D. (2010). Psycho-educational guidelines for the use of music in a group anger management programme for children in residential care. *International Journal of Diversity in Organisations, Communities & Nations, 10,* 25–35.

Landreth, G. L. (2012). *Play therapy: The art of the relationship* (3rd ed.). Routledge.

Lasater, K., & Nielsen, A. (2009). Reflective journaling for clinical judgment development and evaluation. *Journal of Nursing Education, 48*(1), 40–44. https://doi.org/10.3928/01484834-20090101-06

LeBlanc, M., & Ritchie, M. (2001). A meta-analysis of play therapy outcomes. *Counseling Psychology Quarterly, 14,* 149–163.

Lee, K. L., Mustaffa, M. S., & Tan, S. Y. (2017). Visual arts in counselling adults with depressive disorders. *British Journal of Guidance & Counselling, 45*(1), 56–71. https://doi.org/10.1080/03069885.2015.1130797

Lin, D., & Bratton, S. (2015). A meta-analytic review of child-centered play therapy approaches. *Journal of Counseling & Development, 93,* 45–58.

Malchiodi, C. A., & Miller, G. (2003). Art therapy and domestic violence. In C. A. Malchiodi (Ed.), *Handbook of art therapy* (pp. 335–348). Guilford.

May, R. (1975). *The courage to create.* Bantam.

McCarthy, J. (2017). Teaching creativity: A look beyond counseling. *Journal of Asia Pacific Counseling, 7,* 37–45. https://doi.org/10.18401/2017.7.1.4

McCurdy, L. E., Winterbottom, K. E., Mehta, S. S., & Roberts, J. R. (2010). Using nature and outdoor activity to improve children's health. *Current Problems in Pediatric and Adolescent Health Care, 40*(5), 102–117. https://doi.org/10.1016/j.cppeds.2010.02.003

McIntyre, J. (2009). Interactive family music therapy: Untangling the system. *The Australian and New Zealand Journal of Family Therapy, 30,* 260–268. https://doi.org/10.1375/anft.30.4.260

Molina, B., Monteiro-Leitner, J., Garrett, M. T., & Gladding, S. T. (2005). Making the connection: Interweaving multicultural creative arts through the power of group counseling interventions. *Journal of Creativity in Mental Health, 1,* 5–15. https://doi.org/10.1300/J456v01n02_02.

Morrison, M. L. (2007). Health benefits of animal-assisted interventions. *Complementary Health Practice Review, 12,* 51–62. https://doi.org/10.1177/1533210107302397

Orkibi, H. (2018). The user-friendliness of drama: Implications for drama therapy and psychodrama admission and training. *Arts in Psychotherapy, 59*, 101–108. https://doi.org/10.1016/j.aip.2018.04.004

Pilkington, K., Kirkwood, G., Rampes, H., & Richardson, J. (2005). Yoga for depression: The research evidence. *Journal of Affective Disorders, 89*(1–3), 13–24. https://doi.org/10.1016/j.jad.2005.08.013

Pinhasi-Vittorio, L. (2018). Writing, sharing, and healing: The interplay of literacy in the healing journey of the recovering from substance abuse. *Journal of Poetry Therapy, 31*(4), 209–223. https://doi.org/10.1080/08893675.2018.1504668

Rappaport, L. (2011). Focusing-oriented art therapy: Working with trauma. *Person Centered and Experiential Psychotherapies, 9*(2), 128–142. https://doi.org/10.1080/14779757.2010.9688513

Ratts, M. J., Singh, A. A., Nassar-McMillan, S., Butler, S. K., & McCullough, J. R. (2015). *Multicultural and social justice counseling competencies.* http://www.counseling.org/docs/default-source/competencies/multicultural-and-social-justice-counseling-competencies.pdf?sfvrsn=20

Ray, D., Armstrong, S., Balkin, R., & Jayne, K. (2015). Child centered play therapy in the schools: Review and meta-analysis. *Psychology in the Schools, 52*, 107–123.

Ray, D. C, & McCullough, R. (2015; revised 2016). *Evidence-based practice statement: Play therapy* (Research report). Association for Play Therapy. http://www.a4pt.org/?page=EvidenceBased

Robinson, C. W., & Zajicek, J. M. (2005). Growing minds: The effects of a one-year school garden program on six constructs of life skills of elementary school children. *HortTechnology, 15*(3), 453–457.

Rogers, C. R. (1959). A theory of therapy, personality and interpersonal relationships, as developed in the client-centered framework. In S. Koch (Ed.), *Psychology: A study of a science. Vol. 3: Formulations of the person and the social context* (pp. 184–256). McGraw-Hill.

Rogers, N. (1993). *The creative connection: Expressive arts as healing.* Science and Behavior Books.

Rybak, C., & Deuskar, M. (2010). Enriching group counseling through integrating yoga concepts and practices. *Journal of Creativity in Mental Health, 5*(1), 3–14. https://doi.org/10.1080/15401381003626782

Sandmire, D. A., Rankin, N. E., Gorham, S. R., Eggleston, D. T., French, C. A., Lodge, E. E., Kuns, G.C.& Grimm, D. R. (2016). Psychological and autonomic effects of art making in college-aged students. *Anxiety, Stress & Coping: An International Journal, 29*(5), 561–569. https://doi.org/10.1080/10615806.2015.1076798

Satir, V. (1972). *Peoplemaking.* Science and Behavior Books.

Shechtman, Z. (2017). Group intervention with aggressive children and youth through bibliotherapy. *International Journal of Group Psychotherapy, 67*(1), 47–67. https://doi.org/10.1080/00207284.2016.1202682

Silverman, M. J. (2009). The effect of single-session psychoeducational music therapy on verbalizations and perceptions in psychiatric patients. *Journal of Music Therapy, 46,* 105–131. https://doi.org/10.1093/jmt/46.2.105

Swank, J. M., & Lenes, E. (2013). An exploratory inquiry of sandtray group experiences with adolescent females in an alternative school. *The Journal for Specialists in Group Work, 38*(4), 330–348. https://doi.org/10.1080/01933922.2013.835013

Swank, J. M., & Shin, S. (2015a). Garden counseling groups and self-esteem: A mixed methods study with children with emotional and behavioral problems. *Journal for Specialists in Group Work, 40*(3), 315–331. https://doi.org/10.1080/01933922.2015.1056570

Swank, J. M., & Shin, S. M. (2015b). Nature-based child-centered play therapy: An innovative counseling approach. *International Journal of Play Therapy, 24*(3), 151–161. https://doi.org/10.1037/a0039127

Theron, L., Cockcroft, K., & Wood, L. (2017). The resilience-enabling value of African folktales: The read-me-to-resilience intervention. *School Psychology International, 38*(5), 491–506. https://doi.org/10.1177/0143034317719941

Whale and Dolphin Conservation Society. (2007). *Dolphin-assisted therapy: Can you put your faith in DAT?* Author.

Zelenski, J. M., & Nisbet, E. K. (2014). Happiness and feeling connected: The distinct role of nature relatedness. *Environment and Behavior, 46*(1), 3–23. https://doi.org/10.1177/0013916512451901

Zilcha-Mano, S., Mikulincer, M., & Shaver, P. R. (2011). Pet in the therapy room: An attachment perspective on animal-assisted therapy. *Attachment & Human Development, 13*(6), 541–561. https://doi.org/10.1080/14616734.2011.608987

CHAPTER 13

TELEBEHAVIORAL HEALTH

Tricia M. Mikolon, University of the Cumberlands

Debra M. Perez, University of the Cumberlands

Sherry M. Todd, University of the Cumberlands

LEARNING OBJECTIVES

1. Understand the importance and history of online counseling.
2. Apply multicultural competencies to online counseling.
3. Understand the intersection between social justice and online practice.
4. Recognize the limitations of online counseling and understand necessary adaptations for overcoming limitations.

LEARNING OUTCOMES

1. Understand the evolution of online therapy, including the contribution of distance counseling.
2. Identify the impact of affluence in online counseling.
3. Grasp the social justice opportunities in an online environment as well as identify social justice variables.
4. Identify limitations of online counseling and formulate appropriate adaptions to overcome each limitation.

Sigmund Freud (1955), the father of psychoanalysis, was not only the founder of the psychoanalytic theory and the first mental health therapist, but he was also the first distance counselor, as he treated some of his patients through correspondence in letters, including his famous treatment of "Little Hans." Since then, advances in technology have provided new opportunities for counseling across a distance. Skinner and Zack (2004) explain that the invention of the telephone provided a novel treatment modality for counselors that is now supported in the research as an effective treatment option for various clients. With the increased utilization of personal computers and the invention of the internet, distance counseling was again influenced by changing technology (Skinner & Zack, 2004).

Although the initial use was for support groups and answers to mental health questions online, the internet now provides counselors with the technology to meet with their clients face-to-face through confidential videoconferencing platforms (Skinner & Zach, 2004). Unfortunately, many of the opportunities afforded to "Little Hans" and the initial clients of distance counseling were due to their affluence, having access to the telephone or internet, and the opportunity for telehealth may not be available to everyone equally. Counseling professionals understand that the profession of counseling may no longer be limited to in-person, face-to-face interactions. The COVID-19 pandemic in many cases necessitated the shift to other venues to provide counseling services. It is important to understand the evolving nature of the profession with regard to distance counseling, technology, and social media, and how such resources can be used to better serve clients while striving to become knowledgeable about these resources. While counselors need to understand the additional concerns related to the use of distance counseling, or telebehavorial health, as it is often referred to, technology, and social media, they must also make every attempt to protect confidentiality and meet any legal and ethical requirements for the use of such resources. Pursuing the use of a distance platform to provide services requires counselors to participate in continuing education activities specific to telebehavioral health and to remain current in a rapidly changing field. Technology changes at such a fast pace that it is strongly advised counselors update their training in technology and in providing telebehavioral health regularly.

Researchers have found telebehavioral health more accessible to those who previously may have avoided counseling due to the perceived stigma, the lack of accessibility, and the affordability (Mallen et al., 2005; Novotney, 2017; Wong et al., 2018). This increased demand for telebehavioral health brings with it an increased need for counselor training to ensure high-quality ethical treatment and multicultural awareness. The American Counseling Association (ACA, 2014) has addressed the uniqueness of online counseling sessions in stressing the need for counselors to be proficient with technology and understand the special ethical considerations and implications of the online format (standard H).

Online counseling formats require understanding the various nuances unique to tele-behavioral health sessions. The competent counselor will understand and appreciate the legal, ethical, and technological concerns and formulate appropriate solutions prior to beginning telebehavioral health sessions by understanding the local and state laws that apply. The need to appreciate and apply ethical and multicultural considerations in each session tailored to the client is a necessary skill. A competent counselor will also be able to provide culturally sensitive, confidential, and informed counseling through the online venue.

MULTICULTURAL AND SOCIAL JUSTICE CONSIDERATIONS

Inclusion

Historically, only the affluent had access to distance counseling or other mental health treatment. Affluence is the state of having an abundance of money, property, or other material goods (Cambridge Dictionary, n.d.) and has impacted access to distance mental health services in similar ways as it has traditional treatment. Electricity, telephones, computers, and the internet have been available to the elite or well-to-do years before being available to lower socioeconomic groups. A study conducted by Broadband Now found that the Federal Communications Commission (FCC) estimate of 20 million Americans without access to the internet is actually double, and 42 million Americans do not have broadband (Poon, 2020). Public schools moving to online education experienced this disparity. Despite the disparity, telebehavioral health is available to an ever-increasing number of people and the removal of barriers continues.

The American Counseling Association (ACA, 2014) addresses the need for counselors to be nondiscriminatory in that they do not condone or engage in discrimination against prospective or current clients, students, employees, supervisees, or research participants based on age, culture, disability, ethnicity, race, religion/spirituality, gender, gender identity, sexual orientation, marital/ partnership status, language preference, socioeconomic status, immigration status, or any basis proscribed by law (ACA, 2014, C.5). Distance counseling, or telebehavioral health, can offer an opportunity for therapy to people who would otherwise not seek counseling services. The provision of telebehavioral health allows physically challenged people access, if transportation is a barrier, or those who are in rural locations, if access to mental health services is a barrier, and so on. While the provision of telebehavioral health can expand access, it can be exclusionary as well. As the country experienced during the stay-at-home mandate during the COVID-19 pandemic, many school-aged children did not have access to the internet due to socioeconomic status, geographic location, or other barriers often experienced by marginalized people.

Cultural factors can impact the manner in which client problems are defined or experienced (ACA, 2014, E.5.b). Counselors need to be keenly aware of the possible impact of a client's culture when diagnosing mental health disorder. The purpose of diagnosis is to "succinctly capture key characteristics" about a client's symptoms and biopsychosocial status (McAuliffe et al., 2013, p. 561). These cultural considerations need to include the client's culture and social norms, traditions, socioeconomic status, age, spirituality, and gender roles (World Health Organization [WHO], 2013), as well as race, ethnicity, and sex. Counseling services provided on telebehavioral health formats allow the counselor to see the client in their own environment but also increases the need for understanding and appreciation of the individual and their multidimensional makeup. This understanding and appreciation of diversity is important throughout counseling; however, it is especially important to pay particular attention to these variables as they relate to assessment (ACA, 2014, E.8). Counselors need to consider the aforementioned variables and their effects on test administration and interpretation. Without such consideration, the counselor is viewing the results in isolation, losing proper perspective of the client and the impact these variables have on the individual, potentially leading to misdiagnosis. "Intentionally asking clients about the meaning and nature of the cultural dimensions of their lives" is a vital part of the assessment process (McAuliffe et al., 2013, p. 560). Additionally, counselors practicing online will need to administer assessments normed for online use, as tests normed for in-person administration may not be appropriate.

Consideration of social justice is also necessary for the telebehavioral health counselor. Appreciation of the historical and social prejudices a client experiences is of the utmost importance in fully understanding the individual. Advocating for social justice in telebehavioral health involves teaching clients how to connect to services in their communities, providing information on available services, working with various systems the client is in contact with, and encouraging clients to advocate for themselves to increase their feelings of belonging and empowerment (Bradley et al., 2008; Toporek et al., 2005). Telebehavioral counselors can assist clients by providing them with a list of self-help or support groups and encouraging them to work with organizations and individuals in their community to meet treatment goals as well as to explore the client's biases (Kiselica & Robins, 2011; Locke & Kiselica, 1999). Additionally, ACA (2014) encourages counselors to strive to become aware of these implications and address their own, as well as others' biases openly (E.5.c). Additionally, social justice advocacy can include promoting access to technology and internet services in areas and for populations that are without the means to participate in counseling services.

Counselors are expected by the ethics of the profession to be culturally competent but may struggle with what variables influence the multicultural identity of an individual. The RESPECTFUL counseling cube (D'Andrea & Daniels, 2001) outlines the various factors that comprise an individual's identity and include religion/spirituality (R), economic class and background (E), sexual identity (S), psychological maturity (P), ethnic/racial identity (E), chronological stage (C), trauma history/experiences (T), family background/history (F), unique physical characteristics (U), and geographical location (L). By further exploring each of these variables for ourselves, counselors can increase their own awareness and biases regarding each, and thus be able to develop a more robust action plan for how to address each in a healthy and respectful manner (LeBeauf et al., 2009). Increased awareness on behalf of the counselor leads to better appreciation of each variable, guiding the necessary modifications to their interactions with clients and resulting in a therapeutic relationship rooted firmly in both appreciation for and acceptance of the differences of each unique individual.

Professional Competencies

Informed Consent

The ACA (2014) Code of Ethics mandates the counselor to communicate with the client in a manner that is "both developmentally and culturally appropriate by using "clear and understandable language when discussing the issues related to informed consent" (p. 4, A.2.c). This is particularly important when providing telebehavioral health services because the words and technology may not be clear to everyone. "When clients have difficulty understanding the language that counselors use, counselors provide necessary services (e.g., arranging for a qualified interpreter or translator) to ensure comprehension by clients" (p. 4). Counselors should consider the unique cultural composition of the client and the implications of providing informed consent and "adjust their practices accordingly" (p. 4) to ensure client comprehension. Additionally, clients need to understand the technology requirements of participating in services online and the potential risks.

The ACA (2014) Code of Ethics goes on to discuss the need for informed consent and disclosure, stressing the need for clients to have the "freedom to choose whether to use distance counseling, social media, and/or technology within the counseling process" (p. 17, H.2.a). Specifically, this highlights the client's right to choose the modality of treatment they are involved in while fully understanding both the risks and benefits of their chosen platform. Furthermore, it supports the client's decision on the technology they use according to their ability and comfort level as well as their full understanding of the anticipated response time, emergency procedures, and "cultural and/or language differences that may affect delivery of services" (ACA, 2014, p. 17). Advocacy in counseling can occur on this level when counselors encourage clients to express their preferences and support their boundaries and needs (Bradley et al., 2008; Kiselica & Robinson, 2001; Toporek et al., 2006).

The ACA (2014) Code of Ethics also addresses the need for counselors to respect client rights, including the need to maintain consciousness and responsiveness regarding cultural meanings of confidentiality and privacy (B.1.a). In essence, this requires counselors to respect different views toward disclosure of information and to hold ongoing discussions with their clients as to how, when, and with whom information is to be shared. Telebehavioral health providers need to plan for informed consent and release of information forms to be provided in not only English but also in other languages. Providing information in the client's first language assists in clarification of the limits of confidentiality and the exact information to be released, as well as further assists in the development of a therapeutic relationship based in mutual respect and open communication (Gonzalez & Faubert, 2015). Counselors need to also consider the technology necessary for a client to sign an informed consent or release of information form, as not all may have access to the required equipment or programs, and have a plan for clients who struggle to complete these forms in the online format.

Boundaries

Regarding boundaries, the ACA (2014) Code of Ethics states counselors can only practice within the boundaries of their competence (C.2.a). Competency is rooted in the counselor's education, training, supervised experience, state and national professional credentials, as well as professional experience. Multicultural counseling competency is required across all counseling specialties, and counselors gain knowledge, personal awareness, sensitivity, dispositions, and skills pertinent to being a culturally competent counselor in working with a diverse client population. This speaks to the need for counselors to be trained in the best practices of telebehavioral health prior to working with any client. This type of telebehavioral health training goes above and beyond what is currently required by the Council for Accreditation of Counseling and Related Educational Programs (CACREP, n.d.) for accredited counseling programs and requires the counselor to gain additional training and certification to ensure competence in online practice.

Knowledge and Legal Considerations

The ACA (2014) explores the need for both knowledge and competency in the Code of Ethics, which states, "Counselors who engage in the use of distance counseling, technology, and/ or social media develop knowledge and skills regarding related technical, ethical, and legal considerations (e.g., special certifications, additional course work)" (p. 17, H.1.a). Proficient counselors will be keenly aware of not only the ethical and legal considerations, but technical problems that can hinder the use of the chosen online format. The ability to rectify issues for themselves as well as assist clients in doing the same at their location is a necessary skill for any telebehavioral health professional. Counselors need not only adhere to the ethics, but also display competency in differentiating treatment to fit the client in the online platform (Fairburn & Cooper, 2011). This differentiation, based on the needs, comfort level, cultural considerations, and personalization of treatment to fit the client, supports a social justice approach to displaying both knowledge and legal appreciation and understanding.

Telebehavioral health professionals need to be aware of and adhere to laws and regulations at "both the counselor's practicing location and the client's place of residence" (ACA, 2014, p. 17, H.1.b). Counselors are responsible for informing their clients of applicable "legal rights and limitations governing the practice of counseling across state lines and international boundaries." This includes the handling of information in accordance with Health Insurance Portability and Accountability Act (HIPAA) regulations and emergency situations, as well as the lack of anonymity rooted in both legal and ethical mandates (Novotney, 2017). Informing the client not only empowers them with knowledge but also supports them in making healthy, well-informed decisions regarding their treatment and the platform on which it is provided.

Technology and Social Media

When contemplating practicing in an online format, there are specific technological considerations that will need to be addressed prior to online practice establishment. A computer or laptop with a camera and microphone and a fast, secure internet connection is the minimum requirement. Computers need password protection and the ability to remotely destroy information contained on the hard drive should the computer ever be stolen. Online practices utilize videoconferencing for sessions and an electronic medical record for signing paperwork and maintaining client records. The counselor will need to have a signed business associate agreement (BAA) with the videoconferencing platform and the electronic medical record platform (or any electronic business having access to client-protected information) ensuring that the client's privacy will be protected and meet the HIPAA requirements. Some platforms offer only one service, such as videoconferencing, requiring multiple platforms, while others offer multiple services in one platform, allowing the counselor to see clients, sign paperwork, file notes, and bill insurance companies all in one location.

There are other technology requirements necessary to keep the client safe and to protect their privacy and information. There are not only requirements that are important on the counselor's side, but they are also important on the client's end and will need to be explained during the informed consent process in order for the client to have the correct information to provide their consent to treatment. For example, to ensure the safety of the connection, the counselor will need to be hard wired to the modem, not on a wireless connection, to maintain the client's privacy. While the counselor cannot ensure that the client utilizes a hardwired connection, it can be made clear that wireless signals can be hijacked so that the client is able to make an informed decision. Additionally, the speed of the internet connection for both the counselor and the client has to be fast enough to support videoconferencing, which will need to be explained so that the client will understand how slow speeds may affect the therapy session due to freezing and reconnecting.

The counselor can ensure that HIPAA privacy concerns are met on their end, seeing clients on a secure computer using a hardwired high-speed internet connection behind closed doors in their office. However, it must be made clear to the client during the intake and informed consent process that the client's privacy is their own responsibility on their end. Counselors cannot ensure that others will not hear the therapy session if they walk by the room the client is using for therapy. Counselors cannot ensure the security of the client's computer or other device or the client's internet connection. The client will have to understand through the informed consent process that security on their end is their responsibility and that the counselor can only ensure security from the counselor's side. In addition to addressing security and privacy, the counselor will create and share the plan for technology failure that occurs prior to the start of session or during a session so that the client knows what to expect if the connection is lost. The counselor will need to make clear a policy on reaching the counselor outside of therapy times or in case of emergencies and how quickly a client can expect a response, especially if the online platform has messaging capability. Counselors utilizing online platforms, especially email, to connect with clients must ensure encryption methods are in place to protect private information from being inadvertently shared or stolen.

Providing counseling in an online format provides access to services for those who would otherwise be unable to obtain services due to location or other limitations. While the ability to serve those who would otherwise be left out of counseling is a strength of telebehavioral health, the need for a strong internet connection and a device that can access the internet may be a limitation. For many in rural areas with limited or no internet connection or for those who cannot afford the technology, online counseling is exclusionary and continues to prevent access to mental health services. While there are public access locations that provide free internet and libraries where you can borrow a computer, the client must weigh the potential security and privacy risks over the ability to get help, especially in areas where there are little or no counselors. Also, counselors utilizing a business website are required by the ACA (2014) Code of Ethics to provide website accessibility for those who are disabled and translation services, if possible, for those whose first language is not English (H.5.d.). Additionally, for clients who are utilizing their insurance to pay for counseling services, some insurance companies will not pay for telebehavioral health services, and clients will need to be made aware of this financial risk, especially for those of lower socioeconomic status. With the global pandemic, insurance companies have relaxed their rules regarding the use of telebehavioral health services, making access to care even greater. However, the client should understand that insurance companies can choose to deny telebehavioral health services at any time, leaving the client with the bill.

Social Media

The use of social media in counseling practices requires the creation of a public social media policy available to all potential clients and posted on professional social media pages and business websites covering how the counselor utilizes social media and what clients can expect in regard to social media, especially the risks. According to the ACA (2014) Code of Ethics, counselors should create and maintain professional and personal social media accounts separately, ensuring the distinction between the two, or even consider keeping the personal account private (H.6.a). Additionally, ACA also expects counselors to respect their clients' social media accounts, only viewing them with the client's permission and to address various aspects of social media usage during the informed consent process (H.6.b. & H.6.c.). Counselors ensure what is posted on their professional social media accounts are accurate and representative of their education, level of licensure, experience, expertise, and professional memberships (ACA, 2014, C.3.). Finally, it is important to remember that what a counselor posts on social media carries weight and can negatively impact potential clients, current clients, employers, counselor education programs, organizations, other professionals, and the profession as a whole. Counselors need to respect varying values and beliefs and refrain from disclosing confidential information or from diagnosing anyone, even public figures, on social media (ACA, 2014, C.6.c.). Counselors need to be aware of the power that social media has, especially during difficult times, such as the current pandemic and social unrest in 2020. Social media can both promote as well as hinder social justice efforts, supporting or further marginalizing cultural groups and steadying or destabilizing societal dissonance.

Nuances of Online Counseling

There are certain nuances that will need to be mastered for a successful online counseling experience. First, counseling requires attention to the client's body language and other forms of nonverbal communication. When counseling online, the client's body cannot be fully seen, so the online counselor will need to learn to notice the slight changes in positioning, changes in breathing, small facial movements, eye movements, and other similar slight changes that represent the client's limited nonverbal communication on a screen. These limited nonverbal cues are initially difficult to spot but become easier with time and experience. However, it is important to consider the client's cultural influences when evaluating any form of nonverbal communication. Conflict, discomfort, and other avoidant cues maybe evidenced in shifting position, looking away, crossing arms, or touching one's face, although these behaviors can have different meanings for various cultures (McAulifffe et al., 2013). There are additional modifications to counseling skills and techniques to be made in the online environment, many of which take creativity on the counselor's part to ensure a successful transition to online treatment.

Next, developing the counseling relationship requires a bit more intentionality on the counselor's part since there is not the option for the connection built when two people are located in the same room, and it can begin with an initial consultation. Offering a brief meeting approximately 15 minutes long allows the client to see the counselor and experience the online platform to assess comfort before agreeing to an intake, as well as creates an initial bond toward developing the therapeutic relationship. The initial consultation also allows the counselor the opportunity to assess the client for appropriateness for the online platform, recognizing that not all clients and not all presenting problems are appropriate for telebehavioral health. Since the client is not physically located in the counselor's office, the relationship cannot depend on proximity but must depend on welcoming and open behaviors exhibited by the counselor and the counselor's understanding of the client's perspective of the online experience.

Finally, crisis management looks different in an online environment due to the distance between the counselor and the client. The counselor needs to develop a crisis management plan that includes when, how, and where they can be reached in case of urgency or emergency and what to do if the counselor cannot be reached. The plan should include a process in case the session is suddenly ended. Clients are informed of the crisis plan and frequently reminded of the process. The counselor has the flexibility to see a client at any time that fits into their schedule, so a client in crisis should be seen online quickly and an assessment should be made with a clear plan to ensure their safety. Additionally, the counselor can meet with the client online while the client waits for emergency services or family to arrive. The counselor must be mindful of the limitation of not being in the same physical location as the client, causing intervention to be challenging. However, due to the immediacy of the technology, the counselor can simultaneously assess the client, determine their location, and access their files quickly online.

SUMMARY, INSIGHTS, AND ACTIONS

From the founding of psychoanalysis and the birth of counseling, providers have found ways to provide services to clients even when they were separated by distance, originally by letters, later by phone, and now over the internet. Often those services are only available to the affluent because of cost or other barriers. Providing counseling in an online environment offers a flexibility for both counselor and client in the convenience of scheduling a session on a client's lunch break or another convenient time while removing the extra commute times or other transportation barriers. Telebehavioral health extends access to counseling services to those who would not have access due to rural location, the lack of experienced providers in their area, childcare, or a limitation in easily leaving their location for an in-person appointment. Improving access to counseling increases the ability to advocate for or with clients, yet it may further marginalize groups that cannot access the technology to meet online. Despite the limitations, telebehavioral health appears to have significantly improved access to mental health services for a number of marginalized populations.

REFLECTION AND DISCUSSION QUESTIONS

1. Create a timeline of the development of distance counseling to present day online counseling.
2. Define the strengths and limitations for multicultural considerations of online counseling.
3. Discuss the social justice benefits of online counseling.
4. Identify three limitations of online counseling and formulate appropriate adaptations to overcome each.

ADDITIONAL READINGS AND RESOURCES

- ACA information on telebehavioral health: https://www.counseling.org/knowledge-center/mental-health-resources/trauma-disaster/telehealth-information-and-counselors-in-health-care
- Telebehavioral Health Institute (offers education, information, and certification): https://telehealth.org/
- PESI (online classes, webinars, and training): https://www.pesi.com/
- National Board for Certified Counselors (information on board certification): https://www.nbcc.org/resources/nccs/newsletter/the-board-certified-telemental-health-provider-bc-tmh-credential

REFERENCES

American Counseling Association. (2014). *Code of ethics*. Author. https://www.counseling.org/docs/default-source/ethics/2014-code-of-ethics.pdf?sfvrsn=2d58522c_4

Bradley, L. J., Lewis, J., Hendricks, B., & Crews, C. R. (2008). *Advocacy: Implications for supervision training*. (ACAPCD-13). American Counseling Association. https://www.counseling.org/resources/library/ACA%20Digests/ACAPCD-13.pdf

Cambridge Dictionary. (n.d.). *Affluence*. https://dictionary.cambridge.org/dictionary/english/affluence.

Council for Accreditation of Counseling and Related Educational Programs. (n.d.). *Home page*. https://www.cacrep.org/

D'Andrea, M., & Daniels, J. (2001). RESPECTFUL counseling: An integrative model for counselors. In D. Pope- Davis & H. Coleman (Eds.), *The interface of class, culture, and gender in counseling* (pp. 417–466). SAGE.

Fairburn, C. G., & Cooper, Z. (2011). Therapist competence, therapy quality, and therapist training. *Behaviour Research and Therapy*, 49(6–7), 373–378. https://doi.org/10.1016/j.brat.2011.03.005

Gonzalez, E., & Faubert, M. (2015). *Language acquisition theories*. In B. T. Erford & D. G. Hays (Eds.), *The ACA encyclopedia of counseling* (pp. 311-312XX–XX). American Counseling Association.

Kiselica, M. S., & Robinson, M. (2011). Bringing advocacy counseling to life: The history, issues, and human dramas of social justice work in counseling. *Journal of Counseling & Development*, 79(4), 387–397. http://dx.doi.org/10.1002/j.1556-6676.2001.tb01985.x

LeBeauf, I., Smaby, M., & Maddux, C. (2009). Adapting counseling skills for multicultural and diverse clients. In G. R. Walz, J. C. Blaur & R. K. Yep (Eds.), *Compelling counseling interventions: VISTA 2009* (pp. 33–42). American Counseling Association. https://www.counseling.org/Resources/Library/VISTAS/2009-V-Print/Article%204%20LeBeaufSmabyMaddux.pdf

Locke, D. C., & Kiselica, M. S. (1999). Pedagogy of possibilities: Teaching about racism in multicultural counseling courses. *Journal of Counseling & Development*, 77(1), 80–86. https://doi.org/10.1002/j.1556-6676.1999.tb02424.x

Mallen, M. J., Vogel, D. L., Rochlen, A. B., & Day, S. X. (2005). Online counseling: Reviewing the literature from a counseling psychology framework. *The Counseling Psychologist*, 33(6), 819–871. https://doi.org/10.1177/0011000005278624

McAuliffe, G., (Ed.) (2013). *Culturally alert counseling: A comprehensive introduction* (2nd ed.). SAGE.

Novotney, A. (2017). A growing wave of online therapy. *Monitor on Psychology*, 48(2), 48. https://www.apa.org/monitor/2017/02/online-therapy

Poon, L. (2020, February 19). *There are far more Americans without broadband access than previously thought*. Bloomberg CityLab. https://www.bloomberg.com/news/articles/2020-02-19/where-the-u-s-underestimates-the-digital-divide

Skinner, A., & Zack, J.S. (2004). Counseling and the internet. *American Behavioral Scientist*, 48(4), 434–446. http://dx.doi.org/10.1177/0002764204270280

Toporek, R., Gerstein, L., Fouad, N., Roysircar, G., & Israel, T. (2006). *Handbook for social justice in counseling psychology: Leadership, vision and action*. SAGE. http://dx.doi.org/10.4135/9781412976220

Wong, K. P., Bonn, G., Tam, C. L., & Wong, C. P. (2018). Preferences in online and/or face-to-face counseling among university students in Malaysia. *Frontiers in Psychology*, 9, 64. https://doi.org/10.3389/fpsyg.2018.00064

World Health Organization. (2013). *Counselling for maternal and newborn health care: a handbook for building skills*. World Health Organization. https://www.who.int/maternal_child_adolescent/documents/9789241547628/en/.

CHAPTER 14

WELLNESS AND COUNSELING

M. Ann Shillingford, University of Central Florida

Nivischi N. Edwards, Liberty University

Gelawdiyos M. Haile, University of Central Florida

LEARNING OBJECTIVES

1. Understand theories and models of wellness through a multicultural lens.
2. Examine the awareness and knowledge of wellness related to diverse communities.
3. Develop skills to support diverse clients on the importance of wellness practices.

LEARNING OUTCOMES

1. Learn strategies to support client wellness.
2. Understand ethical considerations when addressing wellness with diverse clients.
3. Understand the importance of social justice and advocacy in promoting client self-care.

The concept of wellness has been researched and defined in the counseling literature as well as other disciplines. For example, Hettler (1976) defined wellness as "an active process through which people become aware of, and make choices toward, a more successful existence (para. 1)." Wellness practices have been introduced in classroom settings, counseling supervision, and even as a mode of self-regulation for student success. Models of wellness have also been highlighted in the counseling literature as best practice for enhancing clients' self-care and self-exploration in the counseling setting. Unfortunately, despite the myriad resources available on wellness practices, counseling students still ask questions such as, "How do I talk to my clients about wellness? What if my client's wellness has nothing to do with their presenting problem?" and even more personal to their wellness, "When do I have time to practice wellness?"

In this chapter, we attempt to explain what wellness is and also present strategies that counselors and counseling students can use to promote wellness as part of the therapeutic relationship-building process. These strategies are not exhaustive but will hopefully assist in developing an awareness of holistic wellness, increase knowledge of the different aspects of wellness, improve skills for supporting self and clients in bolstering wellness practices, and finally understand how wellness action plans can be beneficial. These authors briefly mention different models of wellness but will focus on the indivisible self-model of wellness as it has been widely used and supported in counseling research. Finally, as you read this chapter, keep in mind that wellness may look different for everyone and there is no one script to address these practices.

WELLNESS AND WELLNESS MODELS

The practice of wellness identifies an individual's interests and goals of and focuses primarily on health and well-being. Additionally, wellness promotes positive, optimistic attitudes and guides individuals toward achieving life goals (Swarbrick, 2006). Swarbrick explains that wellness is a deliberate and conscious process that requires individuals to take personal responsibility and be proactive in preserving their own health. It appears then that a wellness concept may be a viable approach that students can adopt in order to navigate through the challenges of higher education (Spurgeon & Myers, 2010).

Wellness, however, is not only focused on individuals *being* well but also on functioning positively. In fact, positive functioning means exploring one's strengths; that is, what one *does* well (Schueller, 2009). According to Schueller, upholding strengths-based functioning is especially important for individuals from disenfranchised groups where individual weaknesses have more popularly been highlighted. Furthermore, optimal, positive functioning emphasizes an individual's ability to find internal strength amidst life's challenges (Shillingford et al., 2015). The following sections review two models of wellness, the six dimensions of wellness (Hettler, 1997), a grass-roots model that has paved the way for other models, and the indivisible-self (Myers & Sweeney, 2005).

Six Dimensions of Wellness

Bill Hettler, one of the pioneers of wellness models, developed the six dimensions of wellness. Hettler (1976) believed that individuals encompassed six interdependent dimensions that make us holistic beings: (a) *emotional*, people should be aware and accepting of their feelings; (b) *spiritual*, understanding that there is meaning behind the despair, disappointment, and other challenges we may experience in life; (c) *occupational*, our values, interests, and beliefs play a significant role in the satisfaction we experience from work; (d) *intellectual*, the ability to explore our creativity, problem-solving skills, and learning experiences; (e) *physical*, consideration for healthy eating, regular good exercise, and appropriate self-care practices such as going to the doctor and taking medications when necessary; and finally (f) *social*, contributing positively to your environment, communicating with others, and building personal relationships and safer communities.

The Indivisible Self

Myers and Sweeney (2008) developed an evidence-based wellness approach that focuses on individuals' optimal, positive functioning. The indivisible self (IS-WEL), based on Adler's ideology of a holistic, indivisible self, has been identified as a suitable framework for endorsing self-care and self-awareness in counselor education. The IS-WEL is comprised of one high-order factor (indivisible self) and five second-order factors (creative, coping, essential, social, and physical). Bearing in mind the holistic nature of positive functioning, the IS-WEL can be useful in helping students identify an ideal wellness plan that will not only highlight their overall levels of wellness but also address salient strengths they possess in navigating through higher education. Furthermore, understanding wellness strategies can support counselors in presenting a holistic approach to client support.

Creative Self

The first of the five factors, the creative self, represents one's thinking, emotions, control, work, and positive humor (Myers et al., 2004). Myers and Sweeney (2008) further clarified these five representations of the creative self as (a) one's thinking affecting the emotions, (b) the emotions influencing the cognitive responses to experiences, (c) perceptions of control influencing personal life events, (d) enhancing the capacity to have a successful life through work, and (e) being able to enjoy humor. Individuals who enhance their creative self may be able to promote self-awareness and foster more meaningful social interactions.

Strategies for Enhancing Clients' Creative Selves

Counselors can use numerous interventions to increase clients' emotional wellness. Part of emotional wellness is the individual's ability to recognize and understand their inner world while maintaining a positive self-concept and self-efficacy, as well as regulating emotions in an adaptive and positive way. The goal is to provide clients with coping tools to enhance their ability to deal with the challenges they face.

One way counselors can help their clients is by introducing emotion-regulating skills such as mindfulness (Brown et al., 2013). There are various types of mindfulness exercises counselors can introduce to their clients (e.g., body scan, mindful breathing). Similar to physical wellness, mindfulness exercises should be introduced to clients gradually. Moreover, gratitude interventions such as gratitude writing and gratitude thinking can enhance clients' emotional well-being and overall wellness (Lyubomirsky et al., 2005). Likewise, mindful nature walks or experiencing nature (Anderson et al., 2018), and fostering positive interpersonal relationships can help individuals regulate their emotions in an adaptive way (Williams et al., 2018). Increasing clients' awareness to their inner world and increasing their ability to recognize and use appropriate coping skills can help them foster emotional wellness.

Coping Self

According to Myers and Sweeney (2005), the coping self "is composed of elements that regulate our responses to life events and provide a means for transcending their negative effects" (p. 274). The four components include having realistic beliefs, practicing stress management, maintaining self-worth, and leisure. In essence, positive functioning of the coping self helps individuals realize that irrational thoughts can be key influencers in feelings of frustration and dissatisfaction. The ability to cope by enhancing one's self-worth and self-efficacy as well as being able to manage one's stress is paramount to succeeding in higher education. Finally, individuals should find a healthy balance between work and leisure.

Strategies for Enhancing Clients' Coping Selves

To help clients manage stress and maintain balance between leisure activities and work, counselors can propose interventions that will maintain their clients' novelty, curiosity, and vitality by suggesting a lifestyle change that involves cognitive engagement. Clients should be encouraged to explore and retain new knowledge; counselors could suggest activities such as reading, creative exploration and writing in a form of scriptotherapy (Gladding & Drake Wallace, 2018). Cognitive engaging activities such as crossword puzzles, learning or listening to music, and being engaged in social activities are all good examples of activities that can support a decrease in stress and increase in coping strategies.

Essential Self

The *essential self* represents spirituality, self-care, gender identity, and cultural identity. Broadly speaking, the essential self encompasses individuals' ability to make meaning of their lives (Myers & Sweeney, 2005). Gender and cultural identity play a vital role in how people relate to others and events. Therefore, the higher the level of gender and cultural identity development, the clearer life's purpose and direction becomes. Additionally, it has been noted in the literature that significant positive mental health gains are associated with spiritual beliefs, including benevolent reappraisal, emotional healing, hope for justice, personal sanctification and transformation, positive self-esteem, sense of belonging to a faith community, forgiveness, cultural identity formation, moral development, coping with stress, and empowerment for change (Bowen-Reid & Harrell, 2002; Duffey et al., 2001). Therefore, recognizing the importance of positive functioning of the essential self may lead individuals to more positive mental health as well as the ability to adapt to life's events.

Strategies for Enhancing Clients' Essential Selves

To build and maintain clients' spiritual wellness, counselors can explore with their clients what it means to have a healthy relationship with what they may revere (e.g., God or nature). After exploring and establishing what a healthy spiritual journey looks like, counselors have plethora of interventions they can suggest. For example, spiritual practice such as prayer have been found to enhance individuals' wellness (Stanley, 2009). In addition, contemplative techniques such as meditation and studying sacred scripture are posited to promote well-being (Rana, 2015). Other activities, such as attending religious services, joining spiritual groups, participating in helping ministries, spending time in nature, or gratitude journaling, are also activities that can benefit clients in promoting spiritual wellness. Counselors can also encourage clients to explore their history of ancestry. Mitchell and Shillingford (2016) noted the benefits of ancestry awareness to identity development. The authors suggest that counselors play a significant role in leading clients through this process.

Social Self

The *social* factor represents love and friendship. Love and friendship contribute significantly to enhancing quality of life (Myers & Sweeney, 2005). Myers and Sweeney (2005) posit that feelings of isolation, alienation, and separation contribute to poor health; conversely, developing strong positive relationships outside of academia as well as within academia can foster a sense of belong and support. Wolf et al. (2012) rightly express that although friends and family may be supportive of their graduate students, individuals in academia may better understand the stressors related to completing a graduate counseling program. In fact, Wolf et al. recommended mentoring as a means of securing support.

Strategies for Enhancing Clients' Social Selves

To maintain a client's social wellness dimension, counselors must establish what attaining social wellness means. There is a wide variety of ways counselors can guide their clients in establishing social wellness. First, counselors can help their clients learn how to draw healthy boundaries in relationships. Once healthy boundaries are recognized and understood, clinicians can help clients select activities that enhance their social wellness.

An important example of an activity is allocating time to foster meaningful relationships with supportive friends and family members. Such positive relationships contribute to one's overall well-being and maintain quality of life while avoiding toxic social relationships that jeopardize wellness. It has been reported that perceived social support can serve as a protective factor from mental health disorders such as depression in adolescents (Ehrlich et al., 2014; Luo et al., 2017). As we alluded to earlier, close social support can serve as a healthy way to regulate our emotions (Williams et al., 2018). Joining groups that are aligned with personal hobbies or being engaged in leisure activities (Ábrahám et al., 2012), spending time with positive people, volunteering, and joining exercise groups are other examples of activities to enhance social wellness.

Physical Self

Finally, the *physical self* represents the wellness practice of exercise and nutrition. Practicing regular physical activities have been mentioned in the literature as vital to promoting health and wellness. Individual and group activities further enhance a more active and positive lifestyle (Wolf et al., 2012). Enhancing the physical self does not have to be burdensome. Several resources are available to support individualized physical movement even while sitting at a desk. Although time constraints can hinder intense and regular exercise practices, physical movement on a regular basis, as well as consideration of proper diet, can lower stressors caused by various life demands. Students can enhance their well-being by developing a healthy routine of individualized physical activities and a diet that works for them.

Strategies for Enhancing Clients' Physical Selves

Counselors can support clients in developing an individualized physical wellness plan based on their interests. One factor that contributes to physical wellness is exercise (Cotman & Berchtold, 2002; Hillman et al., 2008; Yamazaki et al., 2018). It is important to allow clients to identify and express the type of physical exercise they prefer to engage in. If clients do not have exercises in which they prefer to engage, they might consider walking, jogging, or running for 30 minutes every other day. Organized sports such as basketball, soccer, or tennis are options as well. Although there is an obvious benefit of exercise (aerobic exercise) to mental well-being, counselors need to pay close attention to a client's physical health before setting or suggesting exercise as a goal. It is critical that the counselor emphasize the gradual development of an exercise routine. While exercise is an important component of maintaining good physical health, counselors should also highlight the importance of attending to other facets of wellness. For instance, Walker (2017) discusses the benefits of getting a sufficient amount of sleep. Moreover, effective nutritional plans and life balance are vital.

Table 14.1   Other Examples of Wellness Practices

WELLNESS FACTOR	EXAMPLES
Creative	• Maintaining work satisfaction • Increasing humor response to decrease stress • Embracing positive thoughts to influence positive emotions • Maintaining the capacity to influence life events
Coping	• Increasing self-worth • Developing positive coping strategies • Learning to enjoy life's moments • Learning how to effectively recognize and decrease stress and stressors

WELLNESS FACTOR	EXAMPLES
Essential	• Practicing spirituality • Finding meaning and purpose in life • Maintaining positive quality of life • Exploring gender and cultural identity for further meaning-making • Promoting healthy self-care habits
Social	• Developing friendships and intimate relationships • Maintaining positive social connections
Physical	• Developing and maintaining physical activity • Healthy exercise routines • Developing health diet and nutritional habits

CHALLENGES IN MAINTAINING SELF-CARE AND WELLNESS

In the previous section, we discussed strategies to enhance wellness. Although the focus was more so on counselors supporting their clients, it should be noted that these practices are helpful to all individuals, counselors and clients alike. To be a source of modeling for clients, counselors themselves should be upholding holistic life balance and self-care practices. The following section shifts the focus of the chapter and highlights challenges counselors face in their own wellness practices that can invariably impact their ability and professionalism in discussing and promoting wellness with clients.

Gaining an enhanced awareness about wellness models and becoming familiar with practical examples and strategies to implement self-care are steps in the right direction. However, the unfortunate reality is that self-care and wellness are not often the first things counselors or those in training think about or implement in their lives. It is often the last thought or the one that sits on the backburner for weeks, months, or even years, with wonderful intentions. Meyers et al. (2012) suggest that the ability to implement self-care activities is a core competency in clinical training, but this most important, sometimes life-saving skill, is rarely taught or implemented programmatically (Newsome et al., 2006).

We live in a society that encourages doing more and being less. The more we have on our plates, the more in which we are actively involved, the more positions we hold, the more we are applauded and commended. Those who connect with the importance of being and work to bring more balance into their lives by implementing wellness strategies are often looked down on or do not receive the rewards readily given to the doers (promotions, raises, praises, etc.). It is no wonder many have a difficult time maintaining self-care and wellness. Some of these challenges include burnout, time, stress, and a lack of mindfulness. Research supports the idea that mindfulness-based self-care approaches positively affect clinical behavior and client outcome in the therapeutic relationship (Newsome et al., 2006; Myers et al., 2012). In the following sections, we will explore how burnout, time, and stress are challenges in maintaining self-care and wellness.

Burnout

Maslach et al. (1996) define burnout as an occupational hazard affecting one's personal and professional well-being, leading to feelings of emotional exhaustion, depersonalization, and reduced personal accomplishment. One challenge in maintaining self-care and wellness is burnout. According to Freudenberger (1975), the three factors of burnout include (a) emotional exhaustion, (b) depersonalization (loss of one's empathy, caring, and compassion), and (c) a decreased sense of accomplishment.

In a field that is focused on helping and supporting others, those providing the help and support oftentimes suffer. It is often the case that because counselors are so passionate about their role of giving help, they neglect helping the person who would benefit most from the help and who needs to be a priority before providing help to other; counselors neglect helping themselves first. As a result, these well-intended, well-meaning givers burn themselves out. Burnout among mental health professionals has become a global problem. Between 21 and 67% of mental health service providers report high levels of burnout (Morse et al., 2012).

It is important to connect with one's environment and self in order to become aware of burnout as this poses a challenge in maintaining self-care and wellness. Burnout often creeps up on the clinician (and client). Oftentimes, before the counselor realizes that life has become unmanageable or they no longer have the energy or desire to do the things that were once important or enjoyable, these things no longer matter. Therefore, intermittent assessment of one's level of wellness aids in maintaining proper health. One way to get ahead of burnout and maintain wellness is to assess what is going on in one's relationship with self and others.

Self-Care Assessment

Kramen-Kahn (2002) suggested the following 15 questions to determine one's current level of personal self-care:

- Do I appear competent and professional?
- Do I appear warm, caring, and accepting?
- Do I regularly seek case consultation with another professional while protecting confidentiality?
- Do I, at the end of a stressful day, frequently utilize self-talk to put aside thoughts of clients?
- Do I maintain a balance between work, family, and play?
- Do I nurture a strong support network of family and friends?
- Do I use healthy leisure activities as a way of helping myself relax from work?
- Do I often feel renewed and energized by working with clients?
- Do I develop new interests in my professional work?
- Do I perceive clients' problems as interesting and look forward to working with them?

- Do I maintain objectivity regarding clients' problems?
- Do I maintain good boundaries with clients, allowing them to take full responsibility for their actions while providing support for change?
- Do I use personal psychotherapy as a means of maintaining and/or improving functioning as a psychotherapist?
- Do I maintain a sense of humor? Can I laugh with my clients?
- Do I act in accordance with legal and ethical standards?

Developing the habit of engaging in regular self-assessment on a monthly or quarterly basis or with clients every other session can minimize the challenges in maintaining self-care and wellness. Being proactive and intentional about maintaining health is vital to maintaining proper perspectives, both personally and when attending to the needs of clients. Oftentimes, burnout is related to an imbalance between work stress and perceived available resources (Demerouti et al., 2001). Burnout and emotional exhaustion have been identified as common risk factors for mental health workers (Jenaro et al., 2007; Senter et al., 2010).

Some major concerns for clinicians include time-consuming and intense work conditions, significant administrative responsibilities, and challenging client issues, including maintaining healthy boundaries and complex client needs (Baker, 2005). Maintaining awareness of these truths and planning ahead can be beneficial to healthy self-care and wellness. Making the time to do what is needed to uphold a proper level of mental health is vital.

Time

Continual, successful time management is even difficult for a person who has achieved much. This can be a challenge for multiple reasons. People often underestimate the amount of time it takes to complete a task, and procrastination can also be a contributing factor (McCrea et al., 2008). When life gets busy and responsibilities increase, oftentimes the first thing that is released is self-care. We tend to let go of the thing(s) that will help promote continual good in our holistic lives and aid in the maintenance of balance and productivity. Zimbardo and Boyd (2008) highlight the importance of managing time by assessing the direction one wants to take and the steps necessary to attain goals before managing time by assigning activities and goals to one's calendar. Also, incorporating a self-care plan of treatment can aid in time management and minimize the challenges in maintaining wellness (Barnett et al., 2006). According to Myers and Sweeney (2005), time management in itself is a form of self-care. It is important that counselors assess how they are using time and the benefits or deficits of the way their time is being implemented. After such assessment, if it is concluded that some things can be done differently for greatly productivity, such changes ought to be implemented. This can be used as a teaching opportunity in work with clients also.

On the surface, practicing time management can seem tedious and calculated. However, with the right techniques and support, it is possible to maintain a healthy self-care plan.

Some examples of executing a carefully drafted self-care plan include sacrifices such as (a) prioritizing responsibilities, (b) blocking time for specific tasks, (c) organizing tasks into manageable portions, (d) designating duties/delegating, (e) and managing distractions such as cell phone use and social media. If after assessing an area of life that is lacking in proper time management, a counselor realizes a need to make adjustments in that specific life area, assigning one's self a treatment as they would a client. This will help minimize feelings of frustration, disappointment, and stress.

Stress

Stress is a normal part of everyday life. It takes on various forms and manifests in varied ways. One can experience stress professionally or personally. Unmanaged chronic stress can have irreversible effects on one's emotional, psychological, and physical health (Schure et al., 2008). It is a contributing factor to numerous health problems and can worsen disorders or diseases. Moate et al. (2016) posit that "stress is one factor that can negatively influence a counselor's ability to achieve and maintain wellness" (p. 161). Stress is a response to a perceived imbalance between the demands of life situations and one's ability to cope (Gandi et al., 2001). Specifically, stress is defined as a "particular relationship between the person and the environment that is appraised by the person as taxing or exceeding his or her resources and endangering his or her well-being" (Lazarus & Folkman, 1984, p. 19). It is important that counselors become aware of personal life stressors and proactively plan for and begin to implement strategies to manage them in healthy ways. Engaging in mindfulness exercises is one such way.

Kabat-Zinn (1993) defined mindfulness as "cultivating awareness with the aim of helping people live each moment of their lives (even the painful ones) as fully as possible" (p. 260). Mindfulness is also paying attention to something, in a particular way, on purpose, in the present moment, nonjudgmentally (Kabat-Zinn, 2003). Incorporating mindfulness exercises as a part of one's life is one healthy way to combat stress and maintain self-care and wellness. Mindfulness-based studies have noted an improvement in overall health, physical, and psychological symptoms (Roth & Robbins, 2014) when these exercises are intentionally implemented. A study by Schure et al. (2008) examined the influence of certain mindfulness exercises for stress reduction on counseling students. The 15-week, three-credit course involved the implementation of three mindfulness practices (twice weekly in-class yoga practice and sitting meditation and qigong—an ancient Chinese method combining gentle physical movement and mediation). Students reported positive experiences as a result of incorporating these practices and the intention to integrate mindfulness practices into their future profession.

Stress can sometimes be overwhelming and negatively affect many life areas. In order to be successful and maintain proper self-care and wellness, it is necessary to learn and implement healthy stress management tools. Incorporating mindfulness practices such as yoga, meditation, as well as mindful walking and eating have demonstrated research efficacy in treating stress (Shapiro et al., 2007). It is important for counselors to work with clients to implement some of these strategies in their own lives and to implement them in their own.

In sum, wellness and self-care practices can be beneficial to everyone. Counselors can promote client wellness by focusing on a holistic therapeutic approach including clients' social, physical, essential, copying, and social self. Counselors also need to maintain holistic life balance as models for their clients, but more so for overall health and wellness. Unfortunately, we are all impacted by varying factors that sometimes get in the way: lack of time, overwhelming stress, and potential for burnout. To support self, counselors should practice being reflective practitioners and putting the knowledge and skills they possess related to wellness into action. Counselors can also support clients by providing culturally related wellness services that highlight clients' needs from a social justice stance.

WELLNESS AND MULTICULTURAL SOCIAL JUSTICE COMPETENCIES

Wellness can be viewed from multiple lenses, but it is vitally important to consider multicultural and social justice implications. Whether counselors are addressing wellness for self, as part of supervision, or for the counselor–client relationship, the constructs of diversity have to be highlighted. According to the multicultural and social justice counseling competencies (MSJCC, Ratts et al., 2016), to be culturally effective practitioners counselors should (a) be self-aware, (b) consider the client's worldview, (c) consider their influence on the counseling relationship, and (d) utilize counseling and advocacy interventions. To address each of these four domains, counselors need to aspire toward the following competencies: attitudes and beliefs, knowledge, skills, and action. In the next sections, we address these multicultural social justice competencies as they pertain to wellness practices for counselors as well as to the therapeutic setting.

COUNSELOR SELF-AWARENESS

Here are three questions that can be asked by counselors to explore self-awareness related to wellness:

1. What role do my assumptions, values, beliefs, and life experiences play in discussing wellness practices with diverse clients (attitude and beliefs)?
2. What do I really know about the benefits of wellness practices with diverse clients (knowledge)?
3. What training have I received to address wellness in a diverse counseling setting (skills)?
4. What do I need to do to improve my awareness, attitude, knowledge, and skills related to wellness with diverse groups (action)?

Counselors' developmental levels can affect their ability to ask these questions and their ultimate reflective responses. If a counselor believes strongly in the benefits of wellness, then most likely that counselor will choose to include a holistic approach to the client treatment plan. Subsequently, counselors who may not necessarily value or practice wellness can overlook client holistic balance in practice. Counselors can work on their attitudes and beliefs regarding wellness in counseling by first exploring their own wellness. It can also be important to understand if there are particular dimensions of wellness that the counselor may uphold more than others. For instance, some counselors are uncomfortable addressing the spiritual needs of their clients, even when the client brings it up in session. As a counseling student, how comfortable would you be in discussing spirituality with your client? What are your attitudes and beliefs regarding spirituality? Do you hold certain assumptions, biases, or social identities about this aspect of wellness? Do these prevent or encourage you to explore with your client? How about occupational wellness? What do you believe about certain cultural groups pursuing particular professions? Do you hold stereotypes regarding particular communities?

DIGGING DEEPER

Your Asian client presents symptoms of depression. He is withdrawn, has poor communication with his family, and does not engage in any social activities. You discover that he is a teacher. You remember reading somewhere that Asian children are strongly encouraged to be medical doctors. As a matter of fact, you are almost positive that your Asian friend from college told you as such. Do you then focus solely on the emotional wellness of your client? How comfortable would you be exploring his occupational wellness? How about your attitude and beliefs toward an Asian career path? After all, you have firsthand information from your college friend. From the MSJCC, the counselor would first need to reflect on their assumptions about this cultural group prior to completing a treatment plan for that client.

SKILLS AND ACTION TO SUPPORT CLIENTS WELLNESS

1. Personal reflection through journaling; write down your thoughts about the matter. Highlight feelings that you experience while discussing with the client.
2. Observe your nonverbal behavior during session. Are you seeing signs of discomfort (e.g., wringing hands, facial expressions, etc.)?
3. Seek peer supervision to discuss what you are experiencing.
4. Be true to your thoughts and feelings. Acknowledge that you may have differing assumptions, values, beliefs, and even worldviews from your client.
5. Be open to learning more about your client and their beliefs about different aspects of wellness. Remember, there is no unified script to wellness; it is individualized.

CLIENT WORLDVIEW

Here are three questions that can be asked of counselors to understand a client's worldview of wellness:

1. How comfortable would I be if my client wants to discuss aspects of wellness (attitudes and beliefs)?
2. What do I know about my client's beliefs, assumptions, and life experiences regarding wellness (**knowledge**)?
3. What culturally relevant skills do I possess to engage in discussions on wellness as initiated by my diverse clients (**skills**)?
4. What do I need to do to increase my awareness of my client's worldview, values, and beliefs regarding wellness (**action**)?

Merriam-Webster's (2020) dictionary defines knowledge as "the facts or conditions of knowing something with familiarity gained through experience or association." Therefore, what a counselor may know about wellness across diverse community could either develop through their own life experiences, cultural immersion, association with others from different cultures, and/or academic learning experiences. In an investigative study on personal interest and knowledge acquisition by Rotgans and Schmidt (2017), the researchers found that knowledge gained about a particular subject matter improved individuals' attitudes and beliefs in that subject matter. In fact, the authors determined that individuals who are acutely aware that they lack knowledge and skills in a given area may engage in information-seeking behaviors to reduce the knowledge gap. That is, counselors who are aware that they lack the knowledge to fully address a client's worldview will most likely seek interventions to address that gap. Again, counselor attitudes and beliefs may play a significant role in pursuing knowledge acquisition and taking subsequent action to cultivate their new knowledge.

DIGGING DEEPER

Your client is a Black male veteran who presents with posttraumatic stress disorder (PTSD). He is disabled and is using a wheelchair. He has shared with you that he is unable to keep a job, maintain long-term healthy relationships, and communicate his feelings to others. You are a practicum student. You have read articles on PTSD and have even watched a few movies on soldiers in Afghanistan. You are nervous because you have already been told that Black men are tough and do not talk about feelings, but you think it is important to address his emotional wellness. What knowledge do you have about (a) military culture, (b) Black culture, and (c) disabled culture? You begin to doubt that the client would even be interested in addressing wellness. Let's pause for a minute. He is experiencing PTSD (emotional wellness), he cannot hold a job (occupational wellness), he is disabled (physical wellness), he feels hopeless (spiritual wellness), and he has limited healthy relationships (social wellness). As you can see, this client is in need of a wellness overhaul. What knowledge do you have to support him?

SKILLS AND ACTION TO SUPPORT CLIENT WELLNESS

1. Develop knowledge about the varying aspects of your client's intersectionalities (military background, ethnicity, gender). This can be done through researching literature, reading related books, supervision, communicating with colleagues, and simply asking the client.
2. Explore different wellness models with your client. Take the time to engage in discussion about each dimension of wellness from the client's perspective. The more knowledge you as the counselor have about the models, the better you prepared you are to explore with your client.
3. Attend professional development sessions that address skills to explore counselor bias and privilege that may arise when working with diverse groups.
4. Know the challenges clients face when working toward improving their wellness practices and support them in developing a plan to anticipate and address these potential challenges.
5. Visit communities that represent your diverse clients to gain a better understanding of the challenges and the marginalization they encounter.
6. Seek supervision in addressing any discomfort that may arise from your new knowledge.

COUNSELING RELATIONSHIP

The following questions can be vital in enabling counselors to develop more meaningful therapeutic relationships with diverse client groups:

1. How aware am I of the influence of my client's worldview and my own attitudes and beliefs regarding wellness on counseling outcomes (**attitudes and beliefs**)?
2. What do I know about the intersection of my beliefs and that of my client regarding aspects of wellness (knowledge)?
3. Do I possess the necessary skills to discuss wellness from a culturally sensitive standpoint with my client without my own privilege hindering the dialogue (skills)?
4. What training do I need to become a more multiculturally competent counselor for my clients (action)?

There are significant benefits to fostering a therapeutic relationship between client and counselor. To do so, one might regard the work of Carl Rogers, who emphasized the necessary conditions for facilitating this counseling relationship. According to Rogers (1957), the following factors are may produce positive client outcomes: (a) counselors' unconditional positive regard for the client, (b) empathy for the client, (c) counselors' congruence and genuineness, and (d), the client's interpretation of the counselor–client therapeutic connection. Another key factor to consider when addressing the client–counselor relationship is ethical issues. The counselor must be cognizant of the role that ethics play in either strengthening or disrupting the therapeutic alliance. Organizations associated with helping professions highlight specific ethical guidelines and standards that serve as a roadmap for counselors in decision-making.

DIGGING DEEPER

Your client is a 14-year-old Latina. You have been working with this client over six sessions now. The client presents with social anxiety and was referred to you, her school counselor, by her special education teacher and her parents. Your client is performing well academically but often has challenges working with classmates on group projects. She is introverted and explains that she does not have many friends at school. The sessions seem to be going well. Your client who at first remained very quiet in previous sessions is now opening up more and sharing more personal details. Today, the client comes to the counseling session and appears excited about something. She shares that her 15th birthday will be in 2 weeks and her family is planning her *quinceañera*. She wants you to attend. You are concerned about the ethical nature of socializing with the client outside of the counseling session. You are also concerned about her emotional and social wellness and how your decline of her offer might impact her.

SKILLS AND ACTION TO CLIENT WELLNESS

Ethical dilemmas can be overwhelming for counselors, particularly when options seem to question the potential effects on the therapeutic relationship. Here are potential actions that should be taken:

1. If in doubt, consult with another professional (e.g., supervisor, colleagues, and instructor).
2. Consult the ACA Code of Ethics and/or that of your counseling division (e.g., ASCA ethical standards, ASERVIC competencies).

3. Discuss your concerns regarding attending the event with the client. Being genuine and open may decrease any psychological impacts on the client.
4. Use your intuition.
5. Do research to educate yourself on the cultural/Indigenous practices of your client.

COUNSELING AND ADVOCACY INTERVENTIONS

In determination of appropriate counseling and advocacy interventions, following are a few questions to ponder:

1. How might my perceived power and privilege affect my ability to intervene for my client outside of the counseling setting (attitude and beliefs)?
2. What do I know and/or need to know about my client's intersectionalities from a historical context (knowledge)?
3. What skills do I possess to address community and institutional policies that are affecting my clients (skills)?
4. What is the best course of action when advocating for my client (action)?

According to Ratts et. al. (2016), counselors are sometimes faced with the decision of interceding for their clients at various levels: intrapersonal, interpersonal, institutional, community, public policy, and international/global. That is, from a systemic standpoint, counselors should understand their clients operate (a) as individuals; (b) as part of a historical unit (e.g., family); (c) as part of a community (e.g., church); and (d) within the bounds of laws, policies, and regulations (local, state, federal) based on global and international affairs. Ratts et al. further highlighted that clients' well-being, and counselors', are affected by these systems in differing ways. In fact, counselors need to understand that counseling extends beyond the walls of the counseling office as clients may be impacted by structures and organizations outside their therapeutic scope.

DIGGING DEEPER

Sonil is of Haitian descent and identifies as a member of the LGBTQIA community. Their parents are aware of Sonil's sexual orientation and have expressed their disappointment. At 5 years old, Sonil came to the United States with their parents in 2010 after the 7.1 magnitude earthquake devastated Haiti. Sonil identifies as Black and holds strong roots in the American culture. Recently, the U.S. government, under the presidency of Donald Trump, announced the potential deportation of thousands of Haitians who had originally been given refuge in the United States. Sonil and their family are at risk for deportation. Sonil reports problems with insomnia, stomach pain, social withdrawal, and depression. You as Sonil's counselor are faced with supporting your client but are unsure of which aspect of wellness is most affected.

SKILLS AND ACTION TO SUPPORT CLIENT WELLNESS

As presented, your client has multiple aspects of wellness that need to be addressed (coping, social, essential, and creative). You also recognize that there are multiple systemic layers that are at play. The following are suggestions noted by Ratts et al. (2016) to address these concerns:

1. Reflect and assess how your own bias, privilege, and marginalization might affect the support you extend to your client.
2. Operate through a critical consciousness lens to better understand what your client is experiencing.
3. Foster relationships with different groups in the community (e.g., family, LGBTQIA, Haitian community elders).
4. Collaborate with community leaders to address systemic barriers that are affecting your client.
5. Engage in research and social action to disrupt public policies that increase client marginalization.
6. Stay current on global events that influence marginalization.
7. Take action to address global and international policies.
8. Seek supervision.
9. Seek personal counseling.
10. Attend professional development workshops.
11. Stay connected with counseling organizations that promote social justice and advocacy as well as internationalization and counseling.

SUMMARY, INSIGHTS, AND ACTIONS

Wellness, as defined by Myers et al. (2000) is a way of life oriented toward optimal health and well-being in which body, mind, and spirit are integrated by the individual to live life more fully within the human and natural community. Ideally, it is the optimum state of health and well-being that each individual is capable of achieving. There is sometimes a disconnect between care for clients and care for self. Self-care can be defined as time for self, time not well spent. Self-compassion is a gift for self. "Wellness conceptualized as the paradigm for counseling provides strength-based strategies for assessing clients, conceptualizing issues developmentally, and planning interventions to remediate dysfunction and optimize growth" (Myers & Sweeney, 2008, p. 482).

In this chapter we have (a) reviewed the theories and models of wellness through a multicultural lens, (b) examined wellness related to diverse communities, and (c) examined the multicultural and social justice competencies (Ratts et al., 2016). Our hope is that this information is beneficial is supporting you, the counselor, in becoming a reflective, culturally sensitive social advocate. We also hope that through this chapter you are supported through developing skills to educate diverse client groups on the importance of wellness practices from the individual level to more institutional and international platforms. We hope you have learned strategies to improve wellness and promote self-care, both for yourself and for the clients you serve. Finally, we hope your attitude, beliefs, knowledge, and skills related to ethical considerations related to diverse clients are enhanced.

REFLECTION AND DISCUSSION QUESTIONS
1. What are three tangible strategies to improve wellness?
2. According to the Multicultural and Social Justice Counseling Competencies, which three domains should counselors embrace in order to be culturally effective practitioners?
3. List the components of Myers and Sweeney's (2008) evidence-based wellness approach, The Indivisible Self (IS-WEL).
4. How will you intentionally enhance your attitude and beliefs regarding wellness with your clients?
5. If you find yourself in a state of impairment, while having a full caseload, and experiencing countertransference with a long-term client, what will you do?

ADDITIONAL READINGS AND RESOURCES

ACA Code of Ethics: https://www.counseling.org/docs/default-source/ethics/2014-code-of-ethics.pdf?sfvrsn=2d58522c_4

ASCA, Ethical standards for school counselors: https://www.schoolcounselor.org/asca/media/asca/Ethics/EthicalStandards2016.pdf https://www.schoolcounselor.org/getmedia/f041cbd0-7004-47a5-ba01-3a5d657c6743/Ethical-Standards.pdf

Granello, J. (2012). *Wellness counseling.* Merrill Counseling.

Health and Wellness Resources, parent toolkit: https://www.parenttoolkit.com/additional-resources/health-and-wellness-resources https://www.parenttoolkit.com/

Jeffrey, A. (2012). The clinical intuition exploration guide: A decision-making tool for counselors and supervisors. *The Family Journal: Counseling and Therapy for Couples and Families, 20,* 37–44.

Mindfulness video with Jon Kabat-Zin: https://www.youtube.com/watch?v=3nwwKbM_vJc

National Institute of Health: https://www.nih.gov/health-information/
science-based-health-wellness-resources-your-community
National Wellness Institute: https://www.nationalwellness.org/
U.S. Department of Health and Human Services: https://www.hhs.gov/programs/
prevention-and-wellness/index.html

REFERENCES

Ábrahám, J., Velenczei, A., & Szabo, A. (2012). Perceived determinants of well-being and enjoyment level of leisure activities. Leisure Sciences, 34(3), 199–216. https://doi.org/10.1080/01490400.2012.669677

Anderson, C. L., Monroy, M., & Keltner, D. (2018). Awe in nature heals: Evidence from military veterans, at-risk youth, and college students. Emotion, 18(8), 1195–1202. https://doi.org/10.1037/emo0000442

Baker, E. K. (2005). Caring for ourselves: A therapist's guide to personal and professional well-being. American Psychological Association.

Barnett, J. E., Johnston, L. C., & Hillard, D. (2006). Psychotherapist wellness as an ethical imperative. In L. VandeCreek & J. B. Allen (Eds.), Innovations in clinical practice: Focus on health and wellness (pp. 257–271). Professional Resources Press.

Bowen-Reid, T. L. & Harrell, J. P. (2002). Racist experiences and health outcomes: An examination of spirituality as a buffer. Journal of Black Psychology, 28, 18- 36. DOI:10.1177/0095798402028001002

Brown, A. P., Marquis, A., & Guiffrida, D. A. (2013). Mindfulness-based interventions in counseling. Journal of Counseling & Development, 91(1), 96–104. https://doi.org/10.1002/j.1556-6676.2013.00077.x

Cotman, C. W., & Berchtold, N. C. (2002). Exercise: A behavioral intervention to enhance brain health and plasticity. Trends in Neurosciences, 25(6), 295–301. https://doi.org/10.1016/S0166-2236(02)02143-4

Demerouti, E., Bakker, A. B., Nachreiner, F., & Schafuli, W. B. (2001). The job demands resources model of burnout. Journal of Applied Psychology, 86, 499–512. https://doi.org/10.1037/0021-9010.86.3.499

Duffey, T. H., Lumbadue, C. A., & Woods, S. (2001). A musical chronology and the emerging life song. The Family Journal, 9(4), 398–406. doi:10.1177/1066480701094007

Ehrlich, K. B., Cassidy, J., Lejuez, C. W., & Daughters, S. B. (2014). Discrepancies about adolescent relationships as a function of informant attachment and depressive symptoms. Journal of Research on Adolescence, 24(4), 654–666. https://doi.org/10.1111/jora.12057

Freudenberger, H. J. (1975). The staff burn-out syndrome in alternative institutions. Psychotherapy: Theory, Research, and Practice, 12, 73–82.

Gandi, J. C., Wai, P. S., Karick, H., & Dagona, Z. K. (2011). The role of stress and level of burnout in job performance among nurses. Mental Health in Family Medicine, 8, 181–194.

Gladding, S. T., & Drake Wallace, M. J. (2018). Scriptotherapy: Eighteen writing exercises to promote insight and wellness AU. Journal of Creativity in Mental Health, 13(4), 380–391. https://doi.org/10.1080/15401383.2018.1486259

Hettler, W. (1976). The six dimensions of wellness. Stevens Point, WI: National Wellness Institute.

Hillman, C. H., Erickson, K. I., & Kramer, A. F. (2008). Be smart, exercise your heart: Exercise effects on brain and cognition. Nature Reviews Neuroscience, 9(1), 58–65. https://doi.org/10.1038/nrn2298

Jenaro, C., Flores, N., & Arias, B. (2007). Burnout and coping in human service practitioners. Professional Psychology: Research and Practice, 38, 80–87. https://doi.org/10.1037/0735-7028.38.1.80

Kabat-Zinn, J. (1993). Mindfulness meditation: Health benefits of an ancient Buddhist practice. In D. Goleman & J. Gurin (Eds.), Mind/body medicine (pp. 259–276). Consumer Reports Books.

Kabat-Zinn, J. (2003) Mindfulness-based interventions in context: Past, present, and future. Clinical Psychology: Science and Practice, 10, 144–156. http://dx.doi.org/10.1093/clipsy.bpg016

Kramen-Kahn, B. (2002). Do you "walk your talk"? The Maryland Psychologist, 44(3), 12.

Lazarus, R. S., & Folkman, S. (1984). Stress, appraisal, and coping. Springer.

Luo, Y., Xiang, Z., Zhang, H., & Wang, Z. (2017). Protective factors for depressive symptoms in adolescents: Interpersonal relationships and perceived social support. Psychology in the Schools, 54(8), 808–820. https://doi.org/10.1002/pits.22033

Lyubomirsky, S., Sheldon, K. M., & Schkade, D. (2005). Pursuing happiness: The architecture of sustainable change. Review of General Psychology, 9(2), 111–131. https://doi.org/10.1037/1089-2680.9.2.111

Maslach, C., Jackson, S. E., & Leiter, M. P. (1996). Maslach Burnout Inventory (3rd ed.). Consulting Psychologists Press.

McCrea, S. M., Liberman, N., Trope, Y., & Sherman, S. J. (2008). Construal level and procrastination. Psychological Science, 19, 1308–1314.

Merriam-Webster (2021). Definition of knowledge. Retrieved from https://www.merriam-webster.com/dictionary/knowledge.

Mitchell, M., & Shillingford, M. A. (2016). A journey to the past: Promoting identity development of African Americans through ancestral awareness. The Family Journal, 25, 63–69.

Moate, R. M., Gnilka, P. B., West, E. M., Burns, K. L. (2016). Stress and burnout among counselor educators: Differences between adaptive perfectionists, maladaptive perfectionists, and nonperfectionists. Journal of Counseling & Development, 94(2), 161- 171. https://doi.org/10.1002/jcad.12073

Morse, G., Salyers, M. P., Rollins, A. L., Monroe-DeVita, M., & Pfahler, C. (2012). Burnout in mental health services: A review of the problem and its remediation. Administration and Policy in Mental Health and Mental Health Services Research, 39(5), 341–352. https://doi-org.ezproxy.liberty.edu/10.1007/s10488-011-0352-1

Myers, J. E., & Sweeney, T. J. (2005). The indivisible self: An evidence-based model of wellness. Journal of Individual Psychology, 61(3), 269–279.

Myers, J. E., Luecht, R. M., & Sweeney, T. J. (2004). The Factor Structure of Wellness: Reexamining Theoretical and Empirical Models Underlying the Wellness Evaluation of Lifestyle (WEL) and the Five-Factor Wel. Measurement and Evaluation in Counseling and Development, 36(4), 194–208. https://doi.org/10.1080/07481756.2004.11909742

Myers, J. E., Sweeney, T. J., & Witmer, J. M. (2000). The wheel of wellness counseling for wellness: A holistic model for treatment planning. Journal of Counseling and Development, 78, 251–266.

Myers, S. B., Sweeney, A. C., Popick, V., Wesley, K., Brodfeld, A., & Fingerhut, R. (2012). Self-care practices and perceived stress levels among psychology graduate students. Training and Education in Professional, 6(1), 55–66.

Newsome, S., Christopher, J. C., Dahlen, P, & Christopher, S. (2006). Teaching counselors self-care through mindfulness practices. Teachers College Record, 108(9), 1881–1900.

Rana, N. (2015). Mindfulness and loving-kindness meditation: A potential tool for mental health and subjective well-being. Indian Journal of Positive Psychology, 6(2), 189–196.

Ratts, M. J., Singh, A. A., Nassar-McMillan, S., Butler, S. K., & McCullough, J. R. (2016). Multicultural and social justice counseling competencies: Guidelines for the counseling profession. Journal of Multicultural Counseling and Development, 44, 28–48. doi: 10.1002/jmcd.12035

Rotgans, J. I. & Schmidt, H. G. (2017). The relation between individual interest and knowledge acquisition. British Educational Research Journal, 43(2), 350- 371. https://doi.org/10.1002/berj.3268

Roth, B., & Robbins, D. (2004). Mindfulness-based stress reduction and health-related quality of life: Findings from a bilingual inner-city patient population. Psychosomatic Medicine, 66, 113–123.

Rogers, C. R. (1957). The necessary and sufficient conditions of therapeutic personality change. Journal of Consulting Psychology, 21, 95–103.

Schueller, S. M. (2009). Promoting wellness: Integrating community and positive psychology. Journal of Community Psychology, 37(7) 922–937. https://doi.org/10.1002/jcop.20334

Schure, M. B., Christopher, J., & Christopher, S. (2008). Mind-body medicine and the art of self-care: Teaching mindfulness to counseling students through yoga, meditation, and qigong. Journal of Counseling & Development, 86, 47–56. https://doi.org/10.1002/j.1556-6678.2008.tb00625.x

Senter, A. W., Morgan, R. D., Serna-McDonald, C., & Bewley, M. (2010). Correctional psychologist burnout, job satisfaction and life satisfaction. Psychological Services, 7, 190–201. https://doi.org/10.1037/a0020433

Shapiro, S. L., Brown, K. W., & Biegel, G. M. (2007). Teaching self-care to caregivers: Effects of mindfulness-based stress reduction on the mental health of therapists in training. Training and Education in Professional Psychology, 1(2), 105–115. https://doi.org/10.1037/1931-3918.1.2.105

Shillingford, M. A., Trice-Black, S., & Butler, S. K. (2015). Wellness of minority female counselor educators. Counselor Education & Supervision, 52(4), 255–269. https://doi.org/10.1002/j.1556-6978.2013.00041.x

Spurgeon, S. L. & Myers, J. E. (2010). African American males: Relationships among racial identity, college type, and wellness. Journal of Black Studies, 40(4), 527–543. https://doi.org/10.1177/0021934708315153

Stanley, R. (2009). Types of prayer, heart rate variability, and innate healing. Zygon: Journal of Religion & Science, 44(4), 825–846. https://doi.org/10.1111/j.1467-9744.2009.01036.x

Swarbrick, M. (2006). A wellness approach. Psychiatric Rehabilitation Journal, 29(4), 311–314. https://doi.org/10.2975/29.2006.311.314

Walker, M. P. (2017). Why we sleep: Unlocking the power of sleep and dreams. Scribner.

Williams, W. C., Morelli, S. A., Ong, D. C., & Zaki, J. (2018). Interpersonal emotion regulation: Implications for affiliation, perceived support, relationships, and well-being. Journal of Personality and Social Psychology, 115(2), 224–254. https://doi.org/10.1037/pspi0000132

Wolf, C. P., Thompson, I. A., Thompson, E. S., Smith-Adcock, S. (2012). Wellness in counselor preparation revisited: Promoting individual well-being. Journal of Individual Psychology, 68(2), 164–181. DOI:10.1353/jip.2014.0001

Yamazaki, Y., Sato, D., Yamashiro, K., Tsubaki, A., Takehara, N., Uetake, Y., & Maruyama, A. (2018). Inter-individual differences in working memory improvement after acute mild and moderate aerobic exercise. PLoS ONE, 13(12), 1–14. https://doi.org/10.1371/journal.pone.0210053

Zimbardo, P., & Boyd, J. (2008). The time paradox: The new psychology of time that will change your life. The Free Press.

CHAPTER 15

RESEARCH AND WRITING

Danica G. Hays, University of Nevada, Las Vegas

Heather Dahl, University of Nevada, Las Vegas

LEARNING OBJECTIVES

1. Become familiar with key concepts and terminology related to counseling research.
2. Be able to distinguish between various quantitative, qualitative, and mixed methods research designs.
3. Gain knowledge about consuming and writing research from a multicultural and social justice lens.

LEARNING OUTCOMES

1. Understand the importance of research to address multicultural and social justice concerns in the counseling profession.
2. Learn how to maximize the four qualities of culturally competent researchers in their work.

The nature of counselors' work, and their need to continue to strengthen their professional identity, requires the ability to understand, conduct, and evaluate research that has implications for their clients. **Research** refers to the systematic exploration or testing of a broad array of theoretical and technical issues using multiple, rigorous data sources and materials. Through research, accepted theories and techniques are investigated and revised to ensure they are culturally relevant. In counseling, researchers develop counseling models, plan and evaluate counseling interventions, and investigate phenomena relating to client attitudes, skills, beliefs, and knowledge. Researchers can use a multitude of research methods, including quantitative, qualitative, and mixed-method designs. Research serves an invaluable purpose in the field of counseling, guiding best practices and providing a better understanding of client and counselor experiences (Kottler & Shepard, 2014).

With the increased diversification of the United States, counselors are called to continually infuse multiculturally competent and socially just principles and actions within counseling practice and research. Thus, fostering their multicultural and social justice counseling competency (MSJCC) is an integral part of counselors' professional identity: They are to continually engage in multicultural and social justice research to identify and work to minimize factors and conditions that might hinder client, group, and systemic well-being. Furthermore, advocacy through research can illuminate individual and community assets and resources in order to re-script as appropriate dominant views of mental health and treatment approaches (Hays, 2020).

In 2016, the Association for Assessment and Research in Counseling (AARC) released the multicultural research standards (O'Hara et al., 2016) with the purpose of addressing multicultural competence and specific diversity considerations in research. These standards specifically address the importance of advocacy in research and multicultural considerations throughout the research process from the literature review to findings and applications. The intent of the standards is to outline ways in which counselors can both attend to diversity issues in all research as well as engage in research specifically intended to respond to multicultural and social justice concerns in counseling (O'Hara et al., 2016).

The American Counseling Association (ACA, 2014) Code of Ethics provides guidance to counselors who engage in research. In section G of the code, "Research and Publication," counselors are to "minimize bias and respect diversity in designing and implementing research" (p. 15) and "describe the extent to which results are applicable to diverse populations" (p., 16, section G.4.a). Furthermore, section G includes standards in terms of researcher responsibilities, rights of participants, managing and maintaining boundaries, reporting results, and publication and presentations. Within these sections of the ACA (2014) Code of Ethics, there is a purposeful approach to respecting diversity as integral to ethical work as a researcher.

Thus, research is a continual process of investigating phenomena and revising and improving practices designed for an increasingly diverse population of both counselors and clients. To engage in inquiry that takes into account diversity and social justice needs of those within the counseling relationship, counselors are to engage in multicultural and social justice research. **Multicultural and social justice research** is the purposeful approach to using culturally appropriate research designs, working within the intersection of power, privilege, and oppression within the counseling relationship and using research as a means of advocacy (O'Hara et al., 2016; Ratts et al., 2016). The purpose of this chapter is to outline key research concepts, qualities of culturally competent researchers, counseling research designs, and strategies for consuming and writing counseling research. Throughout these sections, maximizing multicultural and social justice research activities is a priority.

KEY CONCEPTS IN RESEARCH

Counselors engaged in research should be familiar with several key research concepts. The first concepts presented relate to ethical and legal issues in research. **Ethics** are the guiding principles for counseling researchers when designing a study, conducting data collection and analysis, and reporting and publishing data. When conducting research at an institution that received federal funding (and is best practice at those that do not), 45 CFR is a federal statute that mandates that researchers must submit any research on human subjects for review to the **institutional review board (IRB)**. The IRB reviews project proposals to evaluate the risk on potential participants and under which classification (e.g., exempt, modifications required, denied) the study falls. One of the requirements of any study by the IRB is informed consent. **Informed consent** is a detailed form that explains the details of a study, including relevant information about the principal investigator, risks or benefits of participating in the study, and participant rights. For minors or vulnerable populations who are asked to participate in research but do not have the capacity to read or understand the informed consent, **assent** may also be solicited.

Counselors should also be familiar with concepts related to different components of the overall research design. There are three key terms associated with study participants: population, sampling frame, and sample. The **population** is the specific group of people that is the target of the research. When counselors are not able to specifically identify every individual within a population, they must rely on a **sampling frame**—or list of those who can be identified. From that sampling frame, a **sample**, or smaller subset of the population, is drawn. There are several sampling methods in which counselors can use that involve randomized or purposefully selected cases in which to collect data, and sample size will vary based on the research purpose and sampling method. As an example of these concepts, Shaina—a college counselor—is interested in exploring the resilience strategies of international students concerned about their respective immigration statuses. The population would be international students at U.S. colleges and universities, and the sampling frame would include students who are identifiable and documented. Then, a sample of international students could be drawn from that sampling frame.

Counselors are also to devise a research question appropriate the research purpose. A **research question** is a statement that identifies the key information that guides the research study. The question should be focused on a specific concern or issue that counselors want to address and is to be answerable by the selected research design. A research question can be designed to describe a construct, examine relationships of multiple constructs, or examine a causal link between constructs. Using a hypothetical research study of investigating the constructs of socioeconomic status, academic achievement and presence of school counselors, here are potential research questions: (a) How do school counselors conceptualize fostering academic achievement among children from lower socioeconomic backgrounds? (b) What is the relationship between academic achievement and socioeconomic status? and (c) Does a school counselor–implemented intervention significantly improve academic achievement for a randomized group of lower socioeconomic status students?

A research question tends to reference several research variables to examine their association with one another. A **variable** is a construct influencing the study; there are three primary types of variables: independent, dependent, and extraneous. An **independent**

variable can be manipulated or controlled, has more than one level or category that can vary, and can have an effect on the outcome of the dependent variable. A **dependent variable** is the outcome that may be influenced by the independent and is measured; it cannot be manipulated. Finally, an **extraneous variable** can have an impact on measurement of the independent and/or dependent variable. To the extent possible, counselors seek to identify and control an extraneous variable to minimize measurement error. A specific extraneous variable is a confounding variable. A **confounding variable** is a variable that was not specifically identified and controlled for at the beginning of the study but has a direct impact on the dependent variable.

To illustrate these variable types, consider the following hypothetical research study: Cheyenne wants to investigate the role of after-school programs in middle school prosocial behaviors. With a sample of two middle schools, each involved in different after-school programs, the independent variable could be the after-school program (i.e., two categories), the dependent variable could be the prosocial behavior (e.g., indicated by a score from a prosocial behavior measure), and extraneous variables might include systematic differences between students at the two middle schools, the degree to which the programs were respectively delivered and measured, and events impacting the way students were selected for the study.

When conducting research, counselors hope that their research is valid. **Internal validity** is the understanding that a change in the dependent variable is due to the independent variable as opposed to extraneous variables. **External validity** is the ability to generalize results of a study to a larger group than the sample that was studied. **Validity threats** refer to variables that could impact the internal and external validity of the study. For example, suppose Terrence—a mental health counselor—is interested in exploring the relationship between access to social services and decreases in substance abuse for the homeless population in his city. Internal validity might be strengthened by ensuring the independent variable—access to various social services—and the dependent variable (substance use) are appropriately and consistently defined and measured and that potential extraneous variables (e.g., participant attrition, closure of social service agencies) are controlled to the extent possible. In terms of external validity, Terrence will want to use a sample representative to a larger population of interest with enough heterogeneity in the types of social services per category (e.g., housing, counseling, childcare, unemployment agencies, food banks) included based on a study's focus.

Statistics can be considered tools counselors can use to organize and interpret data obtained from a sample. **Descriptive statistics** is an approach used to organize, summarize, and describe a data set. For example, these may be descriptions of the sample itself (e.g., demographics of refugees entering the southern U.S. border) or descriptions of data from a measure administered to a sample (e.g., mean and standard deviation of a score on a wellness inventory). **Inferential statistics** use descriptive statistics to infer or draw conclusions about a variable or construct about a population from a sample. An example of inferential statistics using the refugee example would be computing the relationship between wellness scores (i.e., dependent variable) and refugees' country of origin (i.e., independent variable). Because the likelihood that a dependent variable measured within a population of interest is estimated by data from the research sample, measurement error is always present.

Oftentimes, as noted by the quantitative research designs presented, counselors want to evaluate, using groups or samples, the degree to which two population means are the same. With the refugee example, a counselor can explore whether there is a statistical significance in wellness scores for refugees originating from two countries. Counselors thus develop a **statistical hypothesis** to test population differences. Statistical hypothesis testing really involves determining if there is no statistical difference between two population means (i.e., **null hypothesis**). Counselors must determine how confident they want to be for rejecting the null hypothesis; they articulate this by setting a **level of significance** or **alpha level**, or the probability they are willing to wrongly reject the null hypothesis. In most counseling research studies, counselors set the alpha level at .05; they are confident in allowing, during inferential statistics, a 5% chance they wrongly reject the null hypothesis. Thus, the alpha level indicates the threshold by which counselors commit two types of decision error: type I and type II error. When a counseling researcher incorrectly rejects the null hypothesis (i.e., notes there is a significant difference between population means when there is not one), a **type I error** has occurred. A **type II error** refers to when a counseling researcher fails to reject the null hypothesis when it is the incorrect decision (i.e., notes there is not a significant difference between population means when there was one).

QUALITIES OF CULTURALLY COMPETENT RESEARCHERS

The MSJCCs (Ratts et al., 2016) and the AARC multicultural research standards (O'Hara et al., 2016) are useful documents to frame the discussion of the qualities of culturally competent counselors. Specifically, counselors interested in engaging in culturally competent research can translate the competency standards to aspirational qualities and actionable steps/sample interventions to promote multicultural and social justice research. The four interdependent qualities are as follows: (a) counseling researcher self-awareness, (b) knowledge of research participant worldview, (c) mutually beneficial counseling research relationship, and (d) engagement in research advocacy. Following a description of the four qualities is a case example highlighting how a counselor can engage in intimate partner violence research in a culturally competent manner.

Counseling Researcher Self-Awareness

A key quality of counselors wanting to engage in multicultural and social justice research is possessing a high degree of self-awareness as practitioners and researchers. Applying the MSJCCs (Ratts et al., 2016) to research activities, counselors should reflect deeply on how their social identities, privilege and oppression experiences, and attitudes and beliefs impact their approach to research and their research experiences in general. Further, they seek knowledge and skills to foster research self-awareness.

During the research process, counselors value fostering their cultural competency and engaging with other counselors in culturally diverse research teams that value multicultural and social justice research. Further, they continually explore their biases throughout data collection, analysis, and reporting (O'Hara et al., 2016).

Knowledge of Research Participant Worldview

A second quality of culturally competent counselors relates to having knowledge about the worldview of potential and actual research participants. Applying the MSJCCs (Ratts et al., 2016), **research participant worldview** can be conceptualized as the values, norms, biases, and assumptions derived from individual social experiences that impact the research process. For example, participants may have previous negative experiences with counseling researchers or may have not been able to participate often in research. Counselors also need to be knowledgeable about the history and events that shape how counseling research is conducted today while gauging whether those practices are conducive to culturally competent research.

To understand participant worldview, counselors need to first understand who the participant is. Depending on the community in which the research is taking place, the participant might be an individual, family, and/or the entire community. Once the participant group is identified, it is important for counselors to gain extensive information about the community they want to investigate and maintain contact with that community before, during, and after the research process (O'Hara et al., 2016).

As counselors prepare to conduct research, they must ascertain how the constructs of interest are conceptualized within a community and whether existing tools are appropriately normed and/or able to be accurately measured for that population. As data are collected, interpreted, and reported, it is also useful for counselors to check in with their respective research team and community of interest to ensure that findings and reporting align with others' understanding and that any reported data is presented in an empowering manner to the extent possible.

Mutually Beneficial Counseling Research Relationship

A third quality of culturally competent counseling researchers is the interest and ability to create a mutually beneficial counseling research relationship where both counselors and participants benefit. To foster a strong research relationship, counselors understand how counselor and participant worldviews, shaped by their respective privilege and oppression experiences, influence that relationship. Both researchers and participants should gain positive outcomes from the research process. Positive outcomes for participants might include access to much-needed clinical or academic interventions, knowledge about the career interests from a tool included in survey research, or an opportunity to provide input on safety needs during a focus group interview session. Some positive outcomes for researchers can include access to data used to publish or to apply for external funding.

Culturally competent counselors who value strong research partnerships can cocreate research goals with research participants, consider them as coresearchers and minimize the researcher–participant power differential, and engage with communities throughout the research process. Building and maintaining trust is a crucial element of research relationships. At the beginning of the potential research relationship, counselors assess participants' previous experiences with research and degree of trust with the research process and then work to build trust by being transparent about research design components as well as the benefits and challenges of the research relationship.

Engagement in Research Advocacy

The fourth quality of culturally competent researchers involves a willingness and commitment to engagement in research advocacy. **Research advocacy** may be defined as the adoption of research practices that serve to empower both researchers and participants; these practices can result in improved client and student services and/or education and training opportunities. Applying the MSJCC (Ratts et al., 2016), advocacy can occur at six levels of intervention: intrapersonal, interpersonal, institutional, community, public policy, and international. In order to engage at these levels, counselors must be informed consumers of published research and critical analysts of their motives for engaging in their own research with implications for marginalized populations.

Counselors serving as research advocates conduct research that promotes cultural understanding and participant and community empowerment. Multicultural and social justice research maximizes equitable participation in research and is thus more likely applicable to the community to which it is intended to apply. Further, counselors identifying with this quality disperse research that is multiculturally responsive while safeguarding against unnecessary participant harm during data collection, analysis, and reporting (O'Hara et al., 2016). By prioritizing empowerment and thus participant and community voice, the community of interest is more likely to benefit from the research. Further, one of the ultimate outcomes of research advocacy is establishing empirically supported treatments that inform professional counseling practice and future counseling research.

CASE EXAMPLE: INTIMATE PARTNER VIOLENCE RESEARCH

The following research study example illustrates some of the ways that counselors might integrate the four qualities of culturally competent researchers. Danielle is interested in studying the prevalence and consequences of high school student dating violence of in a culturally diverse school district in a city in the southern United States.

COUNSELING RESEARCHER SELF-AWARENESS

Prior to fully articulating the research goals and intended population of study, Danielle reflects on why she is interested in studying dating violence among high school students and what she assumes the data will show upon study completion. She also reflects on her relationship to the region of the country and the high schools within that school district. As a White heterosexual female who is working on her master's degree in counseling, she reflects on her privileged (e.g., White, heterosexual, able-bodied, Christian) and oppressed (i.e., female) statuses and how that influences how she thinks about the topic of dating violence and how those statuses will influence the way she approaches the study phases. To help minimize biases she may have during the study, she forms a diverse research team to help with data collection and analysis.

RESEARCH PARTICIPANT WORLDVIEW

As Danielle considers the methodology she will use to examine dating violence prevalence and consequences, she identifies the population of interest as high school students randomly selected from six high schools that constitute the district. She gains additional information about the school district itself as well as the neighborhoods that surround the schools. Before administering a survey, she reviews the tool's psychometric information, including information on whom the tool was normed to ensure the measure is appropriate for the population of interest. In addition, she conducts a small focus group interview with potential participants and local community members to gather their perspectives of how dating violence is defined and any concerns they have with how it is defined and measured in previous research.

COUNSELING RESEARCH RELATIONSHIP

Danielle values involving research participants in the research study as much as possible. Before beginning the study, she reviews the research questions, intended assessment tool, and planned design with the research team as well as with a small group of potential participants. Further, she asks school personnel and a small group of students about their previous experiences with research. She carefully reviews the informed consent document and reminds them of their rights as a research participant. She also discusses her cultural identities and professional background as a counselor trainee as part of the informed consent process.

RESEARCH ADVOCACY

Throughout the research study, Danielle is mindful of minimizing risk to participants and reflecting on how results can be used to inform counseling services and general knowledge about dating violence among high school students in current and similar settings. Because she views her research as a potential form of advocacy, she considers how the research process, relationship, and findings potentially impact her personal and professional worldview, her relationship with the population and community members, the way high schools and the surrounding community might benefit from the study, how data might inform legislation on dating violence prevention, and how the study can inform international urban contexts.

REFLECTION QUESTIONS

After reading the case study, consider the following reflection questions:

- What do you identify as potential ways a diverse research team can help Danielle foster her self-awareness regarding the research topic and sample?
- What are potential topics of conversation within a diverse research team to facilitate culturally competent research team members?
- What are some of the potential cultural strengths and limitations of the way Danielle has chosen to collect data? What might further increase her chances of identifying participants' worldviews on the topic of dating violence?
- Why might it be useful for Danielle to talk with potential participants about their experiences with previous research?
- Using the six MSJCC intervention levels (Ratts et al., 2016) as a framework, identify ways Danielle can strengthen the applicability and utility of her study findings.

COUNSELING RESEARCH DESIGNS

Counselors can use a variety of research designs to address questions that arise in their practice. Designs typically fall into three major categories: quantitative, qualitative, and mixed-methods. **Quantitative research** relies on numerical methods to test hypotheses related to variables or theories, engage in measurement and evaluation, and evaluate associations between or causal effects of variables or constructs. **Qualitative research** is the exploratory approach that examines participant meanings or theoretical processes by analyzing participant narratives or other language-based artifacts. **Mixed-methods research** integrates quantitative and qualitative approaches, developing interpretation from textual and numerical data.

In the following subsections, different quantitative, qualitative, and mixed-methods research designs are presented. For each design described, an example is presented of how a counselor interested in investigating lesbian, gay, bisexual, transgender, and queer (LGBTQ) school bullying would apply a respective design (see Table 15.1).

Quantitative Research Designs

Quantitative research is categorized as experimental or nonexperimental. Research is considered **experimental** if it involves an intervention whereby a counselor manipulates variables and/or conditions. The more stringently a counselor manipulates a variable or condition, the more the design can be considered experimental. Further, experimental designs can study changes for participants within a group (i.e., **within-subject design**) or can compare two or more groups on changes based on group assignment (i.e., **between-groups design**). **Nonexperimental** research involves exploratory designs that do not include a manipulated intervention of variables and/or conditions.

Experimental Designs

There are four experimental designs counselors can apply to their research: pre-experimental, quasi-experimental, true experimental, and single-subject. Within each of these designs are more specific approaches depending on when and if those designs implement and measure an intervention (see Table 15.1). **Pre-experimental designs** are those used when it is not possible for a counselor to randomly assign participants to a group or groups. **Quasi-experimental designs** are those comparing groups that may naturally share characteristics (e.g., Latinos, adolescents, high school students); however, random assignment of groups is not possible. **True experimental designs,** considered the gold standard of experimental designs, involve two or more groups that can be randomly assigned and compared. Finally, **single-subject research designs** (SSRD) allow study of an individual or group of individuals through repeated measures of a target behavior. It is important to note that SSRD can include qualitative design components, although they are typically represented by quantitative designs only.

Nonexperimental Designs

There are several types of nonexperimental designs: descriptive, correlational, and ex post facto designs. A **descriptive design** is detailing a variable of interest at one time (*simple descriptive*) or over a longer period (*longitudinal*). A **correlational design** involves identifying the relationship between two variables or examining group differences on a variable. An **ex post facto research design,** also known as a causal-comparative design, involves examining how an independent variable (measured previously) may have caused differences for a dependent variable. Because data have already been collected, randomization—and thus experimentation—is not possible.

Table 15.1   Counseling Research Designs and LGBTQ Youth Bullying

RESEARCH DESIGN	DESCRIPTION	SCHOOL BULLYING STUDY EXAMPLE
QUANTITATIVE RESEARCH DESIGNS		
PRE-EXPERIMENTAL		
One-group posttest-only design	An intervention is provided to a group and change is then measured.	A group of middle school teachers receives training on recognizing the effects of school bullying on LGBTQ students. The teachers complete a survey to evaluate knowledge and awareness gains.
One-group pre-test-posttest design	A group is measured before and after an intervention.	A third-grade class of students receives a classroom guidance lesson on reporting bullying behaviors. The students are assessed before and after the lesson to detect changes in skills for reporting.
Nonequivalent groups posttest-only design	Two or more groups that are not necessarily similar or equal are studied; one group receives an intervention and one does not. Then, each group is measured at the same time.	A school counselor wants to determine if LGBTQ students gain skills after a group counseling session for responding to bullying incidents. In addition to assessing the students in this group, she also tests, at the same time, another group of LGBTQ students who did not participate in the group counseling session.
QUASI-EXPERIMENTAL		
Nonequivalent groups pretest-posttest control group designs	Two or more groups that are not necessarily similar or equal are studied; one group receives an intervention and one does not. Then, each group is measured before and after the intervention period.	A mental health counselor is interested in determining if a new intervention is effective for families with an LGBTQ child experiencing school bullying. During his parenting group session, he implements the intervention. For a second parenting group, he does not provide the intervention. Both groups are measured before and after the intervention period.
Nonequivalent groups pretest-posttest comparison group designs	Two or more groups that are not necessarily similar or equal are studied; one group receives one intervention and one receives another. Then, each group is measured before and after the intervention period.	A mental health counselor is interested in determining if a new intervention is effective for families with an LGBTQ child experiencing school bullying. During his parenting group session, he implements the intervention. For a second parenting group, he provides another intervention that is well established in the literature. Both groups are measured before and after the intervention period to determine which intervention is effective.

RESEARCH DESIGN	DESCRIPTION	SCHOOL BULLYING STUDY EXAMPLE
Time series designs	A group is measured repeatedly before and after an intervention (i.e., one-group interrupted time series design) or an intervention and control group is each measured before and after the intervention period (i.e., control group interrupted time series design). For both types, observations should be made at equal time intervals and involve an intervention that is clearly distinctive from the baseline experience for the group(s).	A school counselor working with LGBTQ middle school students who have experienced bullying provides a solution-focused therapy technique to alleviate depression symptoms. The counselor collects baseline data (i.e., level of depression prior to treatment) and then measures depression symptoms every week for 6 weeks once the intervention is administered.

TRUE EXPERIMENTAL

RESEARCH DESIGN	DESCRIPTION	SCHOOL BULLYING STUDY EXAMPLE
Randomized pretest-posttest control group design	Groups are randomly assigned, and one group receives an intervention. Both groups are measured before and after the intervention period.	A school counselor is interested in measuring attitudinal changes regarding bullying of LGBTQ youth. She randomly assigns 100 elementary students to two groups and measures them prior to showing a film to one of the groups. The second group does not watch the film or receive another intervention. Both groups are then measured for attitudinal changes to evaluate the impact of the film.
Randomized pretest-posttest comparison group design	Groups are randomly assigned, and one group receives one intervention and the other group or groups receive(s) different interventions. Both groups are measured before and after the intervention period.	A school counselor is interested in measuring attitudinal changes regarding bullying of LGBTQ youth. She randomly assigns 100 elementary students to two groups and measures them prior to showing a film to one of the groups. The second group hears a guest speaker who accounts his bullying experiences as an LGBTQ youth. Both groups are then measured for attitudinal changes to evaluate the impact of each intervention for a respective group.
Randomized posttest-only control group design	Groups are randomly assigned, and one group receives an intervention. Both groups are measured after the intervention period.	Middle school teachers in a school district are randomly assigned to one of two groups. One group receives training on recognizing the effects of school bullying on LGBTQ students. All teachers in both groups complete a survey after the intervention period to evaluate knowledge and awareness gains.

RESEARCH DESIGN	DESCRIPTION	SCHOOL BULLYING STUDY EXAMPLE
Randomized posttest-only comparison group design	Groups are randomly assigned, and every group receives an intervention. Groups are measured after the intervention period.	Middle school teachers in a school district are randomly assigned to one of two groups. One group receives training on recognizing the effects of school bullying on LGBTQ students. The other group receives a training on classroom management skills to prevent LGBTQ bullying. All teachers in both groups complete a survey after the intervention period to evaluate knowledge and awareness gains.
Solomon four-group design	Four groups are randomly assigned to one of the following conditions: (a) pretest, intervention, posttest; (b) pretest, no intervention, posttest; (c) intervention and posttest only; and (d) no intervention and posttest only.	A mental health counselor works with high school students who identify as LGBTQ and who present to counseling with anxiety. He is interested in evaluating the impact of cognitive behavioral therapy (CBT) for anxiety symptoms using the Beck Anxiety Inventory (BAI). He randomly assigns clients to one of four groups: clients receiving CBT and taking the BAI before and after the intervention; clients taking the BAI before and after an intervention period but do not receive CBT; clients receiving CBT and then taking the BAI after the intervention; and clients taking the BAI without an intervention.
Single-Subject Research Design	A target behavior is repeatedly measured, including a baseline measurement (A) prior to treatment (B). Other measurements may occur after the treatment (i.e., C, D, etc.). SSRDs can be within-series (evaluating the effectiveness of one intervention or program), between series (evaluating the effectiveness of multiple interventions or programs), or multiple baseline (evaluating change across multiple individuals, situations, or behaviors).	A couples and family counselor is working with a family with a child who has bullied LGBTQ youth at his school. At the beginning of the counseling relationship, the counselor evaluates the emotional functioning of the family members. The counselor then employs Bowenian family techniques with the family, evaluating the impact on each family member's emotional functioning after the treatment at multiple intervals.
Descriptive Design	Characteristics of a variable are explored.	A middle school counselor conducts a survey of all students to measure attitudes regarding LGBTQ bullying.

RESEARCH DESIGN	DESCRIPTION	SCHOOL BULLYING STUDY EXAMPLE
Correlational Design	The relationship between two variables is investigated, or group differences on a variable are examined.	A counseling researcher conducts a national survey of youth bullying experiences. She is interested in determining if there are differences in responses between those who do and do not identify as LGBTQ.
Ex Post Facto Research Design	The impact of an independent variable on a dependent variable is evaluated using previously collected nonrandomized data.	A counseling researcher wants to determine if those who bullied LGBTQ youth when they were school aged later engaged in other forms of violence as adults. The counselor reviews archived student discipline records and related to them to current violence records.

QUALITATIVE RESEARCH DESIGNS

Case Study	A specific bounded case is described or compared.	Working within a local high school LGBTQ bullying support group, a counseling researcher studies the activities, events, and processes in the support group, as well as the individuals in the group.
Phenomenology	The meaning or essence of a participant(s) experience is explored.	A counseling researcher seeks to understand the essence LGBTQ students and their experiences with bullying at a local high school. The researcher first brackets their biases and sets aside preconceived ideas on what the experience may be for LGBTQ students. The researcher conducts individual interviews with 12 students and works to describe the phenomenon.
Grounded Theory	Theory is formulated to explain a process or action.	A counseling researcher seeks to develop a theory to describe how bulling impacts LGBTQ students in the local school system. The researcher uses an inductive approach and remains close to the data to better understand the processes and to eventually identify a core category.
Consensual Qualitative Research	Consensus is used along with share power between participant(s) and researcher to develop theory.	A counseling researcher works with a local LGBTQ community group to develop a theory on the effect bullying had on participants' overall self-efficacy throughout their K–12 experience.
Participatory Action Research	Outcomes are used as a vehicle for change and shared power between participant(s) and researcher.	A counseling researcher works with school counselors in a school district who need assistance with bullying prevention policies, specifically with LGBTQ students. Over time, the researcher collects data and shares power with the participants of the study, eventually enacting policy change with them.

Qualitative Research Designs

Qualitative research is the study of processes and/or phenomena. Counseling researchers seeks to understand and be immersed in data collection, understanding the context of the process or phenomenon. Often, qualitative inquiry is exploratory and occurs in a **naturalistic setting**, or the context in which participants live and engage with others (Hays & Singh, 2012). Qualitative research focuses on depth as opposed to breadth, or **thick description**, using strategies in data collection and analysis that comprehensively describe the participant perspective. Data collection can include participant interviews, images (e.g., photos, videos), documents, archival data, and field observation. Throughout qualitative inquiry, **trustworthiness** strategies are implemented to increase the validity and truthfulness of findings and include activities such as identifying and minimizing researcher bias and employing multiple data collection methods or investigators (Hays & Singh, 2012). Furthermore, research designs, or **research traditions**, each provide a unique approach to data collection and analysis. Common research traditions are as follows: case study, phenomenology, grounded theory, consensual qualitative research, and participatory action research.

Case Study

Known as the universal research tradition (Hays & Singh, 2012), a case study is a bounded system related to a specific event, process, activity, or individual(s). **Bounded systems** are contained with distinct boundaries, with the case study pertaining to a time period, activity, and/or place. The purpose of using the case study tradition is to thickly describe the bounded system using multiple data collection methods and sources.

Phenomenology

Phenomenology is a research tradition that seeks to understand the **essence** or overall deep description of a participant's lived experience, with a direct purpose of understanding a specific phenomenon collectively from a first-person perspective. Researchers use the process of **epoche** to set aside and bracket researcher bias and values, as well as prior views and explanations of the phenomenon (Hays & Singh, 2012). The distinguishing feature of this tradition is the ability for the researcher to attend to direct experiences of a phenomenon by asking participants questions related to the five senses.

Grounded Theory

A research tradition that is an **inductive approach** means biases or preconceived notions are set aside to formulate a theory about a phenomenon. An influential tradition, counseling researchers seek to formulate a theory that is grounded in the data collected and based on the participants' perspectives. The theory generated from data collection is used to explain a process or action surrounding an experience or sequence of events pertaining to a particular phenomenon.

Consensual Qualitative Research

Consensual qualitative research is a research tradition that approaches data collection and analysis with elements from both phenomenology and grounded theory. Participants selected are typically extremely knowledgeable about the topic being studied. A distinguishing feature of this tradition is a broad focus on consensus: During data analysis, researchers work to develop a consensus between themselves, the participants, and the general audience, with power being shared between all involved in the process (Hays & Singh, 2012).

Participatory Action Research

Participatory action research is a research tradition focused on the change of participants and the researcher throughout the inquiry process. Like consensual qualitative research, power is shared between the participants and researcher. Collaborative problem-solving between the participants and the researcher is a central organizing feature of participation action research, with the goal of emancipation and transformation.

Data Analysis

In qualitative inquiry, counseling researchers often gather large amounts of data that needs to be analyzed. While data are analyzed differently depending on what research tradition is being used, there are eight general steps to the analysis process that can help guide the counseling researcher (see Hays & Singh, 2012):

- *Step 1: Reduce data.* Before a counseling researcher begins the data collection process, the decision must be made on what data will be collected. It is important to make sure the data collected are aimed at answering the research question(s).
- *Step 2: Collect data.* Once the counseling researcher has reduced the breadth of data to collect, data collection begins. In this step the researcher, guided by the research tradition, collects data from different data sources (e.g., individual interviews, photographs, focus group interviews).
- *Step 3: Memo and summarize.* During data analysis, the counseling researcher records details about the data collected, revisions in the research design moving forward, and reflections on the potential research findings.
- *Step 4: Organize text.* Throughout data collection and analysis, the counseling researcher will need to organize the data collected. This can include transcribing data, managing or reducing the data into a usable record, or expanding on already created documents.
- *Step 5: Code.* A **code** is a way to label or "chunk" data, allowing it to be more readily analyzed. The coding process may look different for each research tradition but should often begin as quickly as possible in the data collection process. Coding

can be done individually or with a research team and can occur simultaneously with data collection.

- *Step 6: Identify themes and patterns.* In this step the counseling researcher chunks together codes identified in the coding process into themes or patterns. These higher-order codes begin to better describe the phenomenon and can include explanations, causes, relationships, or theoretical concepts.
- *Step 7: Create a codebook.* In this step, the counseling researcher compiles any codes or patterns into a document called a **codebook**. This step can be started earlier in the process as data collection is occurring, conducting **constant comparison** of the data, or comparing data being analyzed to those data already analyzed to generate and revise codes and themes.
- *Step 8: Develop a main narrative or theory.* The final step of data analysis is when the counseling researcher develops a main narrative or theory based on data analysis. Using the themes and patterns identified, the researcher refers back to the research question(s) and determines the outcome of the research.

Mixed-Methods Research Designs

Counseling researchers may want to use a mixed-methods research design, or an integration of quantitative and qualitative research design components. This "mixing" of designs can provide a more comprehensive answer to a research question as compared to using only one design, addressing some of the limitations of each type of research design. Mixed-methods research designs can involve collecting quantitative or qualitative data at the same time (i.e., **concurrent design**) or collecting either qualitative or quantitative data first depending on the research question (i.e., **sequential design**). Further, counseling researchers consider how much priority or focus each type of data will hold in a study; this will largely depend on the research question. Based on these considerations, here are four common mixed methods strategies (see Creswell & Plano Clark, 2017):

- *Sequential exploratory*: Qualitative data are collected and analyzed first, followed by quantitative data.
- *Sequential explanatory*: Quantitative data are collected and analyzed first, followed by qualitative data.
- *Concurrent triangulation*: Qualitative and quantitative data are collected and analyzed at the same time—and at similar priority levels—to confirm or converge study findings.
- *Concurrent nested*: Qualitative and quantitative data are collected and analyzed at the same time, although one of the research design types holds a greater priority or focus for the researcher.

CONSUMING AND WRITING RESEARCH

As stated at the beginning of this chapter, effective counselors are those who are able to understand, conduct, report, and evaluate research. With foundational knowledge regarding key research concepts, qualities of culturally competent researchers, and research designs, counseling researchers can understand the necessary components of a culturally competent research report as well as evaluate the quality of published research. In this section, characteristics of a culturally competent research report—based on the AARC multicultural research standards and the MSJCCs—are presented. Then, characteristics of a quality manuscript, which are integral to high-quality multicultural and social justice research, are outlined.

The Culturally Competent Research Report

Counselors who seek to foster the qualities of culturally competent researchers are particularly mindful of the quality of published research. Whether they are consuming or writing research, counselors critically examine the rationale, research design, and findings and implications reported in a manuscript or other form of written report (e.g., policy brief, client materials, monograph).

As counselors review and/or conduct research, they continually reflect on the infusion of multiculturalism and social justice in counseling manuscripts and other written outlets (O'Hara et al., 2016). Because the written product is indicative of the research process itself, counselors are to remain up-to-date on recent multicultural literature and research, include diverse researchers and participants in their work, carefully select a research design and measures that will be sensitive to diversity considerations, attend to the needs of diverse participants and communities while addressing specific research goals, and maximize research benefits for the communities and populations they serve. For the written report itself, counselors are to ensure that presented findings are multiculturally responsive and do not further pathologize or marginalize diverse populations. In addition, counselors are to provide practical applications to inform counseling practices using a multicultural and social justice lens (O'Hara et al., 2016).

Counselors are to reflect on the following questions as they review and/or conduct research:

- Are included variables in the report comprehensively defined, including a broad array of literature to represent cultural variations of the constructs?
- Does the report reflect a culturally balanced literature review and set of arguments, as well as identify clearly cultural limitations of previous research designs and findings, to indicate a rationale that is thoughtfully presented?
- What samples or subsamples have been intentionally or unintentionally excluded from the study? What outcomes do these exclusions have on the validity of any findings?
- To what extent is the selected research design potentially marginalizing culturally diverse populations and/or limiting the ability to highlight those populations' assets?

- In what ways, if any, are the study sample benefits and the communities of which implications are developed better off as a result of participating in the research process?
- How can relationships with culturally diverse populations be sustained before, during, and after the research process?
- In what ways can the research report content be shared in multiple formats to expand the informational reach of the findings?

Furthermore, the MSJCCs (Ratts et al., 2016) call for counselor competency for six levels of intervention (intrapersonal, interpersonal, institutional, community, public policy, and international and global affairs). As such, culturally competent counseling researchers can be mindful of these levels of intervention as they produce and review scholarship. For each level, counselors are to reflect on how privilege and oppression experiences of both researcher and participant affect the research process. Further, they ensure that a discussion on the role of power is articulated in the written report.

As an intrapersonal intervention, counselors can ensure that participant voice is reflected in the report and that participants benefit in meaningful ways from the research. **Participant voice** refers to the degree to which participant worldview, thoughts, emotions, and/or behaviors are directly expressed as part of findings. Thus, how much from participants' privilege and/or oppression experiences are directly understood from the data? Or are the data presented solely from the researcher's perspective and worldview? Further, participant data, whether presented as a researcher's summary or through participant direct quotes, should be presented in an empowering manner for the community to which it is intended to apply.

Counseling research as an interpersonal intervention highlights how interpersonal interactions that participants have influence their worldview, how they conceptualize the constructs under investigation, and how the research process and report itself attends to interpersonal dynamics between participants as well as those between researchers and participants. Counselors should consider how participants' relationships within their communities serve to empower or disempower them, how their cultural identities are affected by as well as influence the construct under investigation, and how the privilege and marginalized statuses of participants and researchers intersect with the research process and outcome. In the written report, counselors articulate the degree to which participants were linked to one another interpersonally, how those engagements may have influenced their perspectives on the construct under investigation, and how the researcher–participant relationship was formed and sustained throughout the research process.

As an institutional intervention, counselors attend to or involve in their research inquiry the social institutions such as schools, libraries, and religious institutions of which participants are engaged. Specifically, they explore the degree to which inequities among cultural groups are perpetuated by these social institutions and thus influence participants' experiences with the construct under investigation. In addition, counselors can better link participants to social institutions that may serve as resources for them and advocate within these institutions for changes that empower participants' lives.

Counselors engaged in community interventions are focused on the collectivistic norms and values of a community and how those norms and values either empower or disempower participants. Like the institutional level of intervention, counselors can engage with the community to strengthen it as a resource for participants and advocate within the community for increased empowerment. Counselors should ensure in the written report that there is a discussion of participants' relationships with various social institutions and their communities and how those relationships further marginalize or empower them. Further, counselors should ensure implications are included in the report that serve to guide social institutions and communities to support participants.

The public policy intervention level refers to counselors reflecting on and addressing laws and policies at the local, state, and federal levels and how those affect populations of interest (Ratts et al., 2016). The sixth intervention level, international and global affairs, involves counselors reflecting on how international politics and policies impact participants' well-being as well as other constructs under investigation. For these intervention levels, counselors can conduct research on local, state, federal, and/or international laws and policies and how they empower or disempower participants. To fight marginalization, counselors can publish reports that draw attention to actions that hurt populations of interest and advocate for changes in laws and policies. Further, counselors should ensure that laws and policies that impact how participants experience a construct under investigation are thoroughly described for the reader.

Characteristics of a Quality Manuscript

In addition to counselors engaging in and reporting about any of the six levels of intervention (Ratts et al., 2016), there are some general qualities of counseling research that should be evident in published works:

- *Engaging yet comprehensive literature review*: Counselors are to present previous literature to the reader in a critical manner that includes varying perspectives for a construct under investigation. As such, literature that supports *and* refutes a counseling researcher's argument is included. Counselors present the information in an engaging and concise manner; transitions between paragraphs are included to keep the information organized for the reader. When presenting previous literature, they are intentional about discussing how previous studies may further marginalize particular groups.
- *Strong rationale*: Because counselors want to make a substantial contribution to the literature, they should present a rationale informed by the gaps presented in the literature review that convinces the reader it is necessary to address the construct under investigation immediately. The rationale should point to direct outcomes for clients, counselors, or other relevant stakeholders.
- *Solid research design and questions*: Counselors identify research questions informed by the literature review and that are relevant to the counseling profession. They

select a quantitative, qualitative, or mixed-methods design that is appropriate to address the research questions. When selecting the design, they explain why the design is most appropriate and articulate ways they will ensure typically marginalized participants are protected in the study. When relevant, they recruit participants to serve as coresearchers who help finalize and implement the research design. Further, they outline ways in which they recruited and sampled in a manner that empowered participants.

- *Clear results and use of participant voice*: Counselors present results in a fair and understandable way. As best as possible, they include participant voice. Limitations of the data analysis process or the findings themselves are also outlined.

- *Discussion and advocacy-related implications*: In the discussion section, counselors connect the study findings to the previous literature, noting how the findings add to, support, and/or refute previous research. They call attention specifically to how multicultural and social justice practices were integrated throughout the research process and report. Further, they provide relevant, concrete, and advocacy-oriented implications for the reader and those with which they work.

SUMMARY, INSIGHTS, AND ACTIONS

The MSJCC standards (Ratts et al., 2016), AARC multicultural research standards (O'Hara et al., 2016), and the ACA (2014) Code of Ethics collectively call on the profession to engage in multicultural and social justice research to ultimately promote optimal well-being for clients and the profession. This chapter provides foundational information related to key concepts and quantitative, qualitative, and mixed-methods research approaches. We also discussed research design, process, and outcome. Counselors can strengthen their identities as culturally competent researchers through a focus on their self-awareness as researchers, knowledge of research participant worldview, involvement in a mutually beneficial counseling research relationship, and engagement in research advocacy.

This chapter was intended to serve as a primer for research and writing for counselors who are committed to multicultural and social justice principles as practitioners and researchers. In the first section, we highlighted key concepts associated with research ethics, research design, and statistics. Then, we discussed four qualities of culturally competent researchers: (a) counseling researcher self-awareness, (b) knowledge of research participant worldview, (c) mutually beneficial counseling research relationship, and (4) engagement in research advocacy. The extent to which these qualities can be infused within counseling researchers, the greater the likelihood of conducting multicultural and social justice research.

There are multiple counseling research designs that can be categorized as quantitative, qualitative, or mixed-methods research designs. Quantitative designs can be experimental or nonexperimental: The greater extent that a counseling researcher is able to randomly assign and/or randomly select participants, the closer the design is to a true experiment given its strength in terms of validity. Qualitative research designs typically involve one of these research traditions in counseling: case study, phenomenology, grounded theory, consensual qualitative research, and participatory action research. Furthermore, mixed-methods designs involve the "mixing" of qualitative and quantitative research designs, either concurrently or with one type of design following the other in sequence (i.e., sequential).

Whether counselors are reviewing existing research or conducting their own scholarship, understanding components of a culturally competent report is imperative. In this chapter, we outlined several strategies using the MSJCCs (Ratts et al., 2016) and AARC multicultural standards (O'Hara et al., 2016) as a framework for these strategies. Furthermore, general characteristics of a quality manuscript are foundational to a report that reflects multicultural and social justice research.

Becoming a culturally competent counseling researcher to align with the goals of multicultural and social justice research is ongoing. It is a core component of strengthening our professional identity. It is a reflexive and ethical process that requires us to be intentional about how we design, engage, report, consume, and apply research.

REFLECTION AND DISCUSSION QUESTIONS

1. How can counselors engage in research activities to foster their multicultural and social justice competency?
2. Briefly define the four qualities of culturally competent researchers.
3. When would you use a quantitative versus qualitative research design? What are some potential limitations of each type in terms of engaging in culturally competent research?
4. What are some key quality indicators of published counseling research in terms of multicultural and social justice considerations?
5. Select a research topic and discuss how you might address each of the six levels of intervention described in the MSJCCs (Ratts et al., 2016).

KEY TERMS

Alpha level
Assent
Between-groups design
Bounded system
Case study
Code
Codebook
Concurrent design
Confounding variable
Consensual qualitative research
Constant comparison
Correlational design
Dependent variable

Descriptive design
Descriptive statistics
Epoche
Essence
Ethics
Experimental design
Ex post facto design
External validity
Extraneous variable
Grounded theory
Independent variable
Inductive approach
Inferential statistics

Informed consent

Internal validity

Institutional review boards

Level of significance

Mixed-methods research

Naturalistic setting

Nonexperimental design

Null hypothesis

Participant voice

Participatory action research

Phenomenology

Population

Pre-experimental design

Qualitative research

Quantitative research

Quasi-experimental design

Research advocacy

Research participant worldview

Research question

Research tradition

Sample

Sampling frame

Sequential design

Single-subject research design

Statistical hypothesis

Statistics

Thick description

True experimental design

Trustworthiness

Type I error

Type II error

Validity threats

Variable

Within-subject design

ADDITIONAL READINGS AND RESOURCES

Choudhuri, D., Glauser, A., & Peregoy, J. (2004). Guidelines for writing a qualitative manuscript for the Journal of Counseling & Development. *Journal of Counseling & Development, 82,* 443–446.

Hays, D. G., & Wood, C. (2011). Infusing qualitative research traditions in counseling research designs. *Journal of Counseling & Development, 89,* 288–295. https://doi.org/10.1002/j.1556-6678.2011.tb00091.x

Lambie, G. W., Sias, S. M., David, K. M., Lawson, G., & Akos, P. (2008). A scholarly writing resource for counselor educators and their students. *Journal of Counseling & Development, 86,* 18–25.

Rockwell, S. (2002). Some thoughts on the ethics on research and publication. *Radiation Research, 157,* 1–2.

Trusty, J. (2011). Developing studies for publication in counseling journals. *Journal of Counseling & Development, 89*(3), 261–267.

REFERENCES

Creswell, J. W., & Plano Clark, V. (2017). *Designing and conducting mixed methods research* (3rd ed.). SAGE.

Hays, D. G. (2020). Multicultural and social justice counseling competency research: Opportunities for innovation. *Journal of Counseling & Development, 98*(3), 331–344. https://doi.org/10.1002/jcad.12327

Hays, D. G., & Singh, A. A. (2012). *Qualitative inquiry in clinical and educational settings.* Guilford.

Kottler, J. A., & Shepard, D. S. (2014). *Introduction to counseling: Voices from the field* (8th ed.). Cengage.

O'Hara, C., Clark, M., Hays, D. G., McDonald, P., Chang, C. Y., Crockett, S. A., Filmore, J., Portman, T., Spurgeon, S., & Wester, K. L. (2016). AARC standards for multicultural research. *Counseling Outcome Research and Evaluation, 7,* 67–72. https://doi.org/10.1177/2150137816657389

Ratts, M. J., Singh, A. A., Nassar-McMillan, S., Butler, S. K., & McCullough, J. R. (2016). Multicultural and social justice counseling competencies: Guidelines for the counseling profession. *Journal of Multicultural Counseling and Development, 44,* 28–48. https://doi.org/10.1002/jmcd.12035

CHAPTER 16

TESTING, ASSESSMENT, AND DIAGNOSIS

Catherine Y. Chang, Georgia State University

Nicolas Williams, Georgia State University

Ashlei Rabess, Georgia State University

LEARNING OBJECTIVES

1. Increase awareness of the importance of the cultural backgrounds of both professional counselor and client when accurately testing, assessing, and diagnosing their clients.
2. Increase knowledge related to how cultural biases and stereotypes affect testing, assessments, and diagnoses.
3. Outline culturally relevant and socially just skills and actions for testing, assessing, and diagnosing culturally diverse clients.

LEARNING OUTCOMES

1. Understand how cultural background and worldview affects the testing, assessment, and diagnosis processes.
2. Identify sources of cultural biases in testing, assessment, and diagnosis.
3. Be capable of implementing culturally relevant strategies for testing, assessment, and diagnosis.

Testing, assessment, and diagnosis are essential beginning steps for professional counselors to work effectively with their clients. Before discussing how to test, assess, and diagnose through a multicultural and social justice lens, we need first to define each concept. Testing and assessment are interrelated terms and are often used interchangeably, but they are distinct. **Testing** is the process of generating data to inform the assessment and diagnostic processes. **Assessment** is the utilization of the data to inform decision-making and includes the collection of data from both formal and informal sources. Assessment includes the use of tests and is not limited to using test data to gather information. Sources of data used in the assessment process include standardized tests, diagnostic interviews, projective measures, questionnaires, mental status examinations, behavioral observations, and reports from client, family, friends, and community (Whitson, 2017). **Standardized tests** refer to any form of tests that require that all test takers respond to the same questions or a section of questions from a common bank and that scoring is in a common manner. **Diagnostic interviews** include a range of information-gathering questions and techniques where the mental health professional explores the client's presenting issue and background information with the goal of formulating a diagnosis and developing a treatment plan. **Projective measures** are assessment procedures that utilize ambiguous stimuli designed to elicit unique, idiosyncratic responses. **Mental status examinations** (MSE) are structured assessments of a client's behavioral and cognitive functioning and include historic reports from the client as well as observational data collected from the professional counselor. MSE typically include a description of the client's appearance, attitude, and activity, level of consciousness and attentiveness, speech and language, mood and affect, thought process, thought content, perception, cognition, insight, and judgment (Norris et al., 2016).

Professional counselors will want to gather both the strengths and challenges of the client during the assessment process. Assessment should be used throughout the counseling process and helps professional counselors know what is working with their clients and what areas need to be adjusted. Erford (2013) outlined four purposes for assessment in counseling: (a) screening, (b) diagnosis, (c) treatment planning and goal identification, and (d) evaluation of progress/outcomes. Assessment is a broader concept, and testing is a part of the assessment process. **Diagnosis** refers to the process of identifying the nature of a disease or disorder by examining the symptoms (reported by the client) and signs (observed behaviors) through the use of assessment techniques and other available sources. Mental health professionals make diagnoses based on the standards codified by the *Diagnostic and Statistical Manual of Mental* Disorders (fifth edition, DSM-5) (American Psychiatric Association, 2013).

Without appropriate and culturally competent testing, assessment, and diagnosis, professional counselors are at risk of missing critical information that may lead to misdiagnosis and ineffective treatment. Multiculturally competent counselors are aware of and have the knowledge and skills to integrate an understanding of ability status, age, gender identity, ethnic identity, national origin, race, religion, sexual identity, socioeconomic status, and other personal characteristics to provide effective and appropriate assessment and diagnosis. Additionally, multiculturally competent counselors recognize the importance of social justice and advocacy in providing best practices for their clients.

Addressing social advocacy and multicultural competence in all areas related to counseling, and more specifically to testing, assessment, and diagnosis, are reflected in the 2014 ACA Code of Ethics and the 2016 Council for the Accreditation of Counseling and Related Educational Programs (CACREP) national accreditation standards. Section E of the ACA Code of Ethics addresses evaluation, assessment, and interpretation and is one of the components of the counseling process, and standards E.5.b, E.5.c, and E.8 specifically address the importance of cultural sensitivity and the recognition of prejudices in the diagnostic process. According to E.5.b on **cultural sensitivity**, "counselors recognize that culture affects the manner in which clients' problems are defined and experienced. Clients' socioeconomic and cultural experiences are considered when diagnosing mental disorders" (p. 11XX). Standard E.5.c addresses **historical and social prejudices in the diagnosis of pathology**: "Counselors recognize historical and social prejudices in the misdiagnosis and pathologizing of certain individuals and groups and strive to become aware of and address such biases in themselves and others" (p. 11XX). Finally, E.8 on **multicultural issues and diversity in assessment** states, "Counselors select and use with caution assessment techniques normed on populations other than that of the client. Counselors recognize the effects of age, color, culture, disability, ethnic group, gender, race, language preference, religion, spirituality, sexual orientation, and socio-economic status on test administration and interpretation, and they place test results in proper perspective with other relevant factors" (pp. 11–12). The 2016 ethical standards reiterated the 2009 standards that required advocacy knowledge and skills for counselor training. There are several standards within the core CACREP standards that highlight the importance of addressing diversity and advocacy issues in the training of professional counselors. More specifically, the following core standards directly indicate that student learning should occur in the following domains:

- Multicultural and pluralistic characteristics within and among diverse groups nationally and internationally (section 2; standard F.2.a)
- The impact of heritage, attitudes, beliefs, understandings, and acculturative experiences on an individual's views of others (section 2; standard F.2.d)
- Strategies for identifying and eliminating barriers, prejudices, and processes of intentional and unintentional oppression and discrimination (section 2; standard F.2.h)
- Ethically and culturally relevant strategies for selecting, administering, and interpreting assessment and test results (section 2; standard F.7.m)

The Association for Assessment and Research in Counseling (AARC; formerly the Association for Assessment in Counseling and Education [AACE, 2012]) published the multicultural assessment standards, which specifically address the essential role social advocacy and multicultural competences has in assessment and diagnosis. Multicultural assessment can be defined as assessment practices that consider the cultural background of the counselor and client and the intersectionality of the cultural backgrounds. In **multicultural assessment**, the professional counselor takes into consideration these cultural dynamics when assessing, diagnosing, conceptualizing, and treating their clients. The standards outline five core competencies that speak to the importance of effectively selecting, administering, and interpreting assessments and diagnostic techniques with advocacy. More specifically, the standards (AACE, 2012) state the following:

- Culturally competent professional counselors recognize the importance of social justice advocacy; they integrate understanding of age, gender, ability, race, ethnic group, national origin, religion, sexual orientation, linguistic background, and other personal characteristics in order to provide appropriate assessment and diagnostic techniques.

- Culturally competent professional counselors select assessments and diagnostic techniques that are appropriate and effective for diverse client populations.
- Culturally competent professional counselors recognize challenges inherent in assessment of persons and seek to provide administration and scoring of assessment to clients respecting age, gender, ability, race, ethnic group, national origin, religion, sexual orientation, linguistic background, and other personal characteristics.
- Culturally competent professional counselors acknowledge the importance of social justice advocacy in interpretation and communication of assessment results with diverse populations.
- Culturally competent professional counselors seek training and supervised experience to ensure they provide appropriate assessment and diagnostic techniques for diverse client populations (pp. 2–5).

Multicultural competence and social advocacy are important aspects of professional counselor training, as evidenced by our code of ethics and the accreditation standards for counselor training. As such, in this chapter the authors will discuss how to approach testing, assessment, and diagnosis from a multicultural and social justice lens using the multicultural and social justice counseling competencies (MSJCC; Ratts et al., 2015) as the framework. The chapters are organized around the aspirational competencies: attitudes and beliefs, knowledge, skills, and action. We discuss how the developmental domains of (a) counselor awareness, (b) client worldview, (c) the counseling relationship, and (d) counseling and advocacy interventions, which are embedded within each competency, contribute to multicultural and social justice practice.

MULTICULTURAL SOCIAL JUSTICE COUNSELING COMPETENCIES: ATTITUDES AND BELIEFS

DID YOU KNOW?

Culture shapes how individuals describe their symptoms. Culture influences whether you choose to describe physical or emotional symptoms. Culture also dictates whether we as a society believe that the symptoms are acceptable or whether mental health is real or imagined. For example, researchers have shown that Asian clients tend to present with more somatic symptoms first and later will report emotional distress (Grover & Ghosh, 2014).

THINK ABOUT IT

What symptoms do you experience (or not experience) when you feel stressed or depressed? How might these symptoms be related to social/cultural norms? How do your family and your community support your mental health?

According to the MSJCC, professional counselors must embody certain attitudes and beliefs and commit to practicing within a multicultural and social justice framework (Ratts et al., 2016). Individuals from different cultures have different worldviews that influence how individuals learn and how they perceive the world. Cultural backgrounds and worldview impact the symptoms that clients present with as well as how clients handle their mental health issues, seek treatment, and perform on traditional tests. Symptoms can mean different things in different cultures. The "Glossary of Cultural Concepts of Distress" in the DSM-5 that indicates how similar conditions and symptoms can have different cultural contexts. For example, *ataque de nervios* ("attack of nerves") is a syndrome among individuals of Latinx descent and is characterized by symptoms of emotional upset, including acute anxiety, anger, or grief; screaming and shouting uncontrollably; crying; and fainting-like episodes. Still, similar symptoms may be associated with different conditions in different cultural contexts, such as indisposition in Haiti, blacking out in the Southern United States, and falling out in the West Indies.

Additionally, cultural factors impact how much support the individual has to seek mental health services from their families and communities. Clients are multifaceted, and cultural variables can present opportunities for and challenges to the professional counselor when assessing and diagnosing their clients; therefore, it is important to approach these processes with cultural sensitivity, which includes supporting clients' own understanding, construction, and perception of issues. Cultural factors and worldview influence how professional counselors test, assess, and diagnosis, and therefore it is essential that professional counselors consider cultural schemas when making an accurate assessment of emotions and behaviors (Kress et al., 2005; Whitson, 2017). In this section, the authors discuss how the professional counselor can be aware of their attitude and beliefs that both promote and hinder appropriate and culturally relevant testing, assessment, and diagnosis.

Health care professionals' unconscious and unintentional bias and stereotyping of cultural minorities resulted in racial and ethnic disparities in diagnosis, treatment, and health care outcomes (Aronson et al., 2013; Snowden, 2003). Cultural bias can occur during the testing, assessment, or diagnosis processes, and it is essential that prior to testing, assessing, and diagnosing clients from diverse backgrounds that professional counselors are aware of their values, bias, and worldview and that of their clients.

The developmental domains of the MSJCC include counselor self-awareness, client worldview, and counseling relationship (Ratts et al., 2015). Standard one from the multicultural assessment standards (AACE, 2012) emphasizes the importance of acknowledging cultural information and biases when making assessment and diagnostic decisions. Like other authors have discussed in this book, professional counselors will want to engage in the process of self-reflection and exploration to understand how their cultural lens influences the way they perceive their clients' worldviews and how cultural backgrounds can both enhance and hinder counseling relationships.

Cultural bias in testing can be a result of the test materials or the biases of the evaluator. Professional counselors who are unaware of their cultural values and biases are at risk of interpreting test results based on their expectations and experiences as opposed to the experiences and cultural background of their clients. A part of being culturally aware is understanding issues of oppression and their impact on the mental health of historically marginalized individuals and communities. The conceptual framework of the MSJCC uses quadrants to illustrate the intersectionality of identities and how issues of power, privilege, and oppression impact the counselor–client relationship to varying degrees based on the counselor's and clients' privileged and marginalized statuses: counselor–marginalized client, privileged counselor–privileged client, marginalized counselor–privileged client, and marginalized counselor–marginalized client. Because professional counselors and clients can hold membership in both privileged and marginalized groups simultaneously, they can identify with more than one quadrant at any given time (Ratts et al., 2016). Professional counselors will want to examine their cultural group membership and reflect on the privileges (e.g., heterosexual, nondisabled, Christian) as well as the challenges of being a member of it (e.g., POC, trans, female). Cultural bias is an issue across assessment methods because assessment procedures do not always account for differences based on cultural factors (Erford, 2013). Professional counselors will want to recognize in themselves and others how their biases influence the assessment process for marginalized populations.

Culture is an important component of the diagnostic process. Cultural factors can be a trigger for psychopathology and impact levels of severity of psychiatric symptoms (Alarcón, 2009). Diagnostic error and misdiagnosis are linked to the counselor's judgments of what the counselor believes is pathological and related to stereotyping, self-confirmatory bias, and self-fulfilling prophecy (McLaughlin, 2002). When diagnosing a client, professional counselors must take the additional time to gather cultural information in a meaningful manner. Professional counselors are more attune to cultural factors when they match the cultural characteristics of their clients, and professional counselors are likely to report positive prognoses for their clients if they report an increased level of awareness of cultural bias (Hays et ala., 2010). Alarcón (2009) outlined five main aspects to include in a well-structured clinical interview when making a diagnosis: cultural variables, family data, pathogenic (harmful factors in the development of the mental health concern) and pathoplastic (uniqueness of the symptom expression) factors, explanatory models (idiosyncratic perspective from the client and family members regarding the origin of the symptoms), and client's strengths and weaknesses. In order to reduce the likelihood of imparting cultural biases in the assessment and diagnosis processes, professional counselors will want to be aware of their own cultural identities and the cross-cultural dynamics of their relationship with their culturally different client. In addition, before making any decisions based on assessments or a diagnosis, professional counselors will want to make sure that additional factors such as cultural or systematic and internalized oppression issues are taken into consideration.

Strategies to Increase Awareness

Questions to facilitate self-awareness:

- How does my worldview inform my beliefs about mental health issues?
- How does my privilege impact my understanding of myself and my clients?
- How do my worldview and privileges influence how I utilize tests, engage in the assessment process, and make diagnoses?
- How can a lack of self-awareness impact the therapeutic relationship?

  Activity to increase your awareness of privilege and oppression: Because professional counselors who are socially just address intrapersonal processes that impact privileged and marginalized clients, they will want to increase their awareness of their privilege and oppressed identities.

- Make three columns. In the first column make a list of privileges you personally experienced or witnessed over the past week. In the second column, make a list of oppressive acts you have experienced or witnessed over the past week. In the third column, indicate whether the acts are examples of power/lack of power, access/lack of access, advantages/lack of advantages, and majority/minority status (from Gnilka et al., 2018).

Strategies for understanding client's worldview:

- Professional counselors can immerse themselves in different cultures to gain an understanding of their clients' worldviews and how the clients' worldviews impact the assessment process.
- Before making a diagnosis, professional counselors will want to reflect on the following questions:
  - How does my client define their cultural identities? Which cultural identities are most salient for my client and are these changes based on social context?
  - What are the client's presenting symptoms and how does the client make meaning of those symptoms?
  - To what degree have current societal issues, power, privilege, and oppression contributed to my client's presenting concerns?
  - How are my client's symptoms impacted by their cultural characteristics?
  - What diagnosis best fits for my client? How is the diagnosis impacted by the client's and my cultural characteristics and values?
  - Would I come to the same decision if my client was from a different culture?

Strategies for awareness of the counseling relationship:

- Professional counselors will want to pay close attention to cultural characteristics in general, and most specifically when they are working with clients from a different cultural group than the counselors.
  - How is my cultural background influencing the counseling relationship?

- ◦ How might my client view me culturally?
- ◦ How does my cultural background enhance and hinder my relationship with my client?
- ◦ How do power, privilege, and oppression show up in my relationship with my client?
- ◦ How might the wellness/strengths-based model impact my view of my client and the way I utilize testing/assessment/diagnosis as a counselor (versus the medical model)?
- • Professional counselors will want to explain the purpose of assessment and how those results will be used in a developmentally and culturally sensitive and appropriate manner and provide information regarding how they can impact the assessment results and interpretation of the results (AACE, 2012).

MULTICULTURAL SOCIAL JUSTICE COUNSELING COMPETENCIES: KNOWLEDGE

DID YOU KNOW?

- • Minority students are overrepresented in special education (Zhang et al., 2006).
- • African Americans and Latino Americans are diagnosed with psychotic disorders at a higher rate than Euro-Americans/White Americans (Schwartz & Blankenship, 2014).
- • Gay and bisexual men are more likely to be diagnosed with major depression and panic disorder than heterosexual men (Cochran et al., 2003).
- • There is a disproportionate rate of mental disorders across racial and ethnic groups (Paniagua, 2014).

THINK ABOUT IT

What are your first reactions to learning that there are differences in test results and diagnoses based on race, ethnicity, and gender? Why do you believe there are such differences based on cultural group membership? How do social norms influence these findings?

Multiculturally competent counselors are knowledgeable about relevant multicultural and social justice theories and constructs (Ratts et al., 2016). In this section, the authors provide the knowledge necessary to understand why cultural bias influences assessment and diagnostic outcomes and how to conduct testing, assessment, and diagnosis from a multicultural and social justice lens. Professional counselors may not be aware of how their cultural background and worldview influences their construction of knowledge, the testing and assessment process, and how they interpret data; therefore, professional counselors must find methods for culturally sensitive and culturally informed assessment and diagnosis (Whitson, 2017).

For years, researchers have called for improved validity of assessment instruments and diagnostic accuracies, and this is especially relevant for diverse populations (Liang et al., 2016). Multicultural competence and social justice are central to the counseling process and should play a role in how professional counselors assess the needs of their clients and select culturally relevant interventions, which require appropriate assessments and diagnosis (Chang et al., 2010). Test bias, assessment bias, and diagnostic bias based on cultural factors can lead to inaccurate test and assessment results and misdiagnosis. **Test and assessment biases** refer to qualities within the test or assessment that unfairly or unjustly penalize one group based on cultural or other group characteristics (Whitson, 2017). **Diagnostic bias** occurs when your personal biases, prejudice, or subjective judgment influence your diagnosis (Schwarz & Blankenship, 2014)

Cultural bias in testing can result in different test results in subgroups despite similar ability levels (Kruse, 2016). Cultural bias in testing leads to the overrepresentation of African American students in special education (Reid, 2015). Most commercially available testing materials represent the mainstream, middle-class population and therefore may not be relevant to minority communities (Harry & Klingner, 2006). Standardized tests that measure intelligence and general knowledge are normed on the knowledge and values of the majority groups and therefore can be biased against minority groups who may have a different conceptualization of wisdom and intelligence (Kim & Zabelina, 2015). When working with clients from marginalized groups, professional counselors are charged with understanding the normative group and having technical information about the inventory, benefits, and limitations of the assessments and about the potential bias in the scoring and interpretation process in order to compact cultural bias (AACE, 2012). To reduce cultural bias, professional counselors will want to consider the cross-cultural validity and cultural equivalence of the instrument during the test selection process. An instrument developed to measure a construct in one culture may not measure the same concern or issue accurately in members of another cultural group. The standards for educational and psychological testing (American Educational Research Association [AERA], APA, & National Council on Measurement in Education [NCME], 2014) outline four criteria evaluating the fairness of assessments, which professional counselors will want to be mindful of when selecting testing materials. According to these criteria, tests should be free of bias, all test takers should be treated equitably, individuals with equal standing should score equally regardless of group membership, and all test takers should have an equal opportunity to learn.

Balkin et al. (2014) proposed a model for evaluating test bias and test fairness when selecting test materials to use with diverse populations. The steps of the model are theoretical evaluations of group differences in the test, evaluation of psychometric characteristics, evaluation of normative sample, and factor variance. Prior to test selection, professional counselors should take the time to review the theory and literature behind the test development, which can be found in the test manual for most tests. The next step includes evaluating the normative sample of the test. The norm group is the basis for score interpretation. Client scores should be compared to a normative sample that includes their demographics. Issues of test bias arise when scores from individuals or groups from one group are compared to a normative sample that is qualitatively different or nonrepresented in the normative sample. Professional counselors will want to familiarize themselves with the norm group of the instrument and be cautious of using instruments with norm groups that are qualitatively different than their clients. Like normative samples, factor invariance is important to consider during the testing processes. Simply stated, factor invariance involves statistical tests that evaluate the properties and interpretations of test scores to determine whether they are similar across various groups. If factorial invariance is established, then we can assume that the test is measuring the same construct across groups. Professional counselors should be especially cautious when interpreting test results when the normative sample is not representative of the clients' cultural background, and when factorial invariance is strong comparisons based on different groups is inappropriate (Balkin et al., 2014).

It is outside the scope of this chapter to thoroughly review all the technical information related to selecting, administrating, and interpreting test and assessments that are culturally appropriate; therefore, we encourage professional counselors to seek additional training to be multiculturally competent in making assessments (see AACE, 2012 and AERA, APA, & NCME, 2014).

Misdiagnoses of racial and ethnic minorities contribute to inappropriate and ineffective mental health services (Malgady et al., 1996) and can be psychologically and socially damaging (Schwartz & Blankenship, 2014). Hays et al. (2010) found that the clients' cultural identity, cultural match between a client and counselor, and cultural bias affected the clinical decision-making process. Participants in this study who shared the same race/ethnicity and gender match with the clients in the case study were more likely to discuss these variables in the case conceptualization. A disproportionate number of racial/ethnic minorities were diagnosed as bipolar compared with Whites, and a disproportionate number of women were diagnosed with major depressive disorder, alcohol abuse/dependence, and having a personality disorder compared with men (Hays et al., 2010). African American clients are more likely than non-Hispanic White youth to be diagnosed with psychotic disorders, disruptive behavior disorders, and conduct-related problems (Mak & Rosenblatt, 2002; Nguyen et al., 2007; Schwartz & Feisthamel, 2009). African American and Hispanic/Latino patients in a pediatric psychiatric hospital are more likely to be diagnosed with psychotic disorders and behavioral disorders than White youth (Muroff et al., 2008). African Americans are subject to overdiagnosis of schizophrenia (Office of the Surgeon General, 2001). Misinterpretation of assessment information and racial diagnostic bias on the part of the clinician are potential causes for African American clients being disproportionately diagnosed with several mental disorders (Schwartz & Blankenship, 2014; Schwartz & Feisthamel, 2009).

According to the DSM-5, "Mental disorders are defined in relation to the culture, social and familial norms and values" (APA, 2013a, p. 14); therefore, professional counselors are charged with considering cultural issues when diagnosing their clients. Cultural biases in testing materials and the cultural competence of the clinician have been identified as reasons for mental health professionals' tendency to overdiagnose clients of color (Paniagua, 2014). Behaviors that clinicians deem as unusual or out of the norm from their perspective do not constitute a mental disorder and culturally expected or typical cognitive patterns and psychological and emotional states and behavior do not warrant a mental health disorder (APA, 2013).

Kress et al. (2005) recommend that professional counselors thoroughly and sensitively conduct a cultural assessment with clients, which includes assessment of the clients' worldviews, assessment of clients' cultural identities; identification of sources of cultural information relevant to clients; assessment of the cultural meaning of problems and symptoms; assessment of the impact of clients' complaints on family, work, and the larger community; and assessment of the stigmas associated with the problem. In conducting a cultural assessment, it is important for the professional counselor to consider the relationship between discrimination and racial identity, especially for multiracial people given the relationship between experiences of discrimination and multiracial identity integration (McDonald et al., 2019). Professional counselors will want to openly discuss all the salient identities of their clients and how these identities will impact the counseling relationship (McDonald et al., 2019) and assessment process. As a part of the initial assessment and a way to empower clients, the culturally competent counselor will want to disseminate information regarding assessment and the psychotherapy processes because many clients from underserved populations may be unfamiliar with assessment and psychotherapy processes (Chang & O'Hara, 2012).

The DSM-5 includes the Cultural Formulation Interview (CFI), which contains 16 questions designed to explore clients' experiences and understand their worldview as well as gather information regarding their explanation and interpretations of their concerns. The CFI asks questions in four core areas: (a) cultural definition of the problem ("Sometimes people have different ways of describing their problem to their family, friends, or others in their community. How would you describe your problem to them?"); (b) cultural perceptions of the cause, context, and support ("Why do you think this is happening to you? What do you think are the causes of your [problem]"); (c) cultural factors affecting self-coping and past help-seeking ("Has anything prevented you from getting the help you need?"); and (d) cultural factors affecting current help-seeking. ("What kinds of help do you think would be most useful to you at this time for your [problem]?") (APA, 2013b, pp. 1–3). When working with culturally diverse clients, professional counselors will want to be mindful of the "Glossary of Cultural Concepts of Distress," which can be found in the appendix of the DSM-5 and provides descriptions of common cultural syndromes, idioms of distress, and causal explanations relevant for clinical practice (APA, 2013a). When using any standardized questions, professional counselors need to remember the importance of developing an authentic and caring relationship with their client is essential to accurate diagnosis and culturally relevant counseling interventions.

Now that you have some facts regarding diagnostic inaccuracies based on certain cultural characteristics, what can you do to ensure that when you are assessing or diagnosing clients from diverse populations that you are culturally sensitive and socially just? What information do you need to make an informed assessment and diagnosis that will result in culturally sensitive and effective treatment?

Strategies to Increase Knowledge

- Be intentional about gathering cultural background information from your clients and use that information to inform your assessment and diagnosis. What cultural groups define your client's identity? Which cultural groups are most salient? Which cultural group identities are based on contextual factors? (e.g., an Asian female may be independent and strong-willed at work and appear docile when interacting with her traditional Asian parents).
  - Be familiar with the Cultural Formulation Interview (APA, 2013b) and incorporate these questions into your clinical interview.
- Identify clients' reasons for seeking treatment and understanding of problem etiology (Chang & O'Hara, 2012).
- Integrate Balkin et al.'s (2014) model for evaluation test bias and test fairness into the test selection and interpretation processes.
- Keeping in mind that social factors impact the development of psychiatric diagnostic criteria and the DSM-5 favors some groups over others when making a diagnosis, be knowledgeable of the cultural identities of the client and how their symptoms are culturally based (McLaughlin, 2002).
- Thoroughly research assessment instruments you are interested in using before using them:
  - Who are the stakeholders and what are their beliefs and values?
  - When was the instrument created and for whom?
  - Are there other instruments that measure the same or a similar construct?
  - What makes this instrument a better option to use with your client than another?
  - Who was a part of the initial sample? Who was the instrument "normed" upon?
  - How valid/reliable is the instrument?
  - What critiques have been made of the instrument? By whom?
  - What training is required and/or recommended to administer this instrument effectively?

MULTICULTURAL SOCIAL JUSTICE COUNSELING COMPETENCIES: SKILLS AND ACTIONS

DID YOU KNOW?

- Mental health professionals' cultural competence, compassion, and the sharing of their client's worldview are more important to the counseling relationship than the cultural match between counselor and client (Paniagua, 2014).

THINK ABOUT IT

What skills do you need to be multiculturally competent to assess and diagnose your clients? How can you integrate social advocacy activities that will enhance your ability to be multiculturally competent when assessing and diagnosing your clients?

Multiculturally competent counselors develop culturally relevant interventions based on multiculturally based attitudes, beliefs, and knowledge and use interventions and strategies to enact individual- and community-level changes (Ratts et al., 2016). In this section, the authors discuss the skills necessary to conduct testing, assessment, and diagnosis from a multicultural and social justice lens as well as challenge all professional counselors to take action to aspire to become a multiculturally and social justice–aware professional counselor.

Cultural bias inherent in assessment materials must be considered when selecting and interpreting the most culturally appropriate assessment materials for our clients. When selecting the assessment materials, you are encouraged to reflect on the following questions: What am I assessing? What are some things to look for to determine if the assessment materials are culturally appropriate for my client? If using a standardized test, what is the norm group for the test? When was the test developed? Who developed the test and for what purpose? What are some potential biases from those promoting the test?

Many assessments used in the diagnosis of behavioral and cognitive deficits, substance abuse issues, and mental health disorders are normed using samples that lack diverse representation. Therefore, cultural knowledge must be an essential aspect of assessment and diagnosis (Balkin et al., 2014). For example, alternative assessments to traditional or standardized tests are considered more culturally fair than paper and pencil tests (Kim & Zabelina, 2015). Many authors have recommended that professional counselors adjust their interviewing style to the cultural norms of their clients (e.g., eye contact, personal space, rate of speech, nonverbal behaviors) in order to be more culturally sensitive and to develop an understanding of their clients' worldviews (Chang & O'Hara, 2012; Kress et al., 2005). Kress et al. (2005) provide a list of 10 questions to ask before making any diagnosis. Sample questions are "Have I been able to separate what is important to me and what is important to this particular client? What do I know about this client's cultural heritage? What do I not know about this client's cultural heritage? Have I appropriately consulted with other mental health professionals, members from this particular culture, and/or members of this client's family or extended family? Has this client aided in the construction of my understanding of this problem?" (Kress et al., 2005, p. 103). Other authors have made recommendations for selecting culturally appropriate assessment materials for clients, including but not limited to being aware of theory involved in creating instruments, awareness of basic psychometric properties to validate the instrument, critical evaluation of test reliability, and generalizability of normative groups (Balkin et al., 2014). Additionally, it is important that counselors seek specialized training for administering the tests and assessments they use with clients and discuss potential risks and benefits with clients prior to administration.

The fourth aspirational competency, action, was added to the MSJCC during the revision process in response to scholars who have called for action as a way to operationalize the multicultural competencies (Chang et al., 2010; Ratts et al., 2016). Action includes taking steps to continue our commitment to engage in self-reflection and knowledge-building to continuously examine our values, beliefs, and biases so that we are better attuned to our clients' worldviews. This cultural awareness and cultural knowledge aids in professional counselors' ability to select and interpret assessments and diagnosis within a multicultural and social justice framework. It may also help professional counselors advocate for how their client's test scores are used and interpreted. A part of action can also include our role as advocates for our clients when dealing with managed care and insurance claims as well as educating the general public regarding the clients' rights and responsibilities related to assessment and diagnosis.

Strategies for Skills Development and Action

- When making assessments, professional counselors are encouraged to use "cultural informants" to determine what behaviors are typical in the culture of the client. Cultural informants can be family members or members of the community (Harry & Klinger, 2006).
- Develop relationships with member of diverse communities. This will increase the professional counselor's ability to made clinical judgments, which are socially just and culturally competent. This also will increase the network of cultural informants.
- Appropriate treatment must consider cultural differences in the expression of symptoms and treatment preferences (Snowden, 2003); therefore, professional counselors will want to be mindful of cultural expressions of symptoms and treatment preferences when working with their clients.
- Practice interviewing with people who are culturally different.

- Culturally competent and socially just counselors seek training on how assessment data can be used to make systemic changes that benefit disadvantaged and vulnerable populations (AACE, 2012).
- As a way to increase multicultural awareness, knowledge, and social justice, professional counselors can work collaboratively with community leaders to better understand the needs of that diverse community and provide better access to services (AACE, 2012).
- Professional counselors can work collaboratively with allies and policy makers to educate the general public about culturally appropriate assessments for diverse individuals and groups, thus promoting social justice for diverse groups (AACE, 2012).

CASE STUDY

Cedric is a 31-year-old African American, cisgender, able-bodied male client who identifies as a Christian conservative. He graduated from a local university with a bachelor's degree in business and also holds a master's degree in accounting. Currently, Cedric works as an accountant at a prestigious bank in town. He works 50-plus hours during the week and usually goes out to local bars with his friends on the weekends. He attends church regularly and dedicates his service to helping the church manage their finances. Lately, Cedric has been feeling down. Despite much prayer, an active social life, and a thriving career, he feels guilty for not being happy with where he is in life. Unsure of what to do, he hesitantly seeks a professional counselor through his behavioral health insurance at a local private practice that specializes in spirituality. He presents to counseling in hopes of "getting out of this rut."

Lawrence is a 54-year-old African American, able-bodied, cisgender, heterosexual male counselor. He retired from the military after 20 years of service, then pursued a degree and licensure in clinical mental health counseling. While he strongly identifies with Christian values, he also identifies as more spiritual than religious. As the owner of an established private practice, Lawrence specializes in spirituality and identity work with clients.

As you read their dialogue, think about how both Cedric and Lawrence's identities could impact the process of assessment and diagnosis.

Lawrence: You mentioned earlier that you have been feeling guilty about not being happy with your life. Tell me more about that.

Cedric: I've been feeling unhappy pretty much every day for the past few months. I've lost my appetite, I'm drinking a lot more than usual, and not sleeping well at night. On top of that, I've been feeling very tired at work when I'm usually more alert. I know I should be grateful for everything I have. I mean, what do I really have to complain about? I have a great job, amazing friends, and a strong prayer life. But it still feels like something is missing. I feel like I'm in a rut, but I don't know which way is up or how to get out.

Lawrence: On the one hand, you're able to acknowledge the positive aspects of your life, but on the other hand, you feel guilty for not being happier than you are.

Cedric: Hmm, yeah. I know the Bible says that "weeping may endure for a night, but joy comes in the morning." I figure if I can just hold out, I'll be happy again eventually.

Lawrence: So, you figure if you just hold out, you'll be happy eventually and you took the initiative to come to counseling for your problem. What role do you think God plays in your happiness?

Cedric: (pause) I think that over the years, I've made God responsible for my happiness. Honestly, I'm not so sure that God would approve of my life if I really did what would make me happy.

Lawrence: What aspect of your life do you think God wouldn't approve of?

Cedric: (pause) Well … I recently met this guy named Chris at a bar and we hit it off pretty fast. We've been hanging out a lot lately, and I really enjoy spending time with him. I've been trying to ignore it, but I find myself thinking about him a lot, and there's some attraction there. I don't know what this means for my relationship with God.

Lawrence: You're afraid that your attraction to Chris may change your relationship with God. I wonder how you think this fear is related to the rut that you're in.

Cedric: I don't know, but I think they might be related.

Lawrence: That seems like a really scary place to be. You want to explore this potential relationship with Chris, and your faith contributes to the hesitancy you're feeling. You're also wondering about this rut and how to get out of it. Maybe in our next session we can explore some of your personal beliefs about attraction, how they relate to your religious values, and what this means for your life moving forward.

What is your reaction to the dialogue between Cedric and Lawrence? Based on this interaction, how might you think Lawrence would go about the assessment and diagnosis process with Cedric? How might their shared identities impact Lawrence's diagnosis of Cedric? Their differing identities? Given your own identities and values, would you diagnose Cedric? With what? Why or why not?

SUMMARY, INSIGHTS, AND ACTIONS

As reflected in the MSJCC conceptual framework, the aspirational competencies of the MSJCC (attitudes and beliefs, knowledge, skills, and action) are interrelated, and within each aspirational competency professional counselors are encouraged to reflect on the different domains (counselor self-awareness, client worldview, counseling relationship, and counseling and advocacy interventions). Our attitudes and beliefs about the testing, assessment, and diagnostic processes are informed by and influence our self-awareness, client worldview, counseling relationship, and our implementation of counseling and advocacy interventions. Our knowledge about testing, assessment, and diagnostic processes is enhanced and deepened when we take into consideration our cultural background, values, and biases; clients' worldviews; and the counseling relationships. The use of this cultural relevant knowledge to inform the assessment and diagnostic processes will lead to more effective, culturally sensitive, and socially just counseling and advocacy interventions. Professional counselors working from a multicultural and social justice framework will want to be proactive in gaining the skills necessary to increase their awareness and knowledge base regarding how to assess and diagnose within a cultural context and be proactive in taking action to increase their self-awareness of their cultural identities, to increase their awareness of clients' worldviews, and to increase their awareness of how cultural identities influence the counseling relationship.

REFLECTION AND DISCUSSION QUESTIONS

1. What can you do to combat bias in testing, assessment, and diagnosis?
2. A diagnosis can be an incredible source of information and can aid in making important and multiculturally sensitive and socially just treatment decisions. Discuss the potential dangers for overdiagnosing, underdiagnosing, and misdiagnosing conditions based on cultural and social factors.
3. Review the MSJCC and discuss in a small group how you will apply these competencies when you test, assess, or diagnose your clients.
4. What can you do to gain the necessary skills, awareness, and knowledge to assess and diagnose in a cultural context?

ADDITIONAL READINGS AND RESOURCES

American Educational Research Association, American Psychological Association, & National Council on Measurement in Education. (2014). *Standards for educational and psychological testing.* American Educational Research Association.

American Psychiatric Association (2013). *The Cultural Formation Interview.* https://www.psychiatry.org/File%20Library/Psychiatrists/Practice/DSM/APA_DSM5_Cultural-Formulation-Interview.pdf

Association for Assessment and Research in Counseling (2012). *Standards for multicultural assessment.* http://aarc-counseling.org/assets/cms/uploads/files/AACE-AMCD.pdf

https://secureservercdn.net/104.238.71.109/kxo.052.myftpupload.com/wp-content/uploads/2020/04/AACE-Standards-for-Multicultural-Assessment-2012.pdf.

Paniagua, F. A. (2014). *Assessing and treating culturally diverse clients: A practical guide.* SAGE.

Ratts, M. J., Singh, A. A., Nassar-McMillan, S., Butler, S. K., & McCullough, J. R. (2016). Multicultural and social justice counseling competencies: Guidelines for the counseling profession. *Journal of Multicultural Counseling and Development, 44,* 28–48. https://doi.org/10.1002/jmcd.12035

Websites

American Counseling Association, Assessment, diagnosis and treatment planning resources: https://aca.digitellinc.com/aca/specialties/26/view

American Psychological Association, Testing and assessment: https://www.apa.org/science/programs/testing/.

Association for Assessment and Research in Counseling website: http://aarc-counseling.org/

Association for Multicultural Counseling and Development website: www.multiculturalcounseling.org

REFERENCES

Alarcón, R. D. (2009). Culture, cultural factors and psychiatric diagnosis: review and projections. *World Psychiatry, 8*(3), 131–139.

American Counseling Association. (2014). *ACA code of ethics.* https://www.counseling.org/resources/aca-code-of-ethics.pdf

American Educational Research Association, American Psychological Association, & National Council on Measurement in Education. (2014). *Standards for educational and psychological testing.* American Educational Research Association.

American Psychiatric Association. (2013a). *Diagnostic and statistical manual of mental disorders* (5th ed.). Author.

American Psychiatric Association. (2013b). *The Cultural Formation Interview.* https://www.psychiatry.org/File%20Library/Psychiatrists/Practice/DSM/APA_DSM5_Cultural-Formulation-Interview.pdf

Aronson, J., Burgess, D., Phelan, S. M., & Juarez, L., (2013). Unhealthy interactions: The role of stereotype threat in health disparities. *American Journal of Public Health, 103*(1), 50–56. https://doi.org/10.2105%2FAJPH.2012.300828

Association for Assessment and Research in Counseling. (2012). *Standards for multicultural assessment.* https://secureservercdn.net/104.238.71.109/kxo.052.myftpupload.com/wp-content/uploads/2020/04/AACE-Standards-for-Multicultural-Assessment-2012.pdf.

Balkin, R. S., Heard, C. C. C., Lee, S.H. & Wines, L. A. (2014). A primer for evaluating test bias and test fairness: Implications for multicultural assessment. *Journal of Professional Counseling: Practice: Theory, & Research, 41*(1), 42–52. https://doi.org/10.1080/15566382.2014.12033932

Chang, C. Y., Crethar, H.C., & Ratts, M. J. (2010). Social justice: A national imperative for counselor education and supervision. *Counselor Education and Supervision*, *50*(2), 82–87.

Chang, C. Y., & O'Hara, C. (2012). The initial interview with Asian American clients. *The Journal of Contemporary Psychotherapy*, *39*(3), 33–42. https://doi.org/10.1007/s10879-012-9221-9

Cochran, S. D., Mays, V. M., & Sullivan, J. G. (2003). Prevalence of mental disorders, psychological distress, and mental health services using among lesbian, gay, and bisexual adults in the United States. *Journal of Consulting Clinical Psychology*, *71*(1), 53–61.

Council for the Accreditation of Counseling and Related Educational Programs. (2016). *2016 CACREP standards*. http://www.cacrep.org/wp-content/uploads/2018/05/2016-Standards-with-Glossary-5.3.2018.pdf

Erford, B. T. (2013). *Assessment for counselors* (2nd ed). Brooks/Cole.

Gnilka, P., O'Hara, C., & Chang, C. Y. (2018). Social justice counseling. In D. G. Hays & Erford, B. T. (Eds.), *Developing multicultural counseling competency: A systems approach* (3rd ed.) (pp. 66–91). Pearson.

Grover, S., & Ghosh, A. (2014). Somatic symptoms and related disorders in Asian and Asian Americans. *Asian Journal of Psychiatry*, *7*(1), 77–79. https://doi.org/10.1016/j.ajp.2013.11.014

Harry, B., & Klingner, J., (2006). *Why are so many minority students in special education?: Understanding race and disability in schools.* Teachers College Press.

Hays, D. G., Prosek, E. A., & McLeod, A. L. (2010). A mixed methodological analysis of the role of culture in the clinical decision-making process. *Journal of Counseling and Development*, *88*(1), 114–121. https://doi.org/10.1002/j.1556-6678.2010.tb00158.x

Kim, K. H., & Zabelina, D. (2015). Cultural bias in assessment: Can creativity assessment help? *International Journal of Critical Pedagogy*, *6*(2), 129–147.

Kress, V. E., W., Eriksen, K. P., Rayle, A. D., & Ford, S. J. W. (2005). The DSM-IV-TR and culture: Considerations for counselors. *Journal of Counseling & Development*, *83*, 97–104.

Kruse, A. J. (2016). Cultural bias in testing: A review of literature and implications for music education. *Update: Applications of Research in Music Education*, *35*(1), 23–31. https://doi.org/10.1177/8755123315576212

Liang, J., Matheson, B. E., & Douglas, J. M. (2016). Mental health diagnostic considerations in racial/ethnic minority youth. *Journal of Child Family Studies*, *25*(6), 1926–1940. https://doi.org/10.1007/s10826-015-0351-z

Mak, W., & Rosenblatt, A. (2002). Demographic influences on psychiatric diagnoses among youth served in California systems of care. *Journal of Child and Family Studies*, *11*(2), 165–178. http://dx.doi.org/10.1023/A:1015173508474

Malgady, R. G., Rogler, L. H., & Cortés, D. E. (1996). Cultural expression of psychiatric symptoms: Idioms of anger among Puerto Ricans. *Psychological Assessment*, *8*(3), 265–268. https://dx.doi.org/10.1037/1040-3590.8.3.265

McDonald, C. P., Chang, C. Y., Dispenza, F., & O'Hara, C. (2019). Multiracial identity, color-blind racial ideology, and discrimination: Professional counseling implications. *Journal of Counseling & Development*, *97*, 75–85. https://doi.org/10.1002/jcad.12237

McLaughlin, J. E. (2002). Reducing diagnostic bias. *Journal of Mental Health Counseling*, *24*(3), 256–269.

Muroff, J., Edelsohn, G.A., & Ford, J.S. (2008). The role of race in diagnostic and disposition decision making in a pediatric psychiatric emergency service. *Gen Hosp Psychiatry*, *30*(3), 269–276. https://doi.org/ 10.1016/j.genhosppsych.2008.01.003 DOI: 10.1016/j.genhosppsych.2008.01.003 or https://DOI: 10.1016/j.genhosppsych.2008.01.003

Nguyen, L., Huang, L. N., Arganza, G. F., & Liao, Q. (2007). The influence of race and ethnicity on psychiatric diagnoses and clinical characteristics of children and adolescents in children's services. *Cultural Diversity and Ethnic Minority Psychology*, *13*(1), 18–25. http://dx.doi.org/10.1037/1099-9809.13.1.18

Norris, D. R., Clark, M. S., Shipley, S. (2016). The mental status examination. *American Family Physician*, *94*(8), 635–641. https://www.aafp.org/afp/2016/1015/p635.html

Office of the Surgeon General, Center for Mental Health Services, & National Institute of Mental Health. (2001). *Mental health: Culture, race, and ethnicity: A supplement to mental health.* Substance Abuse and Mental Health Services Administration. https://www.ncbi.nlm.nih.gov/books/NBK44249/

Paniagua, F. A. (2014). *Assessing and treating culturally diverse clients: A practical guide.* SAGE.

Ratts, M. J., Singh, A. A., Nassar-McMillan, S., Butler, S. K., & McCullough, J. R. (2015). *Multicultural and social justice counseling competencies.* https://www.counseling.org/docs/default-source/competencies/multicultural-and-social-justice-counseling-competencies.pdf?sfvrsn=8573422c_20

Ratts, M. J., Singh, A. A., Nassar-McMillan, S., Butler, S. K., & McCullough, J. R. (2016). Multicultural and social justice counseling competencies: Guidelines for the counseling profession. *Journal of Multicultural Counseling and Development*, *44*, 28–48. https://doi.org/10.1002/jmcd.12035

Reid, D. (2015). Disproportionality in special education: A persistent reality for African American student justice. *Spirituality & Education Journal*, *3*(1), 2379–3538.

Schwartz, R. C., & Blankenship, D. M. (2014). Racial disparities in psychotic disorder diagnosis: A review of empirical literature. *World Journal of Psychiatry*, *4*(4), 133–140. https://doi.org/10.5498/wjp.v4.i4.133

Schwartz, R. C., & Feisthamel, K. P. (2009). Disproportionate diagnosis of mental disorders among African American versus European American clients: Implications for counseling theory, research, and practice. *Journal of Counseling & Development*, *87*, 295–301.

Snowden, L. R. (2003). Bias in mental health assessment and intervention: Theory and evidence. *American Journal of Public Health*, *93*(2), 239–243.

Whitson, S. (2017). *Principles and applications of assessment in counseling* (5th ed.). Cengage.

Zalaquett, C. P., Fuerth, K. M., Stein, C., Ivey, A. E., & Ivey, M. B. (2008). Reframing the DSM-IV-TR from a multicultural/social justice perspective. *Journal of Counseling and Development*, *86*, 364–371. https://doi.org/10.1002/j.1556-6678.2008.tb00521.x

Zhang, D., Katsiyannis, A., Ju, S., & Roberts, E. (2014). Minority representation in special education: 5-year trends. *Journal of Child Family Studies*, *23*, 118–127.

CHAPTER 17

UNDERSTANDING COUNSELOR LICENSURE

Implications From a Multicultural Counseling Social Justice Competency Perspective

Gerard Lawson, Virginia Polytechnic and State University

Jyotsana Sharma, Oklahoma State University

LEARNING OBJECTIVES

1. Gain awareness and understanding of the purpose of professional licensure.
2. Gain knowledge regarding the three components required to become licensed (education, supervised experience, examination).
3. Understand what skills the process of licensure can provide for professional counselors.
4. Evaluate the importance of licensure for purposes of advocacy, social justice, and multicultural competencies.

LEARNING OUTCOMES

1. Comprehend the influences of multicultural and social justice counseling competencies (MSJCC) on the development of counselor licensure.
2. Comprehend the importance of professional licensure in the 21st century related to accountability, advocacy, and social justice.
3. Create a personal plan of action for professional and client advocacy and increase the application of the MSJCC.

At the most fundamental level a license to practice as a counselor (or in any profession) is a mechanism for protecting the public and ensuring client welfare. Each state issuing a license has determined there is some level of risk to the general public in the practice of counseling, so individuals must be vetted and approved to practice in that profession (Safriet, 2002). A license sets out the minimum acceptable requirements for becoming licensed in that professional area of practice. The state that issues the license has determined that a specific combination of education, experience, and an examination will help to determine who is allowed to practice in a given field. A license also allows for that profession to take responsibility for ensuring that they can and will monitor the quality and efficacy of the work of their members, to police their own. This is done by ensuring counselors work within their scope of practice and follow the established codes of ethics and standards of practice, which are enforced by licensure boards and professional associations. Practicing as a licensed professional within those parameters is also one of the areas where an understanding of the multicultural and social justice counseling competencies (MSJCC) is most relevant. The process for becoming licensed can vary quite a bit, but there are some common themes in the preparation and how a licensee demonstrates their competence as a counselor. Before we examine the specific requirements, a little history of the counseling profession and counselor licensure will help provide context.

FOUNDATIONS OF THE COUNSELING PROFESSION

In the early part of the 21st century, the counseling profession undertook a year-long process known as the 20/20 Initiative on the Future of the Counseling Profession to establish a common identity for counselors and the counseling profession. As a result of that effort, 29 counseling organizations agreed to a consensus definition of counseling: "Professional counseling is a professional relationship that empowers diverse individuals, families, and groups to accomplish mental health, wellness, education, and career goals" (Kaplan et al., 2014, p. 92). In addition to being a current definition of the work of counselors, the historical roots of the counseling profession are reflected. Those roots are in mental health and prevention, education, and career development.

Much of the formal establishment of the counseling profession began in the early 1900s and can be seen in the work of three pioneers. Frank Parsons, who is often credited with starting the vocational guidance movement, started the Vocational Bureau in Boston, Massachusetts. Parsons believed that young people who had been working on farms and were drawn to the cities during the Industrial Revolution required guidance in order to be productive members of society and to keep them out of trouble. Part of that guidance was about choosing a career that was meaningful and well suited to their skill sets. Around the same time, Jesse Davis was working in Grand Rapids, Michigan, and had a vision for how vocational guidance could be part of the regular services offered in school systems (Pope, 2009). Similar to Parsons, Davis (1956) seized opportunities for guidance in the schools to help young people capitalize on their educational aptitudes and find their career paths, and he saw that discipline issues were often an "opportunity for character building" (p. 122). In that same decade, Clifford Beers wrote about his time being hospitalized in psychiatric facility and the conditions and experiences that he encountered. As a well-educated young man who was hospitalized following a suicide attempt, his perspective was given credence and the experience led him to write a book called *A Mind That Found Itself* (1908). Beers became a strong advocate for individuals with mental illness and the founder of what became known as the mental hygiene movement. One important aspect of the mental hygiene movement was the focus on the prevention of mental health issues. As the profession grew over time each of these influences were retained, and an overarching emphasis on supporting normal human development became part of the work of counselors. As Smith and Robinson (1995) wrote, "Mental health counseling believes that a person does not have to be sick to get better" (p. 158). Over a century into its development, the counseling profession continues to demonstrate that focus on prevention, mental health and wellness continues to be the foundation for the work counselors do, and we realize that the world of the 21st century will be very different than that of the 20th century, and counseling must be responsive to the needs in our communities.

In 1996, Sue, Ivey, and Pederson proposed the theory of multicultural counseling and therapy (MCT) and recognized that professionals working in the fields of counseling and mental health needed to address issues of race, ethnicity, and culture. Professionals had recognized by that time that individual experiences influence the way in which we interact with other individuals, especially minority or marginalized populations. The field of counseling was starting to realize that the theories of psychology were based on Euro-American contexts (Sue et al., 1996), which were not always applicable to individuals born and brought up in different cultures and contexts. Institutions were being challenged to educate and train practitioners who were culturally competent (Sue et al., 1996). By 2001, the Surgeon General's report on mental health as it relates to culture, race, and ethnicity had cautioned practitioners about the efficacy and applicability of using traditional therapeutic models while working with individuals, groups, and families from marginalized and minoritized backgrounds (U.S. Department of Health and Human Services [DHHS], 2001).

Sue and Sue (2008) recognized that cultural competence was a dynamic process a practitioner needed to engage with actively. It was not something that was fully achieved. Ivey et al. (2012) stated key considerations of a culturally competent practitioner. They included active engagement by the practitioner for developing self-awareness and challenging their own assumptions and biases. Second, they proposed that the practitioner should also be actively involved in understanding the context of the individual, family, or group they are working with. Lastly, they recognized that work with a client needs to be relevant to the client and sensitive to their identities and contexts (Ivey, et al., 2012). In the field of counseling, the MSJCC (Ratts et al., 2015) address the salient points proposed by authors before them. When the MSJCC were endorsed by the American Counseling Association (ACA), the message sent to communities across the country was that they are as central to how professional counselors practice as every other competency. To be a competent counselor means to demonstrate multicultural and social justice competence.

It is worth acknowledging that, although the various mental health professions have their own unique approach, and they each have merit, there are some fundamental differences in philosophy and approach among the professions. For example, the psychology profession tends to follow the medical model more so than a developmental model for treating clients (Goodyear et al., 2008). This has been a source of some consternation, especially among counseling psychologists, who are more like counselors than most specialties within psychology, and who would rather have a more person-centered approach. In a large study of the professional identity and work settings of counseling psychologists,

Goodyear et al. (2008) found that "counseling psychologists increasingly seem to have defined themselves and their specialty in terms of clinical remediation and to have given correspondingly less emphasis to the developmental and preventive themes that have historically defined the specialty" (p. 221). Similarly, the social work profession works to ameliorate social conditions that lead to mental distress and challenges, but how that work is conceptualized is different than how counselors would approach it. The National Association of Social Work (NASW) website includes information on clinical social work, which includes the definition: "Clinical social work is the professional application of social work theory and methods to the diagnosis, treatment, and prevention of psychosocial dysfunction, disability, or impairment, including emotional, mental, and behavioral disorders" (Barker, 2003 as cited in NASW, 2005, p. 9). This definition seems to highlight the deficits a client is experiencing (although it does include prevention), whereas the consensus definition of counseling focuses on empowering clients, groups, and families to achieve their goals across domains. Those differences may be subtle but are also reflected in training, scope of practice, codes of ethics, and licensure requirements across professions.

HISTORY OF COUNSELOR LICENSURE

Before Counselor Licensure

The history of counseling licensure is interesting because it began as a response to social issues across the country, and because that history provides interesting context for some of the struggles the counseling profession continues to face. In the 1950s and 60s counselors worked in the community providing mental health services and often would seek licensure as a psychologist if they met the requirements (Goodyear, 2000) or worked without a license at all. The fact that counselors work in the community is especially significant. The work counselors do has historically been more community based and less often in hospitals and residential settings. This means counselors are able to meet clients where they live and work, understand the context of the issues their clients are facing more completely, and help to find solutions that are appropriate within that community. In 1963, the Community Mental Health Centers Act (CMHCA) was signed into law by President Kennedy and was designed to establish community mental health organizations that could serve individuals with mental health needs in their community rather than in large institutions. As more funding was provided for services in the community, pressure began to mount on counselors who had worked in that setting for years.

The CMHCA brought with it the realization for psychologists, who had worked primarily in hospitals and institutional settings, that there were economic implications to allowing individuals trained as counselors to continue to practice under the psychologist licensure (Goodyear, 2000). As a result, boards of psychology began to restrict who was allowed to take the psychology license exam, after years of allowing qualified counselors to become licensed as psychologists (Goodyear, 2000; Sweeney & Witmer, 1977). In addition to regulatory challenges, there were aggressive legal actions taken against counselors who were working in the community, providing low-cost and free counseling services in underserved areas. For example, psychologists brought suit for practicing without a psychology license against a counselor who had been practicing in the community for years (Kress & Barrio Minton, 2015).

Counselors also started facing discrimination at agencies by being refused jobs they were fully capable of performing (Sweeney & Witmer, 1977). Agencies that operated statewide had begun eliminating counseling positions, stating that only psychologists and social workers would be able to provide mental health services in those roles. In addition, there was criminal case brought against a counselor for practicing psychology without a license (*City of Cleveland v. Cook*, as cited in West, Bubenzer, and Osborn, 2003; Cottingham & Swanson, 1976). These actions deprived clients of the services they were receiving, required counselors to close their practices, leaving communities underserved, and changed their careers drastically (West et al., 2003). These actions were also the call to action the counseling profession needed to begin the process of seeking a counseling license. Fortunately, the courts ruled in favor of the counselors and in one case even stated that counseling was a separate profession than psychology and needed its own regulatory board (Sweeney & Witmer, 1977).

Establishing a Counselor License

In 1975, the ACA, which was then known as the American Personnel and Guidance Association (APGA), developed a comprehensive strategy to pursue counseling licensure legislation in every state (Sweeney & Witmer, 1977). The APGA had supporting materials for the leaders involved in advocating for the profession. The precedents set by the court system in favor of the counselors that were being excluded by the psychology profession helped in these advocacy efforts (Lawson, 2016). In 1976, Virginia was the first state to pass a law that supported professional counselors to practice independently (Lawson, 2016; Sweeney & Witmer, 1977). That was the beginning of a process that took over 30 years to complete: achieving licensure in all 50 states. Building off of the court victories, counselors began to approach legislatures and argue that counselors had something distinct to offer clients and that it was in the state's interest to regulate that practice through licensure.

Part of the reason for the slow development is that some states did not have enough counselors or organizational support to pursue legislative change (Sweeney & Witmer, 1977). As the profession grew, that issue became less prominent. In many cases, however, delays were caused by other mental health professions opposing the licensing of counselors (Lawson, 2016). Again, despite the fact that counselors often were providing services not being offered by any other profession, there was opposition. As a result, the licensure laws were cobbled together state by state and often were the product of deal making that often left the counselor license much more diffuse than other professions. For example, nearly all states require a degree from a graduate training program accredited by the Council on Social Work Education in order to become a licensed clinical social worker (Dyeson,

2004). And the Association of State and Provincial Psychology Boards (ASPPB, 2015) has taken a clear stance on the need for psychologists to have graduated from an accredited program, when they state, "The [ASPPB] endorses the position that graduation from an APA/CPA accredited program should be a minimum requirement for doctoral level licensure for health service providers." Alternatively, counseling licensure regulations regularly require a degree from a counseling program, or related profession, which has led to difficulty with professional identity, national recognition, and parity with other professions. When California became the 50th state to license counselors in 2009 (33 years after Virginia began the process; Shallcross, 2009) the counseling profession was prepared to address the next challenges of licensure.

GROWTH OF THE COUNSELING PROFESSION

After licensure laws were passed in all 50 states, the next stage of the profession's development was to begin expanding access for licensed counselors (Lawson et al., 2017). One of the primary advantages of nationwide licensure law coverage is that advocacy for including counselors in federal legislation becomes a little easier. Prior to 2009, federal legislators would frequently dismiss counselors' claims that they should be included in federal mental health options. Following the licensure laws passed in California, counselors approached the U.S. Congress about including counselors as providers under TRICARE, the insurance provider for military families (U.S. Department of Defense [DOD], 2006). As part of this deliberation, Congress directed the Institute of Medicine (IOM, 2010), a nonprofit, nonpartisan research organization, to explore the issue and make recommendations about the inclusion of counselors in TRICARE. The IOM (2010) did explore the issue, and in their report noted that the great variety in the types of educational preparation of licensed counselors made it difficult to recommend that all licensed counselors be included in TRICARE. Instead, the IOM recommended that counselors who graduated from CACREP-accredited clinical mental health graduate programs be included (U.S. DOD, 2014). This was a momentous victory, as it was the first time that counselors were included in a federally administered insurance benefit.

One of the things that was recognized from the success with TRICARE is that it would benefit counselors if there was greater standardization in licensure requirements, and in particular the educational requirements (Lawson et al., 2017). That theme was advanced by several of the associations in the counseling profession, which have individually endorsed or supported the inclusion of a degree from a CACREP-accredited counseling program, as a requirement for licensure as a counselor. The rationale behind these developments is that, having seen the conclusion of the IOM, the counseling profession would be wise to increase standardization of the requirements for licensure so that counselors can be included in more opportunities with fewer barriers. The groups supporting this standardization include the Association for Counselor Education and Supervision (ACES, 2013), the American Association of State Counseling Boards (AASCB, 2015), and the ACA (2015).

PROFESSIONAL IDENTITY

According to Gale and Austin (2003), the term *professional counselor* does not fully convey the scope of what a professional counselor does. This is confusing when a potential client is trying to decide the kind of help they need and trying to distinguish between a variety of other professionals like social workers, psychologists, or paraprofessionals. In "20/20 Initiative on the Future of the Counseling Profession" (Kaplan & Gladding, 2011), representatives of the profession reached a consensus that in order to create a vision of the future of the counseling field there needs to be concerted efforts toward seven critical issues: strengthening identity, presenting as one profession, improving public perception and recognition as well as advocacy for professional issues, licensure portability, expanding and promoting the research base of professional counseling, focusing on students and prospective students, and promoting client welfare and advocacy (Kaplan & Gladding, 2011). The 20/20 process did ultimately find consensus on several important areas, including the recommended licensure title of licensed professional counselor (LPC) (Kaplan et al., 2014).

Currently, all 50 states, as well as the District of Columbia and the U.S. territories of Guam and Puerto Rico, have a licensure procedure established for professional counselors (ACA, 2016). However, the titles for these licensed counselors are quite varied. There are 36 states that recognize the LPC, eight that recognize the licensed mental health counselor (LMHC), and three that recognize the licensed clinical mental health counselor (LCMHC) licensure (ACA, 2016). Additionally, 31 states provide some other specific type of licensure or provisional license for graduates who are under supervision while they work toward their professional license (ACA, 2016). There are some unique variations to the LPC licensure title as well, including states that include the "clinical" designation to show a more advanced level of practice as part of their license (e.g., licensed professional clinical counselor [LPCC] or licensed clinical mental health counselor [LCMHC]; ACA, 2016). Most recently, the U.S. Virgin Islands passed legislation to establish a licensing board for counselors, but it is unclear if that has come to fruition and people have been able to apply for a counseling license (Bray, 2016).

If this jumble of letters, all of which represent counselors who are licensed for independent practice, is confusing, imagine what a client must feel trying to determine whom they are seeing. Seeing a counselor should mean that a client is able to experience the full range of that counselor's identity, training, and expertise. But a client may see a counselor in Maryland, for example, who was a LCPC and benefitted from the experience. Then a short time later, this client moved across the river, to Virginia or the District of Columbia, to see a counselor and could not find any LCPCs (in both neighboring jurisdictions counselors are LPCs, but an LCP is a licensed clinical psychologist). The experience that client would have with a psychologist would likely be very different than that with a counselor. Moreover, counselors who are in practice are denied the benefit of their hard-earned professional identity when that identity is spelled seven different ways in the title of our license. Finally, once again, because of the many licensure titles across the country, the profession has had difficulty getting federal legislators to understand who counselors are from state to state.

INITIAL LICENSURE REQUIREMENTS

As noted, there are typically at least three components to earning a license for independent practice: education, experience, and an examination. Some of the variations in these processes are highlighted, but a prospective licensee must carefully consult the licensure requirements in the state where they plan to practice.

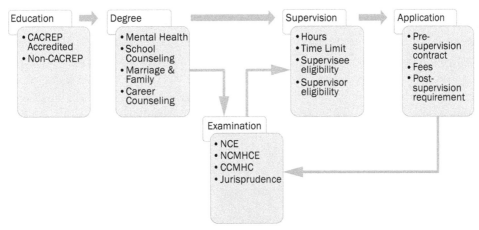

In some cases the licensure exam can be taken before supervised experience is accrued, and in others it must be after.

Figure 17.1

Educational Requirements

There are a variety of paths to earning the degree that will qualify for independent licensure. The majority of states (33 and the District of Columbia; ACA, 2016) require 60 graduate credits to meet the educational requirements for counselor licensure. However, there are states that require as few as 42 credit hours (Wisconsin; ACA, 2016), and states can require specific direction about what must be included in that graduate training. Many states require curricular experiences in specific areas. For example, some states require the core curriculum reflected in the CACREP standards (ACA, 2016). Currently, 22 states specify a CACREP-accredited master's program by name as meeting the requirements for independent licensure but also allow for equivalent degrees (ACA, 2016). A few states also require specific coursework in the laws and legal obligations in that state (often called a jurisprudence exam), and other states require coursework on intimate partner violence, HIV, and avoiding medical errors (Florida; ACA 2016). Most state regulations, along with the curricular requirements, also specify the number of hours of supervised practicum and/or internship experience that must occur in graduate training (ACA, 2016). That can range from 300 hours of internship (e.g., Georgia, Hawaii, Nebraska), to 600 hours (the CACREP standard) in many states, to very specific requirements. For example, Indiana requires a 100-hour practicum, a 600-hour internship, and a 300-hour advanced internship (ACA, 2016). Florida also requires 1,000 hours of practicum and internship experience, but only for applicants who did not complete a degree from a program accredited by CACREP (ACA, 2016).

The idea of requiring a degree from a CACREP-accredited program as a prerequisite for licensure is controversial. That movement reflects the current effort toward achieving standard educational requirements, which would benefit clients and counselors and make advocacy easier for the counseling profession (Lawson et al., 2017). There are already a few states (e.g., Ohio, North Carolina, Kentucky, Bray, 2014) that require a degree from a CACREP-accredited program as a prerequisite for licensure, and there are several other states that are in the process of changing their laws or regulations . As we have noted already, because of the piecemeal way in which counseling licensure laws were adopted, related degree programs are frequently accepted as meeting the licensure requirements for counselors but not for allied professions (e.g., psychology, social work, marriage and family therapy). So, counseling is the only profession where a client could see someone licensed as a counselor, who was in fact trained as a psychologist (or social worker, marriage and family therapist, art therapist, etc.).

Many states identify a degree from a CACREP-accredited program as the preferred standard but also allow "CACREP-equivalent or -related degree programs" (Lawson, 2016, p. 75), which presents a similar problem as the related degrees. Programs that are not CACREP accredited have frequently adopted the CACREP language to describe their curriculum (e.g., course titles). This highlights a concern articulated by Cashwell et al. (2009), who note that programs so frequently describe their programs as equivalent that students in programs that are not accredited by CACREP frequently believe that their program is CACREP accredited. And simply focusing on the titles or content of the courses ignores the parts of the CACREP accreditation process that require ongoing assessment of student learning outcomes, ratios of students to faculty and supervisors, the teaching of the ACA (2014) Code of Ethics, a counselor professional identity, and more. As a result, Cashwell et al. (2009) maintains that "there is no appropriate use of the term CACREP equivalent" (p. 14). Frequently, students who graduate from programs that are not accredited by CACREP will be required to provide additional documentation to demonstrate that they meet the educational requirements.

Supervised Experience

The period of supervised experience following the completion of a master's degree is a critical stage in the development of a counselor's skills and professional identity. Supervision is known as a critical component of developing the skills in assessment, diagnosis, conceptualization, helping skills, and ethical practice that are required to be a counselor. All states require a certain number of years and/or hours of supervised experience after completing a master's degree in counseling to apply for licensure. Hours range between a total of 1,500–4,000 hours of supervised work experience. Most states specify how many of these hours are required to be direct or face-to-face. For example, Massachusetts requires a total of 3,360 hours out of which 960 hours need to be direct hours with clients. They also require 130 hours of supervision concurrent with the clinical practice. Many states have specific requirements for who can provide the supervision, often identifying that a licensed counselor (as opposed to someone licensed in an allied profession) must provide some or all of the supervision (ACA, 2016).

Most states also specify a time limit to supervised clinical experience as well. Two years appears to be the most common time frame, endorsed by 34 states. Some states specify hours completed but also give the latest time period possible for hours' completion. For example, Virginia states that residency must be completed between 21 months and 4 years (Virginia Board of Counseling, 2018). Alternatively, Pennsylvania asks for 3 years or 3,600 hours (ACA, 2016). Even though most states have similar requirements, anyone planning on pursuing licensure would be well advised to become familiar with the specific requirements in the state where they plan to apply.

Testing

In addition to completing both your education and supervised experience, all states require an examination to demonstrate your mastery of specific content areas related to counseling practice. Most states use either the National Counselor Examination for Licensure and Certification (NCE) or the National Clinical Mental Health Counselor Examination (NCMHCE), and some states accept results from either examination. The tests are both offered by the National Board of Certified Counselors (NBCC). The NCE is a 200-item multiple-choice exam that is designed to assess whether the candidate has the knowledge, skills, and abilities essential to providing counseling services. Eight content areas specified in the CACREP standards are tested by the NCE: human growth and development, social and cultural diversity, helping relationships, group work, career development, assessment, research and program evaluation, and professional orientation and ethical practice. The NCMHCE is a test that provides 10 simulations to the candidate that are clinical in nature. It is designed to test a candidate's ability to problem-solve, identify and analyze information presented, and diagnose and provide suggested treatment for the case presented. Some states also accept results of the Certified Rehabilitation Counselor Examination (CRCE) for their state counselor's license, and it is administered by the Commission on Rehabilitation Counselor Certification (CRCC). This exam has 175 multiple-choice questions across 12 domains that underlie rehabilitation counseling (CRCC, 2019). Additionally, some states require a jurisprudence exam, which is designed to ensure that licensed counselors know and understand the relevant laws and procedures in that state. Currently, 11 states require licensed counselors moving to their state from another state to sit for the jurisprudence exam (ACA, 2016).

Scope of Practice

The scope of practice as presented and defined by the 20/20 vision (Kaplan et al., 2014) and endorsed by 94% of the participating counseling organizations states that professional counselors' scope of practice includes providing services to "individuals, groups, families, couples and organizations through the application of accepted and established mental health counseling principles, methods, procedures, and ethics." (Counseling Today, 2014). It is also agreed that counselors work toward promoting wellness across various dimensions of human existence, including mental health, social and career achievement, development across the span of life, and the prevention and treatment of mental health disorders (Counseling Today, 2014). The role of assessment, diagnosis, evaluation, and treatment planning is also mentioned in the scope of practice, which is an important detail. In fact, several states (often through state psychological associations) have challenged counselors' ability to provide psychological testing and/or the ability to provide a client with a diagnosis (e.g., New York; ACA, 2016). These are examples that demonstrate how clients and counselors are being disadvantaged and the need for social justice advocacy on behalf of the profession.

Codes of Ethics

Professional counselors abide by the ACA (2014) Code of Ethics. However, this ethical code is not consistently adopted into licensure policies and procedures by all states. Only 18 states have adopted the ACA (2014) Code of Ethics, but in a possible conflict state laws, regulations, and standards of practice take precedence (ACA, 2016). The inclusion of, or reference to, the ACA (2014) Code of Ethics is an important issue. For example, the ACA (2014) code spells out the core values of the counseling profession: "1. enhancing human development throughout the lifespan; 2. honoring diversity and embracing a multicultural approach in support of the worth, dignity, potential, and uniqueness of people within their social and cultural contexts; 3. promoting social justice; 4. safeguarding the integrity of the counselor–client relationship; and 5. practicing in a competent and ethical manner requires that counselors do not impose their personal values on clients" (p. 3). These core values refer to honoring diversity, embracing a multicultural approach, promoting social justice, and prohibiting imposing a counselor's values onto a client. These values are then reflected in specific requirements for ethical behavior throughout the code. Allied mental health professions share some of these values, and states that do not reference the ACA (2014) Code of Ethics might also endorse similar values. However, we have several states introduce laws that run counter to ACA's, including those that would prohibit a counselor from being sanctioned or losing their license for refusing to work with LGBTQ clients. Codes of ethics and standards of practice should be a reflection of the profession's values and understanding of how people change. When states regulations do not reflect those values, there is a clear opportunity for social justice advocacy.

Portability

Often once a new counselor graduates, they are focused on getting a job and securing their license, and they are not even considering the possibility of moving to a new state in the future. But the variations in licensure laws from state to state, and the lack of reciprocity or consistent endorsement, can make moving very challenging. There are several professionals who have suffered similar difficulties and have had to jump through hoops in order to get licensed in another state(s) (Kaplan, 2012). Some states require that an individual moving into their state be licensed for a specific amount of time (3 to 5 years is common) in order to avoid meeting all of the requirements of the receiving state. If you have not been licensed long enough, you may need to take additional courses, accrue more supervised experience, and/or take another exam. Several national organizations have proposed models in an attempt to begin moving toward easier licensure portability, but none have gained much traction. Recently the ACA (2018) announced an ambitious plan to pursue an interstate compact model. An interstate compact allows individual states to join in an agreement to recognize a specific level of training and supervision. That would allow states to recognize the license of an individual who moves from one compact state to another, without any additional requirements. It would also simplify the process of technology-assisted distance counseling and make it easier for individuals who live close to state borders to serve those in either state. This is a process that will take time and require advocacy but holds great promise to allow for easier movement.

CASE STUDY

Tara completed a 48-credit master's degree from a regionally accredited institute in Colorado in 2013. She secured a job working with adolescents in a residential and outpatient setting in Colorado after graduation and began working toward her license. She became a licensed professional counselor candidate (LPCC) soon after she took the position and entered into a supervision agreement. Two years and 2,000 hours of experience later she attempted the NCE exam, passed, and was able to get licensed as an LPC in the state of Colorado. About a year later, Tara decided that she wanted to move back closer to home in Arkansas, and she wanted to work in an area that had a high need for mental health professionals. She found a job in Arkansas, parts of which are considered high-need areas for mental health services and shortage areas as far as mental health counselors are concerned—parts of the state that have high poverty, challenged educational systems, and an abundance of historically marginalized populations with little to no resources. Tara was extremely excited about her new job; she felt that she could really make a difference with her work in this area. The only stipulation her new position had was to acquire a professional license in Arkansas within a year of her hire date.

When Tara applied for licensure in Arkansas, she was disappointed. They refused her request to grant her licensure by endorsement because she had not been licensed in Colorado for 3 years. The state licensing board stated that she did not have the required 60 credits for her master's degree and that she did not complete the 3,000 hours of supervised experience required in Arkansas. In order to acquire the licensed counseling associate, Tara needed to complete 12 additional credits, and to get her LPC she would need another 1,000 hours of supervised experience. Tara could finish her supervised hours while working and complete the 12 extra credits, but it would be cutting it close with her 1-year timeline to get licensed. Her job could be in jeopardy if she is unable to get her license within a year.

REFLECTION QUESTIONS

1. What are aspects of the licensure process and portability Tara should have considered before moving?
2. Can she make a case for herself with the licensure board in Arkansas on the basis of serving high-need and economically marginalized populations? What can she advocate for?
3. What are some advocacy issues Tara can get involved in as she tries to move toward her licensure in Arkansas?
4. If you were Tara's mentor or supervisor, what would you suggest she do?
5. How can Tara advocate her workplace to provide her with resources and/or time to complete the requirements she needs to fulfill?

CONSIDERATIONS

Throughout this chapter we have seen that one of the current disadvantages professional counselors are facing are the conflicting standards of licensure throughout the United States. In order to progress as a profession and advocate for the needs of our clients as well as professional counselors across the country, it is important that we reach consensus over how the field of professional counseling needs to take shape in the next few years. Through the case study presented we have tried to highlight some of the salient features future counselors-in-training should consider with some intentionality as they progress through their training programs and join the workforce as practitioners, supervisors, educators, and researchers.

SUMMARY, INSIGHTS, AND ACTIONS

At first blush there may not appear to be a great deal of overlap between the multicultural and social justice competencies and counselor licensure. Hopefully, after this discussion of the history, progress, and challenges of establishing counseling licensure in United States (and of practicing as a licensed counselor) the relevance of multicultural counseling and social justice become apparent. For our clients, we should have high confidence that individuals licensed follow the ACA (2014) Code of Ethics and abide by the standards of practice of their state. Those guidelines typically mean we are placing our clients' needs above our own; however, we also see cases when political ideology compromises the way in which we care for our client. Counselors are trained to tread lightly when using assessment instruments and diagnosing to be sure that they are culturally appropriate for the client. However, there have been efforts to prohibit licensed counselors from being able to provide any assessment or diagnosis. And there are structural challenges for counselors seeking to move from state to state even after earning a license. This often creates a barrier to providing services to individuals in high-need areas. Each of these concerns are opportunities for counselors to engage in social justice advocacy to standardize professional counseling licenses across the United States.

REFLECTION AND DISCUSSION QUESTIONS

1. After reading this chapter, what do you think are the primary benefits of the counselor licensure process?
2. What are the three components of securing professional licensure? What challenges are present among those three components? How can you help to make those challenges more manageable?
3. What is the title used for licensed counselors in your state?
4. Does the scope of practice in your state include all of the aspects described by ACA in "20/20: A Vision for the Future of Counseling"? (https://tinyurl.com/CounselingScope)

REFERENCES

American Association of State Counseling Boards. (2015). *Letter on the evolving conversation regarding educational requirements.* http://www.aascb.org/aws/AASCB/pt/sd/news_article/114494/_PARENT/layout_details/false

American Counseling Association. (2015). *Licensure policies.* Author. http://www.counseling.org/knowledge-center/licensure-policies

American Counseling Association. (2016). *Licensure requirements for professional counselors: A state-by-state report.* E. T. Shifflett, Ed. Author.

American Counseling Association. (2018, December 19). *ACA takes action toward interstate licensure portability* [Blog post]. https://www.counseling.org/news/aca-blogs/aca-government-affairs-blog/aca-government-affairs-blog/2018/12/19/aca-takes-action-toward-interstate-licensure-portability

Association for Counselor Education and Supervision. (2013). *ACES's position on educational standards for licensure.* http://www.acesonline.net/sites/default/files/ACESEducationalStandardsAnnouncement.pdf

Association of State and Provincial Psychology Boards. (2015). *APA accredited programs.* http://www.asppb.net/?page=APAAccreditation

Barker, R. (2003). *The social work dictionary* (5th ed.). NASW Press.

Beers, C. (1908). *A mind that found itself.* University of Pittsburgh Press.

Bray, B. (2014, March 13). CACREP degree to be required for counselor licensure in Ohio. *Counseling Today.* http://ct.counseling.org/2014/05/cacrep-degree-to-be-required-for-counselor-licensure-in-ohio/

Bray, B. (2016, February 23). Counseling licensing board to be established in U.S. Virgin Islands. *Counseling Today.* https://ct.counseling.org/2016/02/counselor-licensing-board-established-u-s-virgin-islands/#

Cashwell, C. S., Ritchie, M. H., Rapisarda, C., & Bobby, C. (2009). *AASCB and CACREP: Partners in professionalism and protection.* http://www.aascb.org/aws/AASCB/asset_manager/get_file/37436/cacrep_update.pdf

City of Cleveland v. Cook. (1975). Municipal Court, Criminal Division, No. 75-CRB 11478. (Transcript dated August 19, 1975)

Cottingham, H. F., & Swanson, C. D. (1976). Recent licensure developments: Implications for counselor education. *Counselor Education and Supervision, 16*(2), 84–97. https://doi.org/10.1002/ceas.1976.16.issue-2

Counseling Today. (2014). *20/20 organizations endorse licensure title, scope of practice for counseling profession.* https://ct.counseling.org/2014/10/2020-organizations-endorse-licensure-title-scope-of-practice-for-counseling-profession/

Davis, J. B. (1956). *The saga of a schoolmaster.* Boston University Press.

Dyeson, T. B. (2004). Social work licensure: A brief history and description. *Home Health Care Management Practice, 16*(5), 408–411. https://doi.org/10.1177/1084822304264657

Gale, A. U., & Austin, B. D. (2003). Professionalism's challenges to professional counselors' collective identity. *Journal of Counseling & Development, 81,* 3–9.

Goodyear, R. K. (2000). An unwarranted escalation of counselor-counseling psychologist professional conflict: Comments on Weinrach, Lustig, Chan, and Thomas (1998). *Journal of Counseling & Development, 78*(1), 103–106.

Goodyear, R. K., Murdock, N., Lichtenberg, J. W., McPherson, R., Koetting, K., & Petren, S. (2008). Stability and change in counseling psychologists' identities, roles, functions, and career satisfaction across 15 years. *The Counseling Psychologist, 36,* 220–249. https://doi.org/10.1177/0011000007309481

Institute of Medicine. (2010). *Provision of mental health counseling services under TRICARE.* National Academies Press.

Ivey, A. E., D'Andrea, M., & Ivey, M. B. (2012). *Theories of counseling and psychotherapy: A multicultural perspective.* Thousand Oaks, CA: Sage Publications.

Kaplan, D. (2012, January 25). Licensure reciprocity: A critical public protection issue that needs action. *Counseling Today*. http://ct.counseling.org/2012/01/licensure-reciprocity-a-critical-public-protection-issue-that-needs-action/

Kaplan, D. M., & Gladding, S. T. (2011). A vision for the future of counseling: The 20/20 principles for unifying and strengthening the profession. *Journal of Counseling & Development, 89*(3), 367–372. https://doi.org/10.1002/j.1556-6678.2011.tb00101.x

Kaplan, D. M., Tarvydas, V. M., & Gladding, S. T. (2014). A vision for the future of counseling: The 20/20 principles for unifying and strengthening the profession. *Journal of Counseling and Development, 92*(3), 367–372. https://doi.org/10.1002/j.1556-6676.2014.00164.x

Kress, V. E., & Barrio Minton, C. A. (2015). Thomas J. Sweeney: A visionary leader and advocate for the counseling profession. *Journal of Counseling & Development, 93*(1), 114–118. https://doi.org/10.1002/j.1556-6676.2015.00187.x

Lawson, G. (2016). On being a profession: A historical perspective on counselor licensure and accreditation. *Journal of Counselor Leadership and Advocacy, 3*(2), 71–84. http://dx.doi.org/10.1080/2326716X.2016.1169955

Lawson, G., Trepal, H. C., Lee, R. W., & Kress, V. (2017). Advocating for educational standards in counselor licensure laws. *Counselor Education & Supervision, 56*(3), 162–176. https://doi.org/10.1002/ceas.12070

National Association of Social Workers. (2005). *NASW standards for clinical social work in social work practice.* https://www.socialworkers.org/LinkClick.aspx?fileticket=YOg4q-defLBE %3d&portalid=0

Pope, M. (2009). Jesse Buttrick Davis (1871–1955): Pioneer of vocational guidance in the schools. *Career Development Quarterly, 57*(3), 248–256.

Ratts, M. J., Singh, A. A., Nassar-McMillan, S., Butler, S. K., & McCullough, J. R. (2015). Multicultural and social justice counseling competencies: Guidelines for the counseling profession. *Journal of Multicultural Counseling and Development, 44*(1), 28–48. https://doi.org/10.1002/jmcd.12035

Safriet, B. J. (2002) Closing the gap between can and may in health-care providers' scopes of practice: A primer for policymakers. *Yale Journal on Regulation, 19*(2), 301–334.

Shallcross, L. (2009, December 5). Counseling profession reaches the big 5-0. *Counseling Today.* http://ct.counseling.org/2009/12/counseling-profession-reaches-the-big-5-0/

Smith, H. B., & Robinson, G. P. (1995). Mental health counseling: Past, present, and future. *Journal of Counseling & Development, 74*(2), 158–162. https://doi.org/10.1002/j.1556-6676.1995.tb01842.x

Sue, D. W., Ivey, A. E., & Pederson, P. B. (1996). *A theory of multicultural counseling and therapy.* Brooks/Cole.

Sue, D. W., & Sue, D. (2008). *Counseling the culturally diverse: Theory and practice* (5th ed.). Wiley.

Sweeney, T. J., & Witmer, J. M. (1977). Who says you're a counselor? *Personnel Guidance Journal, 55*(10), 589–594. https://doi.org/10.1002/j.2164-4918.1977.tb04309.x

U.S. Department of Defense. (2006). *Aspects of the use of licensed professional counselors in the military health system* https://www.health.mil/Reference-Center/Reports/2006/08/28/Use-of-Licensed-Professional-Counselors-in-the-Military-Health-System

U.S. Department of Defense. (2014). TRICARE certified mental health counselors. *Federal Register, 79*(137). http://www.gpo.gov/fdsys/pkg/FR-2014-07-17/pdf/2014-16702.pdf

U.S. Department of Health and Human Services. (2001). *Mental health: Culture, race, and ethnicity—A supplement to mental health: A report of the surgeon general.* U.S. Department of Health and Human Services, Substance Abuse and Mental Health Services Administration, Center for Mental Health Services.

Virginia Board of Counseling. (2018). *LPC license process handbook.* https://www.dhp.virginia.gov/Forms/counseling/LPC/LPC_Licensure_Process_Handbook.pdf

West, J., Osborn, C., & Bubenzer, D. (2003). Dimensions of leadership in the counseling profession. In J. West, D. Bubenzer, & C. Osborn (Eds.), *Leaders and legacies: Contributions to the profession of counseling* (pp. 3–22). Brunner-Routledge.

Appendix A. States Licensure List

Alabama (AL)	**Alabama Board of Examiners in Counseling** License application License requirements
Alaska (AK)	**Alaska Board of Professional Counselors** License application FAQ
Arizona (AZ)	**Arizona Board of Behavioral Health Examiners** License application License requirements FAQ
Arkansas (AR)	**Arkansas Board of Examiners in Counseling and Marriage & Family Therapy** License application License requirements
California (CA)	**California Board of Behavioral Sciences** License application FAQ
Colorado (CO)	**Colorado Department of Regulatory Agencies** Online application Pre-License checklist Professional license checklist
Connecticut (CT)	**Connecticut Department of Public Health** Online application License requirements
Delaware (DE)	**Delaware Board of Mental Health and Chemical Dependency Professionals** License application License requirements

District of Columbia (D.C.)	**D.C. Board of Professional Counseling** License application License checklist
Florida (FL)	**Florida Board of Clinical Social Work, Marriage & Family Therapy, and Mental Health Counseling** Online application License requirements FAQ
Georgia (GA)	**Georgia Board of Professional Counselors, Social Workers, and Marriage & Family Therapists** License application FAQ
Hawaii (HI)	**Hawaii Mental Health Counselor Program** License application FAQ
Idaho (ID)	**Idaho State Licensing Board of Professional Counselors and Marriage & Family Therapists** License application FAQ
Illinois (IL)	**Illinois Professional Counselor Licensing and Disciplinary Board** Online exam application License application
Indiana (IN)	**Indiana Behavioral Health and Human Services Licensing Board** License application FAQ
Iowa (IA)	**Iowa Board of Behavioral Science** Online application Pre-license requirements Professional license requirements
Kansas (KS)	**Kansas Behavioral Sciences Regulatory Board** License application FAQ
Kentucky (KY)	**Kentucky Board of Professional Counselors** Online application
Louisiana (LA)	**Louisiana Licensed Professional Counselors Board of Examiners** Online application Online application Pre-License requirements
Maine (ME)	**Maine Board of Counseling Professionals Licensure** Online license & exam applications FAQ
Maryland (MD)	**Maryland Board of Professional Counselors and Therapists** Pre-license application Professional license application License requirements FAQ

Massachusetts (MA)	**Massachusetts Board of Registration of Allied Mental Health and Human Services Professions** License application Online application FAQ
Michigan (MI)	**Michigan Board of Counseling** License application License requirements FAQ
Minnesota (MN)	**Minnesota Board of Behavioral Health and Therapy** License application License requirements
Mississippi (MS)	**Mississippi State Board of Examiners for Licensed Professional Counselors** Online pre-license application Online professional license Pre-license requirements Professional license requirements
Missouri (MO)	**Missouri Committee for Professional Counselors** License application License requirements FAQ
Montana (MT)	**Montana Board of Behavioral Health** Online application Pre-license requirements License requirements FAQ
Nebraska (NE)	**Nebraska Department of Health and Human Services** Examination application Pre-license application License application Independent license application FAQ
Nevada (NV)	**Nevada Board of Examiners for Marriage and Family Therapist and Clinical Professional Counselors** Exam application License application License requirements
New Hampshire (NH)	**New Hampshire Board of Mental Health Practice** License application FAQ
New Jersey (NJ)	**New Hampshire Professional Counselor Examiners Committee** License application License requirements FAQ
New Mexico (NM)	**New Mexico Counseling and Therapy Practice Board** License application FAQ

New York (NY)	**New York State Education Department Mental Health Practitioners Unit** Online application License requirements License checklist FAQ
North Carolina (NC)	**North Carolina Board of Licensed Clinical Mental Health Counselors** Online application Pre-license requirements License requirements
North Dakota (ND)	**North Dakota Board of Counselor Examiners** Pre-license application License application License requirements
Ohio (OH)	**Ohio Counselor, Social Worker, and Marriage and Family Therapist Board** Online application License requirements FAQ
Oklahoma (OK)	**Oklahoma State Board of Behavioral Health** License application License requirements
Oregon (OR)	**Oregon Board of Licensed Professional Counselors & Therapists** License application License requirements Exam requirements
Pennsylvania (PA)	**Pennsylvania Department of State** Online application FAQ
Puerto Rico (PR)	**Puerto Rico Board of Examiners of Professional Counselors** Information available
Rhode Island (RI)	**Rhode Island Board of Mental Health Counselors and Marriage & Family Therapists** License application
South Carolina (SC)	**South Carolina Board of Examiners for Licensure of Professional Counselors, Marriage and Family Therapists, Addiction Counselors, and Psycho-educational Specialists** License application License requirements FAQ
South Dakota (SD)	**South Dakota Board of Examiners for Counselors & Marriage and Family Therapists** License application License-MH requirements Pre-License requirements License-MH requirements

Tennessee (TN)	**Tennessee Board for Licensed Professional Counselors, Licensed Marital and Family Therapists, and Licensed Clinical Pastoral Therapists** Pre-license application Online application License requirements
Texas (TX)	**Texas State Board of Examiners of Professional Counselors** Exam application License application Online application License requirements
Utah (UT)	**Utah Clinical Mental Health Counselor Board** Pre-license application License application Online application License requirements
Vermont (VT)	**Vermont Board of Allied Mental Health** Online application License requirements FAQ
Virginia (VA)	**Virginia Board of Counseling** Pre-license application License application License requirements Exam requirements
Washington (WA)	**Washington Department of Health** Pre-license application License application Online application License requirements FAQ
West Virginia (WV)	**West Virginia Board of Examiners in Counseling** License application License requirements
Wisconsin (WI)	**Wisconsin Marriage and Family Therapy, Professional Counseling, and Social Work Examining Board** License application License requirements
Wyoming (WY)	**Wyoming Mental Health Professions Licensing Board** Pre-license application License application FAQ

BONUS CHAPTER. CLINICAL SKILLS FROM A MULTICULTURAL PERSPECTIVE

Counseling Native/Indigenous Populations

Isaac Burt, Florida International University

Jonathan Yellowhair, Native Americans for Community Action

Allen E. Ivey, University of Massachusetts, Amherst

Picture this scenario:

A small town located in one of the most populated states in the country. The residents of this town have a long and rich history stretching back multiple generations. Peculiarly, few people in this state have ever heard of the residents from this town. Although strong of body and will, their existence went unnoticed by much of the state. That is, until "it" happened. What was "it"? Suicide. Mass suicide attempts. Imagine 20% of a population attempting suicide within a 7-month period. Now, visualize that 50% of those suicides attempted by children (14 and younger) and young adults (25 and younger). That, in and of itself, is horrible, but imagine something even worse: the response from the rest of the state. Yes, people came to help. However, after several weeks or months, they ceremoniously leave, without fully understanding the problem or resolving it. A year later, the issues continue, as the residents received no additional assistance in their time of need.

This scenario may appear as if it was a scene from a grisly horror movie, or if it was real, certainly nothing that could happen in a first-world, industrialized, Western country. The truth, however, is that it did. The example given was the true-life experience of the Attawapiskat, who live on the northern coast of Ontario, Canada. This small Indigenous population of approximately 2,000 was unknown to people until the suicide crisis thrust their presence into the lives of Natives across the world. This emergency arose as a major problem that people could not ignore and that demanded national and international attention. However, the true problem lies with what happened before the mass suicides and suicide attempts. How did it even get to this level? Where were mental health counselors, facilities, or services? Of those that were there, were they even competent to work with Indigenous people? The last question is the dilemma facing practitioners working with Indigenous populations. While every tribe's mental health issues are unique, an overriding issue persists of counselors as neglectful and unaware of how to counsel Indigenous people.

Indigenous communities, especially isolated ones such as the Attawapiskat, have a long history of dealing with generational pain and suffering. This trauma stems from a variety of sources, such as racially motivated practices by Euro-centric cultural incongruence, poverty, alcoholism, and substance. Suicide is incongruent with numerous tribes' beliefs, but what happened at Attawapiskat is a result of when exhausted tribal coping mechanisms meet generations of unaddressed complex trauma.

COUNSELING NATIVE AND INDIGENOUS CULTURES

The U.S. population is currently in a state of change, as more ethnically diverse children are born and immigrant populations continue to grow (Hemmings & Evans, 2018). Although professional counseling has attempted to adapt commensurately (i.e., multicultural and social justice counseling competencies [MSJCCs]), limitations still exist when counseling diverse clients. A major obstacle is that the helping professions primarily began from a predominately White male, middle-class framework (Burt et al., 2016; Vereen et al., 2017). Clients not having this racial, social, and economic background may not fit into or respond to techniques and theories traditional sit-down counseling espouses (Butler & Shillingford, 2014). An example of these types of clients is Native American (Native) or Indigenous clients.

Erroneously thought of as "extinct," "invisible," or only as sport mascots, the Native or Indigenous population is comprised of roughly 8 million men, women, and children (2.9 million single-race and 5.2 million multi-race), with a 39% increase in number since 2000 (Norris et al., 2012). Further, the federal government acknowledges and recognizes over 500 tribes in the United States. Within these tribes, there is a myriad of different languages, religion, and cultural history. However, one factor most tribes have in common is the shared experience of marginalization (e.g., made to perceive themselves as a foreigner in their own country). Truly, this is the epitome of marginalization and increases the risk for mental and physical problems.

Adding to these historical issues, a number of Native/Indigenous tribes are in a constant struggle to maintain traditional cultural beliefs and rituals that define the culture. A shared major aspect of Native/Indigenous culture is an intimate appreciation and connectivity to the land (Mother Earth). Many Native/Indigenous people see their identity and dependence on the land as intertwined. However, due to some legitimate and illegal businesses, coupled with the isolated locales of some reservations, many Native/Indigenous people may perceive their land as defiled. For instance, pollution and unwanted buildings/architecture impact not only identity, but livelihood and their very existence. Taking these factors into consideration, Native/Indigenous people present a multifaceted and complicated clinical issue for counselors working with the population. As such, any counselor providing therapeutic services to Native/Indigenous people must possess factors such as (a) a thorough understanding of the historical perspective and its impact, (b) strong self-awareness, and (c) multiculturally competent clinical skills.

UNDERSTANDING THE HISTORICAL IMPACT

Historically, the Native/Indigenous population of the United States of America has faced several issues, ranging from political oppression to disproportionate incarceration rates. From the early days of European settlers, Native/Indigenous people have encountered an inordinate amount of pressure due to rifts between Indigenous values and beliefs promulgated by others. Making matters worse, the plight of Native/Indigenous people do not receive as much news and social awareness as other groups. However, the Native American population struggles has a myriad of issues that other minority groups deal with as well. Akin to other marginalized groups, Native/Indigenous deal with low socioeconomic status (SES), substance use/abuse, stereotypes, microaggressions, early adolescent pregnancy, and historical abuse from the majority population.

What sets Native/Indigenous people apart from other minorities is the isolation involved and the existing state of affairs of the reservation. The reservation system proved to be a defining moment for Native/Indigenous tribes. This system, created under the auspices of Native/Indigenous people keeping their citizenship and sovereignty, created a caste system that made it easier to control and manipulate Native/Indigenous people. In essence, one of the major critical reasons for the reservation was to be able to control Native/Indigenous people, and, for lack of a better word, "enlighten" them. However, the strict boundaries forced more conflict as tribes begin to wage war for dwindling resources. Thus, the reservation system disconnected the Native/Indigenous population from mainstream America, and this separation still exists in contemporary society. Although this information may be widely known, many counselors are unaware of the extent to which this unequal system has negatively affected Native/Indigenous people. Thus, counselors need to have this understanding of the historical implications of Native/Indigenous people before attempting to conduct counseling.

SELF-AWARENESS

In recent years, instances of racial, religious, gender, and sexual intolerance appear to be rising (Nadal et al., 2014; Pearson et al., 2014; Singh & Walinsky, 2017). Emerging from this trend of prejudice is a culture of increased marginalization and oppression (Burt, 2018). Marginalization and oppression due to race, religion, or sexual orientation is a form of modern-day enslavement affecting many diverse clients (Vereen et al., 2017). Exacerbating the situation is the impact of this phenomenon sometimes goes unnoticed by the very professionals trained to help. Although overlooked at times, the increasing number of public instances (e.g., the Dakota Pipeline) document uprisings and a greater need for practitioners to acknowledge and address the impact of historical racial, religious, gender, and sexual marginalization and oppression. Hence, in today's current climate of social, gender, racial, and ethnic instability, understanding the efficacy of students to work with diverse clients such as Native/Indigenous people is critical. Unconscious biases inhibit the full growth of counseling students, as their predispositions go unchecked and end up potentially damaging clients. Unchecked biases do a disservice to clients as counselors sometimes pay more attention to other characteristics (e.g., race) than to the actual issues clients have. Coupled with this problem, negative biases amalgamate, and beginning counselors can discriminate without consciously realizing what they are doing.

One form of discrimination is microaggressions, which is having an implicit bias (unknown by the person discriminating) against another due to their color, race, or ethnicity. These biases can take many forms, such as a person believing the color of one's skin makes them smarter, more credible, and with better attributes (Sue & Sue, 2013). Although counseling students take classes to increase self-awareness and reduce biases, these prejudices still exist. Counselors need to actively reflect, confront their biases, and immerse themselves in other cultures to increase self-awareness, knowledge, and appreciation for clients from different racial backgrounds such as Native/Indigenous people. Although the major overarching purpose of increasing self-awareness is to assist in creating improvements in counseling students, it can also lead to developing stronger therapeutic bonds with clients (Butler & Shillingford, 2014; Young, 2017). The following misapprehensions can assist in illuminating how a lack of self-awareness can undermine the therapeutic relationship. Many misconceptions exist about Native/Indigenous people that counselors could easily believe and that can inhibit the counseling relationship. For instance, there are the fallacies that there is one overall culture, that mascots honor Native populations, and that they are a "vanished" race (Mihesuah, 2013). If counselors are not continually being reflective and aware of their biases and beliefs, these can damage the therapeutic alliance. Counselors can unwittingly believe these myths and act in accordance with them. Behaving in such a manner can isolate Native/Indigenous people, although the Native client may never bring it up.

HAVING MULTICULTURALLY COMPETENT CLINICAL SKILLS

The purpose of this chapter is to enhance practitioners' in the helping professions (counselor education, clinical psychology, school psychology, social work) knowledge, application, ability, and utilization of multiculturally competent clinical skills with clients. Helping professionals need to be comfortable in integrating and incorporating multiculturally competent clinical skills into their everyday practice and scope (e.g., university, community clinic, school, private practice). However, a lack of application and knowledge inhibit the full utilization of multiculturally competent clinical skills. Thus, beginning counselors need to actively seek, identify, and explore instances to be able to utilize multiculturally competent clinical skills. Several models exist for this purpose. For example, there are the MSJCCs (Ratts et al., 2016) and the relational cultural model (Comstock et al., 2002). Both are viable methods to utilize with Native/Indigenous clients.

Furthermore, micro skills (Ivey et al., 2017) are a fundamental aspect of counseling which one cannot separate from the process.

Micro skills are a core component of education for beginning counselors, as they encompass the elements of basic communications skills. These competencies include paraphrasing, reflecting feelings, summarizing, and asking open/closed questions. Micro skills can also include when counselors provide facts and use minimal prompts. To be multiculturally competent, counselors must also be attentive of body language and facial expressions used to demonstrate listening and interest in what clients communicate. As counselors become more sophisticated in their abilities, they can begin to use more advanced micro skills. These include reframing, interpreting, empathetic confrontation, and strategic self-disclosure (Ivey et al., 2017).

As stated previously, the number of Native/Indigenous people has increased in the United States. However, the number of interventions available for counselors to adequately work with this population has not increased commeasurably. Thus, there is a lack of interventions that are culturally appropriate and suitable for this unique and underserved population. Many culturally sensitive methods exist, such as the relational-cultural model and the MSJCC framework. Both strategies promote positive transformation and healing through a culturally sensitive paradigm. A strengths-based, culturally competent process, this intervention is a viable option for working with this marginalized population. This chapter will focus on connecting clinical skills (i.e., micro skills) within a strengths-based, culturally sensitive framework to enhance counseling with Native/Indigenous populations. A hypothetical case of an Indigenous client will illustrate how a helper can successfully work therapeutically with Native populations.

Recognition of Native/Indigenous Mind-Set

Corresponding with Ivey et al. (2017), counselors must connect to clients to build trust and maintain the therapeutic relationship. Although disclosure is a more complex skill for counselors to utilize, with Indigenous populations it is imperative. Listed as a concrete action tactic, the use of the skill needs to be strategic and logical (Ivey et al., 2017). When counseling Native populations, in addition to the client's story, the counselor must share as well. The following example taken from the Navajo tribe may illustrate the importance of disclosure for Indigenous clients. Navajo tradition encourages tribal members of all ages to introduce themselves in a specific manner when meeting fellow Dine (pronounced di-nay, the Navajo Indigenous word for "the people"). This introduction initiates by disclosing their name and information about clans passed down to them from ancestors (e.g., mother, father, maternal/paternal grandfather). After divulging clan information, Navajos then enunciate the identity of their mother and father. Included in this disclosure is where the person is presently living and where their family's ancestral home presides. The belief is that a Navajo can hear a 15-second introduction and know more about people than they will ever know about themselves. This introduction testifies to the history of the family and can go back generations. This disclosure simultaneously works as not only verification to what your life may presently entail, but also your current endeavors. Amazingly, this process exemplifies the purest form of self-disclosure. It conveys to the Navajo the very fabric of who people are as individuals.

Although this level of personal admission is unheard of in the helping profession and sometimes discouraged (Miller & McNaught, 2016), a sound rationale exists behind the process. This Navajo practice emerges from a perspective of trust and respect for the person met, as they (the Navajo tribe member) will shortly disclose who they are with their introduction. Navajo tradition dictates it is rude to ask someone of their clans and not respond with their own. The Navajo tribes' complex clan system and high-contextual culture foster rapport from the moment a person meets someone by conveying this aspect of vulnerability and humility. While it can be uncomfortable for helpers unfamiliar with the culture to have this level of vulnerability, it is possible to make accommodations. For example, beginning a therapeutic relationship with any client hinges on being genuine (Young, 2017). What helpers can do to build this rapport with Native clients is to tell their story on how they came to be a helping professional. As stated before, there are over 500 tribes in the continental United States alone (U.S. Census Bureau, 2010). Thus, helpers cannot generalize and assume that all tribes react and behave in a similar fashion as the Navajo. However, there are some core commonalities a counselor can use to build rapport utilizing self-disclosure with Native clients. The following case vignette may help to illustrate.

Aki is a vain and physically aggressive Native 13-year-old boy who is regularly engaging in fights and physically aggressive ways to show people he is, in his words, "tough." Born into a family with a long history of producing strong males, Aki is from the Ojibwe/Chippewa tribe. Aki tells people that he wants to get as strong as his father, who left him and his mother at an early age. Aki has the idea that if he beats others, his father will realize how tough he is and love him more. Aki believes that by fighting others, his father will respect him, and this will result in his father coming back to the family he abandoned years ago. Although Aki claims (tells adults) most of the fights he gets into are unintentional, he does tell his closet friends that he looks for people to fight. Aki rarely fights in school; he normally tells the people he wants to fight to meet him in a place outside of class. Additionally, he tells other students to "spread the word" so that there will be people there to watch him. In the last year, he has had several small fractures in his fingers and toes. Child protection agencies visited Aki's home, but ultimately did not do anything because the mother said she was unaware of Aki fighting. Though Aki is physically aggressive, he has shown empathy with friends. Further, he has an extreme degree of loyalty for his friends and higher than average academic abilities (he has B's on his report card).

A way a helper could approach this situation is through a cultural lens, suggested by Ivey et al. (2017), coupled with appropriate self-disclosure. Similar to Navajo tradition, the helper can state their name and information about themselves they are comfortable revealing. For example, the helper can give an honest answer as to the rationale the person has for helping people. Most people have a personal motive for becoming a professional helper (Young, 2017). Being able to discuss this motivation is not something normally taught to students in counseling programs. More than just a professional disclosure statement, the helper could explain their reason for being a therapist, then connect that rationale to Aki's issues. Throughout this process, the helper can reveal professors and/or mentors who influenced them throughout their career. Analogous to the Navajo tradition, the helper is taking Aki through their professional heritage and culture. Although Aki is not Navajo, the same core methods can be effective with him, just modified, as all multiculturally competent helpers should do with clients (Ratts et al., 2016).

Addressing Ways to Show Humility When Counseling Indigenous Populations

Corresponding with the preceding material, the helper must be able and willing to disclose information about oneself. If this is successful, the helper may be able to move to the next level. Keeping with the case of Aki, the helping professional may believe that Aki can benefit by engaging in prosocial behaviors with positive peers. A major factor impacting if Aki will be receptive toward the helper's suggestions is how well they display humbleness. In many Native people's culture, the concept of humility is imperative. It is okay to think that you are equal to others, just not better (Mihesuah, 2013). Thus, it is critical that helpers working with this population understand this tenet. Most Western counseling theories place a high value on the therapist as knowledgeable and in a "superior" position (Young, 2017). Subsequently, novice and experienced counselors alike sometimes struggle with showing competency and control. An easy way to handle both is to be appear overly knowledgeable and erudite. Although some Western ideologies allow for that type of behavior, it may be offsetting to a Native client. To be effective with Indigenous populations, more culturally appropriate approaches need usage (Mihesuah, 2013). Thus, to be effective with Native clients, counselors can start the process of humbling themselves by admitting they are unfamiliar with the culture and need to learn. After initiating this procedure, counselors can begin understanding through cultural storytelling.

In many Indigenous populations, storytelling is a critical aspect of learning and understanding where you are from and what values are important (Curtice, 2019). Although storytelling does have a somewhat negative connotation in counseling (Young, 2017), it is an essential component of Native culture. Even if Natives do not regularly engage in storytelling, it is a concept that is familiar and valued (McFaggan, 2012). With youth, (such as Aki), storytelling can be a link to the past and a connection to the present and future (Simundson, 2012). A counselor may be able to use storytelling to relate with Aki. For example, utilizing a micro skills framework, the counselor can focus on attending and empathy skills. According to Ivey et al. (2017), counselors can hear a client perfectly but still fail to listen effectively. To be able to connect with Aki, the counselor must be able to not only verbally track the client, but recognize there is an intent behind the story. Many counselors receive training and education stipulating limiting storytelling by clients

(Young, 2017). However, with culturally diverse clients (e.g., Indigenous populations), storytelling is essential in understanding the client (Ivey et al., 2017).

An example is the Ojibwe story "the gifts of the seven grandfathers." In this story, the creator selected seven grandfathers to look over the people. With their collective insight, they chose one person (a baby) to disseminate their knowledge. As the baby grew older, each grandfather bestowed an element of acumen to the child: humility, wisdom/ intelligence, love, respect, bravery, honor, and truth. This Ojibwe story is one passed down from generation to generation with several important meanings. If Aki mentioned aspects of this story or referred to the folklore, it could go undetected or ignored by the counselor. To circumvent against this problem occurring, the counselor needs to effectively utilize attending and empathy skills. A common mistake counselors (beginning and advanced) make is trying to make an impact too early with the client. As opposed to indicating how skilled or technical they (or their theory) are, listening to the client's story is more beneficial. In fact, seemingly innocuous behaviors such as sitting on the side as opposed to direct eye contact can assist in building the relationship just as much as staying on the issue/topic (Ivey et al., 2017). Succinctly stated, when counseling Native clients, counselors must take steps to increase their attending/empathy skills (Beitel et al., 2018). In Aki's example, although the counselor may not immediately discern the story's importance, utilizing empathetic skills (e.g., vocal tone) can convey warmth and interest. Thus, a simple understanding of storytelling's significance in the culture and appreciation can build the therapeutic relationship in several different ways.

First, the counselor expresses concern and respect while silently communicating humbleness by listening attentively to the story. Second, if the counselor can match Aki verbally in regard to tone, speed, and rate, that helps strengthen the bond between them. Third, body language expresses people's intent and meaning more candidly than verbal cues (Young, 2017). If the counselor can notice subtle cues from Aki while engaged in storytelling and mirror those mannerisms, that can also build the relationship. Fourth, Ivey et al. (2017) state the following for being a multicultural sensitive and appropriate counselor when working with clients (including Indigenous ones): "Note their patterns of eye contact, their changing vocal tone, their body language, and topics to which your clients attend and those that they avoid. Also note the individual and cultural differences in attending" (p. 76). All the preceding patterns use empathetic and attending skills. Combined, they assist in building the therapeutic relationship between Aki and the counselor. Ultimately, the counselor's multicultural comfort level, coupled with expressing humility, can be effective with Native clients (Beitel et al., 2018).

How to Learn, Respond, and Act to Native/Indigenous Clients

Indigenous people face several microaggressions, one of the most detrimental is being "invisible." Similar to Black/African Americans, this concept of invisibility does not entail people cannot physically perceive them. It goes further and embodies the ideas that the person is not relevant, their culture is useless, and people from that culture have no value in life or society (Burt et al., 2016). An example is the suicide attempts mentioned previously with the Attawapiskat. Although the mass suicides of the Attawapiskat did garner some attention, the help diverged quickly and soon people went on to other issues. In some instances, society neither knew of the Attawapiskat before nor had heard of their predicament. Thus, the plight of the Attawapiskat was, to a certain extent, invisible to people. Commensurate with other races/ethnicities, when Indigenous people present issues and demand acknowledgment, their requests go unheard, or not believed (Coll et al., 2018). Of course, a consequence stemming from this problem is that Native people perceive their concerns receive no attention or are considered irrelevant (Mihesuah, 2013). Imagine the following real-life example, taken from one of the authors of this text:

> Faced with disclosing my full name at my university or in any form of bureaucratic procedure, peoples' first reaction when hearing my name is to make snide comments or remarks to be funny. People feel obligated to comment "but your hair's not yellow," "you're the first Indian I've met," or my favorite "I didn't know that you all still existed." These remarks are all key components to destroying rapport with an Indigenous client. Every time this happens, I personally feel like it is an odd combination of fascination and disrespect that works as a defense mechanism to mask their own anxiety of having never met an Indigenous person before. It has taken place in every capacity where I use my name, or my name is displayed, and people from all regions and cultures have done it.

Although this is one person's personal narrative, it corroborates research documenting shared experiences common among Indigenous people (Mihesuah, 2013). Through this example it is clear problems emerge that many counselors are not aware even exist. Observation/following the client's lead, one of the micro skills illustrated by Ivey et al. (2017), is a tool a counselor can take to avoid running into this problem. In the case with Aki, the counselor needs to learn how to use observation to learn, respond, and act toward him. Aki is not an alien from a different planet. He is a human (young boy) who appears to struggle with paternal issues. This is a problem many young males face in today's world (Burt, 2018). What makes Aki "different" is that he is of Native/Indigenous ancestry. What would be a common problem for the counselor now turns into a complicated issue. Compounding this issue is that a dichotomy exists with counselors. There is an arrogance that manifests as "I can work with all clients," coupled with ignorance, "I've never even met this kind of person; I don't know what to do" (Vereen et al., 2017). This intrapersonal contradiction confuses counselors (novice and experienced alike). Due to this intrapersonal clash, anxiety forms (Sue & Sue, 2013). To alleviate the concern caused by this dichotomy, most counselors fall back and rely on their training when confronted with new situations (Young, 2017). While this default is not bad in and of itself, it does pose a problem when the education and training has not prepared them for Native clients (Coll et al., 2018). In addition to the paternal and behavioral issues Aki presents, the counselor in this example is also having a unique multicultural encounter

(Ivey et al., 2017). Thus, a pragmatic, realistic question emerges for the counselor: "What do I do?"

In this situation, the counselor needs to become a student again. When the counselor was learning, they had previous experience as a person living their life (Gerig, 2018). However, they tempered that experience and accommodated new information when learning counseling. Thus, the counselor in this situation needs to do the same again. They must learn, respond, and act in new ways toward Aki by observing and following his lead. While this sounds simple, it is not easy (Willink & Babin, 2017). For the counselor to undertake this mission, they must throw away arrogance and embrace the idea they do not know anything (Goggins, 2018). It is a process of submitting oneself to humility and the client (Aki). This undertaking is anxiety provoking and not normally taught in academic or professional settings (Willink & Babin, 2018). In the case of Aki, the counselor may need to work much harder to present to Aki. This includes acknowledging limited experience with Native populations. Although the profession encourages self-awareness, a disconnect sometimes emerges with helpers. This chasm materializes between admitting something is awry and doing something about it. When it comes to counseling Indigenous people, the healing does not start in the counseling session, or even with the client, but with the healing of ignorance. Rapport is critical with Indigenous people and cannot start until counselors can be harmonious with themselves.

How Native/Indigenous Clients Think: Why They Think That

"Do you call consider yourself an American?" "So, are you from a tribe?" Asking questions is a critical component of the counseling process. In fact, Ivey et al., (2017) state that helping professionals need to "draw out and enrich client stories by bringing out a more complete description, including background information and needed details" (p. 109). The problem arises when helpers use questions to cover their apprehension. In some instances, many helping professionals have never encountered a Native person. Stereotypes, such as sports mascots (e.g., Washington Redskins), movie depictions (*The Ridiculous 6*), or seemingly innocuous commercials (The Indigenous woman as the face for Land O' Lakes Butter) are the only Native representations they know. Thus, an amalgamation of nervousness, apprehension, and captivation take hold of the helper. As one of the authors of this chapter states when people realize he is Native, "I personally feel like it is an odd combination of fascination and disrespect that works as a defense mechanism to mask their own anxiety of having never met an Indigenous person before." In these circumstances, it may behoove the helper to self-reflect and identify the rationale behind the question and the purpose it serves (if any) (Young, 2017). Obviously, self-awareness and becoming a reflective practitioner is paramount in these cases. Under these circumstances, it is crucial that helpers follow a framework to guide their questions (Ratts, 2017). The newspaper reporting model, suggested by Ivey et al. (2017), recommends using a mixture of open and closed questions. Helpers should focus on the who, what, when, where, how, and why.

Utilizing this model requires helpers to focus on (a) who is the client as an individual (i.e., idiosyncratic traits or characteristics); (b) what the significant multicultural considerations are; (c) when (i.e., times) the issue appear; (d) where (i.e., situations) the problem occurs; (e) how the client behaves when reacting to the issue; and (e) why the problem continues to occur. A word of caution needs mentioning, however. Excessive questioning can give clients the perception they are under interrogation (Burt et al., 2016; Ivey et al., 2017; Young, 2017). Depending on the skill level of the helper, questions can be a double-edged sword. They can assist in facilitating the therapeutic relationship, or they can be invasive to the point where clients refuse to answer. Of primary importance is that the helper first listens to the client and understands their story. As the story unravels and understanding increases, the helper can facilitate the therapeutic process by utilizing the newspaper framework.

In the case of Aki, after hearing aspects of his story, the helping professional can ask questions utilizing the newspaper reporting model. The model is not sequential, nor does every question need asking. Thus, the helper can begin wherever is most essential to the client's issue(s). Due to Aki having documented issues with fighting, the helper can ask him, "What do you get from fighting?" Although this question may appear innocuous and somewhat pedestrian, it is a complex inquiry. As opposed to asking questions like "Why do you keep fighting?" or "Do you like fighting?" this query takes into consideration that Aki gets something positive out of fighting. The critical factor is determining what exactly is the positive reinforcement Aki perceives he receives. The objective of this question is to further develop the therapeutic relationship, as the helper now demonstrates verbal interest in Aki (as opposed to just listening and utilizing observation skills). With questions now focusing on Aki as a unique individual, it makes it now a helping relationship where each person is learning and giving of one another. As the therapeutic relationship develops, the helper makes it clear the ultimate goals are to improve behavioral control and interpersonal awareness. Through the helper, Aki understands that therapy will deal with interpersonal, intrapersonal, and other psychological aspects that affect him (such as fighting and wanting to prove himself to others).

As an addendum to the initial set of questions, the helper can stay in the "what" category of the newspaper reporting model. For example, the helper can ask Aki the following follow-up: "What does it mean to be a male in today's society/community/tribe/family and what do others expect from you?" At this point, it is critical that Aki and the helper work with one another, using techniques and cooperating, adjusting to each other's temperament, openness, and self-awareness. Thus, if used carefully, questioning is a valuable skill. The newspaper reporting model suggested by Ivey et al. (2017) can assist helpers with utilizing effective multiculturally sensitive questions. Of upmost importance is that the helping professional develop an array of questions that complement their unique, or natural, therapeutic style.

Importance of Understanding the Nonconfrontational Aspect of Native/Indigenous Clients (Avoid Telling Counselor They Are Offended)

Popular media and Hollywood stories depict Indigenous people as warlike, combative, and always primed for battle. While every race and ethnicity has those who are more martial in nature, most Indigenous people do not fit this stereotype (Mihesuah, 2013). With 567 federally recognized tribes in the United States alone, variation can and will occur (Norris et al., 2012). Indigenous beliefs, culture, and language vary drastically from one group to the next (Young, 2015). Acknowledging this, most tribes have some overall common characteristics. For instance, there is normally some sort of clan structure, familial system to maintain integrity, and unique accountability measures developed within their own tribe. With that stated, there is at least one overriding characteristic shared among tribes. That one trait is that being an outsider has a negative connotation. Even though this aspect is negative, it only remains that way if the helper accepts it and acts in a way that earns the moniker.

Indigenous communities are more than accommodating to people who desire to help. However, contradictory to the warlike image perpetrated by Hollywood, Indigenous people do not go around looking for conflict (Mihesuah, 2013). In fact, the reason some helpers remain as outsiders is because Natives attempt to avoid conflict. An example is that helpers can unknowingly offend clients due to not knowing cultural norms. The helper violates a norm they did not understand, or even realized existed, and the client is silently offended. Amalgamating the issue is the Native client does not let the helper know they offended them. This causes a problem, as the helper is unaware, and the client holds back information. Although this may seem unfair to the counselor, it needs understanding through a multicultural lens (Hemmings & Evans, 2018). The Indigenous population in the United States has a long and sordid history of people/government breaking promises, taking resources, and not repaying commensurately (Hagar, 2019). Coupled with this, many outsiders have ill-informed/cruel ideas and stereotypes about Natives (Hirschfelder & Molin, 2018). When viewed through this multicultural perspective, it is easy to see the rationale for trepidation and silence as a defense mechanism. Thus, a looming question emerges for the helper: "What do I do?" This is where helpers can use humility, combined with the micro skills of encouraging, paraphrasing, and summarizing.

Humility can be as simple as acknowledging the feelings one is having, or being congruent with one's personal self (Rogers, 1961/1995). As stated previously, disclosing anxiety does not automatically disqualify you in the eyes of a Native client. It is through covering up, and the client sensing deceitfulness, that is harmful to the therapeutic relationship. In addition to the helper finding the courage to acknowledge feelings, the helper must also encourage the client. A key distinction though is that the responsibility is on the helper to initiate the process. For example, the helper's process is self-initiated. However, for the client, the helper partially facilitates their process as well. Analogous to the idea of a catalyst, the helper provides a spark to speed up the reaction. Instead of a chemical reaction, it is an emotional, cognitive, and social effect going on within the client. After beginning this reaction, the helper can sit back as the client takes over and guides the next steps of the relationship. Through effective encouraging (verbal and nonverbal), paraphrasing (succinctly repeating the essence of the story), and summarizing (condensing all the major points essential to the client's issues), clients more readily lower defenses and are willing to change (Young, 2017). Proceeding in this direction leads to a myriad of positive outcomes for the client. One is growth in effective executive brain functioning. Two is that more effective brain functioning leads to improvements in cognitive understanding, and organization of issues. Three is that it increases and facilitates efficient and sound decision-making (Ivey et al., 2017).

In the case of Aki, the helper can encourage him through verbal signs such as statements showing interest in his activities, peers, and friends. The helper can have Aki focus on what group(s) he identifies with and how these groups help shape him. In session, the facilitator can also provide encouragement through nonverbal signs such as head nods or smiles. Due to his primary issue (anger) and ethnic identity, Aki may not receive praise or reassurance regularly (Nadal et al., 2014). As a result, he may be reluctant in trying something novel or attempting new tasks. Thus, the helper needs to be able to utilize encouragement effectively but not abuse it. Bandura (2008) believed this kind of social encouragement is crucial with people, especially angry adolescents. For instance, adolescents labeled culturally diverse and angry sometimes have a self-fulfilling prophecy and live up to negative expectations of others (Burt et al., 2016). Next, through effective paraphrasing, the helper allows Aki the opportunity to be vulnerable and express himself, as he realizes the helper hears him and understands. By simply being present and able to detail Aki's story (e.g., what he thinks is important in his life and what he believes he needs to be the person he wants to develop into) accurate summarization is a powerful tool for growth (Young, 2017). This type of freedom of self-expression is critical for adolescents to mature and develop better self-efficacy and behavioral control (Bandura, 2008). Having the helper be there, in the moment (i.e., here and now), while utilizing these specific micro skills dramatically improves the therapeutic relationship and increases empathy (Ivey et al., 2017).

Understanding of Native/Indigenous Clients by a Helper

Common questions beginning (and advanced) helpers alike have in regard to providing therapeutic services to Indigenous clients are the following: What should I do if the opportunity to counsel clients on a reservation presents itself? How should I act? What should I do? Will they accept me? If you are counseling on a reservation or within an Indigenous community, it is vital to recognize the role of a counselor within the context of the entire culture. Even though this sounds deceptively simple, it is not easy (Willink & Babin, 2017). This is one of the difficult aspects of providing services to Native populations. Problems arise because of friction, which is the theoretical or perfect way something should go in a person's mind and the reality of what actually transpires (Davis, 2016). For example, many training programs strongly suggest avoiding bringing gifts to clients, as it can muddy waters and decrease counselors' objectivity (Young, 2017). Thus, many counselors receive indoctrination into a profession that espouses sharp and distinct boundaries with clients. In many instances, strict professional parameters are appropriate, as diffusing of boundaries can lead to ethical issues, such as dual relationships (Gerig, 2018). When counseling Indigenous populations, however, the idea of friction occurs, and helpers need to consider multiple factors.

First, although reservations are located in the continental United States, they are sovereign nations. Thus, helpers are entering a different culture and customs as soon as they cross into the reservation that differs from where they come from. To give a crude analogy to illustrate the point, it is akin to helpers going into a new country, while still in their own. While this example does not full encapsulate all the nuances, it does suffice in explaining how problems can arise. Basically, helpers fail to perceive that they are no longer operating by American, or Western, counseling principles and must accommodate another culture (Veeren et al., 2017).

Second, Indigenous people have cultural beliefs around being a good host. Third, coupled with the preceding information, Native practices also center around being a good guest. How these principles impact helpers may go against traditional training mandated in academic training settings. For example, when counseling on a reservation, helpers are basically visitors and need an invitation to enter. This is a unique situation, with few parallels in the helping profession. As such, helpers in this situation may need to adapt their professional norms (e.g., parameters around professional boundaries between helper and client [Young, 2017]). These aspects may include helping the host with things such as dishes after a meal or bringing a gift to thank them for being a good host. As a professional helper and guest, it is vital the practitioner acknowledges their growing role in the Indigenous community. Although it may go against traditional training in professional helper programs, when dealing with Native populations, this modification of norms may need consideration (Beitel et al., 2018). When in this situation, it is imperative the helper is cognizant of dual relationships. Further, the helper should have a supervisor providing clinical oversight (Ivey et al., 2017).

In conclusion, helpers must understand and be cognizant of thoughts that dissociate clients as merely clients in their office. This mind-set can not only inhibit opportunity for growth, it can also disavow the fact the helper is a guest in their home. Some Native clients perceive this lack of acknowledgment as a sign of disrespect. As stated previously, some Indigenous clients may not let the helper know they feel this way. Amalgamating these problems is that far too often helpers come from non-Native communities to work on reservations to polish a resume or seek self-validation through volunteering. These helpers will receive or take what they need and leave without considering the damage they are inflicting on future professional relationships by further validating Indigenous stigmas of outsiders and mental health. Indigenous communities are more than accommodating to people who desire to help, but this accommodation comes with a price many outsiders are not willing to pay, such as ego, self-awareness, or humility.

REFERENCES

Bandura, A. (2008). The reconstrual of "free will" from the agentic perspective of social cognitive theory. In J. Baer, J. C. Kaufman, & R. F. Baumeister (Eds.), *Are we free? Psychology and free will.* (pp. 86–127). Oxford: Oxford University Press.

Beitel, M., Myhra, L. L., Gone, J. P., Barber, J. P., Miller, A., Rasband, A., Cutter, C. J., Schottenfeld, R. S., & Barry, D. T. (2018). Psychotherapy with American Indians: An exploration of therapist-rated techniques in three urban clinics. *Psychotherapy, 55,* 45–51.

Burt, I. (2018). Leadership-driven anger management groups for adolescents: Do they really work? *The Journal for Specialists in Group Work, 43,* 57–80. doi:10.1080/01933922. 2017.1411409

Burt, I., Russell, V. E. D., & Brooks, M. (2016). The invisible client: Ramifications of neglecting the impact of race and culture in professional counseling. *VISTAS, 1016,* 1–10.

Butler, S. K., & Shillingford-Butler M. A. (2014). Counseling Black clients. In M.J. Ratts & P.D. Pederson (Eds.), *Counseling for multiculturalism and social justice* (4th ed., pp. 143–157). Alexandria, VA: ACA.

Coll, K. M., Freeman, B. J., Scholl, S., & Hauser, N. (2018), Challenges and culturally relevant treatment strategies for American Indian youth in therapeutic residential care: A pilot study. *Journal of Child and Adolescent Counseling, 4*(3), 253–264. https://doi.org /10.1080/23727810.2018.1425580

Comstock, D. L., Duffey, T., & St. George, H. (2002). The relational-cultural model: A framework for group process. *Journal for Specialists in Group Work, 27,* 254–272.

Curtice, K. B. (2019). *7 grandfather teachings.* https://kaitlincurtice.com/tag/ ojibwe-teachings/

Davis, E. (2016). *Raising men: Lessons Navy Seals learned from their training and taught to their sons.* St. Martin's.

Gerig, M. S. (2018). *Foundations for clinical mental health counseling: An introduction to the profession* (3rd ed.). Prentice Hall.

Goggins, D. (2018). Can't hurt me: Master your mind and defy the odds. Lioncrest.

Hagar, (2019, January 14). *Native American leaders ask Trump to apologize for "shameful" Wounded Knee remarks.* https://abcnews.go.com/Politics/ native-american-leaders-trump-apologize-shameful-wounded-knee/story?id=60374772

Hemmings, C., & Evans, A. M. (2018). Identifying and treating race-based trauma in counseling. *Journal of Multicultural Counseling and Development, 46*(1), 20–39. https:// doi.org/10.1002/jmcd.12090

Hirschfelder, A., & Molin, P. F. (2018). *Stereotyping Native Americans.* https://www.ferris. edu/HTMLS/news/jimcrow/native/homepage.htm

Ivey, A. E., Ivey, M. B., & Zalaquett, C. P. (2017). *Intentional interviewing and counseling: Facilitating client development in a multicultural society* (9th ed.). Cengage.

McFaggan, J. (2012). Native American storytelling. *Tribal College: Journal of American Indian Higher Education, 24*(1). https://tribalcollegejournal.org/native-american-storytelling/

Mihesuah, D. A. (2013). *American Indians: Stereotypes and realities.* Clarity Press.

Miller, E., & McNaught, A. (2016). Exploring decision making around therapist self-disclosure in cognitive behavioural therapy. *Australian Psychologist, 53*, 33–39.

Nadal, K. L., Griffin, K. E., Wong, Y., Hamit, S., & Rasmus, M. (2014). The impact of racial microaggressions on mental health: Counseling implications for clients of color. *Journal of Counseling & Development, 92*(1), 57–66. https://doi.org/10.1002/j.1556-6676.2014.00130.x

Norris, T., Vines, P. L., & Hoeffel, E. M. (2012). *The American Indian and Alaska Native population: 2010.* U.S. Department of Commerce, Economics and Statistics Administration, U.S Census Bureau.

Pearson, M. R., Derlega, V. J., Henson, J. M., Holmes, K. Y., Ferrer, R. A., & Harrison, S. B. (2014). Role of neuroticism and coping strategies in psychological reactions to a racist incident among African American university students. *Journal of Black Psychology, 40*(1), 81–111. https://doi.org/10.1177/0095798412471682

Ratts, M. J. (2017). Charting the center and the margins: Addressing identity, marginalization, and privilege in counseling. *Journal of Mental Health Counseling, 39*, 87–103. https://doi.org/10.17744lm ehc.39.2.01 **https://doi.org/10.17744/mehc.39.2.01**

Ratts, M. J., Singh, A. A., Nassar-McMillan, S., Butler, S. K., & McCullough, J. R. (2016). Multicultural and social justice counseling competencies: Guidelines for the counseling profession. *Journal of Multicultural Counseling and Development, 44*(1), 28–48.

Rogers, C. R. (1961/1995). *On becoming a person: A therapist's view of psychotherapy.* Houghton Mifflin Harcourt.

Simundson, S. (2012). Storytelling has the power to bring people together. *Tribal College: Journal of American Indian Higher Education, 24*(1). https://tribalcollegejournal.org/storytelling-power-bring-people/

Singh, A. A., & Walinsky, D. (2017). Treatment of trauma and nonsuicidal self-injury in transgender adults. *Psychiatric Clinics, 40*, 41–50.

Sue, D. W., & Sue, D. (2013). *Counseling the culturally diverse: Theory and practice* (6th ed.). Wiley.

Vereen, L., Wines, L., Lemberger-Truelove, T., Hannon, M., Howard, N., & Burt, I. (2017). Black Existentialism: Extending the discourse. *The Journal of Humanistic Counseling, 56*, 72–84. doi: 10.1002/johc.12045

Willink, J., & Babin, L. (2017). *Extreme ownership: How US Navy SEALs lead and win.* St. Martin's.

Willink, J., & Babin, L. (2018). *The dichotomy of leadership: Balancing the challenges of extreme ownership to lead and win.* St. Martin's.

Young, B. (2015, June 11). Why I won't wear war paint and feathers in a movie again. *Time.* http://time.com/3916680/native-american-hollywood-film/

Young, M. E. (2017). *Learning the art of helping* (6th ed.). Pearson.

Index

About the Editors

S. KENT BUTLER

Dr. Butler truly believes that successful people build each other up. They motivate, inspire, and push each other. Unsuccessful people just hate, blame, and complain. In an effort to educate the masses, he believes that we must meet each person where they are. His goal is not to change people, but to expose and provide a pathway to self-knowledge, self-love, and ultimately a desire to change. It is his belief that "All that is necessary for evil to triumph, is for good people to do nothing," a quote attributed to Edmund Burke.

Dr. Butler holds a Ph.D. in educational psychology with a concentration in counseling psychology from the University of Connecticut. He is a Licensed Professional Counselor (LPC), Nationally Certified Counselor (NCC), and Nationally Certified School Counselor (NCSC). In February of 2020, Dr. Butler was elected president-elect of the American Counseling Association (ACA). His presidential year is 2021 – 2022. In July of 2019, Dr. Butler was appointed Interim Chief Equity, Inclusion, and Diversity Officer at the University of Central Florida. In March of 2020, he was selected as a fellow within the National Association of Chief Diversity Officer in Higher Education's Chief Diversity Officer Fellows Program (NADOHE-CDOFP). He is a 2020 – 2021 cohort (C-7) member. The professional leadership program mentors new and early career chief diversity officers. Dr. Butler was also recently promoted to Professor of Counselor Education at the University of Central Florida and has served as a Faculty Fellow for Inclusive Excellence within the Office of the Provost.

Dr. Butler presently serves as faculty advisor to Chi Sigma Iota International Honor Society (CSI), the Counselor Education Doctoral Student Organization (CEDSO), Project for Haiti Knights, and the National Association for the Advancement of Colored People (NAACP). He served as the principal investigator for the High-Risk Delinquent and Dependent Child Educational Research Project: Situational Environmental Circumstances Mentoring Program (SEC), which was a partnership between the University of Central Florida and several Florida universities. This grant opportunity has transitioned into the UCF Young Knights Mentoring Project, a program that supports students at Hungerford Elementary School in Eatonville, FL.

On the national level, Dr. Butler has served the Association for Multicultural Counseling and Development (AMCD) as the 2011 – 2012 President and ACA Governing Council Representative (2015 – 2018). He is honored to have been a member of AMCD's Multicultural Counseling Competencies Revisions Committee (2014 – 2015), which produced the ACA-AMCD endorsed Multicultural Social Justice Counseling Competencies (MSJCC).

In April of 2016, Dr. Butler was bestowed with the prestigious ACA Fellow Award. His research and academic interests lie in the areas of multicultural and international counseling, social justice, mentoring, counseling work as it relates specifically to African American males, group counseling, school counseling, and multicultural supervision.

ANNA FLORES LOCKE

This is Dr. Flores Locke's first textbook publication. She was chosen as the junior faculty on this project because of her undying support for multiculturalism and social justice in the field of counseling. Her current and past leadership in the American Counseling Association demonstrates this commitment. She is the past-president of the Counselors for Social Justice (CSJ) division of the American Counseling Association (ACA) and serves on the Diversity and Equity Committee of the Association for Counselor Educators and Supervisors (ACES). She was elected as the first voting graduate student member on the ACA governing council and commissioned the Social Justice Inter-Divisional Summit, which that united more than 50 counseling professions and 6 divisions to discuss how ACA can practice social justice principles.

Dr. Flores Locke graduated from Montclair State University with a doctorate in counseling and is an assistant professor in mental health counseling at Nyack College in New York City. She has been a practicing Licensed Professional Counselor and Approved Clinical Supervisor for more than 15 years and owns Charlandra Counseling Services in New Jersey. Dr. Flores Locke was given the prestigious education award from the New York League of Puerto Rican Women for her positive contributions to the Latino communities of New York City. She was also recognized by Negocios Now as an accomplished professional during their 40 Under 40 event. As a Latina counselor educator and supervisor, Dr. Flores Locke prides herself on being able to collaborate and motivate others to be social change agents. She is a twin mom and enjoys dancing. Her motto is: Embrace life and live judgment free.

JOEL M. FILMORE

Dr. Filmore is a nationally known professional counselor, educator, researcher, author, trainer, and public speaker. Along with his group clinical practice, he is owner and CEO of Lighthouse Professional Counseling Center. He also serves as a senior staff clinical supervisor for IntraSpectrum Counseling located in Chicago, Illinois. Dr. Filmore has served as the president of the National Association for LGBT Issues in Counseling (ALGBTIC) (now known as the Society for Sexual, Affectional, Intersex, and Gender Expansive Identities (SAIGE)) and has served on its national board for the past seven years. As a survivor of human sex trafficking and addiction, Dr. Filmore has dedicated his personal and professional career to addressing other's trauma, focusing on helping them achieve amazing lives, not merely surviving their traumatic experiences. He engages in research related to multiculturalism, LGBT issues, race/gender/sexual orientation identity development, trauma and abuse, sex trafficking, and sex offender issues, as well as addictions/substance abuse.

About the Contributors

Dr. Carla Adkison-Johnson is a tenured professor and interim chairperson for the Department of Counselor Education and Counseling Psychology at Western Michigan University (WMU). She has a Ph.D. in counseling and human development from Kent State University. She has published extensively in the areas of preparing for the professorate, child discipline, culturally competent mental health counseling and African American child rearing practices. Her research has garnered attention in the legal, child welfare, and counselor education literature. She has served as a child discipline expert witness in civil and criminal courts. Dr. Adkison-Johnson is editor-elect for the *Journal of Multicultural Counseling and Development* (JMCD). In 2017, she received the WMU College of Education and Human Development Distinguished Scholar award. Dr. Adkison-Johnson is also the recipient of the Kent State University Outstanding Alumnus award. She is a life member and past national treasurer for Chi Sigma Iota. Dr. Adkison-Johnson is a past member of the Board of Directors for the Council for Counseling and Educational Related Programs (CACREP). In this capacity, she served as chair of CACREP's training committee.

Dr. Monica P. Band is a licensed professional counselor in Washington, DC and Virginia. She holds a doctorate in counselor education and supervision. She is a full-time private practitioner and owner of Mindful Healing Counseling Services, LLC. Dr. Band is Gottman method couples therapy and EMDR trained. She specializes in working with the Asian American Pacific Islander (AAPI) community as well as issues related to grief, loss, and past trauma. She holds several professional certifications as a national certified counselor, certified rehabilitation counselor, approved clinical supervisor, certified career counselor, and certified career counselor educator. Additionally, she is an adjunct professor of counseling. Dr. Band's affinity and commitment to growing as a multicultural and social justice counseling professional are informed by her lived experiences as a third-generation Chinese American and being raised in an interfaith household. Dr. Band is dedicated to healing those who have experienced intergenerational and complex racial trauma.

Dr. Matthew J. Beck is a counselor educator and the school counseling clinical coordinator at Western Illinois University-Quad Cities. Dr. Beck received his Bachelor of Music degree in education from The University of Iowa and his Master of Education degree in school counseling from Western Illinois University. He earned his Ph.D. in counselor education and supervision from The University of Iowa. Prior to his position as an assistant professor, he worked in public education for 12 years as a teacher and professional school counselor at the elementary, middle, and high school settings in Illinois. He is a licensed clinical professional counselor (LCPC) in the state of Illinois, an approved clinical supervisor (ACS), a national certified counselor (NCC), and holds licensure as a professional school counselor in Illinois. Matthew's research interests include school counselor advocacy, professional identity development for school counselors, and the needs of LGBTQ students in K–12 settings.

Michael Brooks is a counselor education associate professor and program coordinator at North Carolina A&T State University (NCAT) in Greensboro, North Carolina. His research centers on Black male success factors, counselor education pedagogy, and ex-offender recidivism and vocational rehabilitation. Dr. Brooks serves as program coordinator of the Rehabilitation Counseling and Rehabilitation Counselor Education Ph.D. program. In addition to his faculty role, he is also the chair of the university's Institution Review Board (IRB) and a member of the North Carolina Board of Licensed Professional Counselors. Since 1999, Dr. Brooks has held several positions (treasurer, southern regional representative, president, JMCD associate editor) in the Association for Multicultural Counseling and Development (AMCD). Also, since 2014, he has been the editor in chief for the *International Journal for Social Science Studies*. Dr. Brooks is a past presenter of the Association for Multicultural Counseling Development, as well as the Alabama Association for Counselor Education & Supervision. Brooks received his BA in psychology from Morehouse College and a MA and Ph.D. in counselor education and supervision from the University of Central Florida. Prior to a beginning a career in higher education, Dr. Brooks worked as a practicing counselor with local community mental health, outpatient substance abuse, and employee assistance agencies. He's treated or provided indirect care to a diverse clientele: couples, families, homeless, those with HIV/AIDS, as well as clients with varying abilities.

Nathaniel (Nathan) Brown is an assistant professor of professional mental health counseling. He teaches in the Department of Counseling, Therapy, and School Psychology. Dr. Brown received his Ph.D. in counselor education and supervision with a focus on P-16 partnerships and social justice (Counseling and Student Personnel Services) from the University of Georgia. He began his college counseling career in 2007 and has served in a variety of positions for the last 17 years: college counselor, university housing resident director, coordinator of academic and student affairs, coordinator of student affairs operations, director of student success, and interim dean of student affairs. Dr. Brown's research interests include college counseling and student affairs, developing a counseling theoretical orientation and approach in counseling, animal-assisted therapy, HIV/AIDS support groups, group counseling, LGBTQIQ+, transition of foster care young adults into postsecondary education, the retention/persistence/graduation rates of college students who experienced foster care, marginalized intersections of queer identity development, college identity development of marginalized/oppressed students, and communities of color experiencing impostor syndrome in postsecondary education. He can be contacted at nbrown@lclark.edu.

Isaac Burt is an associate professor who received his Ph.D. from the University of Central Florida in counselor education. He is a member of the American Counseling Association (ACA), as well as the Association for Counseling and Supervision (ACES), Association for Multicultural Counseling and Development (AMCD), Association of Humanistic Counseling (AHC), Association for Specialists in Group Work (ASGW), and Chi Sigma Iota (CSI). He has dedicated his career to multiculturalism. He has served the counseling profession in several capacities, such as being a member of the membership committee for AMCD, member of the executive board for AMCD, chair of the strategic planning committee for AMCD, and vice president - Native American Concerns for AMCD. He is also an associate editor of the premier journal for multiculturalism in counseling, the *Journal of Multicultural Counseling and Development* (JMCD), and editorial board member for the premier journal for group counseling, the *Journal for Specialists in Group Work* (JSGW). Additionally, he has 17 years' experience in schools, mental health agencies, and community centers, which included counseling individuals, couples and families from the Caribbean, Africa, Latin America, and Bosnia, as well as multicultural populations born in the United States, specifically Black/African Americans, Latinos, Asians, and LGQBT. He has an interest in social justice for historically marginalized populations and culturally sensitive treatments, with numerous publications that explore how counselor educators and counselors alike should rethink policies and approaches when providing therapy to multicultural populations.

Michael P. Chaney is an associate professor in the Department of Counseling at Oakland University. A licensed professional counselor and approved clinical supervisor, he received his Ph.D. in counseling from Georgia State University. He is past president of the Association of LGBT Issues in Counseling, currently serves as editor in chief for the *Journal of LGBT Issues in Counseling*, and is an editorial board member for the *Journal of Addictions and Offender Counseling* and the *Journal of Counseling Sexology and Sexual Wellness*. He has demonstrated competencies and expertise working with clients dealing with substance use and mood disorders, sexual compulsivity, issues related to sexual/affectional orientations, gender identity and expression, male body image, and past trauma. He has numerous publications in prestigious peer-reviewed journals in the areas of substance use disorders, sexual compulsivity, LGBTQ+ issues, male body image, and social justice and advocacy in counseling.

Catherine Y. Chang (Catharina) is a professor at Georgia State University and the director of International Programs for the College of Education and Human Development. Dr. Chang's primary areas of interest include social justice and advocacy, multicultural counseling competence, counselor training and supervision, and counseling implications related to Asian American and Korean American clients. She is an ACA fellow. She is a licensed professional counselor, a national certified counselor, and a certified professional counselor supervisor.

Dr. Dawnette Cigrand is professor and chair of the Counselor Education Department at Winona State University in Winona, Minnesota. Dr. Cigrand received her bachelor's degree in secondary education and English at Cornell College, then taught high school English for 4 years. While teaching, she earned her master's degree in school counseling from the University of Iowa, then served as a school counselor in rural schools for 10 years. Her Ph.D. in counselor education is also from the University of Iowa. Dr. Cigrand currently serves as the chair of the ASCA Positions Statements Committee, is a member of the ACES Ethics Task Force, is former president of the Minnesota School Counselor Association, and is a licensed school counselor in Wisconsin. Her scholarly work focuses on school-based mental health initiatives, school counselor development, and school counselor leadership and advocacy.

Heather Dahl, Ph.D., is an assistant professor in the Department of Counselor Education, School Psychology, and Human Services at the University of Nevada, Las Vegas. Her areas of expertise include suicide prevention and assessment, crisis intervention, research methodology, and integration of career issues into mental health practice. She has held service positions at the local, regional, national, and international level, including president of the Western Association for Counselor Education and Supervision.

Aseelah Davis was born and raised in Brooklyn, New York. She discovered her passion for writing when she was a child and would pick up a pen and write for the love of writing. Aseelah honed her specialty of writing poetry in the fifth grade when she wrote her first poem for her mother. She has participated in multiple spoken word performances at NYACK College for her poetry, delivered a speech to fellow NYACK students during Chapel, and was recently chosen to have two of her poems published in NYACK College's legacy book series entitled "The Fine Print." Aseelah is a former alumnus of New York City College of Technology where she graduated with her associate's degree in liberal arts and art. She went on to achieve her bachelor's degree in early childhood and special education with a concentration in psychology. Aseelah is currently in her last year of graduate school at NYACK College pursuing her master's degree in mental health counseling. She is also currently an intern, has a certification as a prepare enrich facilitator for premarital couples, and is pursuing her certification to become a credentialed alcohol and substance abuse counselor. Aseelah's goals consists of helping individuals struggling with alcohol and substance use disorders and mental health illnesses to persevere through their challenges, help lead people to God's calling over their lives, become a published author of hopefully countless bestseller books, own her own counseling practice, and positively make an impact globally.

Dr. Nivischi N. Edwards is a core faculty member of the Department of Counselor Education and Family Studies at Liberty University. She has done research on Black female faculty success and presented these findings at national and international conferences. She has also presented research on race and mental health, including the impact of microaggressions on persons of color. Additionally, Dr. Nivischi presents on the importance of having courageous conversations about race in counselor education. Dr. Nivischi has provided counseling to people of multiple races, ethnicities, socioeconomic cultures, religion, and gender. Her teaching and research interests include healthy relationships—including those with self and others. Her website is http://drnivischi.com/.

Okenna Egwu is a clinical counselor and doctoral candidate at William & Mary. He completed his master's degree at Bradley University in human development counseling with a focus in clinical mental health. Okenna has worked with a number of populations and in a variety of professional settings with college students, children and families, and juvenile offenders. Okenna's research interests center on multicultural considerations in counseling and the role that personal and systemic biases play in therapy. His work also explores the use of relational approaches in counseling and counselor education.

Dr. Isabel C. Farrell is an assistant professor at Wake Forest University. Dr. Farrell has a master's in counseling psychology from Northeastern State University and a Ph.D. in counselor education from the University of Tennessee, Knoxville. She is also a licensed professional counselor in Oklahoma and a national certified counselor. Dr. Farrell currently resides in Winston Salem, North Carolina. Her clinical expertise lies with working with bilingual Latinx children and families in underserved communities, domestic violence and sexual assault survivors residing at safe shelters, and providing career counseling services in Appalachian communities. Her passion for advocacy and working with underserved populations guides her research. Her research and special interests include bilingual counseling, cultural identity, undocumented clients, advocacy, and legislative professional advocacy.

Regina Finan is a doctoral candidate in the Counseling and Student Personnel Services program at the University of Georgia. After a career in higher education administration, she earned her Master of Science degree in clinical mental health counseling from Georgia State University (GSU). Her career working with college students in higher education, experience with mental health counseling, and current training as a counselor-educator are a great fit in her role as the academic specialist in the Department of Counseling and Psychological Services. Her research interests include diversity and social justice, counselor training, multiracial identity, and graduate student mothers. She currently serves as the vice president for the Multiethnic and Multiracial Concerns Group in the Association for Multicultural Counseling and Development (AMCD). Her previous positions have included serving as the task force chair for Multiethnic and Multiracial Concerns in AMCD and as the cochair for the Southeast Association for Counselor Education and

Supervision's (SACES) Human Rights and Social Justice Interest Network. Regina is a theoretical gardener (*imagining* exquisite landscapes) and occasional "top chef."

David Julius Ford, Jr. holds a bachelor's in psychology and a master's in clinical mental health counseling, both from Wake Forest University. In May 2014, he earned his Ph.D. in counselor education and supervision at Old Dominion University. Dr. Ford is a licensed clinical mental health counselor (LCMHC) in North Carolina and a licensed professional counselor (LPC) in Virginia and New Jersey. He is a national certified counselor (NCC) and approved clinical supervisor (ACS). Dr. Ford taught for 4 years at James Madison University and is now an assistant professor in the Department of Professional Counseling at Monmouth University and serves and the president of the New Jersey Counseling Association.

Dr. Ford's professional interests are Black Greek life, multicultural issues, college students, African American men in higher education, career counseling, addictions counseling, supervision, group work, qualitative research, the LGBTQQIA community, intersectionality, and persons living with HIV/AIDS. He has experience as an instructor for undergraduate human services courses and has taught graduate courses in counseling skills, multicultural counseling, career counseling, testing and assessment, clinical mental health counseling, addictions counseling, practicum supervision, and group counseling. He has also taught a doctoral-level dissertation course and a doctoral-level course in grant writing and program evaluation and advanced theories. He is one of 24 inaugural fellows of the NBCC Minority Fellowship program. He is the 2020 recipient of the AMCD Samuel H. Johnson Distinguished Service award and the 2020 ACES Outstanding Counselor Education and Supervision Article award. Dr. Ford is a classically trained pianist and is a proud, active, and financial member of Kappa Alpha Psi Fraternity, Inc. As an undergraduate, he had the privilege of taking a class taught by the late Dr. Maya Angelou. Dr. Ford currently lives in Ocean, New Jersey.

Dr. Perry C. Francis is a professor of counseling at Eastern Michigan University. In addition to teaching he is the coordinator of the Counseling Training Clinic in the College of Education where he sees clients and supervises students and postgraduate counselors. He is a member of the American College Counseling Association and has served on the leadership team in various capacities for the past 25 years, including serving on the ACA governing board for 6 years. He has presented on ethics in supervision, ethical issues facing college counselors, and suicide prevention at conferences in the United States, Canada, and Europe. Additionally he chaired the ethics revision task force that produced the 2014 ACA Code of Ethics. Perry has written numerous journal articles and book chapters on ethics as they apply to college counseling, couples and family therapy, and how values and ethics collide.

Harriet L. Glosoff, Ph.D., LPC, NCC, ACS, is an ACA fellow and associate professor in the Professional Counseling Program at Texas State University. Her professional background includes extensive experience in providing counseling services in inpatient, community, private practice, and higher education settings. She also has been a researcher, counselor-educator, and clinical supervisor for students and professional counselors for over 25 years. Her research focuses on addressing cultural and spiritual issues in counseling and supervision; professional ethics; and strategies to increase the cognitive complexity of students/supervisees to promote cultural competence. Dr. Glosoff has a long history of service to the profession. Examples of leadership roles include serving as a member of an American Counseling Association (ACA) Presidential Task Force on Cultural Encounters, a board member for the Association for Spiritual, Ethical and Religious Values in Counseling, president and secretary of the Association for Counselor Education and Supervision, cochair of the ACA Ethics Committee, and member of two ACA Code of Ethics Revision Taskforces. Dr. Glosoff's commitment to multiculturalism and social justice counseling is rooted in the Jewish teachings of *Tikkun Olam*, or the responsibility for addressing or "fixing" wrongs in the world. She grew up being taught that no one is free until everyone is free and that it is our individual and collective responsibility to be agents of change and combat social injustice.

Gelawdiyos M. Haile is a Ph.D. student at the University of Central Florida. He completed his master's degree in mental health counseling. He has presented on the topic of addiction and wellness nationally and internationally. He is currently conducting a study that focuses on addiction recovery and quality of life. His research interests include addiction, multicultural counseling, human performance, and interpersonal neurobiology (IPNB) in counseling.

Danica G. Hays, Ph.D., is an interim dean and professor at the University of Nevada, Las Vegas. Her areas of expertise include research methodology and program evaluation, leadership development, domestic violence prevention, assessment and diagnosis, and multicultural and social justice issues in community mental health and counselor preparation. She has extensive leadership history in the Association for Assessment and Research in Counseling (AARC) and the Association for Counselor Education and Supervision (ACES), including serving as AARC president, ACES journal editor for counselor education and supervision, and president of an ACES region. The American Counseling Association has recognized her nationally as a fellow, as well as presented her awards for her research and advocacy as a counselor educator.

Allen E. Ivey, Ph.D., is a distinguished university professor (Emeritus) at the University of Massachusetts, Amherst. Dr. Ivey is the founder and former president of Microtraining Associates, an educational publishing firm focusing on counseling and therapy skills and multicultural approaches to counseling and therapy. He currently serves as a consultant to Microtraining/Alexander Street Press. After his degree from Stanford (Phi Beta Kappa), he studied social work in Denmark on a Fulbright and then earned his doctorate in counseling from Harvard. A diplomate of the American Board of Professional

Psychology, Allen is a past president and fellow of the Society of Counseling Psychology of the American Psychological Association and a fellow of the American Counseling Association. He is also a fellow of APA's Society for the Psychological Study of Ethnic Minority Issues and the Asian American Psychological Association. The author or coauthor of over 40 books and 200 articles, his works have been translated into 21 languages. His major scholarly focus has been on demystifying the counseling and therapy process, and this led to a deep interest in multicultural issues. His first anti-racism workshop was in 1967. The originator of the influential micro counseling framework and the integrative theory developmental counseling and therapy (DCT), Allen has won wide recognition and national and international awards. However, he is most pleased and honored by being named a "Distinguished Multicultural Elder" at the National Multicultural Conference and Summit.

Kalesha D. Jenkins, Ph.D. is a graduate of the University of Cincinnati's (OH) Counselor Education and Supervision program. Her research focuses on the self-awareness process and influence of privilege and marginalization in multicultural competency through community-based practices and culturally informed methodologies. Dr. Jenkins is a licensed professional counselor working primarily with adults in underserved communities that suffer from race-based, historical, and generational trauma using psychodynamic and postmodern psychotherapy. She received her master's degree in clinical mental health counseling from the University of Cincinnati and bachelor's degree in psychology/business from Seton Hill University (PA).

Dr. Erin Lane joined the Counselor Education faculty at Western Illinois University-Quad Cities in 2018. She earned Bachelor of Arts degrees in psychology and theater arts from Beloit College in Beloit, Wisconsin. Dr. Lane received her Master of Arts degree in school counseling from the University of Iowa, along with a certification in gifted education from the Belin Blank Center. She earned her Ph.D. in counselor education and supervision from the University of Iowa. Prior to her doctoral training, Dr. Lane spent over a decade in school settings, serving in the roles of teacher, administrator, and, finally, school counselor. Her research interests include school counselor advocacy and social justice, serving underrepresented gifted students, college and career readiness in PK–12 settings, and school counselor preparation. She is a licensed school counselor in Iowa and is a national certified counselor (NCC).

Dr. Gerard Lawson is a professor in the School of Education at Virginia Tech and was the 66th president of the American Counseling Association, having served in that office from July 2017–June 2018. Dr. Lawson is also past president of the Association for Counselor Education and Supervision (ACES) and of the Virginia Counselors Association. He earned his bachelor's degree from Virginia Tech in human development, his master's in counseling from Longwood College, and his doctorate in counselor education from the College of William and Mary, all in Virginia. He is a licensed professional counselor, a licensed substance abuse treatment practitioner, a national certified counselor, and an approved clinical supervisor. Since joining the faculty at Virginia Tech, Dr. Lawson has published his research in prestigious journals including the *Journal of Counseling and Development, Counselor Education and Supervision*, and *The Clinical Supervisor*. He has presented at national and international conferences on a range of topics, including counselor wellness, crisis response and resilience, and clinical supervision. Dr. Lawson was awarded the inaugural Martin Ritchie award for advocacy in 2015, in 2017 he was awarded the Virginia Tech College of Liberal Arts and Human Sciences Land-Grant Scholar award, and in 2019 he was among the inaugural recipients of the ACES Legacy Awards. He is an American Counseling Association fellow, one of the highest professional recognitions in the counseling profession.

Dr. Patrice Leopold is a recent graduate of the counselor education doctoral program at the University of Florida and is currently an adjunct instructor at Barry University. Her fervor for multicultural awareness and social justice is rooted in her experiences of intersectionality between her marginalized and privileged identities. As a child of Haitian immigrant parents, she often encountered challenges with the stigmas associated with mental health and seeking help. She has established varying initiatives to reduce these stigmas among marginalized populations in her community, one in which includes fostering creativity in her various roles.

Tricia M. Mikolon, Ph.D., CRC, LPC has used her education as a certified rehabilitation counselor and licensed professional counselor to assist in her clients in increasing their personal accountability and responsibility while encouraging them to embrace their own unique cultural values. She has worked with both rural and incarcerated populations throughout her career.

Michelle D. Mitchell is an assistant professor from Wake Forest University, a licensed professional counselor in Pennsylvania, and an NBCC board-certified counselor with clinical experience working with underprivileged and marginalized populations. Dr. Mitchell's passion for multiculturalism and social justice counseling stems from her experiences as a case manager. During that time, she provided outpatient services for clients with severe and persistent mental illness. Unfortunately, many of her clients were subject to clinicians who could provide assistance based on diagnosis but didn't understand who clients were as cultural beings. The aforementioned clinical approach has inspired her to meet the needs of clients through the culturally responsive training of students in counseling programs. Her clinical experience has mainly focused on working with underprivileged and marginalized populations. She is an active member of many counseling and counselor education organizations, including ACA, AMCD, and AARC.

Jennifer Niles holds a Master of Arts in counseling from Wake Forest University and a Bachelor of Science in human development and family studies. Jennifer is a doctoral student of counselor education and supervision at William & Mary. Her clinical experience is in elementary school counseling and with children and families in child welfare. Jennifer's research interests include school counseling, social justice, and mindfulness practices.

Dr. Spencer Niles serves as professor in the Counselor Education program at William & Mary. Previously, he served as dean (2013–2020) and professor at the School of Education at William & Mary. He was also a distinguished professor and department head for Educational Psychology, Counseling, and Special Education at the Pennsylvania State University from 2000–2013 where he led the development and implementation of Penn State's CACREP-accredited master's programs in school counseling, clinical mental health counseling, and career counseling. He also led Penn State's creation and implementation of their first CACREP-accredited Ph.D. in counselor education and supervision. Prior to joining the faculty at Penn State, he served as professor of counselor education at the University of Virginia.

Dr. Niles is a past president of Chi Sigma Iota International and was twice the president of the National Career Development Association (NCDA). He is the recipient of the NCDA Eminent Career award. Dr. Niles is a fellow of the National Career Development Association and the American Counseling Association (ACA). He has received numerous awards from the ACA, including the Thomas Hohenshil Research award, the Thomas Sweeney Visionary Leadership and Advocacy award, the President's award, the David Brooks Distinguished Mentor award, the ACA Extended Research award, and the Visionary Leader and Advocate award. He received the Noted Scholar award from the University of British Columbia. Dr. Niles is a fellow of ACA and NCDA. He served as two-term editor for *The Career Development Quarterly*, editor for the *Journal of Counseling & Development*, and continues to serve on numerous journal editorial boards. He has authored or coauthored approximately 140 publications and delivered over 150 presentations at national and international conferences. His book, *Career Development Interventions* (6th edition), is the best-selling career text in the world. His forthcoming coauthored books are titled *Career Flow and Development: Hope-Action Theory* and *Career Recovery: Creating Careers With Hope in Difficult Times*.

He has taught in over 27 countries and is an honorary member of the Japanese Career Development Association, honorary member of the Italian Association for Educational and Vocational Guidance, a member of the Board of Directors for the International Center for Career Development and Public Policy and a lifetime honorary member of the Ohio Career Development Association.

Amber Norman is a licensed mental health counselor (FL) and visiting lecturer in the Department of Counselor Education and School Psychology at the University of Central Florida. As a clinician, she specializes in working with ethnic and sexual minorities, treating mood disorders and trauma-related impairments. She has served in a variety of community-based settings, including outpatient/residential and sober living facilities; the Department of Juvenile Justice treating substance-related concerns and childhood trauma; and home-based therapy for children in foster care and adults contending with domestic violence. Dr. Norman's research centers on sexuality-related education, queer sexuality, and prejudice-motivated violence.

James P. Norris is a licensed mental health counselor in the state of Washington and a licensed professional counselor in Arizona. Norris is a doctoral candidate at University of the Cumberlands in the School of Social and Behavioral Science. He is the founder of Matumaini Counseling and Community Center, a nonprofit organization that provides psychoeducation, social justice, and advocacy work around mental health in the African American community. Norris has a private practice where he provides counseling services. Norris is a 2019 NBCC fellow and a part of the 2020 WACES cohort for the Emerging Leaders program. Prior to attending University of the Cumberlands, he attended Western Illinois University and completed his degree in liberal studies with a focus in education. After graduation, he pursued a professional football career, signing two Arena Football League contracts with Spokane Shock and Stockton Lightning. Upon the ending of his football career, he served as a corrections officer for 11 years with the King County Jail in Seattle, Washington. Norris's research interests include trauma and the incorporation of hip hop in counseling practice. He can be contacted at jnorris4837@ucumberlands.edu.

Anthony Pacifico, B.A. is a student at Seton Hall University pursuing an M.A./Ed.S. in professional counseling. Anthony's experiences in counseling include working with populations at community agencies and college counseling centers. His research and academic interests are family therapy, identity, and sports psychology.

Dr. Brean'a Parker received her Master's of Education in professional community counseling and her Ph.D. in counselor education from the University of Georgia. She is currently an assistant faculty member in the Department of Educational Leadership, Policy and Human Development at North Carolina State University. Dr. Parker currently teaches within the master's-level counseling program and emphasizes the integration of critical theory and history, intersectionality theory, and social justice in core counseling curriculum courses. Dr. Parker's scholarly interest center the experiences of interpersonal violence and trauma within the Black community; healing and resistance praxis in response to complex trauma within the Black community; and social justice-based counselor education.

Dr. Parker's passion for multiculturalism and social justice practice stems from learning and navigating the world as Black woman and observing the ways Black and African American and other women of color, trans, queer, and folks who live with disabilities engage in critical disruptive scholarship and social justice toward liberation. She is also inspired by Black feminism and womanism embodiment of working in solidarity and dismantling oppression through radial love, healing, discourse, and action.

Debra M. Perez, M.A., LPCC, SCPG, BCTHP is a licensed clinical mental health counselor and holds a special certification in problem gambling treatment and a board certification in telebehavioral health. She provides online counseling to underserved populations in rural New Mexico. She is a doctoral candidate at the University of the Cumberlands. She is proud of her Hispanic heritage and her service to minority and underserved populations throughout New Mexico.

Ashlei Rabess is a doctoral student in counselor education and practice at Georgia State University. She is a licensed associate professional counselor in the state of Georgia and a national certified counselor. Rabess's primary areas of interest include multiculturalism and social justice in counseling and counselor education, generational trauma and healing in African American communities, and trauma-informed group work.

She is dedicated to eliminating the stigma against mental illness and seeking mental health services among marginalized populations. Testing, assessment, and diagnosis often contribute to this stigma and can cause harm to individuals seeking treatment or prevent them from seeking help altogether. Thus, there is a clear need for culturally competent and socially just approaches among all clinicians.

Jyotsana Sharma, Ph.D. is a tenure-track assistant professor at Oklahoma State University. She graduated from her doctoral program in counselor education from Virginia Tech (CACREP-accredited) in 2019. She is a licensed clinical mental health counselor (LCMHC) in the State of New Hampshire, a national certified counselor (NCC) and an approved clinical supervisor (ACS) through the National Board for Certified Counselors (NBCC). Her experience includes working as a clinician in residential treatment for at-risk youth and in anxiety treatment center in New Hampshire, and as a therapist and psychology teacher at a college-prep boarding school in Massachusetts. Her research interests include trauma recovery, post-trauma growth, adverse childhood experiences, patterns of violence and how trauma travels through generations, and social and cultural contexts and their effect on trauma recovery. She is also involved in research related to equity and access to mental health services in aging populations as well as effective training and education for developing socially and culturally sensitive counselors.

M. Ann Shillingford, Ph.D. is an associate professor of counselor education at the University of Central Florida (UCF) in Orlando. She currently serves as coordinator of the counselor education Ph.D. program at UCF. She has several years of experience as a professional school counselor prior to completing her doctorate at UCF. Dr. Shillingford has written several articles and book chapters on multicultural issues particularly focused on disparities among of color. Dr. Shillingford has a keen interest in exploring measures to deconstruct educational, social, and health disparities among marginalized communities. Dr. Shillingford is currently conducting research exploring the effects of media exposure to police and community violence on the physical and mental health of African American mothers raising young Black men. She also facilitates a study-abroad program with counseling students to the island of Dominica, exploring the multicultural competence of counseling students through a cultural immersion experience.

Dr. Shillingford has two coedited books, *The Journey Unraveled: College and Career Readiness of African American Students* Lexington Books, (2015) and *Demystifying the DSM: A Tool for School Counseling Students and Practitioners* (Cognella, 2020).

Dr. Jacqueline Swank is an associate professor of counselor education at the University of Florida. Her passion for creativity and social justice stem from her work with diverse children and their families in residential, inpatient, and outpatient settings and her desire to connect and develop relationships with others. She advocates for the use of creativity to foster awareness, consider diverse perspectives, and empower clients to let their voices be heard using creative methods that extend beyond verbal communication, such as play, especially for clients who struggle with verbal expression.

Dr. Swank's passion for creativity and social justice stem from her work with diverse children and their families in residential, inpatient, and outpatient settings and her desire to connect and develop relationships with others. She advocates for the use of creativity to foster awareness, consider diverse perspectives, and empower clients to let their voices be heard using creative methods that extend beyond verbal communication, such as play, especially for clients who struggle with verbal expression.

Sherry M. Todd, Ph.D., LPC, ATR-BC, CTTS holds several trauma certifications, has worked for 25 years with incarcerated and at-risk youth, and advocates that trauma is a causal diagnosis. Dr. Todd is full-time faculty in a CACREP counseling program, and her research interests include transgenerational trauma and the racial disparities in lethality among adolescents.

Cirecie A. West-Olatunji, Ph.D., serves as full professor and director of the Center for Traumatic Stress Research at Xavier University of Louisiana. She is also a past president of the American Counseling Association (ACA), past secretary of Division E: Counseling and Human Development in the American Educational Research Association (AERA), and a past president of the Association for Multicultural Counseling and Development (AMCD). Dr. West-Olatunji has received numerous awards from national organizations and is an ACA fellow. Nationally, Cirecie West-Olatunji has initiated several clinical research projects that focus on traumatic stress and systemic oppression. Her publications include three coauthored books, several book chapters, and over 50 articles in peer-reviewed journals. Dr. West-Olatunji has delivered research papers throughout Asia, Africa, Europe, and the Americas.

Miss Jo Lauren Weaver is a doctoral student in counselor education at the University of Florida. Her vigor for social justice developed from her experience working at a juvenile detention center with a high percentage of disproportionate minority contact. She worked with young, diverse clients, whose words had often been dismissed or silenced.

As such, she created a safe space of expression through creative interventions, including songwriting, drawing, and dance to empower her clients. Today, she continues to use and expand her creativity in her work as a developing researcher, supervisor, and teacher.

Nicolas Williams is a doctoral student in counselor education and practice at Georgia State University. Williams's primary areas of interest include spiritually integrated supervision and counseling, race-based stress and trauma in African American communities, and liberation-based healing and wellness practices. He is a national certified counselor.

Williams is committed to meeting the mental and behavioral health needs of marginalized communities, reducing health disparities, and improving overall community health and well-being. Developing the knowledge, skills, and awareness necessary to utilize testing and assessment and make diagnoses effectively with cultural sensitivity is the work of every professional counselor and clinician.

Jonathan Yellowhair, M.S, LAC, NCC is currently an addictions counselor and psychotherapist at Native Americans for Community Action (NACA), located in his hometown of Flagstaff, Arizona. He received his Master of Science degree in clinical mental health counseling from Georgia State University and is a Northern Arizona University Alumni with a B.A in International Affairs and B.S in Applied Indigenous Studies. He is a U.S. Marine Corps veteran with deployments to Iraq and Afghanistan who is passionate about addressing and challenging mental health disparities and systemic barriers that preside within his community and others facing marginalization. In 2018, Jonathan was awarded the National Board for Certified Counselors Minority Addictions (MFP-AC) fellowship and was the first Navajo to ever become a Pat Tillman Foundation scholar. As a member of the Navajo Nation, Jonathan finds it imperative to implement cultural teachings from his family in Chilchinbeto, Arizona, directly into his work in Flagstaff. He is passionate about facilitating groups for clients mandated from the courts and individuals navigating substance use disorders and other areas, including adolescence, trauma, domestic violence, cultural identity, depression, and social anxiety. Jonathan emphatically advocates for people in recovery/sobriety and believes that everyone has the innate ability to heal themselves through communal support and by embracing the right process. Jonathan loves his pitbulls Mowgli and Baloo and enjoys taking them for long walks on trails early in the morning. He cherishes spending time with his family and advocating for his tribe and Indigenous people locally and around the globe.

Printed in the USA
CPSIA information can be obtained
at www.ICGtesting.com
LVHW020334280723
753396LV00003B/7